NORTHERN IRELAND

PERSONAL INSOLVENCY

The Servicing the Legal System Programme

The Programme was inaugurated in August 1980 in the School of Law of the Queen's University, Belfast to promote the publication of commentaries on various aspects of the law and the legal system of Northern Ireland. Generous financial and other support for the Programme has been provided by the Northern Ireland Court Service, the Inn of Court of Northern Ireland, the Bar Council of Northern Ireland, the Law Society of Northern Ireland, TSB Northern Ireland plc, and Queen's University. Details of all SLS publications may be obtained from the SLS Office, School of Law, Queen's University, Belfast BT7 1NN, Northern Ireland.

NORTHERN IRELAND

PERSONAL INSOLVENCY

by

JOHN M HUNTER, CBE, LLB, Solicitor, Former Master
(Bankruptcy), Supreme Court of Judicature of Northern
Ireland

SLS

Belfast 1992

*First Published in 1992 by SLS Legal Publications (NI), School of Law,
Queens University, Belfast, BT7 1NN*

ISBN 0 85389 455 8

Typeset by SLS Legal Publications (NI)
Printed by Dataplus, Belfast

Contents

Preface

The Insolvency (Northern Ireland) Order 1989, The Insolvency Rules (Northern Ireland) 1991 and other subordinate legislation effected the most significant changes in insolvency law and procedure in Northern Ireland for over 130 years. They follow closely the corresponding legislation introduced in England and Wales in 1986, but with adaption to reflect the exclusive jurisdication of the High Court in Northern Ireland and differences in related areas of law.

This book is intended to provide a guide to the substantive law and a detailed exposition of the procedure governing the insolvency of individuals and partnerships.

I wish to record my thanks to Mrs Sara Gamble LL.B., Publications Editor of SLS who prepared the Tables of Statutes, Statutory Instructments and Cases, made many helpful suggestions on the layout of the text and personally handled every stage of the publication, and to my wife for assistance with proof reading.

September 1992   JOHN M HUNTER

Table of Cases, Practice Notes and Practice Directions

(N.B. References in this Table are to paragraph numbers.)

Practice Directions

Practice Notes

Table of Statutes

(NB References in this Table are to paragraph numbers.)

Table of Statutory Instruments

Rules and Orders

(N.B. References in this Table are to paragraph numbers.)

Forms in the Appendix to the 1991 Rules

References and Abbreviations

Primary legislation
(a) Insolvency
(i) <u>Northern Ireland</u>

1857 Act	Irish Bankrupt and Insolvent Act 1857
1872 Act	Bankruptcy (Ireland) Amendment Act 1872
1929 Act	Bankruptcy Amendment Act (Northern Ireland) 1929
1980 Order	Bankruptcy Amendment (Northern Ireland) Order 1980
Bankruptcy Acts	1857 Act, 1872 Act, 1929 Act and 1980 Order
the Order	Insolvency (Northern Ireland) Order 1989
Article/Art.	an Article of the Order
Schedule/Sch.	a Schedule to the Order

(ii) <u>Great Britain</u>

IA 1986	Insolvency Act 1986

(b) Other

Land Registration Act/LR Act	Land Registration Act (Northern Ireland) 1970
Registration of Deeds Act/ R of D Act	Registration of Deeds Act (Northern Ireland) 1970
Judgments Enforcement Order/ JEO	Judgments Enforcement (Northern Ireland) Order 1981

Subordinate legislation
(a) Insolvency

the Bankruptcy Rules	Bankruptcy Rules (Northern Ireland) 1983
Deceased Insolvent Estates Order/DIEO	Administration of Insolvent Estates of Deceased Persons Order (Northern Ireland) 1991
Insolvency Regulations/ Ins Regs	Insolvency Regulations (Northern Ireland) 1991
Insolvency Practitioners Regulations/Ins Pract Regs	Insolvency Practitioners Regulations (Northern Ireland) 1991
Insolvent Partnerships Order/IPO	Insolvent Partnerships Order (Northern Ireland) 1991
the Rules	Insolvency Rules (Northern Ireland) 1991
Rule/R.	a rule of the Rules

F.   a form prescribed by the Rules

(b) Other

Land Registration Rules/   Land Registration Rules (Northern
  LR Rules   Ireland) 1977

Insolvency (Registration of
  Deeds) Regulations/Ins R of
  D Regs   Insolvency (Registration of Deeds)
                                    Regulations (Northern Ireland) 1991

the Supreme Court Rules/RSC   Rules of the Supreme Court (Northern
                                    Ireland) 1980

Text books and periodicals

Atkin   Court Forms, 2nd. edn., vol.7, 1988
                                    issue

Hals   Halsbury's Laws of England, 4th. edn.
                                    vol.3 (1973)

JH   Northern Ireland Bankruptcy Law and
                                    Practice, John M.Hunter (1984)

MH   Muir Hunter on Personal Insolvency

Ins Int   Insolvency Intelligence

General

associate   a person who is an associate of the
                                    bankrupt within the definition in
                                    Article 4

authorised insolvency   person authorised under Part XII of
  practitioner   the Order to act as an insolvency
                                    practitioner in relation to the debtor
                                    or bankrupt

bankrupt's estate   the property of the bankrupt
                                    available for the benefit or his
                                    creditors, as defined in Article 11

bankruptcy order   an order adjudging an individual
                                  bankrupt

bankruptcy petition   a petition to the Court for a bankruptcy
                                    order

business   includes a trade or profession

business day   any day other than a Saturday, Sunday,
                                    Christmas Day, Good Friday or a day
                                    which is a bank holiday in Northern
                                    Ireland

Court   the High Court of Justice in Northern
                                  Ireland(Chancery Division) exercising its
                                  jurisdiction under the Order and in

	respect of administrative functions includes the Office
commencement date	the date appointed under Article 1(2) for the provision in question to come into operation
debtor	includes a solicitor against whom a bankruptcy petition is presented by the Law Society of Northern Ireland under Article 238(1)(d)
Department	the Department of Economic
execution	Development includes enforcement of a judgment by the Enforcement of Judgments Office
hearing date	the date fixed for a hearing
insolvency administration order	an order for the administration in bankruptcy of the insolvent estate of a deceased person
insolvency administration petition	a petition for an insolvency administration order
insolvency proceedings	proceedings under the Order or the Rules
Judge	the Chancery Judge
Master	the Master (Bankruptcy)
Office	the Bankruptcy and Companies Office
Official Receiver	an Official Receiver or a Deputy Official Receiver
responsible insolvency practitioner	the person acting as the supervisor of a voluntary arrangement, or as trustee or interim receiver, including the Official Receiver when so acting or when acting as receiver and manager of a bankrupt's estate
Taxing Master	the Master (Taxing Office)
trustee	the trustee of the bankrupt's estate
venue	the time, date and place for any proceeding or attendance before the Court, or for a meeting of creditors
voluntary arrangement	a voluntary arrangement by an individual debtor under Chapter II of Part VIII of the Order

Chapter 1

THE LEGISLATION

THE INSOLVENCY (NORTHERN IRELAND) ORDER 1989

The legislative background

1.01 This Order ("the Order") for the first time brings together in one enactment most of the primary legislation governing the insolvency of individuals and companies in Northern Ireland and also embraces the winding up of solvent companies. It follows very closely the provisions of the Insolvency Act 1986 ("IA 1986") applying to England and Wales, thus achieving, again for the first time, substantial harmonisation of the law of insolvency between the two parts of the United Kingdom. The different law governing individual insolvency in Scotland has been modernised by the Bankruptcy (Scotland) Act 1985.

1.02 The IA 1986 is a consolidation Act. It was preceded by the Insolvency Act 1985, which gave effect to many, but not all of the recommendations of the Insolvency Law Review Committee under the chairmanship of Sir Kenneth Cork GBE, which reported in April 1982,[1] as well as containing other provisions, some of which depart from the recommendations of that committee.

1.03 As regards the insolvency of individuals in England and Wales, the IA 1986 replaces the Bankruptcy Act 1914 (repealed by the 1985 Act) by a radically revised code, which includes new procedures for judicially controlled voluntary arrangements between individual debtors and their creditors. The insolvency of partnerships and the administration of the insolvent estates of deceased persons are not regulated directly by the Act but it enables the Lord Chancellor by order made with the concurrence of the Secretary of State for Trade and Industry to apply its provisions, with modifications. The same approach has been adopted for Northern Ireland by the Order.

1.04 Deeds of arrangement in England and Wales continue to be governed by the Deeds of Arrangement Act 1914, as amended. However, as deeds of arrangement in Northern Ireland were still subject to the Deeds of Arrangement Act 1887, the opportunity has been taken to include in the Order provisions similar to those of the 1914 Act.

Commencement of the Order

1.05 The Order has been brought into operation by Commencement Orders made under Article 1. The Insolvency (1989 Order) (Commencement No.1) Order (Northern Ireland) 1990 provided for the commencement on 1st June 1990 of interim amendments of the Bankruptcy Amendment (Northern Ireland) Order 1980 ("the 1980 Order") relating to preferential debts, which had the effect of applying to insolvencies commencing on or after that date the revised preferential payment provisions of the Order. This Commencement Order also introduced from 1st June 1990 the new provisions in Article 343 of the Order relating to supplies of water, electricity, etc. in individual insolvency. The Insolvency (1989 Order) (Commencement No.2) Order (Northern Ireland) 1991 brought into operation on 5th July 1991 Article 361 (fees orders) and the Insolvency (1989 Order) (Commencement No.3) Order (Northern Ireland) 1991 brought into operation on 9th July 1991 Part XII/and Article 363 (insolvency practitioners) and, Articles 355/357 (Official Receivers). The remainder of the provisions of the Order affecting individual insolvency, with minor exceptions, were brought into operation on 1st October 1991 by the Insolvency (1989 Order) (Commencement No.4) Order (Northern Ireland) 1991.

1.06 The previous legislation relating to bankruptcy and arrangements between debtors and creditors has been repealed by Schedule 10,[2] except in respect of cases to which the Order does not apply.[3] In such a case the Bankruptcy Acts will continue to apply, subject only to the amendments contained in the transitional provisions of Schedule 8, of which the most material relate to debtor's summonses, discharge from bankruptcy and successive bankruptcies.[4]

Application of the Order
1.07 With the exception of the transitional amendments of the Bankruptcy Acts referred to in the preceding paragraph and the provisions introduced on 1st June 1990, the provisions of the Order relating to bankruptcy apply only to a case in which a petition is presented on or after 1st October 1991.[5] The new provisions for deeds of arrangement apply only to such deeds registered on or after that date.[6] No petition for an arrangement under the control of the Court under the Bankruptcy Acts may be presented after 30th September 1991. The new provisions for individual voluntary arrangements operate from 1st October 1991.

1.08 The application of the Order to the Crown is dealt with in Article 378.

Subordinate legislation
1.09 One of the significant features of the new insolvency legislation in Great Britain, which has been adopted also in Northern Ireland, is the volume and range of subordinate legislation made under the Order and other primary legislation affected by the Order.

1.10 The most extensive subordinate legislation is the Insolvency Rules (Northern Ireland) 1991 ("the Rules") dealt with in the next chapter.

1.11 As mentioned above, the application of the Order to insolvent partnerships and the administration of the insolvent estates of deceased persons is governed by orders made by the Lord Chancellor with the concurrence of the Department of Economic Development ("the Department").[7]

1.12   Other important subordinate legislation relating to the insolvency of individuals include -

(a)   Insolvency Regulations (Northern Ireland) 1991; these include regulations in respect of accounts and records to be kept by trustees in bankruptcy, payments into and out of the Insolvency Account, payments of dividends and regulations governing deeds of arrangement;

(b)   Insolvency Practitioners (Recognised Professional Bodies) Order (Northern Ireland) 1991 listing the professional bodies authorised to licence insolvency practitioners;

(c)   Insolvency Practitioners Regulations (Northern Ireland) 1991 regulating the authorisation of insolvency practitioners by the Department, the security required to be provided and the records to be kept by insolvency practitioners;

(d)   Insolvency (Monetary Limits) Order (Northern Ireland) 1991 prescribing monetary limits under provisions of the Order;

(e)   Insolvency (Deposits) (Northern Ireland) Order 1991 prescribing the deposit payable on the presentation of a bankruptcy petition and how the deposit is to be accounted for;

(f)   Insolvency (Fees) (Northern Ireland) Order 1991 prescribing fees payable under the Order, other than Court fees;

(g)   Insolvency (Registration of Deeds) Regulations (Northern Ireland) 1991 prescribing the procedure for the registration in the Registry of Deeds of bankruptcy petitions, bankruptcy orders and other bankruptcy proceedings;

(h)   Land Registration (Amendment No.3) Rules (Northern Ireland) 1991 which include rules prescribing additions to the Land Registration Rules (Northern Ireland) 1977 to provide for the registration in the Land Registry of notices of bankruptcy petitions, bankruptcy inhibitions and other bankruptcy proceedings.

Footnotes

(1) Cmd. 8558

(2) Ss. 13(2), (3) and 18 of the Debtors Act (Ireland) 1872, which do not relate exclusively to bankrupts or debtors entering into arrangements with their creditors, remain unrepealed.

(3) Sch. 8 para. 8(2) re bankruptcy and Sch. 8 para. 22 re arrangements.

(4) Paras. 6.52, 21.52/57, 23.04/05.

(5) Sch. 8, para. 8(1).

(6) Sch. 8, para. 17.

(7) Arts. 364, 365.

Chapter 2

THE INSOLVENCY RULES (NORTHERN IRELAND) 1991

The rule-making authority

2.01 The Insolvency Rules ("the Rules") are made by the Lord Chancellor, with the concurrence of the Department and after consultation with the advisory committee appointed by him.[1] This committee is a continuation of the committee appointed to keep under review the former rules regulating company winding up and bankruptcy.

Provisions which may be included in the Rules

2.02 The general rule-making power is to make rules for the purpose of giving effect to the Order.[2] Powers to make rules on specific matters are also contained in the Order and rules may be made in respect of matters specified in Schedule 6 or which correspond to provisions contained in the Bankruptcy Rules (Northern Ireland) 1983 ("the Bankruptcy Rules") before the commencement date.[3] The Rules may also make provision for enabling the exercise of the jurisdiction of the Court under the Order to be delegated to the Master (Bankruptcy)[4] and for such incidental, supplemental and transitional provision as may appear to the Lord Chancellor or, as the case may be, the Department necessary or expedient.[5]

Prescribed forms

2.03 The forms contained in Schedule 2 to the Rules must be used in insolvency proceedings.[6] However, deviations therefrom not materially affecting the substance nor calculated to mislead, are permitted.[7]

Application of the Rules

2.04 The Rules apply to bankruptcy proceedings where the bankruptcy petition is presented on or after 1st October 1991 and to proceedings for an individual voluntary arrangement or in respect of a deed of arrangement to which the Order applies, commenced on or after that date.[8] They apply to proceedings commenced before that date only where expressly provided[9] or to the extent necessary to give effect to the transitional provisions of Schedule 8.[10]

Application of the rules and practice of the Supreme Court

2.05 Except so far as inconsistent with the Rules, the Rules of the Supreme Court (Northern Ireland) 1980 ("the Supreme Court Rules") and the practice of the High Court apply to proceedings under the Order or the Rules, with any necessary modifications.[11] In some instances the modifications are expressly stated.[12] This follows the pattern of the Insolvency Rules 1986 applying to

5

England and Wales and the Companies (Winding-Up) Rules (Northern Ireland) 1984 and is to be contrasted with the position under the Bankruptcy Rules which provided that the Supreme Court Rules only applied to proceedings under the Bankruptcy Acts where expressly so applied.

2.06   The procedure under other related proceedings which have been assigned to the Chancery Division and the Office[13] remains governed by the Supreme Court Rules. Thus, for example, a partition action by the trustee in the circumstances mentioned in Article 309(3)[14] will be commenced by originating summons.

The Insolvency Rules 1986
2.07   The Rules follow closely the Insolvency Rules 1986 applying to England and Wales. For the convenience of practitioners a reference to the corresponding rule of the 1986 Rules has been noted at the foot of each Northern Ireland rule which is in similar (although not always identical) terms.

Footnotes

(1)   Arts.359(1), 360.
(2)   Art.359(1).
(3)   Art.359(2).
(4)   *Ibid.*
(5)   *Ibid.* The reference in Art.359(2)(d) to the Department appears to be in error, as only the Lord Chancellor may make Insolvency Rules under the Order. Cf. IA 1986, s.411(2)(b) where the corresponding reference to the Secretary of State is appropriate as he makes company insolvency rules in relation to Scotland.
(6)   R.12.08.
(7)   Interpretation Act (Northern Ireland) 1954, s.25.
(8)   R.0.7(1).
(9)   R.7.30(6) re requirement to tax costs, R.7.31(9) re measurement of remuneration by Taxing Master.
(10)   R.0.7(2).
(11)   R.7.45: RSC O.1, r.2(2A),(4).
(12)   E.g. R.7.52(2),(4) re affidavits.
(13)   Paras.5.002, 5.005.
(14)   Para.14.039.

Chapter 3

OFFICIAL RECEIVERS

Introduction

3.01   Under the Order "the Official Assignee for bankruptcy for Northern Ireland"[1] and "the Official Assignee for company liquidations for Northern Ireland"[2] are replaced by Official Receivers, who are to be officers of the Department appointed by the Department.[3] The Department may give directions with respect to the disposal of the business of Official Receivers[4] and it is anticipated that one or more of them will be specifically nominated to discharge the functions of the Official Receiver under the Order in relation to every bankruptcy. If more than one person is so nominated it will be necessary for the Department to nominate the officer authorised to act as the Official Receiver in relation to each bankruptcy and in the event of any change, to nominate his successor.[5]

3.02   The office of Official Receiver is not, as was the office of Official Assignee for bankruptcy for Northern Ireland under the 1980 Order,[6] a corporation sole.

Deputy Official Receivers

3.03   The Department is empowered to appoint one or more officers of the Department as deputy Official Receiver.[7]   Subject to any directions of the Department a deputy Official Receiver has, on such conditions and for such period as may be specified in the terms of his appointment, the same status and functions as an Official Receiver.[8] In the Order and the Rules the term "official receiver" includes any deputy Official Receiver.[9]

Persons entitled to act on Official Receiver's behalf

3.04   In the absence of the Official Receiver authorised to act in a particular bankruptcy, an officer authorised in writing for the purpose by the Department, or by the Official Receiver himself may, with the leave of the Court, act on the Official Receiver's behalf and in his place in the public examination of a bankrupt, in a private examination or in respect of any application to the Court.[10]

3.05   In case of emergency, where there is no Official Receiver capable of acting, anything to be done by, to or before the Official Receiver may be done by, to or before the Master.[11]

Functions and status

3.06   The Order confers numerous specific functions on the Official Receiver.[12] His primary function is to investigate the conduct and financial affairs of the bankrupt and this function continues after the appointment of an insolvency practitioner as trustee. He also has an important function as receiver to protect the bankrupt's assets pending the appointment of a trustee. His various administrative duties include functions in connection with the appointment of a trustee and he will act as trustee if no insolvency practitioner is so appointed and will usually be the trustee in a summary administration.

3.07   Any property vested in the Official Assignee for bankruptcy for Northern Ireland under the Bankruptcy Acts before 1st October 1991 vests on that date in the Official Receiver.[13] Anything which is required or authorised to be done by or to the Official Assignee or an Assistant Official Assignee under those Acts may be done by or to the Official Receiver or a deputy Official Receiver.[14]

3.08   In addition to the Official Receiver's functions under the Order, other functions may be conferred on him by the Department.[15] The Department's functions when acting in place of a creditors' committee may be exercised by the Official Receiver.[16] In the exercise of any of the functions of his office he is required to act under the general authority and direction of the Department, but he is also an officer of the Court.[17] When acting as an official of the Department he is subject to judicial review, but not when acting as an officer of the Court. Any complaint in relation to his conduct as an officer of the Court would fall to be dealt with by the Court.

Application for directions
3.09   The Official Receiver may apply to the Court for directions with regard to the compliance by the bankrupt with any directions of the Court or in relation to any matter arising in insolvency proceedings.[18]

Consultation of creditors
3.10   The Official Receiver may at any time summon and conduct meetings of creditors for the purpose of ascertaining their wishes in all matters relating to the bankruptcy.[19]

Charges and remuneration
3.11   The Official Receiver's charges for services other than as trustee or interim receiver are fixed by the Insolvency (Fees) Order (Northern Ireland) 1991. His remuneration as trustee or interim receiver is prescribed by the Insolvency Regulations.[20]

Expenses
3.12   Any expenses (including damages) incurred by the Official Receiver (in whatever capacity he may be acting) in connection with proceedings taken against him in insolvency proceedings are to be treated as expenses of the proceedings and he has a charge on the insolvent's estate in respect of any sums due to him for such expenses.[21]

Footnotes

(1) 1980 Order, Art.3(1).
(2) Companies (Northern Ireland) Order 1986, Art.488(1).
(3) Art.355(1). Judicial notice is to be taken of such appointments -R.10.1.
(4) Art.355(2).
(5) Art.2(2), definition of "the Official Receiver", and Art.355(2).
(6) 1980 Order, Art.3(1).
(7) Art.357(1). Judicial notice is to be taken of such appointments -R.10.1.
(8) Art.357(2).
(9) Art.2(2), definition of "the Official Receiver".
(10) R.10.2(1).
(11) R.10.2(2).
(12) See MH 3-430 for list of Official Receiver's functions under corresponding provisions of IA 1986. See para. 5.018 re appeal against decision of Official Receiver.
(13) Sch.8, para. 19.
(14) Insolvency (1989 Order) (Commencement No.4) Order (Northern Ireland) 1991, Art.3(2).
(15) Art.356(1).
(16) R.6.163(2): para. 15.03.
(17) Art.356(2).
(18) Art.334(3): R.10.3.
(19) R.6.079(1).
(20) Ins Regs 22/24.
(21) R.10.4.

Chapter 4

INSOLVENCY PRACTITIONERS

Introduction

4.01   One of the most important innovations of the new insolvency law throughout the United Kingdom is the introduction of the requirement that anyone who is to carry out any form of insolvency administration must be duly authorised to do so and that such authorisation is only to be given to persons who fulfil certain requirements directed to demonstrate that they are competent.

4.02   Under the Order a person is not qualified to "act as an insolvency practitioner" unless he is at all times when so acting duly authorised and maintains the required fidelity insurance.[1] He is disqualified from acting at any time when he is an undischarged bankrupt, is subject to a disqualification order or is a mental patient.[2] A person other than the Official Receiver who acts as an insolvency practitioner at a time when he is not qualified to do so is guilty of an offence.[3]

4.03   The requirements of the Order as to acting as an insolvency practitioner do not apply to the Official Receiver,[4] nor do they apply to a person completing an insolvency administration which began before 1st October 1991.[5]

Authorised insolvency practitioner

4.04   In this book the term "authorised insolvency practitioner" refers to a person authorised under Part XII of the Order to act as an insolvency practitioner in relation to the debtor or bankrupt in question.

Acting as an insolvency practitioner[6]

4.05   A person acts as an insolvency practitioner in relation to an individual or a partnership by acting -
- (a)   as his trustee in bankruptcy or interim receiver of his property, or
- (b)   as trustee under a deed of arrangement made for the benefit of his creditors, or
- (c)   as supervisor of an approved voluntary arrangement proposed by him, or
- (d)   as administrator of the estate of a deceased individual administered in bankruptcy under the Deceased Insolvent Estates Order.

Responsible insolvency practitioner

4.06   In the Rules the term "responsible insolvency practitioner" means, in relation to personal insolvency, -
- (a)   the person acting as the supervisor of a voluntary arrangement or as trustee or interim receiver,

(b)   the Official Receiver acting as receiver and manager of a bankrupt's estate.[7]

Qualification of insolvency practitioners
(a) Who may act
4.07   A corporation may not act as an insolvency practitioner,[8] nor may the following persons -

(i)   an undischarged bankrupt (including a person whose estate has been sequestrated in Scotland),

(ii)   a person subject to a disqualification Order made under the Company Directors' Disqualification Act 1986 (applying to Great Britain) or the Companies (Northern Ireland) Order 1989, or

(iii) a mental patient within the meaning of the mental health legislation in Great Britain or Northern Ireland.[9]

(b) Authorisation
4.08   A person who is not ineligible to act as an insolvency practitioner for any of the reasons mentioned above, may obtain authorisation to do so in one of two ways -

(i)   by being a member of or a person subject to the practice rules of a professional body recognised for the purpose by the Department[10] and being permitted so to act by or under the rules of that body (i.e. holding a valid licence issued by it) or,

(ii)   by obtaining an authorisation from a "competent authority".[11]

4.09   In practice almost all insolvency practitioners will be licensed by a recognised professional association. Recognition is granted by the Department by order to bodies which satisfy statutory requirements designed to ensure that licensees are fit and proper persons and meet acceptable requirements as to education and practical training and experience.[12]

4.10   A person applying for authorisation from a competent authority must comply with Part II of the Insolvency Practitioners Regulations which include detailed requirements as to evidence of education, practical training and experience. The only "competent authority" to which application may be made at present is the Department, but the Department may in the future give directions specifying a body or person to issue authorisations in relation to specified cases.[13] An authorisation may be granted for a period not exceeding 3 years[14] and may be withdrawn.[15]

4.11   A person refused authorisation by a competent authority or whose authorisation is withdrawn may, within 14 days of being served with notice of the authority's decision, make representations to the authority, who may then re-consider the decision having regard to such representations.[16] There is no provision, as there is under the IA 1986, for a person refused authorisation or whose authorisation is withdrawn, to appeal to a tribunal. The only remedy in Northern Ireland is by judicial review.

(c) Security

4.12 To be qualified to act as an insolvency practitioner there must be in force security for the proper performance of the practitioner's functions which complies with prescribed requirements.[17]

4.13 Under Part III of the Insolvency Practitioners Regulations, at the time when the insolvency practitioner is appointed to act in relation to any person there must be in force a bond for the general penalty sum of £250,000, complying with Part I, Schedule 2 to the Regulations and there must be issued under the bond, as soon as reasonably possible after the appointment, a certificate of specific penalty in respect of acting in the particular case, under which the specific penalty sum is not less than the value of the assets of the person in question estimated in accordance with Part II of that Schedule, such sum to be increased where that estimate is subsequently revised upwards. The insolvency practitioner must file the certificate of specific penalty in the Court within 14 days of receipt. The bond is retained by the recognised professional body or, as the case may be, the competent authority by which the practitioner has been authorised to act as an insolvency practitioner.

4.14 The cost of the security is chargeable as an expense of the proceedings.[18]

4.15 Any person who, under the Rules, appoints or certifies the appointment of an insolvency practitioner is under a duty to satisfy himself that the person appointed or to be appointed has the required security.[19] It is also the duty of the creditors' committee in a bankruptcy or such a committee established for the purposes of a voluntary arrangement to review from time to time the adequacy of the practitioner's security.[20]

Records to be kept by insolvency practitioner

4.16 The insolvency practitioner must maintain in respect of each case in which he is acting records of matters prescribed by the Insolvency Practitioners Regulations.[21] These relate to his authorisation, his security, the progress of the administration, distribution to creditors and filing of statutory returns and accounts.[22] These records are in addition to the administrative and financial records required to be kept by a trustee in bankruptcy under the Insolvency Regulations.[23] The place where they are maintained must be notified by the practitioner to the authorising body.[24]

4.17 The records must be produced by the insolvency practitioner to the authorising body or its representative on reasonable notice and he must notify that body where and the manner in which they are to be produced.[25] Where the authorisation is by a professional body the practitioner may also be required to produce them to the Department on reasonable notice.[26]

4.18 The records must be preserved for a period of 10 years from the date on which the insolvency practitioner is granted his release or discharge or the date on which any security maintained in respect of the estate expired or otherwise ceases to have effect, whichever shall be the later.[27]

Footnotes

(1)   Art.349(2), (3).
(2)   Para.4.07.
(3)   Art.348.
(4)   Arts.3(5), 348(2).
(5)   Sch.8, para.18.
(6)   Art.3. The nominee under a proposed voluntary arrangement must also
         be qualified to act as an insolvency practitioner - Art.229(1)(d).
(7)   R.0.6.
(8)   Art.349(1).
(9)   Art.349(4).
(10)   Insolvency Practitioners (Recognised Professional Bodies) Order (North-
         ern Ireland) 1991.
(11)   Art.349(2), 350(3).
(12)   Art.350.
(13)   Art.351(2).
(14)   Ins Pract Regs 9.
(15)   Art.352 (4), (5).
(16)   Art.353, 354.
(17)   Art.349(3). Ins Pract Regs10/13.
(18)   R.12.09(3).
(19)   R.12.09(1).
(20)   R.12.09(2).
(21)   Ins Pract Regs15.
(22)   *Ibid* Sch.3.
(23)   Paras.13.128/129.
(24)   Ins Pract Regs17.
(25)   *Ibid*, 16(1), 17.
(26)   *Ibid*, 16(2).
(27)   *Ibid*, 18.

Chapter 5

GENERAL PROCEDURE

The Court
5.001   Jurisdiction under the Order is vested exclusively in the High Court of Justice in Northern Ireland. It is assigned to the Chancery Division[1] and is exercised by the Chancery Judge ("the Judge") under an assignment of business direction by the Lord Chief Justice under section 17 of the Judicature (Northern Ireland) Act 1978, or by any judge of the High Court or of the Court of Appeal acting as Chancery Judge[2] and by the Master (Bankruptcy) ("the Master") under the Rules.[3]

5.002   Applications to the High Court under Article 4 of the Family Law (Miscellaneous Provisions) (Northern Ireland) Order 1984 in the circumstances mentioned in Article 309(2) or 310(1) of the Insolvency Order[4] and under Article 88(3A) or 90(3A) of the Judgments Enforcement Order[5] are also assigned to the Chancery Division.[6]

5.003   The Court has general control of every bankruptcy and has full power to decide all questions of priorities and all other questions, whether of law or fact, arising in any bankruptcy.[7]

5.004   Where a bankruptcy order has been made the Judge may, of his own motion, order the transfer to the Chancery Division of any proceedings pending in another Division of the High Court brought by or against the bankrupt for the purpose of enforcing a claim against the bankrupt's estate, or brought by any person other than the bankrupt for the purpose of enforcing any such claim (including in either case proceedings of any description by a mortgagee).[8] Proceedings so transferred will be dealt with in the Chancery Office and not in the Bankruptcy and Companies Office but, subject to any direction of the Judge, any proceedings in chambers will be disposed of by the Master (Bankruptcy).[9]

The Office
5.005   All business in connection with proceedings under the Order, the associated applications referred to in paragraph 5.002 above and suits for the partition of land[10] maintained by the trustee in the circumstances mentioned in Article 309(3), except in respect of appeals to the Court of Appeal, is transacted in the Bankruptcy and Companies Office ("the Office").[11]

Court and chambers
5.006   The following matters and applications must be heard in open court -
- (a) matters and applications heard by the Judge, except those referred by the Master to be heard by the Judge in chambers or directed by the Judge to be so heard;

(b)   applications by bankrupts for leave to be a director of or directly or indirectly to take part or be concerned in the promotion, formation or management of a company;

(c)   public examinations of bankrupts; and

(d)   opposed applications for discharge of bankrupts or for the suspension or the lifting of the suspension of discharge.[12]

5.007   Every other matter or application before the Master must be heard in chambers.[13]

Judge and Master

5.008   The following applications must be made direct to the Judge -

(a)   applications for the committal of any person to prison for contempt;

(b)   applications for injunctions or for the modification or discharge of injunctions;

(c)   applications for interlocutory relief or directions after a matter has been referred to the Judge; and

(d)   appeals from an order or decision of the Master.[14]

5.009   Any other application must be made to the Master in the first instance.[15] Subject to any general or special direction of the Judge to the contrary, the Master may hear and determine any such application or, after giving any necessary directions, refer to the Judge any matter which he thinks should properly be decided by the Judge, and the Judge may either dispose of it or refer it back to the Master with such directions as he thinks fit.[16] However, any application may be made direct to the Judge in a proper case.[17]

5.010   Subject to the provisions as to applications required to be made to the Judge, anything to be done under or by virtue of the Order or the Rules by, to or before the Court may be done by, to or before the Judge or the Master.[18]

5.011   The provisions of the Supreme Court Rules governing the jurisdiction of other Supreme Court Masters[19] are expressly excluded.[20] Thus, the Master may issue a warrant for the arrest of a bankrupt or other person summoned for examination before the Court who fails to attend without reasonable excuse.[21]

Appeals

(a) From Judge

5.012   An appeal from an order of the Judge lies to the Court of Appeal but, except in cases of contempt of court, only with the leave of the High Court or the Court of Appeal.[22]

5.013   The procedure on such an appeal is regulated by Order 59 of the Supreme Court Rules. The notice of appeal must be filed in the Central Office of the Supreme Court and served on all respondents within 28 days from the date of filing of the order appealed from, unless the time is extended by the Judge or the Court of Appeal or a single Judge of that court.[23]

5.014   Except so far as otherwise directed by the Judge or the Court of Appeal, an appeal does not operate as a stay of proceedings under the order appealed from.[24]

(b) From Court of Appeal
5.015   An appeal from an order of the Court of Appeal lies to the House of Lords, but only with the leave of the Court of Appeal or the House of Lords.[25]

(c) From Master
5.016   An order or decision of the Master may be challenged by an appeal to the Judge.[26]

5.017   Procedure on an appeal from the Master is governed by Order 58 rule 1, paragraphs (2) to (4) of the Supreme Court Rules as modified by the Rules.[27] Unless otherwise ordered by the Judge or the Master, notice of appeal must be issued within 28 days after the order or decision appealed against was given or made, and served on every other party to the proceedings not less than 7 days before the day fixed for hearing the appeal.[28] Except so far as otherwise directed by the Judge or the Master, an appeal does not operate as a stay of proceedings under the decision appealed from.[29]

(d) From Department or Official Receiver
5.018   An appeal under the Order or the Rules against a decision of the Department or the Official Receiver must be brought within 28 days of the notification of the decision.[30]

Review of orders of the Court
5.019   Any order of the High Court made ex parte may be set aside.[31] In addition, the Court may, under Article 371, review, rescind or vary any order made by it in the exercise of its jurisdiction under the Order. This is a continuation of the same unique power enjoyed under the Bankruptcy Acts.[32] A corresponding provision, formerly contained in section 108 (1) of the Bankruptcy Act 1914, had been declared to confer a jurisdiction which, in a proper case, is almost without limit.[33] The power is exercisable by the Judge or the Master, depending on who made the order sought to be reviewed. The application for review should be made by ordinary application on notice to the other parties affected by the order.

5.020   A review under Article 371 is to be distinguished from an appeal and it may take place whilst an appeal is pending.[34] A decision of the Master, as mentioned above, may be appealed to the Judge, but the Judge cannot, under Article 371, review an order of the Master.[35]

Rights of audience
5.021   A solicitor has right of audience in the High Court or the Court of Appeal in all individual insolvency proceedings, whether in court or in chambers.[36] The Master may, in proceedings before him, also permit such right of

audience to be enjoyed by an experienced solicitor's clerk acting on behalf of his principal.[37]

5.022   Official Receivers and deputy Official Receivers have right of audience in all insolvency proceedings.[38]

Title of proceedings
5.023   Proceedings under the Order relating to the insolvency of individuals must be headed -
> "IN THE HIGH COURT OF JUSTICE IN NORTHERN IRELAND
>   CHANCERY DIVISION (BANKRUPTCY)"[39]

5.024   Proceedings relating to individual debtors are to be intituled "Re (*name and short description, including any current trading name, of debtor or bankrupt to which the proceedings relate)*"
To this there should be added any necessary additions.[40] Thus, for example, in an application to the Court the applicant and respondent must be named, as indicated in the prescribed forms of application.[41]

5.025   Proceedings under the Insolvent Partnerships Order[42] must be headed and intituled in accordance with the forms scheduled to that Order.[43]

Orders of the Court
5.026   Every order of the Court must be drawn up, sealed and filed, unless it falls into the categories of orders which the Judge directs need not be drawn up or unless the Judge or the Master who makes the order directs that no order be drawn up.[44] Where no order is drawn up a note or memorandum of the order, signed or initialled by the Judge or the Master making the order and filed, is sufficient evidence of the order having been made.[45] An order will, however, be drawn up and filed upon the request of a party, to be made within 7 days after the order is made, and such a request must be made by a party wishing to appeal against the order.[46]

5.027   Under the "slip rule" clerical mistakes in orders, or errors arising therein from any accidental slip or omission, may at any time be corrected by the Judge or the Master who made the order.[47]

5.028   Orders of the Court are enforceable in the same manner as a judgment to the same effect.[48]

Documents for use in the Court
5.029   All documents for use in the Court must comply with the Supreme Court Rules as to paper quality and size and the Supreme Court Rules regarding furnishing of copies also apply.[49]

Formal defects and irregularities in proceedings: amendments
5.030   Formal defects in proceedings or any irregularity do not invalidate the proceedings, unless the Court considers that substantial injustice has been caused by the defect or irregularity, and that the injustice cannot be remedied by any order.[50]

5.031   The Rules include specific provisions for amendment of documents.[51] In addition, the Court has wide powers of amendment under the Supreme Court Rules.[52]

Court records
(a) Registers
<u>(i) Records to be kept</u>
5.032   The Court is required to keep records of all insolvency proceedings and to cause to be entered in the records (i.e. in a Court register kept in the Office) the taking of any steps in the proceedings and such decisions of the Court in relation thereto as it thinks fit.[53]

<u>(ii) Inspection</u>
5.033   The Court registers are in general open to public inspection.[54] However, if the Master is not satisfied as to the propriety of the purpose for which inspection is required, he may refuse to allow it.[55] A person refused inspection may apply forthwith, ex parte, to the Judge, who may refuse the inspection, or allow it on such terms as he thinks fit.[56] The Judge's decision is final.[57]

(b) Court file
<u>(i) Contents</u>
5.034   There must be opened and maintained in the Office a file of proceedings in each case and, subject to directions of the Master, all documents relating to such proceedings must be placed on the relevant file.[58]

<u>(ii) Inspection</u>
5.035   Each of the following persons, or someone properly authorised by him on his behalf, has the right, at all reasonable times, to inspect the Court's file of proceedings -
   (A) the responsible insolvency practitioner acting in the proceedings;
   (B) any duly authorised officer of the Department;
   (C) any person stating himself in writing to be a creditor of the individual to whom the proceedings relate;
   (D) in individual voluntary arrangement proceedings, the debtor;
   (E) in bankruptcy proceedings, the bankrupt, any person against whom, or by whom, a bankruptcy petition has been presented and any person duly served with a statutory demand.[59]

5.036   In addition, the Court may give any person special leave to inspect the file.[60]

5.037 The Court may, on the application of the Official Receiver, the responsible insolvency practitioner acting in the proceedings or any party appearing to have an interest, direct that the right of inspection is not to be exercisable in the case of documents, or parts of documents (specified generally or specially) without the Court's leave.[61]

5.038 As in the case of the Court registers, the Master may also refuse inspection to any person if not satisfied as to the propriety of the purpose for which inspection is required, subject to the same right of appeal to the Judge.[62]

5.039 The general right of inspection of the Court file is subject to special restrictions in respect of so much of it as shows the grounds of an application under Article 337 (private examination) and to any copy of proposed interrogatories.[63]

5.040 If the Department or the Official Receiver requires to inspect the file, it is to be transmitted upon request, unless it is for the time being in use for the Court's own purposes.[64]

5.041 Any person who has the right to inspect the Court file of proceedings, or his solicitor, may have an office copy of any document from the file, bearing the Court's seal, upon payment of the prescribed fee.[65]

(iii) List of creditors
5.042 In bankruptcy proceedings, where a statement of affairs has not been filed, a creditor who has the right to inspect the Court file may require the responsible insolvency practitioner to send him a list of the creditors and the amounts of their respective debts, on payment of the appropriate fee.[66]

Other insolvency records
(a) Inspection
5.043 Where the responsible insolvency practitioner considers that a document forming part of the records of the insolvency in his custody, except a proof or proxy, should be treated as confidential or is of such a nature that its disclosure would be calculated to be injurious to the interests of the creditors, he may refuse inspection to a person who would otherwise be entitled to inspect it, including the members of a creditors' committee.[67] If he does so refuse, the person wishing to inspect may apply to the Court and on such an application the Court may overrule the insolvency practitioner's determination or sustain it subject to such conditions (if any) as it thinks fit to impose.[68]

(b) Copies
5.044 A person having the right to inspect records held by the responsible insolvency practitioner may take copies on payment of the appropriate fee.[69]

5.045 Where the responsible insolvency practitioner or the Official Receiver is requested by a creditor or member of a creditors' committee to supply copies of any documents, he is entitled to charge the appropriate fee.[70]

False claim of right to inspect documents
5.046 Where under the Rules creditors have the right to inspect any documents, whether on the Court file or in the custody of a responsible insolvency practitioner or other person, it is an offence for a person, with the intention of obtaining the sight of documents which he has not any right to inspect, falsely to claim to be a creditor.[71]

Applications to the Court
(a) Introduction
5.047 The procedure governing applications to the Court under the Order or the Rules otherwise than by petition, is regulated by Chapter 2 of Part 7 of the Rules[72] and is dealt with in the following two paragraphs.

(b) Form and contents of application
5.048 If the application is not made in pending proceedings before the Court it must be made by "originating application".[73] An application in pending proceedings must be made by "ordinary application".[74] The former forms of application by motion or summons or the former special forms of application for particular relief are discontinued in respect of applications governed by the Rules, but will continue to be used in applications to which the Bankruptcy Rules continue to apply and in the applications assigned to the Office which are regulated by the Supreme Court Rules, (e.g. partition suit by trustee)[75]

5.049 The application must be in writing, in the appropriate prescribed form, signed by or on behalf of the applicant's solicitor or by the applicant himself if acting in person, and state -
   (i)   the names of the parties;
   (ii) the nature of the relief or order applied for or the directions sought from the Court;
   (iii) the names and addresses of the persons (if any) on whom it is intended to serve the application or that no person is intended to be served;
   (iv) where the Order or the Rules require that notice of the application is to be given to specified persons, the names and addresses of all those persons (so far as known to the applicant); and
   (v)   the applicant's address for service.[76]

5.050 An originating application must set out the grounds on which the applicant claims to be entitled to the relief or order sought.[77]

5.051 The application is filed in the Office, accompanied by one copy and, where service is required, additional copies for service.[78]

(c) Fixing of hearing

5.052 Subject to the provisions mentioned in the following two paragraphs for the immediate hearing of applications and to any special provision of the Rules under which a particular application is made, the Office must, upon presentation of the application and necessary copies and, unless the Rule under which the application is brought provides otherwise or the Court otherwise orders, fix a "venue" for the application to be heard (i.e. appoint a time, date and place for the hearing[79]).[80] Save in exceptional circumstances, the place for the hearing will be the Royal Courts of Justice, Chichester Street, Belfast.

5.053 Where an application does not require to be served on or notice of it given to, any person, it may be heard ex parte, either forthwith or at a time and place fixed by the Office.[81] An order made ex parte may be set aside by the Court.[82]

5.054 The Court may also, in a case of urgency, hear any application immediately, either with or without notice to, or the attendance of, other parties, and any such application may be heard on terms providing for the filing or serving of documents or the carrying out of other formalities, as the Court thinks fit.[83]

(d) Service

5.055 A sealed copy of the application, endorsed with the venue for the hearing, must be served on each respondent named in the application, unless the Court directs that the giving of notice to any person be dispensed with or that notice be given in some other way.[84] The Court may also direct service of the application upon persons other than those specified by the relevant provision of the Order or the Rules.[85]

5.056 Where a Rule requires notice of the venue fixed for an application to be given, this may (and in practice usually will) be done by service of a sealed copy of the application, endorsed with the venue.[86]

5.057 Unless the provision of the Order or the Rules under which the application is made otherwise provides, or where the application is one which the Court determines to be urgent, an application requiring service must be served at least 14 days before the hearing date.[87] In a case of urgency, but where an immediate hearing is not considered appropriate, the Court may authorise a shorter period of service and may do so on terms providing for the filing or service of documents, or the carrying out of other formalities, as it thinks fit.[88]

(e) Adjournment of hearing: directions

5.058 The Court may adjourn the hearing of an application on such terms (if any) as it thinks fit and it may at any time give such directions as it thinks fit as to -

    (i)   service of notice of the application on or to any person, whether in connection with the venue of a resumed hearing or for any other purpose;

(ii)   whether particulars of claim and defence are to be delivered and generally as to the procedure on the application;

(iii) the manner in which any evidence is to be adduced at a resumed hearing and in particular as to the taking of evidence wholly or in part by affidavit or orally, the cross-examination of any deponents to affidavits, or any report to be given by the Official Receiver or any other person authorised to give evidence by report instead of by affidavit;

(iv)   the matters to be dealt with in evidence.[89]

(f) Affidavits and reports

5.059   Unless any provision of the Rules otherwise provides or the Court otherwise directs, evidence may be given by affidavit.[90] The Court may, on the application of any party, order the attendance for cross-examination of the person making the affidavit, and if a person does not attend when so ordered, his affidavit may not be used in evidence without the leave of the Court.[91]

5.060   Where an affidavit is made by the Official Receiver or the responsible insolvency practitioner, the deponent must state the capacity in which he makes it, the position which he holds, and the address at which he works.[92]

5.061   An affidavit of proof of debt by a creditor may be sworn before his own solicitor.[93] Any affidavit or declaration may be sworn before the Official Receiver or any officer of the Court authorised to take affidavits.[94]

5.062   With the modifications mentioned above, the rules and practice of the High Court with regard to the form, contents and use of affidavits apply.[95]

5.063   The Official Receiver may file a report instead of an affidavit in any case.[96] Unless the application involves other parties, or the Court otherwise orders, this alternative mode of giving evidence may also be used by -

(i)   a trustee in bankruptcy,

(ii)   an interim receiver,

(iii) a nominee or a supervisor of a voluntary arrangement,

(iv)   a special manager, or

(v)   an insolvency practitioner appointed by the Court under Article 247 on the hearing of a bankruptcy petition by a debtor.[97]

5.064   Any report so filed is to be treated as if it were an affidavit.[98] If filed by the Official Receiver in accordance with the Order or the Rules the report is prima facie evidence of any matter contained in it.[99]

5.065   An affidavit supporting an application other than an ex parte application need not be filed with the application. Unless the provisions of the Order or the Rules under which the application is made otherwise provides, or the Court otherwise allows -

   (i)   an affidavit intended to be relied upon at the first hearing of the application must be filed and a copy served on the respondent not less than 14 days before the hearing date, and

  (ii)   where a respondent intends to oppose the application and to rely on affidavit evidence for that purpose, he must file the affidavit and serve a copy on the applicant not less than 7 days before the hearing date.[100]

5.066   The prescribed forms of order do not require affidavits read on an application to be listed. They are embraced by the phrase "upon reading the evidence."

Service and notice of proceedings: general provisions
(a) General
5.067   Where the Rules do not make express provision, the service of documents and the giving of notice in insolvency proceedings is governed by Order 65 of the Supreme Court Rules, with the following modifications -

   (i)   the exclusion in Order 65, rule 7, of originating process from the operation of that rule (which relates to the effect of service after certain hours) does not apply to an application in any insolvency proceedings; thus, any such application (whether an originating application or an ordinary application) served personally or by leaving at the proper address of the person to be served after 12 noon on a Saturday or after 4 00 in the afternoon on any other weekday is deemed to have been served on the Monday following that Saturday or on the day following that other weekday as the case may be;

  (ii)   Order 65, rule 9, relating to dispensing with service of a document on a person who is in default of appearance or has no address for service, does not apply.[101]

5.068   No process may be served in Northern Ireland on a Sunday.[102]

(b) Mode of service
<u>(i) Personal</u>
5.069   Personal service of a document is permitted in all cases[103] and is the primary mode of service of certain documents.[104] An application for committal for contempt of Court must be served personally.

<u>(ii) By post</u>
5.070   Where a Rule refers to giving notice, or to delivering, sending or serving any document and does not expressly require personal service, the notice or document may be sent by post.[105] Any form of post may be used, unless under a particular Rule a specified form is expressly required.[106]

5.071   A document to be served by post must be contained in an envelope addressed to the person to be served and pre-paid for either first or second class post.[107] It may be sent to his last known address.[108]

5.072   Unless the contrary is shown, the document is treated as served on the second business day after the date of posting, if first class post is used, or on the fourth business day after posting if second class post is used.[109] The date of posting a document is presumed, unless the contrary is shown, to be the date shown in the post-mark on the envelope containing it.[110]

(iii) By fax
5.073   Documents not required to be served personally may be served by facsimile transmission.[111]

(iv) Substituted service
5.074   Subject to the special provisions relating to substituted service of a creditor's bankruptcy petition,[112] substituted service of documents in insolvency proceedings is governed by Order 65, rule 4 of the Supreme Court Rules. Thus, the Court may order substituted service of any document which is required by any provision of the Rules to be served personally if it appears to it that it is impracticable for any reason to effect personal service. Accordingly, where difficulty in effecting personal service is anticipated, detailed instructions should be given to the process server as to the steps required to be taken to provide appropriate evidence to support an application for an order for substituted service.[113]

(c) Service out of the jurisdiction [114]
5.075   Order 11 of the Supreme Court Rules which governs the service of a High Court writ of summons, originating summons, notice or petition out of the jurisdiction does not apply to insolvency proceedings.[115]

5.076   Where in insolvency proceedings any process or order of the Court or other document is required to be served on a person who is not in Northern Ireland, the Court may order service to be effected within such time, on such person, at such place and in such manner as it thinks fit, and may also require such proof of service as it thinks fit.[116]

5.077   An application for leave to serve out of the jurisdiction must be supported by an affidavit stating the grounds of the application and in what place or country the person to be served is, or probably may be found.[117]

(d) Service on solicitor
5.078   A notice or other document required or authorised under the Order or the Rules to be served on a person may be served on his solicitor if such person has indicated that his solicitor is authorised to accept service on his behalf.[118]

(e) Service of notices
5.079   All notices required or authorised by or under the Order or the Rules to be given must be in writing, unless otherwise provided or the Court allows the notice to be given in some other way.[119]

5.080   Where the service of notices by the Official Receiver or the responsible insolvency practitioner is required to be proved, proof may be given by a certificate that the notice was duly posted,
signed -
- (i)   where sent or given by the Official Receiver, by him or a member of his staff;
- (ii)   where sent or given by the responsible insolvency practitioner, by him or his solicitor, or a partner or employee of either of them.[120]

5.081   Where a notice is sent or given by any other person, service may be proved by a certificate by that person that he posted the notice, or instructed another person, (naming him) to do so.[121]

5.082   A certificate of posting may be endorsed on a copy or specimen of the notice.[122]

Attendance of insolvency practitioner
5.083   Where the solicitor acting for the responsible insolvency practitioner is required to attend proceedings in the Court, the responsible insolvency practitioner himself need not attend, unless directed by the Court.[123]

5.084   An insolvency practitioner who attends a sitting of the Court unnecessarily risks having his charges for such attendance disallowed.

Attendance of witnesses
5.085   The attendance of witnesses in insolvency proceedings, other than persons summoned for examination under the Order, is secured by the issue of a subpoena under the Supreme Court Rules.

Discovery and interrogatories
5.086   Any party to insolvency proceedings may, with the leave of the Court, to be applied for ex parte, administer interrogatories to, or obtain discovery from, any other party to those proceedings.[124] The procedure is governed by Order 24 or 26 of the Supreme Court Rules.

Security in Court
5.087   Where security has to be given to the Court, otherwise than in relation to costs, it may be given either by bond or by the payment of money into court.[125] The penal sum taken in the bond or the sum paid into court must be not less than the sum for which security is to be given and probable costs.[126] A bond must be entered into with an approved surety company listed in Order 108 of the Supreme Court Rules and in the form prescribed by that Order, but no sureties are necessary unless the Court requires them.[127] Where security is given by lodgment of money in court the Master must forthwith notify the persons for whose protection the security is given that the money has been lodged.[128]

5.088 Security for costs is to be given in such manner, at such times and on such terms (if any) as the Court directs.[129]

5.089 Any money lodged in court under an order of the Court or a certificate of the Master may only be paid out in pursuance of an order of the Court.[130]

Recording of examinations
5.090 The examination of the bankrupt at a public examination or of the bankrupt or other person at a private examination is recorded either by a shorthand writer appointed by the Court or by mechanical recording.

5.091 The shorthand writer appointed is either an official shorthand writer to the Court, nominated by the Judge, or another shorthand writer appointed to record a particular examination.[131]

5.092 An official shorthand writer, at the time of his appointment to the Court, makes a declaration faithfully to record the examination of all persons whose examination he is appointed to take down.[132] Another person is required to make a similar declaration on each occasion on which he is appointed shorthand writer.[133]

5.093 Where a shorthand writer is appointed on the application of the Official Receiver to record an examination, the cost of the written record is deemed an expense of the Official Receiver in the proceedings.[134] Subject to this, the remuneration of the shorthand writer is payable by the party at whose instance he was appointed or out of the bankrupt's estate, or otherwise, as the Court may direct, at the rates payable in the Court of Appeal.[135]

5.094 As an alternative to recording by a shorthand note, an examination may be recorded mechanically. The Rules make provision for certifying such recording and the cost is borne in the same way as for a shorthand record.[136]

Admission of court documents and documents issued from the Department
5.095 Judicial notice is to be taken of the signature of officers of and of the official seals or stamps of courts in the United Kingdom.[137]

5.096 Any document purporting to be, or to contain, any order, direction or certificate issued by the Department is to be received in evidence and deemed to be or (as the case may be) contain that order or certificate, or those directions, without further proof, unless the contrary is shown, and a certificate by the Department confirming the making of any order, the issuing of any document, or the exercise of any discretion, power or obligation arising or imposed under the Order or the Rules is conclusive evidence of the matters dealt with in the certificate.[138]

Gazette notices and newspaper advertisements

5.097   A copy of every issue of the Belfast Gazette is preserved in the Office for at least 2 years.[139]   Accordingly, it is not necessary for a Gazette notice to be vouched by the person inserting it. Where an advertisement relating to insolvency proceedings pending in the Court appears in a newspaper, the person inserting the advertisement is required to file a copy of it in the Office, endorsed with or accompanied by such particulars as are necessary to identify the proceedings and the date of the advertisement's appearance.[140]   An officer of the Court files a memorandum giving the date of and other particulars relating to any notice published in the Gazette and any newspaper advertisement relating to pending insolvency proceedings.[141]   This memorandum is prima facie evidence that any notice or advertisement mentioned in it was duly inserted in the specified issue of the newspaper or the Gazette.[142]

5.098   A copy of the Gazette containing any notice required by the Order or the Rules to be gazetted is evidence of any facts stated in the notice.[143]

5.099   Where notice of an order of the Court is required by the Order or the Rules to be gazetted, a copy of the Gazette containing the notice may be produced in any proceedings as conclusive evidence that the order was made on the date specified in the notice.[144]

5.100   Where an order of the Court which has been gazetted has been varied, the person whose responsibility it was to procure the requisite entry in the Gazette must forthwith cause the variation of the order to be gazetted, and a similar duty is placed on such person to place a further entry in the Gazette to correct any error or inaccuracy in a Gazette entry.[145]

Time

5.101   Where under any provision of the Order, except those relating to deeds of arrangement, or of the Rules, the time for doing anything is limited, the Court may extend the time, either before or after it has expired, on such terms, if any, as it thinks fit.[146]

5.102   The provisions of the Supreme Court Rules excluding the Long Vacation in reckoning any period prescribed for serving, filing or amending any pleadings and requiring notice of intention to proceed after a year's delay do not apply to insolvency proceedings.[147]   Otherwise, Order 3 of the Supreme Court Rules does apply.[148]   Thus, the computation of time is governed by Order 3, rules 1, 2 and 4. The Court may, on such terms as it thinks just, by order extend or abridge the period within which a person is required or authorised by the Rules, or by any order or direction, to do any act in any proceedings.[149]   The period within which a person is so required to serve, file or amend any document may be extended by consent (given in writing) without an order of the Court.[150]

Contempt of Court
5.103   In addition to the Court's power to exercise the general jurisdiction of the High Court to commit for contempt of court,[151] it may commit a bankrupt under specific provisions of the Order making wilful failure to discharge obligations imposed on him a contempt of court.[152]

5.104   An application for committal under the Order may be made by the Official Receiver or the trustee, as appropriate, by ordinary application.[153] The hearing is before the Judge in open court.[154] There is a prescribed form of warrant of committal for contempt[155] and of order of discharge from custody on contempt.[156]

Persons under disability
5.105   Where it appears to the Court that a person affected by the proceedings is incapable of managing and administering his property and affairs either by reason of mental disorder within the meaning of the Mental Health (Northern Ireland) Order 1986, or due to physical affliction or disability, it may appoint such person as it thinks fit[157] to appear for, represent or act for the incapacitated person, either generally or for the purpose of any particular application or proceeding, or for the exercise of particular rights or powers which the incapacitated person might have exercised but for his incapacity.[158]

5.106   The appointment may be made by the Court either of its own motion or on an application by -
  (a)   person who has been appointed by a court in the United Kingdom or elsewhere to manage the affairs of, or to represent, the incapacitated person, or
  (b)   any relative or friend of the incapacitated person who appears to the Court to be a proper person to make the application, or
  (c)   the Official Receiver, or
  (d)   the person who, in relation to the proceedings, is the responsible insolvency practitioner.[159]

5.107   The application may be made ex parte in the first instance, but the Court may adjourn the hearing and direct notice to be given to the person alleged to be incapacitated, or any other person.[160]

5.108   Unless the incapacitated person is a patient within the meaning of the Mental Health (Northern Ireland) Order 1986, the application must be supported by a report from a registered medical practitioner as to such person's mental or physical condition.[161] Where the application is made by someone other than the Official Receiver such report must be made by affidavit.[162] Where the application is by the Official Receiver the report is exhibited to his report to the Court.[163]

5.109   Any notice served on, or sent to, a person appointed to act for an incapacitated person has the same effect as if it had been served on, or given to, the incapacitated person.[164]

Costs
(a) Meaning of "costs"
5.110   By virtue of the Interpretation Act (Northern Ireland) 1954,[165] except where a contrary intention appears,[166] the word "costs" in the Order includes fees, charges, disbursements, expenses and remuneration. Thus, it includes the remuneration of any person employed by the Official Receiver or trustee.

(b) Payment of costs
5.111   All costs incurred in the course of bankruptcy proceedings are to be regarded as expenses of the bankruptcy.[167]

5.112   Subject to the provisions of the Order and the Rules, the costs of proceedings are in the discretion of the Court and the Court may determine by whom and to what extent the costs are to be paid.[168]

5.113   The order of priority of payment of costs payable out of the estate is regulated by the Rules.[169]

5.114   Certain provisions of the Rules protect the Official Receiver from liability for costs of specified proceedings.[170]

(c) Applications for costs
5.115   Where an application is made to the Court for the allowance of costs, otherwise than at the time of the proceedings, the applicant must serve a sealed copy of the application on the responsible insolvency practitioner and in a bankruptcy, on the Official Receiver.[171] The insolvency practitioner and, where appropriate, the Official Receiver, may appear at the hearing of the application.[172] No costs are allowable to the applicant unless the Court is satisfied that the application could not have been made at the time of the proceedings.[173]

(d) Witnesses' expenses
5.116   No allowance as a witness in any examination or other proceeding before the Court may be made to the bankrupt except by a direction of the Court.[174] In a proper case the Official Receiver will no doubt advise the bankrupt, if he is not represented, to apply for such a direction.

5.117   A petitioner is not entitled to witness expenses for attending the hearing of the petition, but if his costs are taxed the Taxing Master may allow his expenses of travelling and subsistence.[175]

(e) Expenses of attendance by insolvency practitioner
5.118   Where, otherwise than by direction of the Court, the responsible insolvency practitioner attends proceedings in the Court when the attendance of his solicitor is required, his expenses of attending will not be chargeable against the insolvent's estate.[176]

(f) Costs of Official Receiver or insolvency practitioner as party to proceedings
5.119   Where the Official Receiver or the responsible insolvency practitioner is made a party to any proceedings on the application of another party to the proceedings, he is not personally liable for costs unless the Court otherwise directs.[177] On a construction of a similar provision in the English Bankruptcy Rules 1915, it was held that "the court" meant the court having jurisdiction in bankruptcy and that, notwithstanding the rule, a trustee in bankruptcy who was the unsuccessful defendant in an action should pay the plaintiff's costs.[178]

5.120   In its application to the Official Receiver, this provision is without prejudice to other provisions of the Order or the Rules by virtue of which the Official Receiver is not in any event to be liable for costs.[179]

(g) Costs of successive bankruptcy petitions
5.121   Where a bankruptcy petition is presented by a person other than the debtor and, before it is heard the debtor presents such a petition on which a bankruptcy order is made, no costs may be allowed to the bankrupt or his solicitor out of the estate unless the Court considers that the estate has benefited by the debtor's conduct or that there are otherwise special circumstances justifying the allowance of costs.[180]

(h) Fixing of costs by the Court: measurement by Taxing Master
5.122   Under certain provisions of the Rules the Court is required to fix, or is authorised to allow, the remuneration of a responsible insolvency practitioner or of a person employed by him in insolvency proceedings. Thus, for example, the remuneration of an interim receiver or of a special manager is fixed by the Court. [181] In any such case the Court may either fix the remuneration itself or direct that it be measured by the Taxing Master.[182]

5.123   Where a direction for measurement by the Taxing Master is given the person whose remuneration is to be measured must lodge in the Taxing Master's Office a bill containing particulars of his charges and disbursements and a copy of the Court's direction.[183] The Taxing Master then notifies the person lodging the bill and any other persons to whom he considers notice ought to be given of the time and place appointed for the measurement to take place.[184] Upon receiving such notice the person lodging the bill must attend in accordance with the notice and produce such information as the Taxing Master may require.[185]

5.124   Upon completion of the measurement the Taxing Master issues a certificate in accordance with the Supreme Court Rules relating to a certificate of taxation.[186] Any party dissatisfied with any decision of the Taxing Master may apply to him to review his decision, which review is conducted in accordance with the Supreme Court Rules governing the review of taxation.[187]

5.125   The procedure for measurement by the Taxing Master under the Rules applies also to the remuneration of an accountant in bankruptcy proceedings under the Bankruptcy Rules.[188]

(i) Taxation of costs[189]
<u>(i) When required</u>
5.126   Taxation of costs payable out of the insolvent's estate in insolvency proceedings is no longer mandatory in every case. The Court may in any proceedings order costs to be taxed but, subject to any such order, taxation is only necessary if the responsible insolvency practitioner cannot agree the costs with the person entitled to payment or if the creditors' committee requires taxation.[190]

5.127   The provisions mentioned in the preceding paragraph apply not only to insolvency proceedings under the Order but to bankruptcy proceedings commenced before the Rules came into force.[191]

<u>(ii) Taxation procedure</u>
5.128   Order 62 of the Supreme Court Rules regulates the procedure for taxation, subject to the special provisions of the Rules and with any necessary modifications.[192] Unless otherwise directed or authorised, the costs of the trustee are allowable on the standard basis.[193]

5.129   If costs cannot be agreed between the responsible insolvency practitioner and the person entitled to payment or if the creditors' committee requires taxation, the responsible insolvency practitioner may require taxation by serving a notice in writing on that person requiring him to deliver his bill of costs to the Taxing Master for taxation.[194]

5.130   A person whose costs are required to be taxed must deliver his bill of costs to the Taxing Master for taxation, and if he does not do so within 3 months of being so required in writing, or within any extended time granted by the Court on his application, the insolvency practitioner may deal with the insolvent's estate without regard to any claim by that person, whose claim is also forfeited, as is any claim against the insolvency practitioner in his personal capacity.[195] These provisions are designed to prevent a distribution of an insolvent's estate being delayed because of avoidable delay in determining the amount of costs payable out of the estate. If the person whose costs are required to be taxed is unable to procure delivery of his bill of costs to the Taxing Master within the prescribed time and cannot obtain an extension of time from the responsible insolvency practitioner, he should apply to the Court for an extension of time.

5.131   The bill of costs of any person employed in insolvency proceedings by a responsible insolvency practitioner must, before it can be taxed, be endorsed with a certificate of employment signed by the insolvency practitioner stating the name and address of the person employed, details of the functions to be carried out under the employment, and a note of any special terms of remuneration which have been agreed.[196]

5.132   A solicitor acting for a debtor who presents his own bankruptcy petition must in his bill of costs give credit for any sum or security received from the debtor as a deposit on account of the costs to be incurred in respect of the filing and prosecution of his petition, and the deposit must be noted by the Taxing Master on the certificate of taxation.[197]

5.133   Where the Court directs that costs be paid otherwise than out of the insolvent's estate, the Taxing Master must note on the certificate of taxation by whom, or the manner in which, the costs are to be paid.[198]

(j) Payment on account of costs
5.134   Where the costs of any person employed by an insolvency practitioner in insolvency proceedings are required to be taxed or fixed by an order of the Court,[199] the insolvency practitioner may nevertheless make payments on account to such person, subject to an undertaking to repay immediately any money which may, on taxation, or when fixed by the Court prove to have been overpaid, with interest at the rate applicable to a money judgment of the High Court on the date payment was made and for the period from the date of payment to that of repayment.[200]

Footnotes

(1)   RSC O.1, r.10(b).

(2)   Judicature (Northern Ireland) Act 1978, ss. 5(3), 6(1).

(3)   R.7.03(2), made under Art.359(2)(c).

(4)   Paras.14.037, 14.042.

(5)   Para.28.37.

(6)   RSC O.1, r.10(d),(e).

(7)   Art.334(1): MH 3-345. As to exercise of similar powers under previous legislation, see JH 2.33/36.

(8)   R.7.04(1)-(3).

(9)   R.7.04(4).

(10)   All partition actions are assigned to the Chancery Division - RSC O.1, r.10 (a)(ix).

(11)   RSC O.1, r.15.

(12)   R.7.02(1).

(13)   R.7.02(2).

(14)   R.7.03(1).

(15)   R.7.03(2).

(16)   R.7.03(3).

(17)   R.7.03(4). E.g. where the Judge is already seized of the matter.

(18)   R.7.03(5).

(19)   RSC O.32, rr. 11 & 12.

(20)   R.7.03(6).

(21)   Paras.11.38, 11.70. Other Supreme Court Masters are restrained from issuing arrest warrants by RSC O.32 r.11(1)(b).

(22)   Judicature (Northern Ireland) Act 1978, ss.35,44. In an exceptional case an appeal may lie from the High Court direct to the House of Lords under the Administration of Justice Act 1969, ss.12-15.

(23)   RSC O.59, rr. 3(4), 4(1)(b), 15. O.3,rr. 5(1),(4). Judicature (Northern Ireland) Act 1978 s.37(2).

(24)   RSC O.59,r. 13(1).

(25)   Judicature (Northern Ireland) Act 1978, s.42. See fn.(22) re appeals direct to House of Lords from High Court.

(26)   R.7.42(1). Following the terminology of Art. 359(2)(c) this Rule refers to appeal as the method of reviewing decisions of the Master by the Judge. Such review is in addition to the Master's power to review his own decisions under Art. 371 (para. 5.019 below). See Atkin Form 432 for precedent of appeal against a bankruptcy order.

(27)   R.7.42(2). The grounds of appeal should be set out in the notice of appeal - Atkin Form 430.

(28)   RSC O.58, r. 1(2),(3) as modified by R.7.42(2): Hals726.

(29)   RSC O.58, r. 1(4).

(30)   R.7.44. The relevant decisions of the Secretary of State under the corresponding provisions of the IA 1986 are listed in MH 7-627. They include

decisions re appointment, removal and release of trustees, decisions of
the Secretary of State acting through the Official Receiver when func-
tioning in place of a creditors' committee and decisions on applications
for certificates under s. 332(2)(c) (Art. 305(2)(c)) that it would be inappropriate or inexpedient for the trustee to apply for a charge on the bankrupt's home - para.14.114.

(31) RSC O.32, r.8.
(32) JH 3.05/08.
(33) *Re Thomas* [1984] 1 WLR 232, 235, per Dillon L.J. see para. 22.02 re
       rescission of bankruptcy order.
(34) *Re Wike, ex p. Keighley* (1874) 9 Ch App 667.
(35) *Re Maugham* (1888) 21 QB 0.214 - (1888) 21 QBD 21.
(36) Judicature (Northern Ireland) Act 1978 s. 106(1)(a).
(37) Judicature (Northern Ireland) Act 1978 s. 106(3).
(38) R.7.46.
(39) R.7.01(2).
(40) *Ibid.*
(41) FF.7.01, 7.02.
(42) Ch 24.
(43) IPO Sch.3.
(44) R.7.49(1),(2).
(45) R.7.49(3).
(46) R.7.49(4).
(47) RSC O.20, r.11. See Supreme Court Practice 1991 20/11/1 - 20/11/8 for
       commentary on corresponding rule of English Supreme Court Rules.
(48) R.7.19.
(49) RSC O.66, rr. 1-4.
(50) R.7.50. This Rule does not apply to a statutory demand - *Re a Debtor
       (No.190 of 1987)*, The Times, 21 May 1988.
(51) E.g. RR 6.019, 6.032, 6.045.
(52) RSC O.2, O.20, rr.5,7,8. Supreme Court Practice 1991, 2/1/1 - 2/2/4, 20/5
       - 8/1, 20/5 - 8/33.
(53) R.7.24.
(54) R.7.25(1).
(55) R.7.25(2).
(56) *Ibid.*
(57) R.7.25(3).
(58) R.7.26.
(59) R.7.27(1)-(3).
(60) R.7.27(4).
(61) R.7.27(5),(6).
(62) R.7.27(8).
(63) R.9.5(3).
(64) R.7.27(7).
(65) RR.7.55, 12.16.
(66) R.12.19. "Appropriate fee" is defined in R.0.2.
(67) R.12.14(1),(2),(4).

(68)   R.12.14(3).
(69)   RR.12.16, 0.2 ("Appropriate fee").
(70)   R.12.17.
(71)   R.12.20.
(72)   R.7.05. For procedure on bankruptcy petitions see Ch. 70
(73)   R.7.06(1).
(74)   *Ibid.*
(75)   Paras.5.002, 5.005.
(76)   RR.7.06(2), 7.07(1),(3): FF.7.01, 7.02.
(77)   R.7.07(2).
(78)   R.7.08(1).
(79)   R.0.2.
(80)   R.7.08(2).
(81)   R.7.09. Where a venue is fixed R.7.08 (paras.5.052, 5.055/057) applies (so far as relevant).
(82)   RSC O.32, r.8.
(83)   R.7.08(6).
(84)   R.7.08(3),(4).
(85)   R.7.08(4).
(86)   R.0.3(4).
(87)   R.7.08(5).
(88)   R.7.08(6).
(89)   R.7.13.
(90)   R.7.10(1).
(91)   R.7.10(1),(2).
(92)   R.7.52(3).
(93)   R.7.52(4).
(94)   R.7.52(5).
(95)   R.7.52(1),(2): RSC O.41.
(96)   R.7.12(1)(a).
(97)   R.7.12(1)(b).
(98)   R.7.12(2).
(99)   R.7.12(3). MH 7-546.
(100) R.7.11.
(101) R.12.12. See paras 5.070/072 re postal service, paras 6.17/30 re service of statutory demand and paras.7.072/080 re service of creditor's bankruptcy petition.
(102) Sunday Observance Act (Ireland) 1695, s.7.
(103) R.0.3(3).
(104) Statutory demand (para.6.17) and creditor's bankruptcy petition (para.7.074).
(105) R.0.3(1).
(106) R.0.3(2).
(107) R.12.11(1).
(108) R.12.11(2).
(109) R.12.11(3),(4).

(110) R.12.11(5).
(111) *Hastie and Jenkerson v. McMahon* [1990] 1 WLR 1575.
(112) Para.7.075.
(113) Supreme Court Practice 1991 para. 65/4/7.
(114) See para.7.076 re service of creditor's bankruptcy petition out of the jurisdiction.
(115) R.12.13(1): *Re Harrods (Buenos Aires) Ltd.* [1990] BCC 481, 484: *Re Tucker* [1988] 1 WLR 497, 502.
(116) R.12.13(3). See Ian Fletcher's note in 1988 JBL p.341 re validity of the rule in the light of the Court of Appeal decision in *Re Tucker* [1988] Ch 148.
(117) R.12.13(4): Atkin Form 210.
(118) R.0.4.
(119) R.12.04(1).
(120) R.12.04(2).
(121) R.12.04(3).
(122) R.12.04(4).
(123) R.7.48.
(124) R.7.54. Atkin Forms 311-318: MH 7-647: *Re Primlaks (UK) Ltd. (No.2)* [1990] BCLC 234.
(125) R.7.53(1),(3). For proceedings to enforce bond, see Atkin Forms 354, 356.
(126) R.7.53(2).
(127) Judicature (Northern Ireland) Act 1978, s.110.
(128) R.7.53(4).
(129) RSC O.23, r.2.
(130) RSC O.22, r.8(1).
(131) R.7.14: F.7.04. An appointment appears to be required in each case, whether the appointee is the official shorthand writer or another person.
(132) F.7.03.
(133) F.7.05.
(134) RR.7.15, 6.222(2).
(135) RR.7.16, 6.222(2). Note different priorities of payment of costs between appointment at instance of Official Receiver and other cases.
(136) R.7.17.
(137) Art.376.
(138) R.12.07.
(139) R.7.28(1).
(140) R.7.28(2).
(141) R.7.28(3) Atkin Form 10.
(142) R.7.28(4).
(143) R.12.21(1).
(144) R.12.21(2).
(145) R.12.21(3). But see RR 6.032(3), 6.045(3) re gazetting amendment of full title.
(146) Art.344.
(147) R.12.10.
(148) *Ibid.* See *Re Virgo Systems Ltd.* [1990] BCLC 34.
(149) RSC O.3, r.5(1), (2).

(150) RSC O.5, r.5(3).
(151) RSC O.52.
(152) Arts. 264(6), 265(4), 306(4), 334(4).
(153) Atkin Form 338. A form of supporting affidavit is prescribed (F.7.13). If the applicant is the Official Receiver he may give evidence by report. If the application is not under the Order it is made by notice of motion under RSC O.52.
(154) Para.5.008.
(155) F.7.14.
(156) F.7.15.
(157) The Official Solicitor may be appointed.
(158) RR. 7.38, 7.39(1),(2).
(159) R.7.39(3): F.7.16.
(160) R.7.39(4).
(161) R.7.40.
(162) R.7.40(1).
(163) R.7.40(2).
(164) R.7.41.
(165) S.46(2).
(166) E.g. R.7.30(7) re taxation does not apply to the remuneration of the responsible insolvency practitioner: specific provision for fixing such remuneration is provided elsewhere in the Rules.
(167) R.12.02.
(168) Judicature (Northern Ireland) Act 1978, s.59(1).
(169) R.6.222.
(170) RR.6.102(7), 6.174(2), 6.220.
(171) R.7.36(1),(2).
(172) R.7.36(3).
(173) R.7.36(4).
(174) R.7.37(1).
(175) R.7.37.
(176) His attendance in such circumstances not being required (para. 5.084).
(177) R.7.35.
(178) *Hill v. Cooke Hill* [1916] WN 61.
(179) R.7.35.
(180) R.7.33(2),(3).
(181) RR.6.054(1), 6.164(5).
(182) R.7.31(1).
(183) R.7.31(3).
(184) R.7.31(4).
(185) R.7.31(5).
(186) R.7.31(6).
(187) R.7.31(7),(8).
(188) R.7.31(9).
(189) In paras. 5.126/133 "costs" does not include the remuneration of the responsible insolvency practitioner - R.7.30(7).
(190) R.7.30(1),(2),(4).

(191) R.7.30(6). Reference to the Official Assignee now applies to the Official Receiver - Insolvency (1989 Order) (Commencement No.4) Order (Northern Ireland) 1991.
(192) R.7.29.
(193) R.7.30(5).
(194) R.7.30(1).
(195) R.7.32(3)-(5).
(196) R.7.32(1),(2): Atkin Form 392.
(197) R.7.33(1).
(198) R.7.34.
(199) This would include the remuneration of an interim receiver or special manager - fn.(181) above.
(200) R.7.30(3).

Chapter 6

STATUTORY DEMAND

Introduction

6.01   Where a creditor's bankruptcy petition is based upon a debt immediately payable the debtor's inability to pay the debt[1] will most frequently be proved by evidence of non-compliance with a statutory demand by the creditor served on the debtor. Where such debt is not immediately payable such evidence is the only permissible proof that the debtor appears to have no reasonable prospect of being able to pay it.[2]

6.02   Unlike a debtor's summons under the old law, the statutory demand is an extra-judicial document. It is not issued out of a court and there is no register in which the service of such a demand will be recorded unless and until the debtor applies to the Court to set it aside.[3] It does not come within the definition of an insolvency proceeding in the Rules.[4]

6.03   Like the debtor's summons, but unlike the bankruptcy notice under the Bankruptcy Act 1914, a statutory demand may be served in respect of a non-judgment debt. Although it is not a pre-requisite to a statutory demand (as it was in respect of a debtor's summons) that the creditor be unaware that the debt is disputed, a creditor who serves a demand without having obtained a judgment for the debt does so at his own risk as regards the cost of a successful application by the debtor to set it aside on the ground that the debt is disputed on substantial ground.[5]

Compliance with demand

6.04   A debtor served with a statutory demand for payment of a debt payable immediately complies with the demand if he pays the debt or secures or compounds for it to the satisfaction of the creditor within 3 weeks after service.[6] Where the debt is not immediately payable the debtor, in order to comply with it, must within the same period establish to the satisfaction of the creditor that there is a reasonable prospect that he will be able to pay it when it falls due.[7] If the amount of the debt is overstated in the demand, the debtor is deemed to have complied with it if, within the time allowed for compliance, he pays the creditor the correct amount, not having within that period given notice to the creditor disputing the validity of the demand on the ground that it is excessive.[8]

6.05   The debtor cannot be required to pay the costs of a statutory demand, but if he is adjudged bankrupt for non-compliance with the demand it appears that the costs of the demand will be allowable as part of the costs of the petition.

Amount of debt

6.06   A statutory demand may be served in respect of a debt of any amount. If the debt is less than the minimum petitioning creditor's debt (currently £750), in any bankruptcy petition following non-compliance the debt will have to be aggregated with another debt or debts to make up that amount.[9] A statutory demand may include more than one debt.[10]

Form of demand

6.07   The demand must be in a form prescribed by the Rules.[11] It must not bear a heading which might suggest that it had been issued out of a court. There are three prescribed forms, depending on the nature of the debt, -
  (a)   Form 6.01 bebt for a liquidated sum payable immediately, not under a court judgment or order;
  (b)   Form 6.02 - debt for a liquidated sum payable immediately following a court judgment or order;
  (c)   Form 6.03 - debt payable at a future date.

6.08   The statutory demand must be dated and be signed either by the creditor himself or by a person stating himself to be authorised to make the demand on the creditor's behalf.[12]

    A solicitor or other agent signing the demand on behalf of the creditor must do so in his own name and not that of his firm, but the firm name should be added.

Contents of demand

(a) General requirements

6.09   The Rules contain detailed requirements as to the contents of a statutory demand,[13] all of which are provided for in the text of and notes to the prescribed forms and these forms also contain some additional requirements which must be complied with.

6.10   Although the Court will adopt a considerable degree of flexibility as regards the consequences of technical defects in a statutory demand, care should be taken in its preparation. If the Court concludes that mistakes have caused or will cause any prejudice to the debtor, the demand will be set aside on the application of the debtor.[14] Even if it is satisfied that no such prejudice has occurred and that therefore the demand should not be set aside, it may penalise the creditor in the exercise of its discretion in relation to the costs of the debtor's application.

6.11   The particulars of debt to be inserted at page 2 of each form must include the following information -
  (i)   when the debt was incurred,
  (ii)   the consideration for the debt[15] or, if there is no consideration, the way in which it arose,
  (iii) the amount due at the date of the demand if the debt is payable immediately, or the amount of future debt and the date payment is due,

(iv) the particulars regarding a partly secured debt or interest or other periodically accruing charges referred to below.[16]

6.12 If the debt is a future debt the demand must state the grounds on which it is alleged that the debtor appears to have no reasonable prospect of paying it.

6.13 If the demand is founded on a judgment or order of a court it must give details of such judgment or order.

6.14 The demand must give the name and address (and telephone and fax numbers, if any) of one or more individuals with whom the debtor may, if he wishes, communicate with a view to securing or compounding for the debt to the creditor's satisfaction or (in the case of a future debt) establishing that there is a reasonable prospect that the debt will be paid when it falls due.

(b) Partly secured debt
6.15 If the creditor holds any security[17] for the debt the amount of the debt of which payment is claimed by the demand must be the sum which the creditor is prepared to regard as unsecured, i.e. the full amount of the debt, less his valuation of the security. He is required to give brief details of the full amount of the debt and to specify the nature of the security and the value which he puts upon it at the date of the demand. These should be stated in the particulars of the debt.

(c) Interest and other accruing charges
6.16 If the amount claimed includes any interest not previously notified to the debtor as his liability or any other charge accruing from time to time, the amount or rate of charge must be separately identified and the grounds on which payment is claimed must be stated. No interest or other charge which may accrue after the date of the demand may be claimed. The amount claimed must be limited to that which has accrued due at the date of the demand.

Service of demand
(a) Mode of service
6.17 The Rules impose on the creditor an obligation to do all that is reasonable for the purpose of bringing the statutory demand to the debtor's attention and, if practicable in the particular circumstances, to have it served personally.[18]

6.18 However service is effected it will be good if acknowledged in writing by the debtor or by some other person (e.g. the debtor's solicitor), provided such person states in the acknowledgement that he is authorised to accept service on the debtor's behalf.[19]

6.19 Where it is not practicable to effect personal service of the demand the creditor may adopt a mode of substituted service calculated to bring it to the debtor's attention. Thus, service may be by post or by insertion through a letter box. However, in view of the serious consequences of publishing an alleged debt, substituted service by advertisement in a newspaper may only be effected where the demand is for payment of a sum due under a judgment or order of a court and the creditor knows, or believes with reasonable cause -

(i)   that the debtor has absconded or is keeping out of the way with a view to avoiding service, and

(ii)   there is no real prospect of the sum due being recovered by execution or other process.[20]

6.20   Unless he has made an arrangement for service of the demand to be acknowledged by or on behalf of the debtor, the creditor must, before adopting a mode of substituted service, be confident that he can satisfy the Court that personal service is impracticable. To do so he must take such steps with a view to effecting personal service as would have sufficed to justify an order for substituted service of a bankruptcy petition.[21] As personal service of the demand is not mandatory no order for substituted service of it may be made.[22]

(b) Proof of service
6.21   Where a bankruptcy petition is based on non-compliance with a statutory demand, the affidavit or affidavits proving service of the demand must be filed with the petition.[23]

6.22   The Court may decline to file the petition if not satisfied that the creditor has discharged his obligation to do all that is reasonable to bring the statutory demand to the attention of the debtor.[24] Thus, the affidavit(s) proving service of the demand must prove acknowledgement of service in due form, personal service or adequate substituted service. Where substituted service has been used and in any other case where the clerk receiving the documents in the Office is in any doubt as to the adequacy of proof of the service of the demand it is anticipated that he will refer to the Master for directions as to whether or not the petition is to be filed. Because of the serious consequences of the filing of a bankruptcy petition proof of service of the statutory demand has to be carefully examined by the Court before filing and not left for consideration only on the hearing of the petition.

6.23   The copy of the demand must be exhibited to the affidavit of service.[25]

6.24   Where the demand has been served personally the affidavit of service must be made by the person who effected that service,[26] unless service has been duly acknowledged in writing,[27] in which case the affidavit is to be made by the creditor or a person acting on his behalf (whether or not he is the person who effected service) and the acknowledgement of service must be exhibited to the affidavit.[28]

6.25   Where substituted service of the demand has been effected by a mode other than advertisement the affidavit of service must -

(i)   where a written acknowledgement of service in due form has been
        obtained, be made by the creditor or by a person acting on his behalf
        and exhibiting the acknowledgement,[29] or
(ii)   otherwise be made by a person having direct personal knowledge of
        the means adopted for serving the demand and must -
        (A)   give particulars of the steps which have been taken with a view
                to serving the demand personally, or refer to an accompanying
                affidavit containing such particulars,
        (B)   state the means whereby (those steps having been ineffective) it
                was sought to bring the demand to the debtor's attention, and
        (C)   specify a date by which, to the best of the knowledge, information
                and belief of the deponent, the demand will have come to the
                debtor's attention.[30]

6.26   Where the demand has been advertised, the affidavit of service must
be made either by the creditor himself or by a person having direct personal
knowledge of the circumstances; and there must be specified in the affidavit -
(i)   the means of the creditor's knowledge or (as the case may be) belief that
         the debtor has absconded or is keeping out of the way with a view to
         avoiding service, and that there is no real prospect of the sum de-
         manded being recovered by execution or other legal process, and
(ii)   the date or dates on which, and the newspaper in which, the demand
         was advertised.[31]
A copy of the advertisement must be exhibited to the affidavit.[32]

(c) Effective date of service
(i) Personal service
6.27   RSC, Order 65, rule 7 applies to the service of a statutory demand.[33]
Consequently, where it has been served personally after 12 noon on a Saturday
or after 4.00 p.m. on any other weekday, for the purpose of computing the
periods after service for compliance or for applying to set aside it is deemed to
have been served on the Monday following that Saturday or on the day
following that other weekday, as the case may be.

(ii) Substituted service
6.28   Where a mode of substituted service other than by advertisement has
been adopted the date specified in the affidavit of service as the date by which
the demand will have come to the debtor's attention is deemed to have been
the date on which it has been served on the debtor, unless the Court otherwise
orders.[34] Where service is effected by first class post a suitable date to be so
specified would be the 7th day after posting, which is the usual provision made
in an order for substituted service by post, although a shorter period (being not
less than that specified in Rule 12.11(3)) may be acceptable to the Court. Whilst
there is no requirement to inform the debtor of the date on which the creditor
will consider service by post to have been effected, it is desirable that he should
have this information so that he is in a position to know how long he has to
comply with the demand or to apply to have it set aside. It is advisable,

therefore, for the creditor to give this information in a letter accompanying the demand.[35]

6.29   Where substituted service is effected by advertisement the time limited for compliance with the demand runs from the date of the advertisement's appearance or (as the case may be) its first appearance.[36]

(d) Service out of the jurisdiction
6.30   As a statutory demand is an extra-judicial document, leave of the Court for its service out of the jurisdiction is not required.[37] However, it should not be served on a debtor against whom a bankruptcy petition may not be presented because he is not subject to the Court's jurisdiction under Article 239. Where such service is appropriate, the periods of 3 weeks after service for compliance with the demand and of 18 days after service for applying to have it set aside require to be appropriately enlarged. Pending the issue of any general directions on this the direction of the Master should be sought.[38]

Setting aside statutory demand
(a) Introduction
6.31   A debtor served with a statutory demand to which he considers he has a good defence must, if he wishes to prevent the creditor presenting a bankruptcy petition against him based on non-compliance with the demand, apply within the time allowed to set aside the demand.[39] However, his failure to do so does not prevent him disputing a petition on grounds which he could have put forward on such an application, except that if his only ground of dispute is that the amount of the debt was over-stated in the demand, the petition may not be dismissed unless, within the time allowed for compliance with the demand, he gave notice to the creditor disputing the validity of the demand on that ground.[40]

(b) Grounds for application
6.32   The Rules prescribe four grounds on which the Court may set aside a statutory demand, namely -
  (i)   the debtor appears to have a counterclaim, set-off or cross demand which equals or exceeds the amount of the debt or debts specified in the demand; or
  (ii)   the debt is disputed on grounds which appear to the Court to be substantial; or
  (iii) it appears that the creditor holds some security in respect of the debt claimed by the demand and either the demand does not comply with the requirement of the Rules regarding claiming a secured debt[41] or the Court is satisfied that the value of the security equals or exceeds the full amount of the debt; or
  (iv)   the Court is satisfied, on other grounds, that the demand ought to be set aside.[42]

6.33   A Practice Note has been issued in the High Court in England which includes a statement as to how the court's discretion under the first two of these grounds will be exercised.[43] It states that where the demand is not based on a judgment or order, the court will normally set it aside if, in its opinion, on the evidence there is a genuine triable issue and that where the demand relates to a debt which is the subject of a judgment or order the court will not at that stage go behind the judgment or order and inquire into the validity of the debt nor, as a general rule, will it adjourn the application to await the result of an application to set aside the judgment or order. The Practice Note draws no distinction between a debt founded on a default judgment and one founded on a judgment or order after a hearing. In the case of a default judgment, if the Master considers that the debtor's application discloses a triable issue, it would appear to be just and convenient to adjourn the application pending the hearing of an application by the debtor to the court in which the judgment was given to have the judgment set aside, subject to an appropriate undertaking as to expedition. This was the practice adopted in relation to an application to dismiss a debtor's summons under the Bankruptcy Acts.

6.34   Under the first of the prescribed grounds for setting aside a statutory demand the amount of the counterclaim etc. must be not less than the amount of the debt or debts specified in the demand. Where it is not, to avoid the risk of having a bankruptcy petition presented against him, the debtor may have to pay the whole sum demanded and then seek to recover his own debt from the creditor serving the demand.[44]

6.35   If the Court considers that the debt is disputed on substantial grounds the statutory demand will be set aside and the creditor, if he wishes to pursue the claim, must institute proceedings in the appropriate court to have it determined. In contrast as to the practice in relation to an application to dismiss a debtor's summons under the Bankruptcy Acts, the dispute may not be determined by the Master.

6.36   There has been a decision in the High Court in England [45] that a statutory demand is liable to be set aside on the ground that it is disputed on substantial grounds unless the whole and not a part only of the debt demanded is undisputed. However, in delivering the judgment of the Court of Appeal in the later case referred to in paragraph 6.38 below, Nicholls L.J. said -

"In the present case the amount stated was wrong, but in my view the mere over-statement of the amount of the debt in the statutory demand is not by itself and without more, a ground for setting aside a statutory demand."

He considered that this was implicit from the terms of the Rules corresponding to our Rules 6.005(4), (a) to (c) and 6.022(4).

6.37   An indication of some of the "other grounds" which may be put forward in an application to set aside a statutory demand is to be found in the marginal notes to the prescribed form of supporting affidavit.[46] These include:

    (i)   debt admitted but not immediately payable, or part only so payable and debtor prepared to pay that part;

    (ii)   debt admitted and debtor prepared to secure or compound to the creditor's satisfaction;

    (iii) debt is a secured debt;

    (iv) enforcement of the judgment on which the demand is based has been stayed;

    (v)   demand does not comply with the Rules.

6.38   The Court of Appeal in England has upheld the refusal of a Registrar (and Warner J. on appeal) to set aside a statutory demand for a judgment debt made in the wrong form and where the amount of money still outstanding had been calculated incorrectly.[47] The judgment of the court, delivered by Nicholls L.J., has given guidance as to how the residual discretion to set aside a statutory demand on "other grounds" will be exercised. The court will have regard to all the circumstances as they are at the time of the hearing. These circumstances must be such as to make it unjust for the demand to give rise to the consequence that non-compliance may found the ability of the creditor to present a bankruptcy petition. Defects in the form of the demand, provided they are not so serious that the demand cannot sensibly be regarded as a statutory demand at all or which result in it being so confusing or misleading that, having regard to all the circumstances, justice requires that it should not be allowed to stand, will not justify its being set aside unless the debtor is prejudiced by the defects. Significantly, the judgment states that if the debtor is wholly unable to pay a debt which is immediately payable, either out of his own resources or with financial assistance from others, so that if the statutory demand were set aside he would be unable to comply with a revised demand served on him, the court will not adopt this course. The Court of Appeal endorsed the refusal of Warner J. in the court below and Vinelott J. in a later case[48] to import into the new code the technical objections which surrounded bankruptcy notices under the old law. This approach to the construction of the new insolvency legislation has since been approved by the House of Lords.[49]

(c) Time for application

6.39   An application by a debtor served with a statutory demand to have it set aside must be made to the Court within 18 days[50] from the date of service or, where the demand is advertised in a newspaper, from the date of the advertisement's appearance or (as the case may be) its first appearance.[51]

6.40   Under Rule 6.004 (3) as from (inclusive) the date on which the application is filed in the Court, the time limited for compliance with the statutory demand ceases to run, subject to the terms of any order made if the application is dismissed.

6.41   The Court may, under its general power to extend time limits,[52] extend the time for filing the application, although it is anticipated that such an extension will not be readily granted.[53] If an extension of time is granted after the expiry of the period allowed for compliance with the demand,[54] Rule 6.004(3) cannot operate and, unless the debtor has obtained, on application to the Judge, an injunction against the presentation of a petition based on non-compliance with the demand,[55] the petitioning creditor would be free to present such a petition up to the time when the application to set aside the demand is filed, after which it could not be presented.[56] In practice the occasion for the debtor to seek an injunction should rarely occur. An application for extension of time will usually be heard by the Master as a matter of urgency and, if granted, the application to set aside the demand can be filed immediately thereafter. However, if the extension of time is refused by the Master and the debtor proposes to appeal against this decision, he may wish to apply for an injunction pending the determination of the appeal unless he obtains a satisfactory undertaking from the creditor not to present a bankruptcy petition in the meantime.

6.42 An application for extension of time is made ex parte by originating application. The supporting affidavit should include the date the debtor received the demand, the grounds to be put forward in the application to set it aside and, where the time for such an application has expired, the reasons for delay in making such application.[57]

6.43 The application for an extension of time may be adjourned for notice to be given to the respondent (the creditor). Before any order extending time is made the debtor will be required to undertake not to dispose of any assets (save expenditure such as ordinary living expenses and legal expenses specified in the order), pending the hearing of the application to set aside the demand, and the order will direct that notice of it be given to the respondent forthwith.[58]

6.44 If the creditor's petition is presented before an application to set aside the statutory demand is filed, the debtor may still apply for an extension of time to make the application; alternatively, he may wait until the hearing of the petition to raise his defence.

(d) Mode of application
6.45 An application to set aside a statutory demand is made by a prescribed form of originating application.[59] The supporting affidavit[60] must specify the date on which the demand came into the debtor's hands, state the grounds on which he claims that it should be set aside and exhibit a copy of the demand.[61] Additional copies of the application and affidavit should be prepared, to enable notice of the hearing to be given to the applicant, the creditor and the person named in the demand as the person with whom the debtor may communicate with reference to the demand.

(e) Hearing of application
6.46 To prevent the debtor using an application to set aside a statutory demand merely as a delaying tactic and the creditor from being put to the trouble and expense of answering unsustainable objections to the demand, the

Court is required to examine the application and supporting affidavit to ascertain whether sufficient cause is shown for it and, if satisfied that it is not, may dismiss it without notice to the creditor.[62] Before making a decision the Master may hear the debtor or his solicitor ex parte or may deal with the matter on reading the documents without a hearing. If the application is dismissed summarily without notice to the creditor the time limited for compliance with it runs again, i.e. remains as if no application to set it aside had been made.[63]

6.47 If the application is not dismissed summarily, the Court fixes a venue for the hearing and gives at least 7 days notice of it to -
- (i) the debtor's solicitor, or the debtor if acting in person,
- (ii) the creditor, and
- (iii) the person named in the statutory demand as a person with whom a debtor may communicate with reference to it (or if more than one, the first named).[64]

6.48 The hearing will be published in the Court list under the record number only and not under the debtor's name. On the hearing the Court considers the evidence filed and may either determine the application at once or adjourn it, giving any appropriate directions.[65]

6.49 Where the creditor holds some security for the debt and has complied with the requirements of the Rules as to disclosing the security and valuing it, but the Court is satisfied that he has under-valued it, the creditor may be required to amend the demand accordingly, but without prejudice to his right to present a bankruptcy petition by reference to the original demand.[66]

6.50 Where a partly secured creditor inadvertently fails to disclose his security or to value it the Court may, in the exercise of its general power to waive formal defects or irregularities,[67] give the creditor leave to amend it and dismiss the debtor's application but, under the power referred to in the succeeding paragraph, direct that the creditor should not be entitled to present a bankruptcy petition until the debtor has had a further 21 days to comply with the amended demand.[68]

6.51 If the Court dismisses the application it must make an order authorising the creditor to present a bankruptcy petition either forthwith or on or after a specified date and send a copy of the order to the creditor forthwith.[69]

(f) Transitional provisions
6.52 If a creditor has served a debtor's summons under the Bankruptcy Acts before 1st October 1991 he may, on or after that date, proceed on the debtor's summons as if it were a statutory demand duly served under the Rules, provided that -
- (i) the debt in respect of which the debtor's summons was served has not been paid, secured or compounded for in the terms of the summons and the 1872 Act;

(ii)   the date by which compliance with the debtor's summons was required was not more than 6 months before the date of presentation of the petition; and

(iii)   a bankruptcy petition founded upon non-compliance with the debtor's summons has not been presented before that date.[70]

6.53   If, whether before or on or after 1st October 1991, an application is made under the old law to set aside a debtor's summons, that application is to be treated, on and after that date, as an application duly made to set aside a statutory demand duly served on the date on which the debtor's summons was in fact served.[71]

Footnotes

(1)   Paras.7.044, 7.052.

(2)   Paras.7.044, 7.055.

(3)   Para.6.31.

(4)   *Re a Debtor (No. 190 of 1987)*, The Times, 21 May 1988, per. Vinelott J.

(5)   Para.6.32. See *Re Cannon Screen Entertainment Ltd.* [1989] BCLC 660 re costs of injunction to restrain winding-up petition against a company served with a statutory demand.

(6)   Art.242(1)(a). See para.6.30 re demand to be served out of the jurisdiction.

(7)   Art.242(2).

(8)   R.6.022(4).

(9)   Paras.7.044, 7.047.

(10)   MH 7 - 062/2. See R.6.005(4)(a).

(11)   Art. 242(1)(a), 2(a). For adaptations of the prescribed forms to particular situations see Atkin Forms 16-26. In England and Wales minor variations in the prescribed forms of demand have been agreed with the High Court. For special forms of demand under the IPO see IPO Sch.3, Forms 2,3.

(12)   R.6.001(1). See note to forms re signature.

(13)   RR. 6.001, 6.002.

(14)   *Re a Debtor (No. 1 of 1987)* [1989] 1 WLR 271, 280.

(15)   This should reflect the statement of consideration required to be stated in a creditor's bankruptcy petition (para.7.059) but may be expressed less formally. In no case may costs of the demand be claimed.

(16)   Paras.6.15/16.

(17)   I.e. security over any property of the debtor, not of a 3rd person - Art. 10(1): *Re a Debtor (No. 310 of 1988)* [1989] 1 WLR 452. See MH 7 - 062/3 re creditor holding security equalling or exceeding amount of petition debt but who is willing to give up the security.

(18)   R.6.003(2).

(19)   RR.6.003(1). 6.010(4).

(20)   R.6.003(3). "Execution" includes enforcement under the JEO - R.0.2. For suggested form of advertisement, see *Practice Note (Bankruptcy: Substituted Service) (No.4/86)* [1987] 1 WLR 82.

(21)   R.6.010(6). Ch.7, fn.(116).

(22)   RSC O.65, r.4.

(23)   R.6.010(1).

(24)   R.6.010(9).

(25)   R.6.010(2).

(26)   R.6.010(3): F.6.13.

(27)   Para. 6.18.

(28)   R.6.010(4): F.6.12.

(29)   *Ibid.*

(30)   R.6.010(5).

(31)   R.6.010(8).

(32)   *Ibid.*
(33)   R.12.12.
(34)   R.6.010(7).
(35)   MH 7 - 090.
(36)   R.6.003(3).
(37)   See Atkin p. 84 re method of service.
(38)   In England and Wales the periods are regulated by reference to the Extra-Jurisdiction Tables governing service of a writ of summons out of the jurisdiction: *Practice Note (Bankruptcy: Service Abroad) (No.1/88)* [1988] 1 WLR 461.
(39)   R.6.004(1): paras.6.04,6.30 above.
(40)   R.6.022(4).
(41)   Para.6.15.
(42)   R.6.005(4).
(43)   *Practice Note (Bankruptcy: Statutory Demand: Setting Aside) (No. 1/67)* [1987] 1 WLR 119.
(44)   MH 7 - 075: *Re a Debtor (No. 10 of 1988)* [1989] 1 WLR 405, 407.
(45)   *Re a Debtor (No. 10 of 1988)* [1989] 1 WLR 405, per Hoffmann J. Incorrect decision later acknowledged in his judgment *Re a Debtor (No.490-SD-1991)* [1992] TLR 179.
(46)   F.6.05.
(47)   *Re a Debtor (No. 1 of 1987)* [1989] 1 WLR 271.
(48)   *Re a Debtor (No. 190 of 1987)* The Times, 21 May 1988.
(49)   *Re Smith (a bankrupt) ex p. Braintree DC* [1990] 2 AC 215, 238.
(50)   See para.6.30 above re extension of this period when demand is to be served out of the jurisdiction.
(51)   R.6.004(2).
(52)   Art. 344.
(53)   Atkin at p.88 suggests that powerful and compelling reason will be needed.
(54)   MH 7 - 071. *Re a Debtor (No.53 of 1991 Kingston upon Thames), ex p. F G Smith (Interiors) Ltd.* (1991) The Independent, 19 August, (1991) 4 Ins Int 80.
(55)   Atkin Forms 32, 33, 35.
(56)   Art.241(2)(d).
(57)   Atkin Form 33.
(58)   Atkin Form 35.
(59)   F.6.04. No court fee is payable on this application. If proceedings are already pending because of an application for extension of time, the application will be an ordinary and not an originating application.
(60)   F.6.05.
(61)   R.6.004(4).
(62)   R.6.005(1).
(63)   R.6.005(1).
(64)   R.6.005(2).
(65)   R.6.005(3).
(66)   R.6.005(5).

(67)   R.7.50.
(68)   MH 7 - 075/2.
(69)   R.6.005(6),(7).
(70)   Sch.8, paras.10, 16(2): R. 6.033(1),(2),(4).
(71)   R.6.033(3),(4).

Chapter 7

BANKRUPTCY PETITION

I. PROCEDURE APPLICABLE TO ALL PETITIONS

Introduction

7.001 A bankruptcy order may only be made on a petition presented to the Court by a person authorised to do so by the Order.[1] Thus, the failure of a debtor to obtain the approval of his creditors to a voluntary arrangement will not inevitably result in his being adjudged bankrupt, as would such failure of an attempted arrangement under the control of the Court under the Bankruptcy Acts. Bankruptcy will only ensue in these circumstances if a bankruptcy petition is presented by or against the debtor.

7.002 A bankruptcy petition may not be presented or proceeded with if the debtor to whom it relates has obtained an interim order under the voluntary arrangement procedure and the order remains in force.[2]

The debtor

7.003 In the Order and the Rules the term "debtor", in relation to a bankruptcy petition, means the individual to whom the petition relates.[3] Thus, it may refer to a solicitor against whom a petition is presented by the Law Society of Northern Ireland under Article 238 (1)(d), notwithstanding that on such a petition the petitioner is not required to allege or prove that any debt is owed by such solicitor.[4]

7.004 A petition may not be presented by a creditor or the debtor himself unless the debtor against whom it is presented satisfies certain conditions entitling the Court to exercise jurisdiction in relation to him. He must qualify under at least one of the following requirements -
  (a) be domiciled in Northern Ireland,
  (b) be personally present in Northern Ireland on the day in which the petition is presented, or
  (c) at any time in the 3 years immediately preceding that day -
    (i) have been ordinarily resident or have had a place of residence, in Northern Ireland, or
    (ii) have carried on business[5] in Northern Ireland in person or by a firm or partnership of which he is a member or by an agent or manager for him or for such a firm or partnership.[6]

7.005 These jurisdictional requirements do not apply to petitions presented by petitioners other than a creditor or the debtor, although in most, if not in all, of such cases they will in fact be satisfied.

The petitioner

7.006　A bankruptcy petition may be presented by -

　(a)　a creditor or creditors jointly,

　(b)　the debtor,

　(c)　the supervisor of or any person (other than the debtor) for the time being bound by, an approved voluntary arrangement, or

　(d)　the Law Society of Northern Ireland, against a solicitor in respect of whom the Society has been appointed his attorney by virtue of Part III of the Solicitors (Northern Ireland) Order 1976.[7]

Where a person is qualified to present a petition under more than one of these four categories (e.g. a person bound by an approved voluntary arrangement who is qualified to present a creditor's petition or the Law Society of Northern Ireland where it is a creditor of the solicitor in respect of whom it has been appointed attorney and is qualified to present a creditor's petition) the petition is treated as a petition under the category specified in the petition.[8]

Deposit[9]

7.007　Before a bankruptcy petition may be presented to the Court a deposit must be paid to the Official Receiver. This sum is security for the fee payable for the performance by the Official Receiver of his general duties on the making of a bankruptcy order ("the administration fee") or, in the case of a debtor's petition, for the fee payable to an insolvency practitioner who has prepared a report under Article 248.

7.008　Where a petition is dismissed or withdrawn the deposit must be repaid in full to the person who paid it, unless a bankruptcy order has been made or a fee has become payable to an insolvency practitioner.

7.009　If the bankrupt's estate is sufficient to pay the whole or part of the administration fee, the deposit is to be repaid to the extent that it is not required for payment of that fee.

7.010　Where a bankruptcy order is annulled, rescinded or recalled, the deposit is to be repaid to the extent that it is not required for payment of the administration fee, unless a fee has become payable to an insolvency practitioner for a report under Article 248.

Notice and registration of petition

7.011　The Court is required, forthwith after the filing of a bankruptcy petition, to send notice of its presentation to the Enforcement of Judgments Office and to register it in the Registry of Deeds in accordance with section 3A of the Registration of Deeds Act.[10] Where the petition (whoever is the petitioner) is against a solicitor, the Court must also notify the Law Society of Northern Ireland.[11]

7.012   Registration is effected by the lodgment in the Registry of Deeds of 2 copies of a document prescribed by the Insolvency (Registration of Deeds) Regulations, one of which must be certified by the Master.[12]

7.013   Registration of the petition in the Registry of Deeds is required in every case, whether or not it is known that the debtor has an interest in any land.[13]

7.014   The registration of the petition may be vacated pursuant to an order of the Court permitting such vacation. To procure vacation the debtor must obtain a prescribed certificate from the Court and lodge it in the Registry of Deeds.[14]

7.015   Registration in the Registry of Deeds has no effect on any registered land or charge.[15] Consequently, the Court is required to notify the Registrar of Titles if it appears to it that the debtor by or against whom the petition is presented is the registered owner of any land[16] and notice of the petition is thereupon to be entered in the appropriate register.[17] The prescribed form of notice requires the relevant folio number to be stated. It is anticipated that the Master will only issue such a notice on receipt of an appropriate certificate by the petitioner's solicitor (or the petitioner, if acting in person) or the Official Receiver. Where the debtor is known to have an interest in registered land under a settlement and where, therefore, he is not the registered owner, the petitioner should consider the advisability of registering an inhibition.

7.016   The notice may be cancelled by the Registrar of Titles on lodgment in the Land Registry of a certified copy of an order of the Court directing or permitting such cancellation.[18]

Amendment of petition
7.017   Any person aggrieved by words in the petition which wrongly associate him with the debtor may apply to the Court for an order amending the petition.[19] If the amendment affects the particulars of the registration of the bankruptcy petition in the Registry of Deeds or the Land Registry the order should give directions for registration of the order.

Withdrawal of petition
7.018   No bankruptcy petition may be withdrawn without leave of the Court.[20] As discussed below,[21] this provision is particularly significant in relation to a creditor's petition.

Dismissal of petition or stay of bankruptcy proceedings
7.019   The Court has a general power to dismiss a bankruptcy petition or to stay proceedings on it on such terms and conditions as it thinks fit, on the grounds of contravention of the Rules, or for any other reason.[22] This provision recognises the discretionary nature of a bankruptcy order, although a discretion which must be exercised judicially in accordance with established principles of insolvency law. There are also other provisions in the Order and

the Rules relating specifically to the dismissal of a petition by a creditor or by the Law Society of Northern Ireland.[23]

Notice and registration of dismissal or withdrawal of petition or of stay of proceedings

7.020   An order dismissing a bankruptcy petition, staying proceedings on it or giving leave to withdraw it must include provision for vacating the registration of the petition in the Registry of Deeds and, if notice of the petition has been given to the Registrar of Titles, for the cancellation of any entry in the register of such notice.[24] A note appended to the prescribed form of order[25] directs the debtor's attention to the advisability of procuring such vacation and cancellation (where appropriate) and to enable him to do so the Court is required to send him 2 sealed copies of the order, together with the certificate signed by the Master required for vacating the registration in the Registry of Deeds.[26]

7.021   If the petition is dismissed or withdrawn, or if proceedings on it are stayed, the Court must send notice of the making of the order of dismissal or stay or of the withdrawal (pursuant to an order giving leave) to the Enforcement of Judgments Office.[27]

Disposition of property of debtor after presentation of petition

7.022   Under Article 257(1) any disposition of property[28] made by the debtor between the day the petition is presented and the vesting of his estate in a trustee following the making of a bankruptcy order on the petition is void except to the extent that it is or was made with the consent of the Court or is or was subsequently ratified by the Court.[29] This prohibition extends to property not comprised in a bankrupt's estate, but not to property held by the debtor on trust for another.[30]

7.023   Some of the consequences of this general rule are alleviated by a provision preventing proceedings being taken to recover any property or payment received by a person before the making of the bankruptcy order in good faith for value and without notice that the petition had been presented, and protecting subsequent transferees of property so received, irrespective of notice of the petition by them.[31]

7.024   In their application to dispositions of land by the debtor, these provisions must be read in conjunction with section 3A of the Registration of Deeds Act in respect of unregistered land and section 67A of the Land Registration Act in respect of registered land.

7.025   A purchaser[32] of unregistered land who has acted in good faith without actual knowledge of the petition is not bound or affected by it until after a period of 21 days from registration of the petition, but thereafter he will be bound or affected notwithstanding the absence of notice of the petition.[33]

7.026 When a notice of the presentation of a bankruptcy petition is registered in a Land Registry folio the lands in the folio become subject to the rights of the creditors of the debtor (subject to any certificate of the result of a priority search and unless cancelled by the Registrar of Titles in accordance with Land Registry Rules[34]) until a bankruptcy inhibition is registered following notice to the Registrar of Titles of the making of a bankruptcy order against the debtor, or until the trustee is registered as owner.[35]

7.027 Registration of the petition may be vacated by the lodgment in the Registry of Deeds of a certificate of the Court.[36] If not vacated earlier, the registration ceases to have effect after 5 years from registration, but may be renewed from time to time and, if renewed, has effect for a further 5 years.[37]

7.028 Notice of the registration of the petition in the Land Registry may be cancelled by the Registrar of Titles on lodgment in the Land Registry of a certified copy of an order of the Court directing or permitting such cancellation.[38] If not cancelled or replaced by a bankruptcy inhibition, the notice ceases to have effect after 5 years from registration, but may be renewed from time to time and, if renewed, has effect for a further 5 years.[39]

7.029 The general rule referred to in paragraph 7.022 above is modelled on the law which has for long governed dispositions by a company after the presentation of a winding-up petition affecting it. Consequently, it is anticipated that the Court's discretion will be exercised on similar principles in respect of commercial transactions.[40] Dispositions by the debtor which are necessary for the maintenance of himself and his family will also, no doubt, be readily approved or ratified.[41]

7.030 If the petitioning creditor receives an offer of payment from the debtor after presentation of the petition, and unless he is satisfied that any such payment would not be made from the debtor's own property, he should not accept the offer without leave of the Court. In considering whether to seek such approval or to reject the offer he should bear in mind the provisions of Article 245(3) as to unreasonable refusal of an offer.[42]

7.031 It is to be noted that transfers of property or payments to a debtor, even with knowledge of the petition, are not within Article 257. Therefore a person owing a debt to the debtor may obtain a good discharge for a payment of the debt notwithstanding that he knows of the petition, subject in the event of the debtor being an adjudged bankrupt, to the provisions of the Order regarding voidable preferences.

7.032 An application for approval or ratification of a transaction under Article 257(1) is made by ordinary application, either by the debtor himself or the other party to the transaction, on notice to the petitioner. In many cases there will be an element of urgency and short service of the application will have to be sought.

Proceedings against the debtor

7.033   The effect of the presentation of a bankruptcy petition on proceedings against the debtor (including the enforcement of judgments) is dealt with in Chapter 28.

Appointment of interim receiver

7.034   If necessary for the protection of the debtor's property, the Court may, at any time after the presentation of a bankruptcy petition and before making a bankruptcy order, appoint an interim receiver of such property.[43] The procedure for such an appointment is dealt with in Chapter 8. In certain circumstances a special manager may also be appointed on the application of the Official Receiver, as such interim receiver.[44]

Rights of occupation of dwelling house

7.035   If a bankruptcy order is made on the petition, the bankrupt's spouse may not acquire any rights of occupation of a dwelling house comprised in the bankrupt's estate under the Family Law (Miscellaneous Provisions) (Northern Ireland) Order 1984 by reason only of anything occurring between the presentation of the petition and the vesting of the bankrupt's estate in a trustee. [45]

Arrest of debtor and seizure of records and goods

7.036   At any time after the presentation of a bankruptcy petition a warrant may be issued by the Court for the arrest of the debtor and for the seizure of any books, papers, records, money or goods in his possession if it appears to the Court that -

   (a)   there are reasonable grounds for believing that he has absconded, or is about to abscond, with a view to avoiding or delaying the payment of any of his debts or his appearance to a bankruptcy petition or to avoiding, delaying or disrupting any proceedings in bankruptcy against him or any examination of his affairs, or

   (b)   he is about to remove his goods with a view to preventing or delaying possession being taken of them by the Official Receiver or the trustee of his estate, or

   (c)   there are reasonable grounds for believing that he has concealed or destroyed, or is about to conceal or destroy any of his goods or any books, papers or records which might be of use to his creditors in the course of his bankruptcy or in connection with the administration of his estate, or

   (d)   he has, without the leave of the Official Receiver or the trustee of his estate, removed any goods in his possession which exceed a prescribed amount, or

   (e)   he has failed, without reasonable excuse, to attend any examination ordered by the Court.[46]

7.037   The procedure for execution of such a warrant is dealt with in Chapter 11 in relation to the arrest of a bankrupt for failure to attend a public examination.[47]

Consolidation of proceedings

7.038 Where two or more bankruptcy petitions are presented against the same debtor the Court may order the consolidation of the proceedings, on such terms as it thinks fit.[48] An application for an order of consolidation will usually be made by the Official Receiver, but may be made by a creditor.[49]

Listing petition

7.039 Although a bankruptcy petition will be heard by the Master in chambers[50] it is anticipated that, as in England and Wales,[51] the hearing will be published in the Court list under the name of the debtor and not identified only by a serial number.

II. CREDITOR'S PETITION [52]

Grounds of petition

7.040 With the abolition of acts of bankruptcy a creditor presenting a bankruptcy petition is now only required to allege that a debt which satisfies requirements specified in the Order is owed to him by the debtor.[53]

Joint petitioners

7.041 More than one creditor may join in the petition.[54] The usual reason for such joinder would be to make up the minimum amount of the debt required to ground a petition.

Joint debtors

7.042 A petition may not be presented against joint debtors.[55] A creditor who wishes to institute bankruptcy proceedings against two or more joint debtors must present a separate petition against each of them.

Restriction on judgment creditor's petition

7.043 If an administration order has been made by the Enforcement of Judgments Office under Part VI of the Judgments Enforcement Order no creditor scheduled to the order may, whilst it is in force, present or join in a bankruptcy petition against the debtor whose estate is the subject of the order without the leave of that Office unless -

(a) his name was, before the date of the order, notified to that Office by such debtor for the purposes of the order; and

(b) the notice given to him by that Office that he has been so notified was received by hi 28 days before presentation of the petition; and

(c) the debt by virtue of which he presents or joins in the petition exceeds a prescribed amount (currently £1500).[56]

The petitioning creditor's debt

(a) General requirements

7.044 The debt or debts specified in the petition must satisfy the following requirements-

(i)   the amount (or aggregate amount, if more than one) must be equal to or exceed "the bankruptcy level",[57]

(ii)   the debt, or each of the debts, must be for a liquidated sum payable to the petitioning creditor, or one or more of them, either immediately or at some certain, future time,

(iii)   the debt, or each of the debts, must either be unsecured or satisfy the requirements with respect to security referred to below.[58]

(iv)   the debt, or each of the debts, must be one which, if it is immediately payable, the debtor appears to be unable to pay or, if it is not immediately payable, to have no reasonable prospect of being able to pay, and

(v)   there must be no outstanding application to set aside a statutory demand[59] served in respect of the debt or any of the debts.[60]

7.045 Neither the Order nor the Rules expressly require that the debt of the petitioning creditor be one which is provable in bankruptcy. However, a petition based on a non-provable debt may be an abuse of process and a ground for dismissal of the petition.[61]

7.046 With the qualification referred to below[62] in respect of an expedited petition, the requirements in relation to the petitioning creditor's debt must be satisfied at the time the petition is presented.[63]

(b) The specified amount
7.047 The minimum amount of the debt or of the aggregate amount of the debts of the petitioning creditor or creditors (in the Order referred to as "the bankruptcy level") is at present £750, but this figure may be varied from time to time by order of the Department, subject to affirmative resolution.[64]

(c) Interest
7.048 Where a debt claimed includes any interest not previously notified to the debtor as a liability of his or any other charge accruing from time to time, the amount or rate of the charge (separately identified) and the grounds on which it is claimed to form part of the debt must be stated in the petition.[65] Where the petition is based upon non-compliance with a statutory demand, only the debt claimed in the demand may be included in the petition; no subsequently accrued interest or other charge may be added.[66]

(d) Security
7.049 If the petitioning creditor holds any security for his debt the petition must either -
(i)   contain a statement that he is willing, in the event of a bankruptcy order being made, to give up his security for the benefit of all the bankrupt's creditors, or

(ii)   be expressed not to be made in respect of the secured part of the debt and contain a statement of the estimated value at the date of the petition of the security for the secured part of the debt, in which case the secured and unsecured parts of the debt are to be treated for the purposes of the requirements of the petition, as separate debts.[67]

7.050 Where the petition contains a statement by a secured creditor in the terms of (i) above, and a bankruptcy order is subsequently made on the petition, the creditor is deemed, for the purposes of the Order, to have given up the security specified in the statement.[68]

7.051 If a secured creditor puts a value on his security in the petition, he may subsequently revalue it only with the leave of the Court.[69]

(e) Inability to pay
(i) Debt payable immediately
7.052 Where a debt alleged in the petition is payable immediately, the apparent inability of the debtor to pay must be based upon one or other of the following circumstances -
(A) that the petitioning creditor to whom the debt is owed has served on the debtor a statutory demand[70] requiring him to pay the debt or to secure or compound for it to the satisfaction of the creditor, that at least 3 weeks have elapsed since the demand was served and the demand has been neither complied with nor set aside; or
(B) that a certificate of unenforceability has been granted under Article 19 of the Judgments Enforcement Order in respect of the debt on a judgment or order of any court in favour of the petitioning creditor, or one or more of the petitioning creditors to whom the debt is owed.[71]

7.053 Unlike a creditor's petition to wind up a company,[72] inability to pay may not be established in any other way.

7.054 As in the case of a debtor's summons under the Bankruptcy Acts, but unlike a bankruptcy notice under the Bankruptcy Act 1914, a statutory demand can only be relied upon by the creditor serving it. Similarly, but effecting a change in the previous law,[73] only a certificate of unenforceability in respect of a judgment or order in favour of a petitioning creditor is relevant.

(ii) Debt not immediately payable
7.055 Where a debt alleged in the petition is not immediately payable, the apparent lack of reasonable prospect that the debtor will be able to pay it must be based on the facts that the petitioning creditor to whom the debt is owed has served on the debtor a statutory demand requiring him to establish to the satisfaction of the creditor that there is a reasonable prospect that he will be able to pay it when it falls due, that at least 3 weeks have elapsed since the demand was served and the demand has been neither complied with nor set aside.[74]

Form and contents of petition

7.056   There are 3 prescribed forms of creditor's petition (other than the special forms applicable to an insolvent partnership -
- (a)   where it is based upon failure to comply with a statutory demand for a liquidated sum payable immediately,[75]
- (b)   where it is based upon failure to comply with a statutory demand for a liquidated sum payable at a future date,[76]
- (c)   where it is based upon a certificate of unenforceability of a judgment debt.[77]

Each form includes detailed instructions as to how it has to be completed. It is to be noted that the petition does not require to be dated, signed or witnessed. The date and time of filing will be included in the endorsement made by the Office.[78]

7.057   The Rules prescribe detailed requirements as to the identification of the debtor and the petitioning creditor's debt[79] which are reflected in the body and/or the instructions in the margin of each prescribed form.

(a) Identification of debtor

7.058   The title should state only the debtor's name and short description, including any current trading name, e.g. "Re John William Wilson, electrical contractor, trading as J. W. Electrics".[80]   Where the debtor's forenames are unknown he may be named as "Re J. W. Wilson (male/female)". However, in the body of the petition the following particulars of the debtor, in so far as they are within the petitioning creditor's knowledge, must be given -
- (i)   his name[81] (and any other name to the personal knowledge of the petitioner used by the debtor), place of residence[82] and occupation (if any);
- (ii)   the name or names in which he carries on business[83] if other than his true name, and whether, in the case of any business of a specified nature, he carries it on alone or with others;
- (iii)   the nature of his business, and the address or addresses at which he carries it on;
- (iv)   any name or names, other than his true name, in which he has carried on business at or after the time when the debt was incurred, and whether he has done so alone or with others;
- (v)   any address or addresses at which he has resided or carried on business at or after that time, and the nature of that business.[84]

These particulars determine what in the Rules is referred to as "the full title" of the proceedings.[85]

(b) Identification of debt

<u>(i) General requirements</u>

7.059   The petition must contain the following particulars of each debt in respect of which it is presented -

(A) its amount, the consideration for it[86] (or if there is no consideration, the way in which it arises) and the fact that it is owed to the petitioner;

(B) when it was incurred or became due;

(C) if it includes interest not previously notified to the debtor or any other accruing charge, the information referred to in paragraph 7.048 above;

(D) either that the debt is for a liquidated sum payable immediately and the debtor appears to be unable to pay it, or that it is for a liquidated sum payable at some future time (to be specified) and that the debtor appears to have no reasonable prospect of being able to pay it;

(E) where the debt is partly secured, the information referred to in paragraph 7.049 above; otherwise, a statement that it is unsecured.[87]

(ii) Debt claimed by statutory demand

7.060   Where the debt is one for which a statutory demand must have been served on the debtor, the date and manner of service of the demand must be specified and the petition must contain a statement that, to the best of the creditor's knowledge and belief, it has neither been complied with nor set aside and that no application to set it aside is outstanding.[88] Where personal service of the demand has been effected, the day of the week and the time of service, as well as the date, must be stated in the petition so that the effective date of service, in accordance with Order 65, Rule 7 of the Supreme Court Rules, may be calculated. Where a mode of substituted service, other than by advertisement, has been used, the date of service will be the date required to be specified in the affidavit of service as the date by which, to the best of the knowledge, information and belief of the deponent, the demand will have come to the debtor's attention.[89] Where substituted service has been by advertisement, the date of service will be the date of the advertisement's appearance or, as the case may be, its first appearance.[90]

(iii) Debt arising under unenforceable judgment

7.061   Where the petition is based on a certificate of unenforceability granted in respect of the debt, it must state the date of the judgment, the court in which it was obtained, the date the certificate was granted and that the debt in respect of which the petition is presented is the amount remaining due on foot of the judgment.[91]

Verification

7.062   The petition must be verified by a prescribed form of affidavit[92] that the statements in it are true, or are true to the best of the deponent's knowledge, information and belief, and if the petition is in respect of debts to different creditors, the debts to each creditor must be separately verified.[93] The original petition must be exhibited to the affidavit.[94]

7.063   The verifying affidavit must be made by one of the following persons:

(a)   the petitioner, or one of joint petitioners,

   (b)   some person such as a director, company secretary or similar company officer, or a solicitor, who has been concerned in the matters giving rise to the presentation of the petition,

   (c)   some responsible person who is duly authorised to make the affidavit and has the requisite knowledge of those matters.[95]

7.064   Where the deponent is not a petitioner he must in the affidavit identify himself and state the capacity in which, and the authority by which, he makes it and the means of knowledge of the matters sworn to.[96]

7.065   If the petition is based upon a statutory demand which has been served more than 4 months before the presentation of the petition, the verifying affidavit must state the reasons for the delay.[97]

7.066   The verifying affidavit is prima facie evidence of the truth of the statements in the petition.[98] No further affidavit proving such matters, other than an affidavit proving service of a statutory demand,[99] is required.

Presentation and filing
7.067   As a general rule inability to pay a debt in respect of which a petition is presented must, in accordance with the criteria laid down in the Order, be apparent at the time the petition is presentation.[100] This rule is, however, subject to an exception where the debt is the subject of a statutory demand. In such a case the petition may be presented before the expiration of the period of 3 weeks from service of the demand if it contains a statement that there is a serious possibility that the debtor's property, or the value of any of his property, will be significantly diminished during that period.[101]

7.068   The petition and verifying affidavit is presented to the Office, where it is filed.[102] Where it is based upon a statutory demand the petitioner must also file an affidavit or affidavits of service of the demand, with a copy of the demand as served exhibited to each affidavit.[103] In such a case the Court may decline to file the petition if not satisfied that the creditor has discharged his obligation as to service of the demand.[104]

7.069   There must be produced with the petition -
   (a)   the receipt for the deposit payable on presentation,[105]
   (b)   two copies of the petition, one for service on the debtor and the other to be exhibited to the affidavit of such service, and
   (c)   if a voluntary arrangement is in force for the debtor, an additional copy of the petition for the supervisor.[106]
Such copies are sealed with the seal of the Court and issued to the petitioner.[107]

7.070   The Office endorses on the petition and copies the date and time of filing and the venue fixed by it for the hearing.[108]

Amendment

7.071 In addition to its general power to order amendment of a petition,[109] the Court has a specific power to authorise a petition presented by more than one creditor or in respect of more than one debt to be amended by the omission of any creditor or any debt and to be proceeded with on the basis of the remaining creditors or debts.[110] Such amendment may be authorised on such terms, if any, as the Court thinks fit to impose.[111]

Service

7.072 A creditor's bankruptcy petition under the Bankruptcy Acts, unlike such a petition under the Bankruptcy Act 1914, was ex parte. A significant change in procedure is that under the Rules such a petition must be served on the debtor.[112]

7.073 If the petitioner is aware that a voluntary arrangement for the debtor is in force, and he is not himself the supervisor of the arrangement, he must send a copy of the petition to the supervisor.[113]

(a) Mode of service

7.074 Unless an order for substituted service is made the petition must be served personally on the debtor by the petitioner or his solicitor, or by a person instructed by the petitioner or his solicitor for that purpose.[114] Personal service is effected by delivering to the debtor a sealed copy of the petition.[115]

7.075 The Court may order substituted service of the petition to be effected in such manner as it thinks fit if it is satisfied by affidavit or other evidence on oath that prompt personal service cannot be effected because the debtor is keeping out of the way to avoid service of the petition or other legal process, or for any other cause.[116] Where such an order has been carried out, the petition is deemed duly served on the debtor.[117]

(b) Service out of the jurisdiction

7.076 Provided that the debtor is a person over whom jurisdiction may be exercised under Article 239[118] an order may be made for service of the petition out of the jurisdiction in such manner as the Court may direct.[119]

(c) Death of debtor before service

7.077 If a debtor against whom a petition has been presented dies, the bankruptcy proceedings continue as if he were alive, unless the Court otherwise orders, although with certain modifications.[120] Reasonable funeral and testamentary expenses have priority over preferential debts.[121] If the death occurred after the petition has been presented but before it is served, the Court may order service on his personal representative, or on such other persons as it thinks fit.[122]

(d) Time for service

7.078   Subject to the provision for an expedited hearing referred to below, the petition must be served on the debtor at least 14 clear days before the hearing.[123]

(e) Proof of service

7.079   Service of the petition is proved by affidavit in the appropriate prescribed form,[124] exhibiting a sealed copy and, if substituted service has been ordered, a sealed copy of the order.[125] The affidavit must be filed immediately after service.[126]

7.080   Where substituted service by advertisement has been ordered, a copy of the advertisement, appropriately marked to identify the proceedings and the date the advertisement appeared, must also be filed.[127]

Date for hearing

7.081   The Court may, on such terms as it thinks fit (e.g. as to notice to the debtor and/or to any creditor who has given notice of intention to appear at the hearing[128]), hear the petition earlier than the prescribed period after service on the debtor if it appears that the debtor has absconded, or the Court is satisfied that it is a proper case for an expedited hearing, or if the debtor consents to such an earlier hearing.[129] However, where the presentation of a petition based on a statutory demand has been expedited under the provision referred to above,[130] no bankruptcy order may be made on that petition within 3 weeks from service of the statutory demand.[131]

7.082   Where the petition has not been served on the debtor the petitioning creditor may apply to the Court for an extension of time for the hearing.[132] The application must state the reasons why the petition has not been served.[133] If another date for the hearing is appointed, the petitioning creditor must forthwith produce to the Office the petition and all copies for amendment accordingly and notify any creditor who has given notice of intention to appear at the hearing.[134] No costs of such application are allowable unless ordered by the Court.[135]

Security for costs

7.083   Where the petitioning creditor's debt is for a liquidated sum payable at some future time, which it is claimed in the petition that the debtor appears to have no reasonable prospect of being able to pay,[136] the debtor may apply to the Court for an order requiring the creditor to give security for costs.[137] The nature and amount of the security is in the Court's discretion.[138] If such an order is made, the petition will not be heard until the whole amount of the security has been given.[139] This provision is additional to the general powers of the Court to order security for costs under the Supreme Court Rules.[140]

Debtor opposing petition

7.084   If the debtor intends to oppose the petition he must, not later than 7 days before the hearing date, file a notice in the prescribed form,[141] specifying the grounds on which he will object to the making of a bankruptcy order and send a copy of the notice to the petitioning creditor or his solicitor.[142]

7.085   After a notice of dispute has been filed the practice in the High Court in London is for the word "disputed" to be added after the debtor's name in the court hearing list.

7.086   Grounds on which a debtor may oppose a bankruptcy petition include-
   (a)   that he is not subject to the jurisdiction of the Court,
   (b)   that the debt has been paid, secured or compounded for,[143]
   (c)   that the petition is materially defective or is an abuse of process or has not been duly served,
   (d)   that the debt alleged in the petition does not satisfy one or more of the requirements listed in paragraph 7.044 above (e.g. debt not owing to creditor or less than £750 so owing, statutory demand not duly served, application to set aside statutory demand pending),
   (e)   that he is able to pay all his debts,[144]
   (f)   that he has made an offer to secure or compound for the petitioning creditor's debt the acceptance of which would have required the dismissal of the petition and that such offer has been unreasonably refused,[145]
   (g)   that he has made an application for an interim order with a view to making a proposal to his creditors for a voluntary arrangement or is about to do so.[146]

Application for dismissal or withdrawal of petition

7.087   Where the petitioner applies to the Court for the dismissal of the petition,[147] or for leave to withdraw it,[148] he must, unless the Court otherwise orders, file an affidavit specifying the grounds of the application and the circumstances in which it is made.[149]

7.088   If, since the petition was filed, any payment has been made to the petitioner by way of settlement (in whole or in part) of the debt or debts in respect of which the petition was brought, or any arrangement has been entered into for securing or compounding it or them, the affidavit must state -
   (a)   what dispositions of property have been made for the purposes of the settlement or arrangement,
   (b)   whether, in the case of any disposition, it was property of the debtor himself, or of some other person, and
   (c)   whether, if it was property of the debtor, the disposition was made with the approval of, or has been ratified by, the Court (if so, specify the relevant Court order).[150]

7.089   The statutory requirement of leave to withdraw a bankruptcy peti-tion[151] has the same objective as the former provisions against compounding after bankruptcy,[152] namely that the collective procedure of bankruptcy, which is designed to secure that the property of the bankrupt is made available for the benefit of all his creditors, should not be used by the petitioning creditor to put pressure on the debtor to pay such creditor in priority to other creditors. Hence the importance of a disclosure of the source of any payment made to the petitioning creditor after the presentation of the petition. In considering an application for leave to withdraw a petition or to dismiss it the Court will have this primary objective in mind and will seek to ensure that, if a payment has been made from the debtor's own property (i.e. property which would be available for the benefit of all creditors in the event of a bankruptcy order being made on the petition) without Court approval or ratification under Article 257(1)[153] the petition is not withdrawn or dismissed without other creditors having an opportunity of pursuing the bankruptcy proceedings under the procedures of substitution or change of carriage referred to below.[154] Conse-quently, no order giving leave to withdraw a petition may be given before the petition is heard.[155] It is understood that when an application for dismissal of a petition is made in the High Court in London the practice is to adjourn the hearing of the petition and in the court list for the adjourned hearing add ("for dismissal") after the debtor's name, to help to draw the attention of other creditors to the opportunity of applying to continue the proceedings. Leave to withdraw the petition may be given where it has not been served; if it has been served, the appropriate order is dismissal of the petition.[156]

7.090   It appears that the Court is not precluded from making a bankruptcy order by the provisions of Article 245(1)(a) where the petitioning creditor's debt has been paid from the debtor's own property without Court approval or ratification, because such a payment, being liable to be rendered void under Article 257(1), is not an unconditional payment that the petitioning creditor was bound to accept.[157] If, however, the petitioning creditor whose debt has been paid does not wish to proceed and no other creditor takes advantage of the procedures to adopt the petition, leave to withdraw the petition will be given.[158]

Notice by creditors intending to appear at hearing[159]
7.091   Although, unlike a company winding-up petition, a bankruptcy peti-tion is not advertised, any creditor who gets to know of it is entitled to appear and be heard, provided he has given to the petitioning creditor the prescribed notice of intention to do so (160) or, if he fails to do this, obtains the leave of the Court to appear.[161]

7.092   The notice must specify -
   (a) the name and address of the creditor giving it, and any telephone number and reference which may be required for communication with him or with any other person (to be also specified in the notice) authorised to speak or act on his behalf;

(b)   whether he intends to support or oppose the petition; and
(c)   the amount and nature of his debt.[162]

7.093   It must be sent so as to reach the addressee not later than 16.00 hours on the business day before that which is appointed for the hearing, (or where the hearing has been adjourned, for the adjourned hearing).[163]

Report by supervisor of voluntary arrangement
7.094   Where a petition contains a request for the appointment of the former supervisor of a voluntary arrangement as trustee, in accordance with Article 270(4)[164] such person must, not less than 2 days before the hearing date, file a report including particulars of the date on which he gave notice to the creditors of his intention to seek such appointment (such notice to be given at least 10 days before filing his report) and details of any response from creditors to that notice, including any objections to his appointment.[165]

Hearing
(a) Appearances
7.095   In addition to the petitioning creditor(s), the following persons may appear and be heard on the hearing of the petition-
   (i)   the debtor,
   (ii)   where a voluntary arrangement is in force for the debtor, the supervisor of such an arrangement,
   (iii) any creditor who has given notice of intention to appear or, having failed to do so, obtains the leave of the Court to appear.[166]

7.096   The petitioning creditor is required to prepare a list of the creditors (if any) who have given notice of intention to appear, a copy of which is to be handed to the Court before the commencement of the hearing.[167] In the list[168] the names and addresses of the creditors and (if known to the petitioning creditor), their respective solicitors, must be specified, and against each name there must be a statement as to whether he intends to support or oppose the petition.[169] If the Court gives leave to appear to a creditor who has not given the petitioning creditor notice of his intention to appear the petitioning creditor must add to the list the required particulars in respect of such persons.[170]

7.097   The costs of creditors appearing on the hearing may be allowed out of the bankrupt's estate.[171]

7.098   If the petitioning creditor fails to appear on the hearing, he is precluded from presenting a subsequent petition against the debtor in respect of the same debt, either alone or jointly with any other person, without the leave of the Court.[172]

(b) Adjournment
7.099   If the hearing is adjourned, the petitioning creditor must, unless the Court otherwise directs, forthwith send to the debtor and to any creditor who

has given notice of intention to appear but was not present at the hearing, notice of the order of adjournment and the venue for the adjourned hearing.[173]

(c) Substitution of petitioner

7.100   The Court may, on such terms as it thinks just, order the substitution of another creditor as petitioner where the petitioning creditor -

    (i)   is found not entitled to petition, or

    (ii)   consents to withdraw his petition or to allow it to be dismissed or to an adjournment of the hearing, or

    (iii)   fails to appear in support of the petition on the original hearing date, or on a date to which it is adjourned, or

    (iv)   appears, but does not apply for a bankruptcy order.[174]

7.101   To qualify for substitution a creditor must -

    (i)   have given notice of his intention to appear or have been given leave to appear,

    (ii)   be desirous of prosecuting the petition, and

    (iii)   have been, at the date of presentation of the petition, entitled to present a bankruptcy petition in respect of a debt or debts owed to him by the debtor.[175]

7.102   Thus, the creditor applying to be substituted must, at the date of the presentation of the petition, be owed a debt or debts satisfying the requirements of Article 241(2)[176] and either have served a statutory demand on the debtor which has not been complied with within 3 weeks of service and no application to set aside the demand is pending, or have obtained a certificate of unenforceability in respect of a judgment for such a debt.[177]

7.103   If an order for substitution is made it will give the substituted petitioner leave to amend the petition.[178] The amendment will be the substitution for the particulars of the original petitioner, his debt and the grounds of his petition of the corresponding particulars in respect of the substituted petitioner. The order will require the substituted petitioner to file, within 7 days, an affidavit verifying the petition and exhibiting thereto a sealed copy of the amended petition.[179]   To afford to the debtor an opportunity to dispute the debt of the substituted petitioner the order will adjourn the hearing of the amended petition and direct service of a sealed copy of the amended petition on the debtor at least 14 days before the date of the adjourned hearing.[180] However, if the debtor is prepared to consent to an immediate bankruptcy order on the petition when amended and the substituted petitioner undertakes to effect the amendments and to file a verifying affidavit forthwith, the Court may be prepared to make the bankruptcy order without an adjournment, directing that the order be not drawn up until the amendments have been made and the verifying affidavit filed.

7.104 The prescribed form of order for substitution reserves the question of the costs of the original petitioner until the final determination of the amended petition. As regards the statutory deposit, the form of order has alternative provisions. Under the first the Official Receiver is ordered to repay the deposit paid by the original petitioner upon receipt of such deposit from the substituted petitioner. Under the second, the question of the deposit is, like the costs of the original petitioner, reserved until the final determination of the amended petition.

7.105 For the purposes of the Rules the terms "petitioner" or "petitioning creditor" include any person who has been substituted as petitioner.[181]

(d) Change of carriage order
7.106 Because only a creditor who can satisfy the requirements mentioned above[182] may be substituted for the petitioning creditor on a bankruptcy petition, the restraint of abuse of the collective procedure of bankruptcy by the petitioning creditor referred to earlier[183] has been further strengthened by the introduction of a novel procedure whereby, in certain circumstances, the carriage of a bankruptcy petition may be given by the Court to any other creditor in place of the original petitioning creditor, but without any amendment of the petition.[184] In contrast to the position following an order for substitution, the petition will continue to be founded on the petitioning creditor's debt.

7.107 An application for a change of carriage order may be made by any person who claims to be a creditor of the debtor, whether or not at the date of the petition he would be entitled to present it in respect of his debt, provided he has given notice of his intentionto appear at the hearing or has been given leave to appear.[185]

7.108 Whether or not the petitioning creditor appears at the hearing,[186] the Court may make the order[187] on such terms as it thinks just, if satisfied that -
    (i) the applicant is an unpaid and unsecured creditor of the debtor, and
    (ii) the petitioning creditor either intends by any means to secure the postponement, adjournment or withdrawal of the petition, or does not intend to prosecute it diligently or at all.[188]

7.109 However, the Court may not make a change of carriage order if satisfied that the petitioning creditor's debt has been paid, secured or compounded for by means of a disposition of property made by some person other than the debtor (i.e. by money or security from a third party), or a disposition of the debtor's own property made with the approval of, or ratified by the Court.[189] Thus, where the petitioning creditor's debt has been paid or provided for the order will only be made where, on the making of a bankruptcy order, the petitioning creditor may be required, by the operation of Article 257, to account for the money or security received for the benefit of the debtor's creditors generally.

7.110   As, following a change of carriage order the proceedings remain grounded on the petition as presented, the creditor given carriage will have to satisfy the Court that the facts in the petition are true and deal with any dispute by the debtor of the petitioning creditor's debt. For this purpose he may rely on all evidence previously adduced in the proceedings, whether by affidavit or otherwise.[190]

7.111   The prescribed form of change of carriage order provides for the hearing of the petition to be adjourned and directs the creditor given carriage to serve a sealed copy of the order on the debtor and the petitioning creditor within a specified period. Like the form of order for substitution, the question of the costs of the petitioning creditor is reserved until the final determination of the petition. However, no provision is made in the prescribed form for refunding the statutory deposit.

7.112   For the purposes of the Rules the terms "petitioner" or "petitioning creditor" include any person who has been given carriage of the petition.[191]

(e) Decisions on the hearing
<u>(i) General procedure</u>
7.113   The proceedings on the petition are conducted before the Master in chambers who may, at the date originally fixed for the hearing of the petition or at an adjourned hearing, and subject to his power to refer the hearing to the Judge, dispose of the petition by making a bankruptcy order, dismissing the petition, staying proceedings on it or giving the petitioner leave to withdraw it. However, where the petition is based upon non-compliance with a statutory demand and was presented within 3 weeks of service of the demand, under the expedited procedure mentioned above,[192] no bankruptcy order may be made before that period has expired.[193]

7.114   If the petition, the affidavit verifying it and the affidavit(s) of service of the petition and, where appropriate, of the statutory demand, are in order and the Court is satisfied that the debt on which it is founded is still due and owing, no further evidence will ordinarily be required for the making of a bankruptcyorder on the petition, if it is not disputed. If the debtor attends and disputes the petition, further evidence (usually oral) on his behalf and on behalf of the petitioning creditor will usually be necessary and in a complicated case may be called for by the Court.[194] The creditor should have received prior notice of the grounds of any dispute.[195] If the debtor has not complied with the requirement to give such notice but attends and wishes to dispute the petition, the Master may decline to permit him to do so, allow the hearing to proceed on the debtor's oral statement of the grounds for dispute[196] or adjourn the hearing and direct that notice of the grounds of dispute be served on the petitioning creditor before the adjourned hearing.

7.115   A debtor served with a statutory demand who fails to apply to have it set aside may, nevertheless, with one qualification referred to below,[197] dispute a petition based on non-compliance with the demand on grounds which he could have put forward on such an application.

7.116 The Court has power to enquire into the validity of a judgment debt, but not to re-open a tax assessment.[198]

7.117 The hearing should not be adjourned solely with the object of giving the debtor further time to pay the petitioning creditor's debt unless the Court considers that there is a reasonable prospect of payment within a reasonable time.[199]

(ii) Making of bankruptcy order

7.118 The Court may make a bankruptcy order if satisfied that the statements in the petition are true and that the debt, or one of the debts in respect of which the petition was presented, satisfies the statutory requirements and, in particular, that it is either a debt which, having become payable at the date of the petition, or having since become payable, has been neither paid nor secured or compounded for, or is a debt payable in the future which the debtor has no reasonable prospect of being able to pay when it falls due.[200] If at the time there is a supervisor of an approved voluntary arrangement in relation to the debtor, he may be appointed as trustee.[201]

7.119 The Court may accept as proof that the petitioning creditor's debt has not been paid or secured or compounded for a certificate by the person representing him at the hearing to that effect, in the prescribed form.[202] A fresh certificate will be required for any adjourned hearing. However, if the debtor alleges that the debt has been paid or secured or compounded for, oral evidence will be required to resolve the dispute.

7.120 In determining whether the debtor has a reasonable prospect of being able to pay a debt payable in the future when it falls due, the Court is to assume that the prospect given by the facts and other matters known to the creditor at the time he entered into the transaction resulting in the debt was a reasonable prospect.[203]

(iii) Dismissal of petition or stay of proceedings

7.121 In addition to the general statutory power to dismiss or stay proceedings on any bankruptcy petition on the grounds of non-compliance with the Rules or for any other reason[204] there are provisions relating specifically to the dismissal of a creditor's petition.

7.122 An over-statement of the amount of the debt in a statutory demand is not, of itself, a ground for dismissal of the petition based on non-compliance with the demand, unless the debtor, within the time allowed for compliance, gave notice to the creditor disputing the validity of the demand on that ground.[205] If no such notice is given the debtor is deemed to have complied with the demand if he has paid the correct amount within the time allowed.[206]

7.123   If the petition is presented in respect of a debt due on a judgment or order, the Court may stay or dismiss the petition on the ground that an appeal is pending from the judgment or order, or that execution[207] of the judgment has been stayed.[208]

7.124   The Court may also dismiss the petition if the debtor satisfies it that –

   (A) he is able to pay all his debts, taking into account his contingent and prospective liabilities, or

   (B) he has made an offer to secure or compound for a debt in respect of which the petition is presented, that the acceptance of that offer would have required dismissal of the petition, and that the offer has been unreasonably refused.[209]

7.125   Before dismissing the petition on the ground that the debtor is able to pay all his debts the Court will require to be satisfied that this is so and if necessary will adjourn the hearing[210] to give the debtor an opportunity to produce sufficient evidence that the debts presently due have been paid or will be paid promptly and that satisfactory provision has been made for contingent and prospective liabilities.

7.126   In the first reported case on unreasonable refusal of an offer as a ground for dismissal of a creditor's bankruptcy petition under the corresponding provision of the Insolvency Act 1986,[211] Harman J. said:

"The registrar observed that a petitioning creditor is entitled to be paid his debt in full on the hearing of a petition unless it is adjourned on the ground that there is a reasonable prospect of him being paid within a reasonable time. In the circumstances of this case I think he was correct to take that as the basic test and to say that the prospects of the debt being paid within a reasonable time were not such as anybody could say were reasonable prospects."

Death of creditor
7.127   Where the petitioning creditor dies after the petition is filed but before the making of an order dismissing it or making a bankruptcy order, his personal representative may continue the proceedings on obtaining an order from the Court to carry on.[212] Such order must be served on the debtor.[213]

III. DEBTOR'S PETITION

When debtor may petition
7.128   The only ground for a bankruptcy petition by a debtor is that he is unable to pay his debts.[214] The petition must contain a statement to this effect and a request that a bankruptcy order be made against the debtor.[215]

Joint debtors

7.129 Except in the case of a petition by partners under the Insolvent Partnerships Order,[216] a petition by joint debtors is not permitted and each debtor who wishes a bankruptcy order to be made against him must present his own petition.

Form and contents

7.130 The petition must be in the prescribed form,[217] which is printed with detailed instructions as to how it is to be completed. Unlike the creditor's petition, it must be signed and dated, but it does not require to be verified by affidavit.

(a) Identification of debtor

7.131 The Rules prescribe detailed requirements as to the identification of the debtor similar to those required in the case of a creditor's petition,[218] the requirement to state any former trading name or former residential or business address being related to the period in which any of the debtor's bankruptcy debts were incurred. The required particulars of the debtor's identity determine the full title of the proceedings.[219]

(b) Admission of insolvency

7.132 The debtor is required to disclose recent insolvency proceedings affecting him, whether compulsory or voluntary, as these constitute one of the circumstances which the Court must take into account to determine whether or not the possibility of a voluntary arrangement in lieu of bankruptcy should be considered.[220]

7.133 If within 5 years before the date of the petition the debtor has been adjudged bankrupt or has made a composition with his creditors in satisfaction of his debts or a scheme or arrangement of his affairs,[221] or has entered into any voluntary arrangement or been subject to an administration order under Article 80 of the Judgments Enforcement Order, the petition must contain particulars of these matters.[222] If a voluntary arrangement is in force for the debtor at the date of the petition, these particulars are to include a statement to that effect and the name and address of the supervisor of the arrangement.[223]

Statement of affairs

7.134 The circumstances governing whether or not the debtor qualifies for consideration of the possibility of a voluntary arrangement in lieu of bankruptcy also require the Court to have information as to the debtor's assets and liabilities. Consequently, the petition must be accompanied by a statement of affairs in the prescribed form, containing all the particulars required by that form and verified by affidavit[224] The verifying affidavit may be sworn before an authorised officer of the Office.[225] Copies of the form of statement of affairs together with guidance notes on its completion may be obtained from the Official Receiver's office.

7.135   It appears that the costs of a statement of affairs is not payable out of the bankrupt's estate. The prescribed form has been designed to enable it to be prepared without professional assistance in most cases. If the debtor obtains a Legal Aid Certificate in respect of the petition, this will probably cover such costs where the debtor could not reasonably be expected to prepare the statement of affairs himself, having regard to the fact that the filing of a statement of affairs is a necessary requirement of the presentation of the petition. However, the application for Legal Aid should request express provision for the costs of the statement of affairs where professional assistance is considered to be necessary.

Presentation and filing

7.136   On presenting the petition to the Court for filing, the petitioner must produce -

   (a)   the statement of affairs,

   (b)   the receipt for the deposit payable on presentation,

   (c)   3 copies of the petition, one to be returned to the petitioner, endorsed with any venue fixed, another so endorsed, to be sent by the Court to the Official Receiver and the third to be retained by the Court, to be sent to an insolvency practitioner, if appointed under Article 247(2),[226]

   (d)   2 copies of the statement of affairs, one to be sent by the Court to the Official Receiver and the other to be retained by the Court, to be sent to an insolvency practitioner, if appointed under Article 247(2).[227]

7.137   An officer of the Office will examine the statement of affairs before filing the petition to see that the statement has been duly completed, contains all the particulars required by the prescribed form and is verified by affidavit. If it is materially defective, for example, by not stating the full names and addresses of creditors and the amounts owing to them, the Office may decline to file the petition until the errors or omissions have been rectified.

7.138   Where the petition is heard immediately upon presentation, or if the Court considers that in any case the delivery of any document to the Official Receiver will be expedited if it is delivered by the bankrupt rather than being sent by the Office, it may direct the bankrupt to do so forthwith.[228]

Report by supervisor of voluntary arrangement

7.139   Where the petition contains a request for the appointment of the former supervisor of a voluntary arrangement as trustee, the supervisor is required to file the same report and within the same time as in the case of a creditor's petition.[229]

Death of debtor after presentation of petition

7.140   If a debtor who has presented his own petition dies, bankruptcy proceedings continue as if he were alive, unless the Court otherwise orders, but reasonable funeral and testamentary expenses notified to the trustee before final distribution of the estate have priority over preferential debts.[230]

Hearing
(a) Date
7.141 Except where the petition contains particulars of a voluntary arrangement in force for the debtor, it may be heard forthwith.[231] If not so heard, a venue for the hearing must be fixed.[232] Where a voluntary arrangement is in force for the debtor a venue must be fixed and the Court must give at least 14 days notice of it to the supervisor of the arrangement.[233] The supervisor may agree to abridge this time or the Court, on application, may do so.

(b) Appearances
7.142 Where a voluntary arrangement is in force for the debtor the supervisor of the arrangement may appear and be heard.[234] Otherwise the hearing is ex parte. Creditors have no right to appear, as they have in the case of a hearing of a creditor's petition.[235]

(c) Decisions on the hearing
(i) Dismissal of petition or stay or proceedings
7.143 The Court may dismiss or stay proceedings on the petition in exercise of its general power under Article 240(3).[236] One of the grounds for a dismissal would be that the petition is an abuse of process.[237]

(ii) Appointment of insolvency practitioner
7.144 The Order contains provisions intended to avoid bankruptcy proceedings following as a matter of course on the presentation by a debtor of his own bankruptcy petition in circumstances where his liabilities are reasonably modest and there appears to be a reasonable prospect that assets can be made available for a voluntary arrangement.

7.145 Thus, before making a bankruptcy order on a debtor's petition the Court must examine the statement of affairs to see whether it discloses that if a bankruptcy order were made the unsecured bankruptcy debts would be less than a specified amount (in the Order referred to as "the small bankruptcies level", at present £20,000) and the value of the bankrupt's estate would be at least a specified amount (at present £2,000).[238] In such a case the petition must then be examined to see whether it shows that the debtor has not within the previous 5 years either been adjudged bankrupt or made a composition with his creditors in satisfaction of his debts or a scheme of arrangement of his affairs.[239] The Court may also question the debtor regarding his assets and liabilities and any other matter relevant to the feasibility of a voluntary arrangement.

7.146 If the three conditions mentioned in the preceding paragraph are satisfied the Court must consider whether it would be appropriate to appoint an insolvency practitioner to prepare a report, with a view to the debtor making a proposal to his creditors for a voluntary arrangement.[240]

7.147   The Court will not exercise its discretion to appoint an insolvency practitioner for this purpose unless the debtor indicates that he is prepared to consider, in consultation with such practitioner (who will be selected by the Court, not by the debtor), making a proposal to his creditors for a voluntary arrangement, nor where it appears clearly that, by reason of the value of the debtor's assets, and taking into account the amount of his preferential creditors, no proposal acceptable to the ordinary unsecured creditors could be made without the introduction of adequate third party money, unless there is reliable evidence that such additional funds will be forthcoming.

7.148   If the necessary conditions are satisfied and the Court does consider it appropriate to do so, it will appoint (from a panel of insolvency practitioners willing to accept such appointments) a person qualified to act as an insolvency practitioner in relation to the debtor to prepare a report and (unless subsequently replaced by a meeting of creditors[241]) to act in relation to any voluntary arrangement proposed in the report either as trustee or otherwise for the purpose of supervising its implementation.[242] It may also, in an appropriate case, upon application of a creditor, the debtor or the appointed insolvency practitioner, appoint either the Official Receiver or the insolvency practitioner as interim receiver.[243]

7.149   The procedure following the appointment of an insolvency practitioner is dealt with below.

(iii) Making of bankruptcy order

7.150   If on a consideration of the petition and statement of affairs the conditions for the appointment of an insolvency practitioner with a view to the debtor making a proposal to his creditors for a voluntary arrangement are not satisfied or where, although they are, the Court does not consider it appropriate to make such an appointment, a bankruptcy order may (subject to the Court's discretionary power to dismiss the petition[244]) be made forthwith. Such an order may also be made at a later hearing held to consider the report of the insolvency practitioner, if appointed.[245]

7.151   In making a bankruptcy order the Court may, in the circumstances mentioned in Chapter 9,[246] issue a certificate for the summary administration of the bankrupt's estate.

7.152   Where a bankruptcy order is made and at the time of the petition a voluntary arrangement for the debtor is in force, any expenses properly incurred as expenses of the administration of the arrangement are a first charge on the bankrupt's estate.[247] If at the time when a bankruptcy order is made there is a supervisor of a voluntary arrangement in relation to the debtor, he may be appointed as trustee.[248]

Procedure following appointment of insolvency practitioner

7.153 Where the Court appoints an insolvency practitioner to prepare a report the order appointing him will fix the venue for the consideration of the report and may direct the debtor to attend that hearing.[249] After such an appointment has been made the debtor may not apply for an interim order under the arrangement procedure whilst the bankruptcy petition is pending.[250]

7.154 The Court must forthwith send to the insolvency practitioner appointed a sealed copy of the order of appointment and copies of the petition and statement of affairs.[251] It is also required to send to the insolvency practitioner and the debtor notice of the venue of the hearing to consider the report.[252] As regards the insolvency practitioner, this requirement is satisfied by sending him the copy of the order appointing him. Notice of the venue to the debtor may also be conveniently given by sending him a sealed copy of the order and service of such order is essential if it directs the debtor to attend the hearing.

7.155 The Official Receiver is required to pay to the appointed insolvency practitioner the prescribed fee for the preparation of the report from the deposit paid on presentation of the petition.[253]

7.156 The insolvency practitioner appointed is required to enquire into the debtor's affairs[254] and to report to the Court whether the debtor is willing to make a proposal for a voluntary arrangement and, if he is so willing, whether, in the opinion of the insolvency practitioner, a meeting of creditors should be summoned to consider the report and, if so, the venue he proposes for the meeting.[255]

7.157 If the insolvency practitioner requires further time to complete his report, he may apply to the Court for an extension of time and postponement of the date for consideration of the report.

7.158 The insolvency practitioner must file his report in the Court and send one copy to the debtor so as to reach him not less that 3 days before the date fixed for consideration of the report, and send a further copy to the Official Receiver.[256]

7.159 The debtor is entitled to attend the hearing to consider the report and must attend if so directed by the Court.[257] If he attends he may make representations with respect to any of the matters dealt with in the report.[258]

7.160 If, on a consideration of the report of the insolvency practitioner, the Court decides that the debtor should be given an opportunity to put a proposal for a voluntary arrangement to his creditors, it will make an interim order under the voluntary arrangement procedure.[259] This order must specify the period during which the interim order is to operate, which is to be such period as is required to enable the debtor's proposal to be considered by his creditors.[260]

7.161   Where the report recommends the summoning of a meeting of creditors, the insolvency practitioner must, subject to any order of the Court, summon the meeting for the venue proposed in his report.[261] The meeting is deemed to have been summoned under Article 231 and the matter thenceforth proceeds under the voluntary arrangement procedure. If the debtor's proposal is approved at the creditor's meeting the petition is, unless the Court otherwise orders, deemed to be dismissed when the interim order ceases to have effect in accordance with Article 234(6).[262] If not so approved, the Court will make a bankruptcy order at the hearing to consider the chairman's report of the result of the meeting or at an adjournment of such hearing to await the outcome of a pending appeal against a decision of the chairman of the meeting as to entitlement to vote or of an application to challenge the decision of the meeting.[263] If no certificate for summary administration is issued, the Court may, on making the bankruptcy order, appoint the insolvency practitioner as trustee.[264]

7.162   Where the petition is deemed to be dismissed under Article 234(6) the Court, on the application of the debtor, makes an order permitting the vacation of the registration of the petition in the Registry of Deeds and, where appropriate, cancellation of the entry in the Land Registry of notice of the petition.[265] The Court sends 2 sealed copies of such order to the debtor and sends notice of the dismissal of the petition to the Enforcement of Judgments Office.[266]

7.163   If, on a consideration of the insolvency practitioner's report, the Court is of the opinion that a voluntary arrangement by the debtor is not appropriate, it may make a bankruptcy order.[267] In such a case the deposit paid on presentation of the petitions will not be available to the Official Receiver as it will have been paid to the insolvency practitioner.[268]

IV. PETITION BY SUPERVISOR OF OR PERSON BOUND BY VOLUNTARY ARRANGEMENT

When and by whom petition may be presented
7.164   No bankruptcy petition may be presented or proceeded with against a debtor who has obtained an interim order under the voluntary arrangement procedure whilst that order remains in force.[269] Thereafter the supervisor of an approved arrangement or any person (other than the debtor) bound by it may present a petition against the debtor.[270] A creditor bound by an approved voluntary arrangement may present a bankruptcy petition in that capacity notwithstanding that his debt does not satisfy the requirements for a creditor's petition.[271]

Bankruptcy order on petition

7.165 No bankruptcy order may be made on such a petition unless the Court is satisfied that -

(a) the debtor has failed to comply with his obligations under the arrangement, or

(b) information which is false or misleading in any material particular or which contains material omissions was contained in any statement of affairs or any document which, under the arrangement procedure, was supplied by the debtor to any person or was otherwise made available by him to his creditors at or in connection with a creditors' meeting in the arrangement, or

(c) the debtor has failed to do all such things as may for the purposes of the arrangement have been reasonably required of him by the supervisor.[272]

7.166 Where a bankruptcy order is made on such a petition, any costs properly incurred as costs of the administration of the voluntary arrangement are a first charge on the bankrupt's estate.[273]

Application of Rules

7.167 Except where otherwise indicated the Rules relating to a bankruptcy petition by a creditor, where applicable, apply to such a petition, with any necessary modifications.[274] A form of petition is prescribed.[275] Where in any Rule or paragraph of a Rule the letters "CP" follow the number that Rule or (as the case may be) that paragraph applies only to a creditor's petition.[276]

V. PETITION BY LAW SOCIETY OF NORTHERN IRELAND

The petition and bankruptcy order thereon

7.168 The Order continues the procedure, unique to Northern Ireland, first introduced by Article 41(2) of the Solicitors (Northern Ireland) Order 1976, whereby, following an order of the High Court appointing the Law Society of Northern Ireland ("the Society") attorney of a defaulting solicitor under Part III of that Order, the Society may present a petition to the Court for that solicitor to be adjudged bankrupt.[277] A bankruptcy order may be made on such a petition on production of an office copy of the order appointing the Society as attorney.[278] The petition is not required to allege, nor is the Society required to prove, that any debt is owing by the solicitor to the Society.[279] If the solicitor is indebted to the Society and the Society's debt satisfies the requirements of a creditor's petition, it may, alternatively, present such a petition.

Meaning of "debtor"

7.169 A solicitor against whom such a petition is presented is included in the definition of "debtor" in the Order in relation to a bankruptcy petition, so that all references to a debtor in the Order and the Rules relating to such a petition may be read as embracing such a solicitor.[280]

Application of Rules

7.170   Except where otherwise indicated, the Rules relating to a bankruptcy petition by a creditor, where applicable, apply to such a petition, with any necessary modifications.[281] A form of petition is prescribed.[282] Where in any Rule or paragraph of a Rule the letters "CP" follow the number, that Rule or (as the case may be) that paragraph applies only to a creditor's petition.[283]

7.171   The Society, whether or not it is a creditor of the bankrupt solicitor, may be represented at any meeting of creditors and is to be given or sent any notice or report under the Order or the Rules which is required or authorised to be given or sent to creditors.[284]

Dismissal of petition

7.172   In addition to the general power of the Court to dismiss a bankruptcy petition or to stay proceedings thereon,[285] the Court may dismiss a petition by the Society as attorney of a solicitor if, at the hearing, the solicitor satisfies it that he is able to pay all his debts.[286]

Footnotes

(1)   Art.238.
(2)   Art.226(2)(a).
(3)   Art.9(1).
(4)   Art.251(1).
(5)   "Business" includes a trade or profession (Art.2 (2)). As to the extended meaning of "carrying on business" under the corresponding provision of the Bankruptcy Act 1914, see Williams and Muir Hunter on Bankruptcy (19th edn) p.53.
(6)   Art.239.
(7)   Art.238.
(8)   Art.240(1).
(9)   Art.361(2): The Insolvency (Deposits) Order (Northern Ireland) 1991: R.6.009(2).
(10)   RR.6.012(1), 6.039(2). See paras.7.025/026 and Ch.28, Pt.V re-effecting registration.
(11)   R.6.012(1).
(12)   R of D Act, s.3A(1): RR. 6.012(2), 6.039(2). See para.7.027 re vacation of registration.
(13)   R of D Act, s.3A(1).
(14)   R of D Act, ss.3(4), 3A(3).
(15)   LR Act, s.72.
(16)   LR Act, s.67A(1): RR. 6.012(3), 6.039(3).
(17)   LR Act, s.67A(1). See para. 7.028 re cancellation of notice.
(18)   LR Rule 150A: para.7.028.
(19)   Para.5.031: Atkin Forms 129/131. See para.9.09 re amendment of title after making of bankruptcy order.
(20)   Art.240(2).
(21)   Para.7.089.
(22)   Art.240(3). For dismissal on ground of abuse of process, see Hals 176, 185.
(23)   Paras.7.121/126 and 7.171.
(24)   RR.6.024(1), 6.040(1).
(25)   F.6.24.
(26)   RR.6.024(1), 6.040(1).
(27)   RR.6.024(2), 6.040(2).
(28)   Including the continued operation by bankers of the debtor's overdrawn account - Re Gray's Inn Construction Co Ltd. [1980] 1 WLR 711.
(29)   MH 3-153/3-159/2 See Ch.28, Pt. V re operation of this provision in respect of bankrupt's land.
(30)   Art.257(6).
(31)   Art.257(4). Notice of non-compliance with a statutory demand may constitute lack of good faith - MH 3-157: Hals 205, fn.4.
(32)   As defined in R of D Act, s.3A(6).
(33)   R of D Act, s.3A(5).
(34)   LR Rule 150A.
(35)   LR Act, ss.67A(2), 81(3), (4).

(36) R of D Act, ss.3(4), 3A(3).
(37) R of D Act, ss. 3(6), 3A(3).
(38) LR Rule 150A.
(39) LR Act, Sch.6, Pt.II, para.6A.
(40) See Buckley on the Companies Acts, 14th edn. 571/5: Palmer's Company Law, 1982 edn. 85-75/76: Paget, Law of Banking, 10th edn. pp. 211/2, 307/10. See also Practice Direction by the Vice-Chancellor which includes a standard form of order made in England under I.A. 1986 s.127 - *Practice Direction (Companies Court: Contributory's Petition) (No.1 of 1990)* [1990] 1 WLR 490.
(41) Roger Gregory, "Bankruptcy of Individuals and Partnerships", para.427.
(42) Paras.7.124, 7.126.
(43) Art.259.
(44) Art.341: para 8.20/21.
(45) Art.309(1): paras.14.037/041.
(46) Art.335.
(47) Para.11.40.
(48) R.6.228.
(49) Atkin p.145, Forms 371/373.
(50) R.7.02(2).
(51) *Practice Direction (Bankruptcy: Business: Distribution) (No.5/88),* [1988] 1 WLR 1404, para.5.
(52) See useful flow chart for proceedings on a creditor's bankruptcy petition at (1991) 4 Ins Int 23.
(53) Art.241. There must be no interim order under the arrangement procedure in force - para.7.002 above.
(54) Art.241: para.7.047.
(55) Only against "an individual" - Art.238(1).
(56) JEO, Art.84: Judgment Enforcement (Amendment) Rules (Northern Ireland) 1985 (SR 1985 No. 164).
(57) Para.7.047.
(58) Para.7.049.
(59) Paras.6.31/51. *Re a Debtor (No 53 of 1991 Kingston upon Thames), ex p. F G Smith (Interiors) Ltd.* (1991) The Independent, 19 August (1991), 4 Ins Int 80.
(60) Art.241(2).
(61) MH 3-073, 3-388.
(62) Para.7.067.
(63) Art.241(2).
(64) Art.241(3).
(65) R.6.008(1).
(66) *Ibid.*
(67) Art.243. MH 3-089.
(68) Art.10(2).
(69) R.6.112(2).
(70) Ch. 6.

(71)   Art.242(1).
(72)   Art.103(1)(e) and (2).
(73)   1872 Act. s.21(5A).
(74)   Art.242(2).
(75)   F.6.07.
(76)   F.6.08.
(77)   F.6.09.
(78)   R.6.009(5).
(79)   RR.6.007, 6.008.
(80)   R.7.01(2).
(81)   Where name differs from that in judgment or statutory demand, see Atkin Form 62.
(82)   Where debtor's residence is unknown, see Atkin Form 64.
(83)   Including a trade or profession - Art.2(2).
(84)   R.6.007(1), (3).
(85)   R.6.007(2).
(86)   For precedents of statements of consideration, see Atkin Forms 66/69.
(87)   R.6.008(1).
(88)   R.6.008(2).
(89)   Paras.6.19, 6.28.
(90)   Paras.6.19, 6.29.
(91)   R.6.008(3). Enforcement costs are not provable and cannot be included in the petitioning creditor's debt - JH 29.028.
(92)   F.6.15.
(93)   R.6.011(1), (2).
(94)   R.6.011(3).
(95)   R.6.011(4).
(96)   R.6.011(5).
(97)   R.6.011(7).
(98)   R.6.011(6).
(99)   Paras.6.21/26.
(100) Art.241(2).
(101) Art.244.
(102) R.6.009(1).
(103) R.6.010(1),(2).
(104) R.6.010(9).
(105) R.6.009(2): para 7.007.
(106) R.6.009(3).
(107) R.6.009(4).
(108) R.6.009(5), (6).
(109) Para.5.031.
(110) Art.245(5).
(111) R.6.019.
(112) R.6.013(1).
(113) R.6.013(4).
(114) R.6.013(1).
(115) *Ibid.*

(116) R.6.013(2): FF.6.16, 6.17. Note that the requirement for substituted service of a bankruptcy petition is more stringent than under RSC O.65 (Para.5.074). See *Practice Note (Bankruptcy: Substituted Service) (No. 4/86)* [1987] 1 WLR 82 as to evidence which in most cases will justify an order for substituted service by the High Court in England, and N.I. Practice Note by Master dated 1 May 1984 re substituted service of a debtor's summons. For precedents of application and supporting affidavit see Atkin Forms 87, 88.

(117) R.6.013(3).

(118) Para.7.004.

(119) R.12.13(2).

(120) DIEO Art.5(1).

(121) DIEO Art.5(2).

(122) R.6.015: DIEO Art.5(3).

(123) R.6.017(1).

(124) FF.6.18, 6.19.

(125) R.6.014.

(126) *Ibid.*

(127) R.7.28(2).

(128) Para.7.091.

(129) R.6.017(2): Atkin Forms 115/117.

(130) Para.7.067.

(131) Art.245(2).

(132) R.6.025(1).

(133) R.6.025(2).

(134) R.6.025(4).

(135) R.6.025(3).

(136) I.e. when the debt falls due - Art.242(2)(a).

(137) R.6.016(1), (2): Atkin Forms 101/103.

(138) R.6.016(3).

(139) R.6.016(4).

(140) RSC O.23: MH 7-104.

(141) F.6.20.

(142) R.6.018.

(143) Art.245(1).

(144) Art.245(3).

(145) *Ibid.* MH 3-095.

(146) If an interim order has been made and is in force the bankruptcy petition cannot proceed - Art.226(2).

(147) Para.7.019.

(148) Para.7.018.

(149) R.6.029(1). But see MH 7-139 re English High Court practice readily to dispense with this affidavit in certain circumstances.

(150) R.6.029(2).

(151) Art.240(2).

(152) JH 7.09/12.

(153) MH 3-154.

(154) Paras.7.100/112. And perhaps a bankruptcy order might be made on the petition on the application of the trustee in a later bankruptcy so as to enable him to reclaim any such payment, by analogy with the decision in *Re Thomas [1984]* 1 WLR 232, decided under the Bankruptcy Act 1914.

(155) R.6.029(3). Cf. R.4.015 re company winding-up petition.

(156) MH 7-139.

(157) See a most valuable discussion of the payment off of the petitioning creditors' debt in "Individual Insolvency - The Insolvency Acts 1985 and 1986" by Sir John Vinelott (Current Legal Problems 1987, p.1 at pp.17-21).

(158) *Re Mann* [1958] 1 WLR 1272, decided under the Bankruptcy Act 1914. But see possible qualification mentioned in fn.(154) above.

(159) MH 7-116, 7-118, 7-137.

(160) F.6.21.

(161) RR.6.017(3), 6.020(1), (4).

(162) R.6.020(2).

(163) R.6.020(3).

(164) Para.13.036.

(165) R.6.009(7).

(166) RR.6.017(3), 6.020(4).

(167) R.6.021(1), (3).

(168) F.6.23.

(169) R.6.021(2).

(170) R.6.021(4).

(171) R.6.222(1),(h).

(172) R.6.023.

(173) R.6.026: FF.6.25, 6.26. See Hals 172, fn. 1 re exercise of Court's discretion to adjourn.

(174) R.6.027(1).

(175) R.6.027(2).

(176) Para.7.044.

(177) Art.242.

(178) F.6.27.

(179) *Ibid*.

(180) Note to F. 6.27 states that service will be personal, unless otherwise ordered.

(181) R.0.2.

(182) Para.7.101.

(183) Para.7.089.

(184) R.6.028.

(185) R.6.028(1).

(186) R.6.028(4).

(187) F.6.28.

(188) R.6.028(2).

(189) R.6.028(3).

(190) R.6.028(5).

(191) R.0.2.

(192) Para.7.067.

(193) Art.245(2). In the meantime, if appropriate, an interim receiver may be appointed to protect the debtor's property.
(194) See *Re A.B.C. Coupler and Engineering Co. Ltd.* [1962] 1 WLR 1236 at pp 1243/4 per Buckley J - a company winding-up petition.
(195) Para. 7.084.
(196) In exercise of the power to waive non-compliance with Rules - RSC O.2, r.1(2).
(197) Para.7.120.
(198) JH 7.25.
(199) *Re Gilmartin* [1989] 1 WLR 513, 516: para.7.126 below.
(200) R.6.022(1); Art 245(1): paras.7.044/049. See dicta of Nicholls L.J. in *Re Marr* [1989] Ch 773 at 783. See para.7.019 re Court's discretion to dismiss the petition.
(201) Art.270(4).
(202) R.6.022(2): F.6.22.
(203) Art.245(4). See MH 3-085 re problems of creditor's proofs and debtor's defence in the case of such a debt.
(204) Art.240(3): para. 7.019.
(205) R.6.022(4).
(206) *Ibid.*
(207) "Execution" includes enforcement under the JEO - R.0.2.
(208) R.6.022(3).
(209) Art.245(3): MH 3-095: *Re a Debtor (No.2389 of 1989)* [1991] Ch 326,333: (1991) 4 Ins Int 76. Presumably views of any other creditor who appears at the hearing as to the reasonableness of any offer by the debtor will be taken into account by the Court.
(210) See para 7.099 re notice.
(211) *Re Gilmartin* [1989] 1 WLR 513, 516.
(212) RSC O.15, r. 7: Atkin Forms 104/106.
(213) Atkin Form 107.
(214) Art.246(1). There must be no interim order under the arrangement procedure in force - para.7.002.
(215) R.6.036(1).
(216) Para.24.020.
(217) F.6.30.
(218) R.6.035(1),(3): para.7.058.
(219) R.6.035(2).
(220) Paras.7.144/148.
(221) Including an arrangement under the control of the Court under the 1857 Act.
(222) R.6.036(2).
(223) R.6.036(3).
(224) Art.246(2): RR. 6.037, 6.066: F.6.31.
(225) R.6.038(6).
(226) Paras.7.144/148.
(227) R.6.038(1), (4), (5).
(228) R.6.038(7).

(229) R.6.038(8): para.7.094.
(230) DIEO Art.5(1), (2).
(231) R.6.038(2).
(232) *Ibid.*
(233) R.6.038(3).
(234) *Ibid.*
(235) Para.7.095.
(236) Para.7.019.
(237) JH 12.09.
(238) Art.247(1)(a), (b): Insolvency (Monetary Limits) Order (Northern Ireland) 1991.
(239) Art.247(1)(c).
(240) Art.247(1)(d).
(241) Para.26.066.
(242) Art.247(2).
(243) Art.259(2): R.6.049(1): para.7.034.
(244) Para.7.143.
(245) Para.7.163.
(246) Para.9.10.
(247) R.6.044.
(248) Art.270(4).
(249) R.6.041(1),(3). F.6.32. In England and Wales the date fixed is normally 14 days from the date of the order - Atkin p.139.
(250) Art.227(5).
(251) R.6.041(1).
(252) *Ibid.*
(253) Insolvency (Fees) Order (Northern Ireland) 1991, Art. 7: Insolvency (Deposits) Order (Northern Ireland) 1991, Art 3.
(254) Art.248(1).
(255) Art.248(1), (2).
(256) R.6.041(2).
(257) R.6.041(3).
(258) *Ibid.*
(259) Art.248(3)(a).
(260) Art.248(4).
(261) Art.248(5).
(262) Para.26.090.
(263) Para.26.088.
(264) Para.13.036.
(265) R.6.040(3).
(266) *Ibid.*
(267) Art.248(3)(b).
(268) Para.7.155.
(269) Art.226(2)(a).
(270) Art.238(1)(c).
(271) Para.7.044.
(272) Art.250(1). See also para.7.019 re Court's discretion to dismiss petition.

(273) Art.250(2).
(274) R.6.006(2).
(275) F.6.10.
(276) R.6.006(3).
(277) Art.238(1)(d).
(278) Art.251(1). See para.7.019 re Court's discretion to dismiss petition.
(279) Art.251(1).
(280) Para.7.044.
(281) Art.9(1).
(282) R.6.006(2).
(283) F.6.11.
(284) R.6.006(3).
(285) R.6.093.
(286) Para.7.019.
(287) Art.251(2).

Chapter 8

INTERIM RECEIVER

Introduction
8.01   Although a receiver could be appointed after the presentation of a bankruptcy petition under section 68 of the 1872 Act, the occasion for such an appointment rarely arose because an adjudication order was, in most cases, made on an ex parte application shortly after the filing of the petition and the bankrupt's property vested in the Official Assignee immediately upon adjudication. Under the new procedure a bankruptcy petition, other than by the debtor, is no longer heard ex parte and a considerable period may elapse between the presentation of the petition and the hearing, during which the debtor, although subject to the restrictions of Article 257 as regards dispositions of his property,[1] will remain in control of it until a bankruptcy order is made, unless an interim receiver is appointed. A petitioner should, therefore, always consider whether such an appointment is desirable to safeguard the debtor's estate against improper dispositions before the Official Receiver takes control on the making of the bankruptcy order.[2]

Power to appoint
8.02   At any time after the presentation of a bankruptcy petition and before the making of a bankruptcy order the Court may appoint an interim receiver of the debtor's property,[3] if it is shown to be necessary to do so for the protection of such property.[4] Only the Official Receiver may be appointed except where, on a debtor's petition, the Court has, under Article 247(2), appointed an insolvency practitioner with a view to consideration of a voluntary arrangement in lieu of bankruptcy,[5] in which case that practitioner may be appointed interim receiver instead of the Official Receiver.[6]

Application for appointment
8.03   An application for appointment of an interim receiver may be made by -
   (a)   a creditor,
   (b)   the debtor,
   (c)   where the petition is by the debtor, by an insolvency practitioner appointed under Article 247(2), or
   (d)   where the petition is by the Law Society of Northern Ireland against a solicitor under Article 238(1)(d), by the petitioner.[7]

8.04   The application must be supported by an affidavit stating -
   (a)   the grounds for the appointment,
   (b)   whether or not the Official Receiver has been informed of the application and, if so, has been furnished with a copy of it,
   (c)   whether, to the applicant's knowledge, there has been proposed or is in force a voluntary arrangement in respect of the debtor,

(d) the applicant's estimate of the value of the property or business in respect of which the interim receiver is to be appointed, and

(e) where an insolvency practitioner has been appointed following the presentation of a debtor's petition and it is proposed that he be appointed interim receiver, and he is not himself the applicant, that he has consented to act.[8]

8.05   The Official Receiver and (if appointed) the insolvency practitioner may attend the hearing of the application and make representations.[9]

8.06   Usually the application is urgent and will be heard on the day it is filed. However, the Official Receiver or the insolvency practitioner proposed to be appointed as interim receiver, as the case may be, must be informed of the intended application in sufficient time to enable him to be present at the hearing: where practicable this must be done by sending him copies of the application and supporting affidavit.[10] Where an insolvency practitioner has been appointed under Article 247(2) but it is proposed to appoint the Official Receiver as interim receiver, copies of the application and affidavit must be sent to the insolvency practitioner.[11]

Order of appointment
8.07   If the Court is satisfied that sufficient grounds are shown (i.e. that it is necessary for the protection of the debtor's property[12]) it may make the appointment on such terms as it thinks fit.[13]

8.08   The order[14] is required to state the nature and a short description of the property of which the interim receiver is to take possession and the duties to be performed by him in relation to the debtor's affairs.[15] It must require the receiver to take immediate possession of that property.[16]

8.09   The interim receiver has, in relation to the debtor's property, all the rights, powers, duties and immunities of the Official Receiver when acting as receiver and manager of the estate of a bankrupt between the date of the bankruptcy order and the vesting of the bankrupt's estate in a trustee, unless the order of appointment expressly limits or restricts such powers in any respect.[17] The provisions of the Order and the Rules relating to the private examination of a bankrupt apply to such an examination on the application of the interim receiver, except that no order may be made for the production of documents by the Inland Revenue.[18]

8.10   For the period between the appointment of the interim receiver and the making of a bankruptcy order on the petition, or the dismissal of the petition, the order of appointment has the effect of restricting the remedies of a creditor of the debtor in respect of a debt which would be provable in bankruptcy, as if it were a bankruptcy order.[19] If a bankruptcy order is made, the date of the first appointment of an interim receiver is the date at which preferential debts are determined.[20]

8.11 Forthwith after the order is made the Court must send 2 sealed copies to the interim receiver, one of which he is required to send forthwith to the debtor.[21]

Deposit

8.12 Where the Official Receiver is appointed interim receiver, the order appointing him will fix an amount to be deposited with him or otherwise secured to his satisfaction, to cover his remuneration and expenses, and the order will not issue until this has been done.[22]

8.13 If the sum deposited or secured subsequently proves to be insufficient, the Court may, on the application of the Official Receiver, order that an additional sum be deposited or secured, and if such order is not complied with within 2 days after service on the person to whom it is directed, the Court may discharge the order appointing the interim receiver.[23]

8.14 If a bankruptcy order is made after an interim receiver has been appointed, any money so deposited (unless it was made by the debtor out of his own property or is required because the bankrupt's assets are insufficient to pay the remuneration and expenses of the interim receiver) be repaid to the person depositing it, or as that person may direct, out of the bankrupt's estate, in the prescribed order of priority.[24]

Security by insolvency practitioner

8.15 Where, on a debtor's petition, an insolvency practitioner appointed under Article 247(2) is appointed interim receiver, he is required to provide security.[25] The cost of providing such security is to be paid in the first instance by the interim receiver; but-
  (a) if a bankruptcy order is not made, he is entitled to be reimbursed out of the debtor's property, and the Court may make an order on the debtor accordingly, and
  (b) if a bankruptcy order is made, he is entitled to be reimbursed out of the bankrupt's estate in the prescribed order of priority.[26]

8.16 If the insolvent practitioner fails to give or to keep up his security, the Court may remove him, and make such order as it thinks fit as to costs.[27] If such an order is made, or if the order appointing the interim receiver is discharged, the Court must give directions as to whether any, and if so what, steps should be taken to appoint another person in his place.[28]

Remuneration and expenses

8.17 Where an insolvency practitioner is appointed interim receiver his remuneration is fixed by the Court from time to time on his application.[29] The factors to be taken into account in doing so are listed in the Rules.[30] The Court may refer the measurement to the Taxing Master.[31]

8.18   Without prejudice to any order as to costs, the remuneration of the interim receiver (whether the Official Receiver or an insolvency practitioner) is to be paid to him, and the amount of any expenses incurred by him (including the remuneration and expenses of any special manager[32]) reimbursed-

(a)   if a bankruptcy order is not made, out of the debtor's property, and

(b)   if a bankruptcy order is made, out of the bankrupt's estate in the prescribed order of priority.[33]

If, in either case, the relevant funds are insufficient, such remuneration and expenses are payable out of the deposit required on the appointment of the Official Receiver as interim receiver.[34] Where a bankruptcy order is not made, the interim receiver may, unless the Court otherwise directs, retain out of the debtor's property such sums or property as are or may be required for meeting his remuneration and expenses.[35]

Termination of appointment

8.19   The appointment of the interim receiver may be terminated by the Court on his application or on the application of the Official Receiver (where not the interim receiver) the debtor, any creditor or, on a petition by the Law Society of Northern Ireland under Article 238 (1)(d), the petitioner.[36] It terminates automatically on the dismissal of the petition or on the making of a bankruptcy order.[37] On any termination of the appointment of an interim receiver the Court may give such directions as it thinks fit with respect to the accounts of his administration and any other matters which it thinks appropriate.[38]

Special manager

8.20   Where the Official Receiver has been appointed interim receiver of the debtor's property he may apply to the Court for the appointment of a special manager of the property or business of the debtor.[39]

8.21   The provisions of the Order and (with appropriate modifications) the Rules relating to the appointment of a special manager of a bankrupt's estate[40] apply to such an appointment. Where a bankruptcy order is not made, the Court may order the debtor to reimburse the special manager for the costs of providing security.[41] The appointment terminates if the bankruptcy petition is dismissed or if the interim receiver is discharged without a bankruptcy order having been made.[42]

Supplies of water, electricity etc.

8.22   The interim receiver has the same right as a trustee to request a supply of water, electricity, telephone or other public telecommunication services for the purpose of carrying on a business, without being required to pay any outstanding charges.[43]

Duties of debtor

8.23   When an interim receiver is appointed, the debtor is required to give the receiver such inventory of his property and such other information, and to attend on the receiver at such times as he may reasonably require for the purpose of carrying out his functions.[44]

Footnotes

(1)   Paras.7.022/023.
(2)   Para.12.27.
(3)   This embraces all his property and is not confined to property which would be comprised in his estate if adjudged bankrupt-Art.259(8).
(4)   Art.259(1).
(5)   Paras.7.146/148.
(6)   Art.259(2).
(7)   R.6.049(1): Atkin Form 139.
(8)   R.6.049(2),(3).
(9)   R.6.049(6).
(10)   R.6.049(4),(5).
(11)   R.6.049(4).
(12)   Art.259(1).
(13)   R.6.049(7).
(14)   F.6.35.
(15)   R.6.050(1).
(16)   Art.259(4).
(17)   Art.259(3).
(18)   Arts.339, 340(7).
(19)   Art.259(6).
(20)   Art.347(6)(a).
(21)   R.6.050(2).
(22)   R.6.051(1).
(23)   R.6.051(2).
(24)   RR.6.051(3), 6.222(1)(g).
(25)   Arts.3(2)(a), 349(3): Ins Pract Regs, Pt III.
(26)   RR.6.052, 6.222(1)(e).
(27)   R.6.053(1).
(28)   R.6.053(2).
(29)   R.6.054(1).
(30)   R.6.054(2).
(31)   Paras.5.122/125.
(32)   Para.8.20.
(33)   RR.6.051(3), 6.222(1)(e),(7).
(34)   R.6.054(3).
(35)   R.6.054(4).
(36)   Art.259(7): RR. 6.055(1).
(37)   Art.259(7).
(38)   R.6.055(2).
(39)   Art.341(1)(c).
(40)   Paras.12.36/47.
(41)   R.6.165(5).
(42)   R.6.168(1).
(43)   Art.343: para.14.034.
(44)   Art.259(5).

Chapter 9

BANKRUPTCY ORDER

Preliminary
9.01   Except where otherwise stated, this Chapter applies to a bankruptcy order made on any petition.

Settlement and contents of order
9.02   The bankruptcy order[1] is settled by the Court.[2] It must state the date of presentation of the petition and the date and time of the making of the order, and contain a notice to the bankrupt requiring him to attend the Official Receiver at a specified place (which will be the Official Receiver's office).[3] Subject to Article 88 of the Judgments Enforcement Order (effect of bankruptcy on enforcement proceedings) the order may include a provision staying any action or proceedings against the bankrupt.[4] Where the petitioning creditor is represented by a solicitor the order must be endorsed with the solicitor's name, address, telephone and fax number (if any) and reference (if any).[5] Where the costs of any creditor appearing on the petition are allowed,[6] these should be provided for in the order.

Action by Court following order
9.03   The Court is required forthwith after the making of the bankruptcy order, to send at least 5 sealed copies (one of which, required for the Registry of Deeds, must be certified by the Master) to the Official Receiver, one sealed copy to the Clerk of the Crown (for recording in relation to disqualification of a bankrupt as a Justice of the Peace) and where the order is made against a solicitor, send a sealed copy of the order to the Law Society of Northern Ireland.[7]

Action by Official Receiver following order
9.04   On receiving the copy orders from the Court the Official Receiver must forthwith send one of the uncertified copies to the bankrupt.[8] Unless otherwise ordered by the Court, he must also
(a)   send notice of the making of the order to the Enforcement of Judgments Office,
(b)   register the order in the Registry of Deeds,
(c)   cause the order to be advertised in such newspaper as he thinks fit and file a copy of the advertisement in the Court, and
(d)   cause the order to be gazetted.[9]

9.05   The Official Receiver will also serve on the bankrupt a notice directing attention to the bankrupt's obligations under the Order.[10]

9.06   Notification of the order to the Enforcement of Judgments Office, registration of it in the Registry of Deeds and the advertising and gazetting of it may be suspended by order of the Court on the application of the bankrupt, supported by an affidavit stating the grounds on which it is made.[11] The application is ex parte but the Court will ensure that the Official Receiver is notified and attends.[12] Such an order is unlikely to be made unless the Court is satisfied that all the debts of the bankrupt have been or will promptly be paid or where an appeal against the bankruptcy order is pending. If made, the order will usually be subject to conditions, e.g. filing of a statement of affairs, where not already filed, and notice to the bankrupt's bankers.[13] The bankrupt must forthwith deliver a copy of the order to the Official Receiver.[14]

Registration of order
9.07   The bankruptcy order must be registered in the Registry of Deeds, whether or not the bankrupt's estate is known to include land.[15] Registration is effected by the Official Receiver lodging in that Registry 2 of the copies of the order received from the Court, one of which must be the copy certified by the Master, and 2 copies of a document prescribed by the Insolvency (Registration of Deeds) Regulations, one of which must be certified by the Official Receiver.[16]

9.08   Where at any time after a bankruptcy order is made it becomes known to the Official Receiver or the trustee that the bankrupt is the registered owner of land (and whether or not notice of the presentation of the petition has previously been given by the Court[17]), he is required to notify the Registrar of Titles.[18] The notice is given in a form prescribed by the Land Registry Rules. Upon receipt of the notice the Registrar of Titles enters a bankruptcy inhibition against the title of the registered owner of the land.[19]

Amendment of title of proceedings
9.09   Where the particulars of the debtor as set out in the petition (constituting the full title of the proceedings[20]) are subsequently found to be materially inaccurate, the Official Receiver, the trustee or any person aggrieved may, at any time after the making of the bankruptcy order, apply to the Court for amendment of the full title.[21] Where such an order is made the Official Receiver must forthwith send notice of it to the Enforcement of Judgments Office and to the Registrar of Deeds and also, if applicable, to the Registrar of Titles, for registration.[22] If so directed by the Court, he must also have notice of the amending order gazetted and advertised in such newspaper as he thinks fit.[23] The Official Receiver should apply for such a direction where he considers that it is desirable that a correction of the particulars in an earlier publication should be published.

Certificate for summary administration
9.10   On making a bankruptcy order on a debtor's petition (but not on any other petition), the Court may in certain circumstances issue a certificate for the summary administration of the bankrupt's estate.[24] This may be done where it appears to be Court that -

(a)   if a bankruptcy order were made the aggregate amount of the unse-
      cured bankruptcy debts[25] would be less than "the small bankruptcies
      level",[26] and
(b)   the debtor has not within the 5 years preceding the presentation of the
      petition been adjudged bankrupt nor made a composition with his
      creditors in satisfaction of his debts or a scheme of arrangement of his
      affairs.[27]

9.11   The certificate may, and usually will be included in the bankruptcy
order.[28] If not so included, the Court must forthwith send copies of it to the
Official Receiver and the bankrupt.[29]

9.12   Whilst a certificate is in force the following consequences ensue -
(a)   the Official Receiver becomes the trustee of the bankrupt's estate
      immediately the certificate is issued and remains trustee unless and
      until the Court, or on the application of the Official Receiver, the
      Department, appoints another person in his place;[30]
(b)   if a trustee has been appointed and a vacancy in the office subsequently
      occurs, the Official Receiver again becomes trustee until, on his appli-
      cation, the vacancy is filled by the Court or, if the appointment is made
      by the Department, either by the Court or the Department;[31]
(c)   if a trustee has been appointed, he may only be removed by the
      Court;[32]
(d)   the Official Receiver need only investigate the bankrupt's conduct and
      affairs if he thinks fit;[33]
(e)   if the bankrupt qualifies for discharge without an order of the Court,[34]
      he obtains his discharge 2 years after the making of the bankruptcy
      order.[35]

9.13   A certificate is to be issued by the Court in the specified circumstances
only if it appears to be appropriate to do so.[36] If circumstances are disclosed
which require an investigation of the bankrupt's conduct or affairs or which
would make it inappropriate that he should obtain an automatic discharge in
2 years instead of 3, the certificate will not be issued.

9.14   Where a trustee has been appointed following the issue of a certificate
the Official Receiver must send a copy of the certificate (whether or not included
in the bankruptcy order) to him.[37]

9.15   Within 12 weeks after the issue of a certificate the Official Receiver must
give notice to creditors of the making of the bankruptcy order, insofar as he has
not already done so.[38] A form of proof of debts[39] must accompany the
notice.[40]

9.16   The Court may at any time revoke a certificate if it appears to it that,
on any grounds existing at the time the certificate was issued, it ought not to
have been issued.[41] Such a revocation may be ordered by the Court of its own

motion or on the application of the Official Receiver.[42] If the Official Receiver applies for a revocation he must give at least 14 days notice to the bankrupt.[43]

9.17   If the Court revokes a certificate it must forthwith give notice to the Official Receiver and the bankrupt.[44] If at the time of revocation there is a trustee other than the Official Receiver, the Official Receiver must send a copy of the Court's notice to such trustee.[45]

Discharge of bankruptcy order
9.18   If a bankruptcy order is discharged on appeal or on a review, the discharge order should provide for the dismissal of the petition and (if applicable) the vacation of registration of the petition and bankruptcy order in the Registry of Deeds and cancellation of any entries in the Land Registry of notice of the petition and/or of a bankruptcy inhibition.[46]

Consequences of bankruptcy order
9.19   The bankruptcy of the debtor commences on the day the bankruptcy order is made and continues until he is discharged.[47] There is no longer any relation back of the bankruptcy to an earlier date.[48]

9.20   Other significant consequences of the making of the order include-
   (a)   dispositions of the bankrupt's property made since the presentation of the petition, and before the vesting of the bankrupt's estate in a trustee, become subject to the restrictions of Article 257;[49]
   (b)   all property belonging to or vested in the bankrupt at the date of the order (with the exception of excluded articles or their replacements, or trust property) is comprised in the bankrupt's estate available for the benefit of his creditors;[50]
   (c)   the Official Receiver becomes receiver and manager of the bankrupt's estate and the bankrupt must deliver possession of his estate to him,[51] subject to limited rights of his spouse and himself to remain in occupation of a dwelling house;[52]
   (d)   the bankrupt becomes subject to the directions of the Court[53] and is required to co-operate with the Official Receiver and the trustee in the investigation of his affairs and the handing over of his property for the benefit of his creditors[54] and he may be examined by the Court publicly[55] or privately[56] and may be required to attend to be questioned at a creditors' meeting;[57]
   (e)   the bankrupt continues to be liable to arrest under Article 335 (2);[58]
   (f)   the bankrupt becomes liable to prosecution for criminal offences in relation to his conduct before and after bankruptcy;[59]
   (g)   the rights of creditors and others to proceed against the bankrupt are affected;[60]
   (h)   the bankrupt is subject to the disabilities and disqualifications mentioned below.[61]

Disabilities and disqualifications of bankrupt

(a) Leaving the jurisdiction

9.21   An undischarged bankrupt may not leave Northern Ireland without the prior leave of the Court, except that with the written consent of the Official Receiver he may travel to Great Britain or the Republic of Ireland.[62]   If he remains outside Northern Ireland with the leave of the Court or the consent of the Official Receiver for a period exceeding 2 weeks he must inform the Official Receiver in writing of his address and of any change of address.[63]

(b) Obtaining credit

9.22   It is an offence for a bankrupt, alone or jointly with any other person, to obtain credit of a prescribed amount (currently £250) or more without disclosing to the person from whom he obtains such credit that he is an undischarged bankrupt.[64]

9.23   Obtaining goods under a hire-purchase or conditional sale agreement for securing payment in advance (whether in money or otherwise) for the supply of goods or services constitutes obtaining credit for the purpose of this offence.[65]

(c) Engaging in business under another name

9.24   It is an offence for an undischarged bankrupt to engage, directly or indirectly, in any business under a name other than that in which he was adjudged bankrupt without disclosing to all persons with whom he enters into any business transaction the name in which he was so adjudged.[66]

(d) Acting as director etc. of company

9.25   An undischarged bankrupt may not, except with the leave of the Court, act as director of, or directly or indirectly take part in or be concerned in the promotion, formation or management of, a company.[67]

(e) Practising as a solicitor

9.26   When a solicitor is adjudged bankrupt his practising certificate is suspended and he may be refused a renewal of his certificate even after he is discharged.[68] Notice of his suspension and of termination of such suspension is published by the Law Society of Northern Ireland in the Belfast Gazette.[69] Adjudication of a solicitor bankrupt is one of the grounds on which the Society may exercise extensive powers of control in relation to his practice.[70]

(f) Acting as insolvency practitioner

9.27   An undischarged bankrupt may not act as an insolvency practitioner.[71]

(g) Practising as an estate agent

9.28   It is an offence for a bankrupt to practise as an estate agent on his own behalf.[72] The prohibition ceases on the annulment of the adjudication or on the discharge of the bankrupt.[73]

(h) Membership of Local Authority
9.29 A bankrupt is disqualified from election to or being a member of a District Council.[74] The disqualification ceases on the annulment of the adjudication or on the discharge of the bankrupt.[75]

(i) Election to or serving in parliament
9.30 A bankrupt is disqualified for being elected to the House of Commons.[76] Formerly a Northern Ireland bankrupt was not so disqualified.[77] No writ of summons may be issued to a bankrupt peer.[78]

9.31 A bankrupt may not sit or vote in the House of Lords or House of Commons or in a committee of either House.[79]

9.32 Where a member of the House of Commons remains an undischarged bankrupt for a period of 6 months after the adjudication his seat is vacated at the end of that period.[80]

9.33 Where the Court makes a bankruptcy order against a peer or a member of the House of Commons it must forthwith certify the adjudication to the Speaker of the House of Lords or, as the case may be, to the Speaker of the House of Commons.[81]

9.34 Where the Court has so certified an adjudication to the Speaker of the House of Commons it must certify to him when the period of 6 months from the adjudication expires without the adjudication having been annulled or immediately any annulment order is made within that period.[82]

9.35 Parliamentary disqualification ceases on the discharge of the bankrupt or earlier annulment of the adjudication.[83]

(j) Election to or serving in Northern Ireland Assembly
9.36 Article 370 of the Order applies to the Northern Ireland Assembly provisions corresponding to those relating to disqualification for election to or sitting or voting in the House of Commons.

(k) Acting as a Justice of the Peace
9.37 A Justice of the Peace adjudged bankrupt is disqualified from acting until he has again been appointed and a bankrupt may not be appointed a Justice of the Peace unless his bankruptcy is annulled or he obtains from the Court either at the time of or subsequent to his discharge from bankruptcy a certificate that, in the opinion of the Court, his bankruptcy was caused by misfortune without any misconduct on his part.[84]

Footnotes

(1) FF.6.29, 6.33.
(2) RR.6.030(1), 6.042(1).
(3) RR.6.030(2), 6.042(2).
(4) Art.258(1): RR.6.030(3), 6.042(3).
(5) RR.6.030(4), 6.042(4).
(6) Para.7.097.
(7) RR.6.031(1), 6.043(1).
(8) RR.6.031(2), 6.043(2).
(9) RR.6.031(2), 6.043(2), 7.28(2). Where the Official Receiver makes a prompt decision with regard to the first meeting of creditors (para.13.016), expense may be saved by combining the advertisement of the bankruptcy order with the notice of such meeting.
(10) For form used in England, see Atkin Form 241.
(11) RR.6.031(3),(4), 6.043(3),(4).
(12) Atkin pp. 144/5.
(13) *Ibid.* In Northern Ireland the Official Receiver will have notified the bankruptcy order to the Head Offices of the Irish banks.
(14) RR.6.031(5), 6.042(5).
(15) R of D Act s. 3B(1): RR. 6.031(2), 6.043(2).
(16) R of D Act s. 3B(1): RR. 6.030(5), 6.042(5).
(17) Para.7.015.
(18) LR Act, s 67A(3).
(19) *Ibid.*
(20) RR.6.007(2), 6.035(2).
(21) RR.6.032(1), 6.045(1): Atkin Forms 129, 130.
(22) RR.6.032(2), 6.045(2).
(23) RR.6.032(3), 6.045(3).
(24) Art.249(1).
(25) Art.9(1): para.19.03.
(26) At present £20,000 - Insolvency (Monetary Limits) Order (Northern Ireland) 1991.
(27) Art.249(2).
(28) R.6.046(1): F.6.33.
(29) R.6.046(2).
(30) Arts.269(1),(2), 270(1),(2).
(31) Art.273(2),(5).
(32) Art.271(1),(2).
(33) Art.262(5).
(34) Para.21.030.
(35) Art.253(2)(a).
(36) Art.249(1).
(37) R.6.047(1).
(38) R.6.047(2).
(39) F.6.40.

(40) R.6.095(2).
(41) Art.249(3).
(42) R.6.048(1): F.6.34: Atkin Form 137.
(43) R.6.048(2).
(44) R.6.048(3).
(45) R.6.048(4).
(46) Atkin Forms 432 and 436.
(47) Art.252.
(48) Cf. former law - J H 21.25/32.
(49) Para.7.022.
(50) Para.12.010.
(51) Paras.12.27, 12.29.
(52) Paras.14.037/047.
(53) Art.334(2).
(54) Arts.264, 285, 306: paras.11.04, 14.022, 14.030.
(55) Paras.11.07/43.
(56) Paras.11.44/77.
(57) Para.16.12.
(58) Paras.7.036, 11.38.
(59) Pt. IX, Ch. VI of Order.
(60) Para.28.16/23.
(61) Paras.9.21/37.
(62) R.6.230(1), (2): Atkin Forms 389, 390.
(63) R.6.230(3).
(64) Art.331(1)(a): Insolvency (Monetary Limits) Order (Northern Ireland) 1991 (reference in Sch. to this Order to Art.333(1) is an obvious misprint for Art.331(1)).
(65) Art.331(2).
(66) Art.331(1)(b).
(67) Companies (Northern Ireland) Order 1989, Art.14(1).
(68) Solicitors (Northern Ireland) Order 1976, Arts.13(1)(c),(k), 15(1). Suspension ceases an annulment of the adjudication and may be terminated by the Council of the Law Society on application of solicitor - Art.16(21),(3) of 1976 Order.
(69) *Ibid.* Art.17.
(70) *Ibid.* Art. 36(2)(a).
(71) Art.349(4).
(72) Estate Agents Act 1979, s. 23(1).
(73) *Ibid*, s.23(2).
(74) Local Government Act (Northern Ireland) 1972, s.4(1)(b).
(75) *Ibid*, s.5(1).
(76) IA 1986, s.427 (1).
(77) JH 13.78.
(78) IA 1986 s. 127(3).
(79) *Ibid*. s.427(1).
(80) *Ibid*. s.427(4).
(81) *Ibid*. s.427(5): Atkin Form 283.

(82)   *Ibid.* s.427(6): Atkin Form 284.
(83)   *Ibid.* s.427(2).
(84)   Magistrates' Courts Act (Northern Ireland) 1964, s.6(2),(3).

Chapter 10

DISCLOSURE BY BANKRUPT OF HIS AFFAIRS: INFORMATION TO CREDITORS

I. STATEMENT OF AFFAIRS

A. DEBTOR'S PETITION

10.01   A debtor's bankruptcy petition must be accompanied by a statement of affairs in the prescribed form, verified by affidavit.[1]

B. OTHER PETITIONS

Duty to submit
10.02   Where a bankruptcy order is made otherwise than on a debtor's petition the bankrupt is required to submit a statement of affairs to the Official Receiver within 21 days from the date of the order.[2] However, the Official Receiver has a discretion to release the bankrupt from this duty or to extend the time, and the Court may do so if the Official Receiver refuses.[3]

Form
10.03   The statement of affairs must be in the prescribed form,[4] contain all the particulars required by that form, and be verified by affidavit,[5]

10.04   The forms of statement of affairs and guidance notes for the preparation of the statement must be given to the bankrupt by the Official Receiver.[6] This will be done when the bankrupt attends the Official Receiver pursuant to the direction to do so in the bankruptcy order.[7] The verifying affidavit may be sworn before the Official Receiver or Deputy Official Receiver, or a duly authorised officer of the Department or the Court.[8]

10.05   Where the Official Receiver thinks that it would prejudice the conduct of the bankruptcy for the whole or part of the statement of affairs to be disclosed, he may apply to the Court for an order limiting disclosure.[9] On such an application the Court may order that the statement or a specified part of it be not filed or that it be filed separately and not be open to inspection except by leave of the Court.[10]

Delivery and filing
10.06   The bankrupt must deliver the verified statement of affairs and a copy to the Official Receiver, who files the verified statement in the Court.[11]

Dispensation or extension of time
10.07   The Official Receiver's power to release the bankrupt from his obligation to deliver a statement of affairs or to grant him an extension of time to do so may be exercised at his own discretion or at the bankrupt's request.[12]

10.08   If the Official Receiver refuses a request by the bankrupt, the bankrupt may apply to the Court.[13] If the Court thinks that no sufficient cause is shown for the application it may dismiss it on an ex parte hearing of which the bankrupt has been given at least 7 days notice.[14] Otherwise the Court must fix a venue for the hearing of the application and notify the bankrupt accordingly.[15] The bankrupt must then send to the Official Receiver, at least 14 days before the hearing date, a notice stating the venue and a copy of the application and of any evidence which he (the bankrupt) intends to adduce in support of it.[16]

10.09   The Official Receiver may appear and be heard on the application and, whether or not he appears, he may file a written report of any matters which he considers ought to be drawn to the Court's attention, sending a copy to the bankrupt at least 5 days before the hearing date.[17]

10.10   The Court must send sealed copies of any order made on the application to the bankrupt and the Official Receiver.[18]

10.11   The bankrupt must pay his costs of the application in any event and, unless the Court otherwise orders, no allowance may be made out of the estate.[19]

Expenses
10.12   The expenses of the preparation of the statement of affairs cannot be paid out of the bankrupt's estate except under the provisions mentioned in the following paragraph.

10.13   If the bankrupt cannot himself prepare a proper statement of affairs the Official Receiver may, at the expense of the estate, employ some person or persons to assist the bankrupt in the preparation.[20] Alternatively he may, at the bankrupt's request made on the grounds that he cannot himself prepare a proper statement, authorise an allowance out of the estate (to be paid in the prescribed order of priority[21]) towards the expenses of the bankrupt in employing some person or persons to assist him in the preparation.[22] Any such request must be accompanied by an estimate of the expenses involved and the Official Receiver may only authorise the employment of a named person or firm approved by him.[23] In giving his authorisation for such an allowance the Official Receiver may impose conditions as to the manner in which the person employed by the bankrupt may obtain access to the relevant books and papers.[24]

Responsibility for statement of affairs etc.
10.14   The employment either by the Official Receiver or the bankrupt of a person to assist in the preparation of the statement of affairs does not relieve the bankrupt of his obligations in relation to the statement of affairs or to provide information to the Official Receiver or the trustee.[25]

Admissibility in evidence of statement of affairs etc.

10.15 In any proceedings (whether or not under the Order) a statement of affairs and any other statement made in pursuance of a requirement imposed by or under any provision of the Order or the Rules may be used in evidence against any person making or concurring in making the statement.[26]

II. ACCOUNTS

10.16 The bankrupt is obliged to give the Official Receiver such information as he may reasonably require.[27] In particular he must, in addition to preparing a proper statement of affairs, furnish to the Official Receiver on request such accounts relating to his affairs of such nature, as at such date and for such period as the Official Receiver may specify.[28] The Official Receiver may require accounts for any period up to 3 years before the presentation of the petition and the Court may, on his application, require accounts in respect of any earlier period.[29]

10.17 The accounts must be delivered to the Official Receiver within 21 days of being requested, or such longer period as he may allow.[30] He may require them to be verified by affidavit.[31] Two copies of the accounts and (where required) the verifying affidavit, must be delivered by the bankrupt to the Official Receiver, who files one copy in the Court.[32]

10.18 The provisions governing the expenses of a statement of affairs and access to books and papers by a person employed by the bankrupt under authorisation by the Official Receiver[33] apply also to accounts directed by the Official Receiver.[34] Likewise, the bankrupt is not relieved of his obligations in relation to such accounts by the employment of some person to assist in their preparation.[35]

10.19 The Official Receiver may at any time require the bankrupt to submit in writing further information amplifying, modifying or explaining any matter contained in his statement of affairs or accounts.[36] He may require the information to be verified by affidavit.[37] The bankrupt is required to deliver to the Official Receiver 2 copies of the documents containing the information and (if required) the verifying affidavit within 21 days of the request, or such longer period as the Official Receiver may allow.[38] The Official Receiver files one copy in the Court.[39]

III. ENFORCEMENT OF DUTY TO DISCLOSE

10.20 Where, on a bankruptcy order made otherwise than on a debtor's petition, the bankrupt fails, without reasonable excuse, to submit a statement of affairs complying with the prescribed requirements within the prescribed time, or where in any case the bankrupt, without reasonable excuse, fails to submit accounts or further information required by the Official Receiver, he is guilty of contempt of court and, where the bankrupt is entitled to an automatic discharge,[40] on the application of the Official Receiver the Court may order that such discharge be suspended.[41]

10.21   Before taking proceedings to have a defaulting bankrupt committed to prison for contempt of court or to have his discharge suspended the Official Receiver will usually apply to the Court for an order requiring the bankrupt to submit the statement of affairs, account or other information within a specified time.[42]   Such an order, duly endorsed as required by the Supreme Court Rules,[43] must be served personally on the bankrupt, unless substituted service is ordered.

IV. INFORMATION TO CREDITORS

10.22   The Official Receiver is required, at least once after the making of a bankruptcy order, to send to all creditors known to him or, where the bankrupt has submitted a statement of affairs, identified in the statement, a report with respect to the bankruptcy proceedings and the state of the bankrupt's affairs, file a copy in the Court and send a copy to the trustee, when appointed.[44] Such duty ceases in the event of the bankruptcy order being annulled.[45]

10.23   Where a statement of affairs has been filed in the Court the Official Receiver's report is to contain a summary of the statement (if he thinks fit, as modified or explained by any further information the bankrupt has been required to furnish), together with any observations he wishes to make with respect to it or to the bankrupt's affairs generally.[46]

10.24   Where the bankrupt has been released from the obligation to submit a statement of affairs the Official Receiver must, as soon as may be after the release has been granted, send to the creditors a report containing a summary of the bankrupt's affairs (so far as within his knowledge) and any observations he wishes to make with respect to it or the bankrupt's affairs generally.[47]

10.25   The Official Receiver need not, however, comply with these reporting obligations where he has previously reported to creditors with respect to the bankrupt's affairs (so far as known to him) and he is of opinion that there are no additional matters which ought to be brought to their attention.[48] Also, the Court may, on his application, relieve him of any duty to report or authorise him to carry out the duty in a way other than required by the Rules, and in exercising this discretion the Court is to have regard to the cost of carrying out the duty, to the amount of the funds available in the estate and to the extent of the interest of creditors or any particular class of them.[49]

Footnotes

(1) Para.7.134.
(2) Art.261(1).
(3) Art.261(3): paras.10.07/11.
(4) F.6.36.
(5) Art.261(2): RR.6.057, 6.058(2).
(6) R.6.058(1).
(7) Para.9.02.
(8) R.6.058(4).
(9) R.6.059(1).
(10) R.6.059(2).
(11) R.6.058(2), (3).
(12) R.6.060(1).
(13) Art.261(3): R.6.060(2).
(14) R.6.060(3).
(15) R.6.060(4).
(16) R.6.060(5).
(17) R.6.060(6), (7).
(18) R.6.060(8).
(19) R.6.060(9).
(20) R.6.061(1).
(21) R.6.222(1)(k).
(22) R.6.061(2).
(23) R.6.061(3).
(24) R.6.061(4).
(25) R.6.061(5).
(26) Art.375.
(27) Art.264(4).
(28) RR.6.062(1), 6.067(1): Atkin Forms 143/145.
(29) RR.6.062(2), (3), 6.067(2), (3).
(30) RR. 6.063(1), 6.068(1).
(31) *Ibid.*
(32) RR.6.063(2), 6.068(2).
(33) Paras.10.12/13.
(34) RR.6.062(4), 6.069.
(35) *Ibid.*
(36) RR.6.064(1), 6.070(1).
(37) RR.6.064(2), 6.070(2).
(38) RR.6.064(2), (3), 6.070(2), (3).
(39) RR.6.064(3), 6.070(3).
(40) Para.21.03.
(41) Arts. 261(4), 264(6), 253(3).
(42) Atkin Forms 146, 147.
(43) RSC O.45, rr.4, 5.
(44) RR.6.071, 6.072, 6.122(8).

(45)   R.6.076.
(46)   R.6.073(1).
(47)   R.6.073(2), 6.074(3).
(48)   *Ibid.*
(49)   R.6.075.

Chapter 11

INVESTIGATION OF BANKRUPT'S CONDUCT
AND AFFAIRS

I. DUTY OF OFFICIAL RECEIVER

11.01   It is the duty of the Official Receiver to investigate the conduct and affairs of every bankrupt (including his conduct and affairs before he was adjudged bankrupt) and to make such report (if any) to the Court as he thinks fit, except in the case of a bankrupt in respect of whom a certificate for summary administration is in force,[1] in which case the Official Receiver carries out such investigation only if he thinks fit.[2] Such investigation is particularly important where the bankrupt is a person who may only obtain his discharge by an application to the Court, because on such an application the Official Receiver is required to report to the Court.[3]

II. ASSISTANCE OF TRUSTEE

11.02   Where the Official Receiver is not the trustee, the trustee must -
  (a)   give the Official Receiver such information,
  (b)   produce such books, papers and other records for inspection by the Official Receiver, and
  (c)   give the Official Receiver such other assistance as the Official Receiver may reasonably require to enable him to carry out his functions.[4]

11.03   If necessary, the Official Receiver may apply to the Court for an order requiring the trustee to carry out any of these duties and such order may impose the costs of such an application on the trustee personally.[5]

III. EXAMINATION OF BANKRUPT BY OFFICIAL RECEIVER

11.04   When a bankruptcy order is made the bankrupt is obliged to give the Official Receiver such inventory of his estate and such other information and to attend on the Official Receiver at such times as the Official Receiver, in the execution of his duties to protect the bankrupt's property and to investigate the bankrupt's affairs, may reasonably require.[6] This obligation continues to apply after the bankrupt's discharge.[7] Failure by the bankrupt, without reasonable excuse, to discharge this obligation is contempt of court[8] and, where he is entitled to automatic discharge, may result in his discharge being suspended.[9]

11.05   The bankruptcy order, a copy of which the Official Receiver is required to serve on the bankrupt, contains a notice to the bankrupt requiring him to attend on the Official Receiver immediately after receiving the order.[10]   On

119

such attendance and subsequently as required by the Official Receiver the bankrupt may be examined by an examiner of the Official Receiver's Office and will be given instructions for the preparation of his statement of affairs.[11]

11.06 Unless a certificate for summary administration has been issued and the Official Receiver decides not to conduct an investigation, such an investigation will initially be carried out in the office of the Official Receiver by one of his examiners. A formal examination before the Court, either publicly or privately, discussed below, may follow. Investigation will concentrate on the period leading up to the bankrupt's insolvency, with a view to discovering the cause of the insolvency and whether or not there is evidence of unfit conduct or criminal offences. The examiner will also seek to ascertain whether the bankrupt has made a full disclosure of his assets and liabilities.

IV. PUBLIC EXAMINATION OF BANKRUPT

(a) Introduction
11.07 Prior to the Order every bankrupt was required to submit to a public examination as to his conduct, dealings and property, unless the Court, on application under provisions of the 1980 Order, dispensed with such examination.

11.08 Under the Order no public examination will be held unless and until the Official Receiver, at any time before the discharge of the bankrupt, applies for an order of the Court for such examination.[12]

11.09 In most cases the Official Receiver will, in his own discretion, decide whether or not a public examination is appropriate and it is anticipated that he will apply for such examination only in a relatively small number of cases. These will be cases where he considers that a rigorous examination of the bankrupt under oath is required because, from the examination of the bankrupt by his examiner or otherwise, there appear to be matters requiring full investigation of suspected misconduct, or where there is otherwise an element of significant public interest in the case, or where the bankrupt has failed to attend for examination or to answer questions satisfactorily. Such an examination may also be necessary in the case of a bankrupt who is not entitled to an automatic discharge if the Official Receiver has not otherwise obtained sufficient information to prepare a report to the Court on the bankrupt's application for discharge.[13]

11.10 Where a public examination is ordered the bankrupt must attend and be examined.[14] If he fails to do so without reasonable excuse he is guilty of contempt of court, and, where he is entitled to automatic discharge, his discharge may be suspended.[15]

(b) Requisition by creditors

11.11 The Official Receiver is required to apply for an order for the public examination of the bankrupt if he receives a notice given in accordance with the Rules by one of the bankrupt's creditors, supported by not less than one-half, in value, of all the creditors, unless the Court otherwise orders.[16]

11.12 The request must be in writing and be accompanied by a statement of the reasons why the examination is required and, unless the requisitioning creditor's debt itself amounts to at least one-half, in value, of the debts of all the creditors, by a list of the creditors concurring with the request and the amount of their respective claims, together with written confirmation of concurrence from each supporting creditor.[17]

11.13 The creditor requisitioning the examination must deposit with the Official Receiver such sum as the Official Receiver determines as security for the expenses of the examination, if ordered.[18]

11.14 If the Official Receiver considers that the creditor's requisition is unreasonable he may apply to the Court for an order relieving him from the obligation to make the application.[19] This application, supported by a report by the Official Receiver[20] may be made on notice to the requisitioning creditor or ex parte, but if he obtains such an order ex parte the Court may order the Official Receiver to give notice of it forthwith to the requisitioning creditor.[21]

11.15 Unless the Official Receiver has been relieved by the Court of the obligation to apply for an order for a public examination at the request of the requisitioning creditor he must make such application within 28 days of receiving the requisition.[22] If he applies to be relieved of the obligation and his application is dismissed, he must thereupon apply for the public examination forthwith.[23]

(c) Application for order

11.16 On receipt of an application by the Official Receiver for the appointment of a time and place for the holding of a public examination [24] the Court must make an order accordingly and directing the bankrupt to attend.[25] The Court has no discretion to refuse to do so.[26]

(d) Notice of order

11.17 Forthwith after the making of an order for the public examination of the bankrupt the Official Receiver must serve a copy on him[27] If the bankrupt cannot be served in Northern Ireland, leave of the Court to serve out of the jurisdiction must first be obtained.[28]

11.18 The Official Receiver must give at least 14 days notice of the hearing -
   (i)   if a trustee has been nominated or appointed, to him;
   (ii) if a special manager has been appointed, to him; and

(iii) unless he obtains a contrary direction from the Court, to every creditor known to him or identified in the bankrupt's statement of affairs.[29]

11.19   The Official Receiver is not obliged to advertise the public examination, but if he thinks fit he may do so in one or more newspapers at least 14 days before the hearing date.[30]

(e) Bankrupt unfit for examination
11.20   Where the bankrupt is suffering from any mental disorder or physical affliction or disability which renders him unfit to undergo or attend for public examination, the Court may, on application, either stay the order for his public examination or direct the manner in which and the place at which it is to be conducted.[31]

11.21   The application may be made by the Official Receiver ex parte, supported by his report.[32]

11.22   Such an application may also be made by -
(i)   a person who has been appointed by a court in the United Kingdom or elsewhere to manage the affairs of, or to represent the bankrupt, or
(ii)   by a relative or friend of the bankrupt whom the Court considers to be a proper person to make the application.[33]

11.23   Where the Official Receiver is not the applicant, he and the trustee (if any) must be given at least 7 days notice of the application.[34] In such a case, unless the bankrupt is a patient within the meaning of the Mental Health (Northern Ireland) Order 1986, the application must be supported by an affidavit of a registered medical practitioner as to the bankrupt's mental and physical condition.[35] Before an order can be made the applicant is required to deposit with the Official Receiver such sum as the Official Receiver certifies to be necessary for the additional expenses of any examination that may be ordered, and the order may provide that a specified portion of such expenses be paid out of such deposit, instead of out of the estate.[36]

(f) Procedure at hearing
11.24   The examination is heard in open court before the Master unless, exceptionally, it is adjourned to the Judge.[37] The bankrupt may be examined concerning his affairs, dealings and property and the causes of his failure.[38] He is examined on oath (or affirmation) and is obliged to answer such questions as the Court may put, or allow to be put to him.[39] If he refuses to answer such questions or answers unsatisfactorily the Court may adjourn the examination generally or, if it considers the bankrupt's conduct warrants such a course, order him to answer, any failure to comply with such an order, without reasonable excuse, being a contempt of court.[40]

11.25   The examination is conducted primarily by the Official Receiver or by an officer authorised in writing by the Department to act in his place,[41] but the

following may also take part in it and question the bankrupt -
  (i)   the trustee, if his appointment has taken effect,
  (ii)   the special manager of the bankrupt's estate or business, if one has been
         appointed, or
  (iii) any creditor who has tendered a proof.[42]

11.26   The Official Receiver or any other person so authorised to question the
bankrupt may appear by solicitor or counsel, but only with the approval of the
Court given either at the hearing or previously.[43]   Any such person is also
entitled, alternatively, in writing to authorise another person (who need not be
a person otherwise having a right of audience) to question the bankrupt on his
behalf.[44] A proxy given by a creditor only authorises the proxy-holder to speak
and vote as the creditor's representative at a meeting. Accordingly, a proxy
cannot be used as an authorisation to question the bankrupt at a public examination on behalf of a creditor; a specific authorisation for this purpose is
required.

11.27   The bankrupt may, at his own expense, employ a solicitor, with or
without counsel, to put such questions as the Court may allow for the purpose
of enabling him to explain or qualify any of his answers and to make representations to the Court on his behalf.[45]   The bankrupt may be able to obtain
legal aid for this purpose.

11.28   When the examination is completed an order will be made concluding
it.

(g) Record of examination
11.29   The examination must be recorded in writing.[46] This is usually done
either by a shorthand writer or by mechanical recording.[47] The practice under
the former Bankruptcy Rules of inviting the bankrupt to accept the notes of his
preliminary examination by the Official Assignee's examiner as his evidence at
his public examination has been discontinued.

11.30   The Court notifies the bankrupt of the time and place fixed for him to
attend for the record of his examination to be read over to or by him[48] and he
is then required to sign it and swear an affidavit agreeing that it is correct.[49]

11.31   The written record is open to inspection[50] and is admissible in evidence against the bankrupt in any proceedings, whether under the Order or
otherwise.[51] The former exclusion, for this purpose, of use in an action against
the bankrupt in a representative capacity or in proceedings in respect of an
offence under the Theft Act (Northern Ireland) 1969[52] no longer applies.
Although the bankrupt's answers are not evidence against third parties, if the
trustee calls the bankrupt as a witness in bankruptcy proceedings by him
against a third party and the bankrupt, in giving evidence, contradicts answers
that he gave at his public examination (or private examination) he may be
questioned on those answers by counsel for the trustee.[53]

(h) Adjournment of examination

11.32   The public examination may be adjourned by the Court from time to time, either to a fixed date or generally.[54] Where the Official Receiver has obtained the order for the public examination because of the bankrupt's failure to attend for examination and the bankrupt does attend under the order, the Official Receiver may ask for an adjournment to a later date, together with directions from the Court for the bankrupt to attend him and, if appropriate, to file a statement of affairs and/or accounts. If the bankrupt then fulfils the Official Receiver's requirements, no public examination may be necessary and the Official Receiver may ask the Court, at the adjourned hearing, to rescind the order.[55]

11.33   The hearing may be adjourned if criminal proceedings have been instituted against the bankrupt and the Court considers that the continuance of the hearing would be calculated to prejudice a fair trial of those proceedings.[56] Under the Bankruptcy Rules,[57] such an adjournment could be ordered where criminal proceedings were "likely to be instituted". The new Rule is narrower in its operation, being confined to a situation where such criminal proceedings have actually been instituted.

11.34   Where the examination is adjourned generally because the bankrupt has failed to attend or is otherwise failing to comply with his obligations and he is entitled to an automatic discharge, the Official Receiver may, there and then, apply for a suspension of such discharge.[58]

(i) Resumption of adjourned examination

11.35   Where the examination has been adjourned generally the Official Receiver or the bankrupt may apply to the Court to fix a venue for the resumption of the examination and for directions as to giving notice of the resumed hearing to persons entitled to take part in it.[59] Where the application is made by the bankrupt, it may be granted on terms that the expenses of giving such notices shall be paid by him and that he must deposit with the Official Receiver such sum as the Official Receiver considers necessary for this purpose, before an appointment for the resumed hearing is made.[60]

(j) Re-opening of examination

11.36   If, after the public examination has been concluded, further information comes to the knowledge of the Official Receiver or the trustee which makes it desirable that the bankrupt be further examined publicly, an application may be made to the Court by the Official Receiver or the trustee, on notice to the bankrupt, for an order for the re-opening of the public examination on a fixed date.[61]

(k) Failure to attend examination

11.37   Failure by the bankrupt, without reasonable excuse, to attend his public examination is a contempt of court.[62] As noted above,[63] where the bankrupt is entitled to an automatic discharge such failure may also be a ground for an application by the Official Receiver for suspension of such discharge.

11.38 The Court may issue a warrant for the arrest of a bankrupt who fails, without reasonable excuse, to attend his public examination[64] and the Official Receiver would usually request a general adjournment of the public examination on the issue of such a warrant, rather than taking contempt of court proceedings. The Master has power to issue such a warrant.[65] The request may be made either orally at the sitting or later by application in writing.

11.39 Before issuing a warrant for the arrest of the bankrupt the Court will require to be satisfied that the order for the examination has been duly served on him. The practice in the High Court in London is to require the Official Receiver, in his application for the order, to state how he proposes to serve it on the bankrupt, at what address(es) and how such address(es) have come to his notice. The Official Receiver is also required to send a copy of the order to the bankrupt at any further address which subsequently comes to his knowledge (if necessary requesting an adjournment of the hearing for this purpose). Although service is effected by prepaid ordinary post,[66] it is understood that the practice is for the Official Receiver, if he contemplates non-attendance of a bankrupt and that in such an event he would wish to apply for a warrant for his arrest, to send an additional copy (or copies) by prepaid first class recorded delivery post and to annexe to the postage certificate the postal receipt for each envelope containing a copy of the order so sent. The Registrar requires an Official Receiver asking for the issue of an arrest warrant to give an assurance that he has no other or better address for the bankrupt than the address(es) to which the copy orders were posted.

11.40 Where the bankrupt is arrested under a warrant, the constable effecting the arrest hands him over to the governor of the prison named in the warrant.[67] He is kept in custody until the Court otherwise orders and the governor is required to produce him to the Court from time to time when so directed.[68] The warrant may require the constable executing it to seize any books, papers, records, money or goods in the possession of the bankrupt.[69] Any property so seized is to be lodged with or otherwise dealt with as instructed by the person specified in the warrant as authorised to receive it[70] or, alternatively, to be kept by the constable pending the receipt of written orders from the Court as to its disposal.[71] The warrant must direct which of these alternatives is to be carried out[72] and it will usually specify the first.

11.41 If, after the warrant is issued and before it is executed, the bankrupt is prepared to attend a resumed hearing the Court may, upon his application, order the discharge or suspension of the warrant and appoint a date for the public examination to be resumed, subject to payment of the Official Receiver's expenses.[73] If the issue of the warrant induces the bankrupt to co-operate, the Official Receiver may no longer require the public examination to be resumed, in which case the Official Receiver may apply to the Court to discharge the warrant and to adjourn the public examination to a fixed date, with a view to the examination being concluded if it has commenced or, if not, for the order for the examination to be rescinded.

11.42   After the bankrupt has been taken into custody under the warrant, and unless he applies to the Court for his release, the Official Receiver will report to the Court the arrest and detention of the bankrupt and apply for the appointment of an early date for the resumption of the public examination and for an order to the governor of the prison where the bankrupt is detained to produce the bankrupt at that hearing.[74] If the bankrupt applies for his release and the appointment of a date for the resumption of the public examination before he has been brought to Court for examination, the practice in England and Wales is that such release is only granted on the bankrupt undertaking to file his statement of affairs (if not already done), to attend on the Official Receiver as and when required and to pay the fees for the resumption of his public examination, and the Court may require such undertaking to be supported by a bond.[75]

(l) Expenses of examination
11.43   The expenses of the public examination are normally payable out of the bankrupt's estate as expenses incurred by the Official Receiver, but where the examination has been ordered on a creditor's requisition, the Court may order that a specified portion of such expenses be paid out of the deposit required to be made by the requisitioning creditor.[76] In no case do the costs of a public examination fall on the Official Receiver personally.[77]

V. PRIVATE EXAMINATION[78]

(a) Introduction
11.44   The Order has continued the power of the Court under the Bankruptcy Acts to summon to appear before it for examination the bankrupt and certain other persons, with a view to assisting in the investigation of the bankrupt's affairs, with particular regard to the discovery and recovery of assets and the ascertainment of liabilities. The categories of persons who may be so summoned have been enlarged to include specifically the bankrupt's former spouse.

(b) Extent of Court's powers
11.45   The Court has power, on the application of the Official Receiver or the trustee[79] to summon to appear before it for examination
  (i)   the bankrupt[80] or the bankrupt's spouse or former spouse,
  (ii)   any person known or believed to have any property comprised in the bankrupt's estate in his possession or to be indebted to the bankrupt,
  (iii) any person[81] appearing to the Court to be able to give information concerning the bankrupt or the bankrupt's dealings, affairs or property.[82]

11.46   The Court may order that any person so liable to be summoned be examined on oath, either orally or by interrogatories, concerning the bankrupt or the bankrupt's dealings, affairs and property.[83] The examination is held in chambers before the Master and is usually referred to as a "private examination", to distinguish it from the public examination of the bankrupt.

11.47   Any person so liable to be examined under (ii) or (iii) above may also be required to produce any document in his possession or under his control relating to the bankrupt or the bankrupt's dealings, affairs or property[84] or to submit an affidavit to the Court containing an account of his dealings with the bankrupt.[85] This last-mentioned power is new, as is the power to order production of documents without summoning the custodian for examination.

(c) The application
11.48   The application[86] is made ex parte.[87] It must sufficiently identify the person in respect of whom an order is applied for ("the respondent") and state whether it is for the respondent -
(i)   to be ordered to appear before the Court, or
(ii)   to answer interrogatories (if so, particulars to be given of the matters in respect of which answers are required), or
(iii)   to submit affidavits (if so, particulars to be given of the matters to which he is required to swear), or
(iv)   to produce books, papers or other records (if so, the items in question to be specified), or for any two or more of those purposes.[88]

11.49   The application must be accompanied by a brief statement of the grounds on which it is made.[89] This statement is not filed and is not open to general inspection.[90]

(d) The order
11.50   The Court has a wide discretion whether or not to make an order. It will not allow an examination if it would be oppressive, vexatious or unfair.[91] The bankrupt or his spouse may be summoned without the applicant establishing that he or she has failed to provide required information, but this will usually be a pre-requisite of an order in other cases, particularly if it is desired to summon a professional witness.[92] Such a request should refer to the power of the Court to order the payment of the costs of an examination against a person who unjustifiably refuses to give information.[93]

11.51   The Order does not contain the provision found in IA 1986, section 367(3) empowering the Court to order that any person who if within the jurisdiction of the Court would be liable to be summoned to appear before it under section 366 shall be examined in any part of the United Kingdom where he may be for the time being, or in any place outside the United Kingdom.[94]

11.52   It appears that the Court will not give leave to serve outside the jurisdiction an order for an examination of anyone other than the bankrupt.[95]

If the proposed examinee is resident in Great Britain or in a country designated under IA 1986, section 426[96] and he cannot be served whilst present in Northern Ireland, an application should be made to the appropriate court for an order for his examination by that court under that section.[97]

11.53   If the Court makes the attendance order,[98] the date specified for the appearance of the respondent must be not less than 14 days from the date of the order.[99]

11.54   If the order requires the respondent to submit affidavits, it must specify the matters to be dealt with in his affidavits and the time within which they are to be submitted to the Court.[100] If he is ordered to produce books, papers or other records, the order must specify the time and manner of compliance.[101] If the respondent is ordered to answer interrogatories, the order must direct him as to the questions he must answer and as to whether his answers are to be made on affidavit.[102]

(e) Service of order
11.55   Unless the Court gives leave for substituted service, the attendance order must be served forthwith on the respondent by personal service.[103] Conduct money must be tendered.[104]

(f) Procedure at examination
11.56   The applicant may attend the examination in person or by a solicitor, with or without counsel, and question the respondent, subject to the Court's power to disallow any questions.[105]   A person examined, other than the bankrupt, will not be compelled to answer incriminating questions and the applicant will not be allowed to conduct a fishing enquiry.[106]

11.57   With the leave of the Court, and if the applicant does not object, any other person who could have applied for the order and, where the application has been made on information provided by a creditor, that creditor, may attend and have questions put to the respondent, but any such questions must be put through the applicant.[107]

11.58   The respondent may be represented by a solicitor, with or without counsel, but only at his own expense.[108] Such solicitor or counsel may put such questions to the respondent as the Court may allow for the purpose of enabling him to explain or qualify any answers given by him, and may make representations on his behalf.[109]

(g) Orders for delivery of property or payment of debt
11.59   Under Article 338, where it appears to the Court, on consideration of the evidence obtained at the examination or by interrogatories or affidavit that "any person" has in his possession any property comprised in the bankrupt's estate or is indebted to the bankrupt, the Court may, on the application of the Official Receiver or the trustee,[110] order that person -

(i)   to deliver the whole or any part of the property to the Official Receiver or the trustee at such time, in such manner and on such terms as the Court thinks fit, or

(ii)   to pay to the Official Receiver or the trustee at such time and in such manner as the Court may direct, the whole or part of the amount due, whether in full discharge of the debt or otherwise as the Court thinks fit.

11.60   The Court may make either of these orders whether or not the initial application was made with a view to obtaining that particular order.[111] It may also order the respondent to pay the costs of the application for such an order.[112]

11.61   It seems that "any person" in Article 338 must be limited to a person examined either orally or by interrogatories or who has submitted an affidavit under an order of the Court.

11.62   The power to order a witness at a private examination to deliver property is new, as is the extension of the power to order payment of a debt to cover a debt which has not been admitted by the person examined.[113] Where such an admission is made the person examined should be invited to sign a written admission.[114]

11.63   It is anticipated that the Court will be reluctant to make orders under these provisions in the absence of a clear admission by the respondent, either orally or in writing,[115] except in a straightforward case where it is satisfied that the respondent has had a proper opportunity to contest the application and that he has no credible defence to the claim.[116]

(h) Record of examination

11.64   The examination is recorded in the same way as at a public examination.[117] Similarly, the respondent is notified of a time and place to attend to have the record read over to or by him and for him to sign it, but it is not required to be verified by affidavit, as is the record of a public examination.[118]

11.65   The written record is admissible in evidence against the respondent in any proceedings, whether under the Order or otherwise.[119]

11.66   Unless the Court otherwise orders, the record of the respondent's examination, any answers given by him to interrogatories and any affidavits directed by the order are not to be filed in the Court.[120] Such documents may be inspected by the applicant and any other person who could have applied for an order for examination of the respondent, but may only be inspected by any other person by an order of the Court.[121] The same restriction on inspection applies to so much of the Court's file as shows the grounds of the application and to any copy of proposed interrogatories.[122]

11.67 The Court may from time to time give directions as to the custody and inspection of the documents protected by these provisions and as to the furnishing of copies of, or extracts from, them.[123]

(i) Enforcement of order

11.68 Where the respondent fails to comply with an order to attend for examination, to answer interrogatories, to submit affidavits or to produce books, papers or other records, an application may be made to have him committed for contempt of court.[124]

11.69 The Court may grant an injunction to restrain a person summoned for examination from leaving the jurisdiction.[125]

11.70 Where a respondent is ordered to attend for examination the Court may issue a warrant to a constable for his arrest and for the seizure of any books, papers, records, money or goods in his possession, where -
   (i)   without reasonable excuse, he fails to appear before the Court, or
   (ii) there are reasonable grounds for believing he has absconded or is about to abscond, with a view to avoiding his appearance before the Court.[126]

11.71 An application for the issue of a warrant must be supported by adequate evidence of due service of the order.[127]

11.72 A person arrested under such a warrant may be kept in custody and anything seized held until he is brought before the Court or until such other time as the Court may order.[128]

11.73 The constable effecting an arrest must forthwith bring the person arrested before the Court for examination.[129] The warrant requires him to bring the arrested person before the Court for examination at such time and place as the Court directs.[130] If the arrested person cannot immediately be brought for examination he is to be delivered to the custody of the governor of the prison named in the warrant, who is required to keep him in custody and produce him before the Court as it may direct.[131] Forthwith after making the arrest the constable must report to the Court the arrest or delivery into custody (as the case may be) and apply to the Court to fix a venue for the examination.[132] The Court must appoint the earliest practicable time for the examination, forthwith give notice of the venue to the applicant for the warrant and issue a direction to the governor of the prison to produce the person for examination at the time and place appointed.[133]

11.74 Any property seized is to be dealt with in the same way as in the case of the execution of a warrant of arrest of a bankrupt failing to attend his public examination.[134]

(j) Costs of examination
11.75   The Court has a new power to rder that the costs of the examination
be paid by the respondent where it appears that the examination was made
necessary because information had been unjustifiably refused by him.[135] It
would appear that this power may be exercisable not only when the respondent
is examined orally but where he is ordered to answer interrogatories or to
submit affidavits.[136] Subject to this power, the applicant's costs are payable
out of the bankrupt's estate, unless the Court otherwise orders.[137]

11.76   A person summoned to attend for examination is entitled to his reasonable travelling expenses, which must be tendered when a summons is
served.[138] Other costs falling on him (but possibly excluding the costs of
solicitor or counsel representing him at the examination[139]) are at the Court's
discretion.[140]

11.77   Where the examination is on the application of the Official Receiver,
otherwise then as trustee, he cannot be required to pay costs.[141]

VI. PRODUCTION OF DOCUMENTS BY INLAND REVENUE

(a) Introduction
11.78   The Order introduces a significant addition to the means of enquiry
open to the Official Receiver or the trustee in investigating the bankrupt's
affairs. Provision is made for the production to the Court of certain documents
relating to the bankrupt's tax affairs held by the Inland Revenue and for the
Court to authorise their disclosure.[142]

11.79   Hitherto, access to tax returns, accounts, correspondence or assessments issued by the Inland Revenue could only be obtained insofar as such
documents or copies were in the bankrupt's custody. Statutory restrictions
protecting confidentiality prevented disclosure by the Inland Revenue.

11.80   The new power is exercisable by the Court only for the purposes of a
public examination of the bankrupt or for proceedings under Articles 337 to 339
(private examination and order at such an examination).[143] Thus, where the
Official Receiver proposes to apply for an order for a public examination he
should consider (in conjunction with the trustee, if he is not himself the trustee)
whether an order for production of documents by the Inland Revenue is
desirable. Where no public examination is held, the Official Receiver or the
trustee may have to request an order under Article 337 or 338 so that he may
then be in a position to apply also for an order for production of documents by
the Inland Revenue.

11.81   The initial order which the Court may make is to order any inspector
or collector of taxes appointed by the Commissioners of Inland Revenue ("the
Commissioners") or any person appointed by the Commissioners to serve in

any other capacity ("an Inland Revenue official") to produce to the Court any return, account or accounts submitted by the bankrupt to any Inland Revenue official or any assessment or determination made in relation to the bankrupt by any such official or any correspondence between the bankrupt and any such official, whether any of these documents originated before or after the making of the bankruptcy order.[144]

(b) Application for order
11.82   The application must be made by the Official Receiver or the trustee.[145] An order cannot be made on the application of an interim receiver.[146] It must specify with as full particulars as possible, the documents to be produced and name the official to whom the order is to be addressed.[147]

11.83   The applicant must, at least 28 days before the hearing, send notice of the venue fixed by the Court and a copy of the application to the Commissioners and the notice must require the Commissioners to inform the Court, not later than 7 days before the hearing date, whether they concur or object to the making of the order.[148]

11.84   If the Commissioners consent to the making of the order applied for but wish the order to be directed to an official other than the one named in the application they must name that official.[149] If they object to the making of the order they must, not less than 7 days before the hearing date, deliver to the Court a statement in writing of their grounds of objection and forthwith send a copy of it to the applicant.[150]   In such event they must also secure the attendance of an officer of theirs at the hearing.[151]

11.85   At the hearing the Court is to have regard to any representation made by the Commissioners.[152]

(c) Order for production
11.86   Before making an order the Court must be satisfied that the office of the Inland Revenue official to which the order is addressed is dealing with, or has dealt with, the bankrupt's affairs[153] and the order may be addressed to an Inland Revenue official other than the one named in the application.[154]

11.87   The order[155] must specify a time for compliance not less than 28 days after service, and may include requirements as to the manner in which documents are to be produced.[156]

11.88   To avoid the necessity of a further application for an order for the disclosure of documents produced to the Court under the order for production,[157] the order should adjourn the application to an appropriate date after the expiry of the date for compliance.

11.89   The applicant must serve the order on the official to whom it is addressed.[158]

11.90   If the official served does not have any of the documents ordered to be produced in his possession he has a duty to take all reasonable steps to secure possession of them and any other Inland Revenue official who has them in his possession must hand them over to him, but if he does not have them and is unable to obtain them, he must deliver a written statement to the Court giving his reasons for non-compliance with the order and send a copy forthwith to the applicant.[159]

(d) Disclosure of documents produced
11.91   At any time after a document has been produced under the order for production, the Court may make a further order[160] authorising the disclosure of the document or of any part of its contents to the Official Receiver, the trustee or the bankrupt's creditors.[161]

(e) Custody of documents
11.92   Where original documents and not copies are produced, any person who by the order for production has them in his possession or custody is responsible to the Court for their safe keeping and return as and when directed.[162]

VII. RE-DIRECTION OF BANKRUPT'S LETTERS ETC.

11.93   If the Official Receiver or the trustee considers that he may obtain useful information as to the bankrupt's affairs from an examination of mail addressed to the bankrupt, he may apply to the Court for an order requiring the Post Office to re-direct and send or deliver to the applicant or otherwise at such place or places as specified in the order any postal packet which would otherwise be sent or delivered to the bankrupt.[163]

11.94   The order continues for the period specified in it, not exceeding 3 months.[164] If a continuation is required after that period, an application may be made for a further order.

Footnotes

(1)   Para.9.10.
(2)   Art.262(1),(4),(5). See para. 14.028 re investigation by trustee.
(3)   Art.262(2): para.21.22.
(4)   Art.278(3).
(5)   R.6.146.
(6)   Art.264(4).
(7)   Art.264(5).
(8)   Art.264(6): paras.5.103/104.
(9)   Para.21.07.
(10) RR.6.030(2), 6.031(2), 6.042(2), 6.043(2): FF. 6.29, 6.33.
(11) Para.10.04.
(12) Art.263(1).
(13) Para.21.22.
(14) Art.263(3).
(15) Art.263(5): fn.(8) above.
(16) Art.263(2).
(17) R.6.170(1), (2): F.6.59: Atkin Form 206.
(18) R.6.170(3).
(19) R.6.170(5): Atkin Form 207.
(20) Atkin Form 208.
(21) R.6.170(6).
(22) R.6.170(4).
(23) R.6.170(6).
(24) Atkin Form 204.
(25) R.6.169(2): F.6.58.
(26) Art. 263(3).
(27) R.6.169(1). Service is by post (para. 5.070).
(28) Paras.5.075/077: Atkin Form 210.
(29) R.6.169(3).
(30) R.6.169(4).
(31) R.6.171(1): F.6.60.
(32) R.6.171(2), (5): Atkin Form 212.
(33) R.6.171(2).
(34) R.6.171(3).
(35) *Ibid:* Atkin Forms 213, 214.
(36) R.6.171(4).
(37) R.7.02(1).
(38) Art.263(4).
(39) R.6.172(1). See *Re Gordon* (6 ACLC 698), a decision of the Federal Court of Australia, briefly reported in (1988) 1 Ins Int 62, re bankrupt's obligation to answer incriminating questions.
(40) Art.334(2),(4): Atkin Form 216 (Report to Judge of unsatisfactory answering).
(41) R.10.2(1).

(42) Art.263(4).
(43) R.6.172(2).
(44) *Ibid*.
(45) R.6.172(3).
(46) R.6.172(4).
(47) RR. 7.14, 7.17. See MH 7-407 re desirability of verbatim recording.
(48) Atkin Form 220.
(49) R.6.172(4): F. 6.61.
(50) R.7.25.
(51) R.6.172(5).
(52) 1980 Order, Art.11(10).
(53) *Re a Debtor, Jacobs v. Lloyd [1944] Ch 344*.
(54) R.6.173(1): F.6.62.
(55) Art.371.
(56) R.6.172(6). See *Re Gordon* sited in fn.(39) above.
(57) Rule 85.
(58) Art.253 (3): R. 6.173(4): para.21.07.
(59) R.6.173(2): F.6.63: Atkin Forms 235/238.
(60) R.6.173(3).
(61) Atkin Forms 242, 244, 245.
(62) Art.263(5).
(63) Para.11.34.
(64) Art.335(2): R.7.21: F.7.07.
(65) The restriction of a Master's powers under RSC O.32 r. 11(1)(b) does not apply - R.7.03(6).
(66) RSC O.65 r.5: para. 5.070.
(67) R.7.21.
(68) *Ibid*.
(69) Art.335(1)(b): F.7.07.
(70) This will usually be an officer of the Official Receiver's Department.
(71) R.7.21.
(72) *Ibid*.
(73) Atkin Forms 224, 225.
(74) Atkin Forms 231/234.
(75) Atkin Forms 226/230.
(76) R.6.174(1).
(77) R.6.174(2).
(78) MH 3-351/3-355.
(79) An application may also be made by an interim receiver before a bankruptcy order has been made - Art.339: para. 8.09. See MH 3-351/1 and Atkin Form 291 re application by creditor in name of trustee.
(80) Even after discharge - *Re Coulson* [1934] Ch 45.
(81) A company may be summoned by its proper officer - *Penn Texas Corpn. v. Murat Anstalt* (No.2) [1964] 2 QB647.
(82) Art.337(1).
(83) Art.338(3). Note the difference from the corresponding IA 1986 s.367(4) which refers to a person who appears or is brought before the court.

(84)   See MH 3-351/5 and *Re Aveling Barford Ltd.* [1989] 1 WLR 360 re production of documents subject to a lien.

(85)   Art.337(2).

(86)   Atkin Form 290.

(87)   R.9.2(4).

(88)   R.9.2(2), (3).

(89)   R.9.2(1): Atkin Form 292.

(90)   Para.11.66.

(91)   See cases cited by MH at 3-351/3, particularly recent Court of Appeal decision in *Cloverbay Ltd v. B.C.C.I. Ltd.* [1991] Ch 90 applied in *Re British and Commonwealth Holdings plc* (1991) Financial Times, 6 August): Hals 295/6.

(92)   See MH 3-351/5 re professional privilege.

(93)   Para.11.75.

(94)   In *Re Tucker* [1990] Ch 148 it was held that the court would not make an order under a similar provision of the Bankruptcy Act 1914 for the examination in England of a person it could not compel to attend: Hals 298. But see "Jurisdictional Reach: the Retreat from Re Tucker" Ian Fletcher (1992) 4 Ins Int 27.

(95)   *Re Tucker* supra: MH 3.353.

(96)   Paras.28.45/46.

(97)   Atkin Forms 296/298.

(98)   F.9.1.

(99)   R.9.3(2).

(100) R.9.3(3).

(101) R.9.3(4).

(102) R.9.4(3).

(103) R.9.3(5).

(104) R.9.6(4).

(105) R.9.4(1).

(106) MH 3-351/4.

(107) R.9.4(2), (4).

(108) R.9.4(5).

(109) *Ibid.*

(110) An application may also be made by an interim receiver before a bankruptcy order has been made - Art 339.

(111) R.9.3(1).

(112) R.9.6(2).

(113) For former law, see JH 20.31 and MH 3-353.

(114) Atkin Form 302.

(115) *Ibid.*

(116) See MH 3-353 for a discussion of the problems of determining a contested claim under this procedure.

(117) Para.11.29.

(118) R.9.4(6).

(119) R.9.4(7).

(120) R.9.5(1).

(121) R.9.5(2).
(122) R.9.5(3): MH 7-670.
(123) R.9.5(4).
(124) Paras.5.103/104.
(125) *Re Oriental Credit Ltd.* [1988] Ch 204.
(126) Art.337(3), (4).
(127) Atkin Forms 304, 305.
(128) Art.337(5).
(129) R.7.22(1).
(130) F.7.08.
(131) R.7.22(2). See Atkin Form 309 for application by person arrested for his release.
(132) R.7.22(3).
(133) R.7.22(4): F.7.09.
(134) R.7.22(5): para.11.40.
(135) R.9.6(1).
(136) *Re Aveling Barford Ltd.* [1988] 1 WLR 360 at 366, dictum of Hoffman J.
(137) R.9.6(3).
(138) R.9.6(4).
(139) Para.11.58.
(140) R.9.6(4): MH 7-672.
(141) R.9.6(5).
(142) Art.340.
(143) Art.340(1).
(144) Art.340(1), (6). MH at 3-357 refers to the omission of power to order production of internal Inland Revenue memoranda and notes of interviews with the bankrupt.
(145) Art.340(1).
(146) Art.340(7).
(147) R.6.191(1): Atkin Form 274.
(148) R.6.191(2),(3),(4).
(149) R.6.191(5).
(150) R.6.191(6), (7).
(151) R.6.191(6).
(152) R.6.192(1).
(153) Art.340(3).
(154) R.6.192(2).
(155) F.6.72.
(156) R.6.192(2).
(157) Para.11.91.
(158) R.6.192(3).
(159) Art.340(4), (5): R.6.192(4), (5).
(160) F.6.73.
(161) Art.340(2).
(162) R.6.193.
(163) Art.342(1): F.6.83: Atkin Forms 368, 369.
(164) Art.342(2).

Chapter 12

BANKRUPT'S ESTATE

Definitions

12.01   The property of a bankrupt which is available for the benefit of his creditors ("the bankrupt's estate") comprises -

    (a)   all property belonging to or vested in the bankrupt at the date of the bankruptcy order, and

    (b)   any property which becomes part of the bankrupt's estate by virtue of specific provisions of the Order or of Article 88(3) or 90(3) of the Judgments Enforcement Order, with the exception of -

        (i)   certain categories of personal property, subject to the right of the trustee to replace any item of excess value,[1]

        (ii)   property held by the bankrupt in trust for any other person,[2] and

        (iii)   any property excluded from a bankrupt's estate by statutory provisions outside the Order (e.g. certain pensions and social security benefits).[3]

12.02   "Property" includes money, goods, things in action, land and every description of property wherever situated and also obligations and every description of interest, whether present or future or vested or contingent, arising out of, or incidental to, property.[4]

12.03   The property comprised in the bankrupt's estate is subject to the rights of any person other than the bankrupt, including the rights of secured creditors, except to the extent that such rights have been surrendered by the creditor voluntarily[5] or involuntarily.[6]

Excluded property

12.04   The following property does not form part of the bankrupt's estate and therefore remains the property of the bankrupt, subject to the replacement rights of the trustee referred to below, -

    (a)   such tools, books, vehicles and other items of equipment as are necessary to the bankrupt for use personally by him in his employment, business or vocation;

    (b)   such clothing, bedding, furniture, household equipment and provisions as are necessary for satisfying the basic domestic needs of the bankrupt and his family.[7]

12.05   It is to be noted that in respect of the excepted items of clothing, furniture etc. an objective test has been substituted for the opinion of the Official Assignee or trustee under section 298 of the 1857 Act, thus making it easier for the bankrupt to challenge in the Court the trustee's assessment of the "basic domestic needs" of the bankrupt. It is not clear whether the categories of items which the bankrupt may retain under this heading have been altered by the substitution of "satisfying basic domestic needs" for "essential for domestic purposes".

12.06   Where the trustee considers that the realisable value of the whole or any part of property excluded from the bankrupt's estate under these provisions exceeds the cost of a reasonable replacement for it, he may claim it for the bankrupt's estate.[8] The claim must be made by notice in writing to be served on the bankrupt within 42 days from the day on which the property in question first came to the trustee's knowledge, unless the Court gives leave to serve outside that period.[9] Upon service of such a notice the property to which it relates vests in the trustee as part of the bankrupt's estate and, except against a purchaser in good faith, for value and without notice of the bankruptcy, the trustee's title to it relates back to the date of the bankruptcy order.[10]

12.07   The trustee is required, in priority to his obligation to distribute the bankrupt's estate, to provide funds from the bankrupt's estate for the purchase by or on behalf of the bankrupt of a reasonable replacement for any such property.[11] The property to be purchased as the replacement must be reasonably adequate for meeting the needs met by the property claimed by the trustee.[12] Such a replacement may be purchased before or after the realisation of the property being replaced, but the trustee is not obliged to purchase a replacement unless and until he has sufficient funds in the estate for that purpose.[13]

12.08   However, the replacement of excluded property of excess value may be avoided if a third party provides the estate with a sum of money which the trustee is satisfied represents the value of the property in question, less the cost of a reasonable replacement.[14] If agreement cannot be reached between the trustee and the bankrupt as to the property which the bankrupt is entitled to retain or as to the replacement or payment in lieu of replacement of any such property claimed by the trustee to be of excess value, either the trustee or the bankrupt may have the dispute resolved by the Court.[15] Property claimed by the trustee for the bankrupt's estate under these provisions may not subsequently be disclaimed, except with the leave of the Court.[16]

Title to the estate
12.09   The bankrupt's estate remains vested in the bankrupt (but subject to restrictions on dispositions,[17]) until the Official Receiver becomes trustee or a trustee is appointed, when it vests in the trustee without any conveyance, assignment or transfer.[18] This is a significant change from the former law. Under sections 267 and 268 of the 1857 Act the bankrupt's estate vested in the assignees in bankruptcy immediately upon the making of an adjudication order. Under the transitional provisions of the Order any unrealised property so vested at the commencement of the Order vests in the Official Receiver.[19]

12.10   Where the Official Receiver becomes trustee on the occurrence of a vacancy any unrealised property forming part of the estate vests in him.[20] In the event of the Official Receiver in whom property is vested dying, ceasing to hold office or being otherwise succeeded in relation to the bankruptcy by another Official Receiver, the property vests in his successor without any conveyance, assignment or transfer.[21]

12.11   The doctrine of election, which was based on the terms of section 271 of the 1857 Act,[22] whereby land held under a fee farm grant or lease did not vest in the assignees on the bankruptcy of the grantee or lessee unless and until they elected to take the land or the benefit of the lease, has not been continued in the Order. Such land will vest in the trustee in bankruptcy of the grantee or lessee in the same way as any other part of the bankrupt's estate. The trustee can only avoid any potential detriment to the estate arising from liabilities under such a fee farm grant or lease by disclaiming the property.

12.12   Where registered land is comprised in the bankrupt's estate, the trustee is entitled to be registered as owner of the land or, where the bankrupt was registered as a joint owner, as a tenant in common of the land with another or others.[23]   When so registered, the trustee is in all respects, and in particular as respects registered dealing with the land, in the same position as if he were a transferee for valuable consideration, but he holds the land for the purposes upon and subject to which the land is applicable by law, and subject to all unregistered rights subject to which the bankrupt held the land.[24]   Such registration is effected by production to the Registrar of Titles of a certified copy of the bankruptcy order, accompanied by -
   (a)   where the Official Receiver is the trustee, a certificate by him that the land is comprised in the bankrupt's estate, has vested in him as trustee and has not been disclaimed,[25] and
   (b)   where another person is appointed trustee, the relevant proof of his appointment and a certificate by him that the land is comprised in the bankrupt's estate and has not been disclaimed.[26]

12.13   The Official Receiver or trustee may be registered in place of a deceased registered owner on production of such evidence as the Registrar of Titles requires.[27]

12.14   Where a trustee who has been registered as owner vacates his office, the Official Receiver, or, if some other person is appointed trustee, such person may be registered as owner on production of the evidence required on the original registration of a trustee.[28]

After-acquired property
12.15   Property acquired by or devolving upon the bankrupt since the date of the bankruptcy order ("after-acquired property") does not form part of the bankrupt's estate unless and until it is claimed for the estate by the trustee by a notice in writing.[29]   Property excluded from the bankrupt's estate under the Order or any other statutory provision may not be so claimed, nor (subject to any order of the Court imposing conditions on discharge) may property ac-

quired by or devolving upon the bankrupt after his discharge.[30] As a general rule damages obtained by a bankrupt in respect of personal injuries or personal inconvenience or damage to reputation may not be claimed by the trustee.[31]

12.16   A notice claiming after-acquired property must be served within 42 days from the day on which it first came to the knowledge of the trustee that the property in question had been acquired by or had devolved upon the bankrupt, unless the Court gives leave to serve outside that period.[32]

12.17   Subject as mentioned below with regard to property acquired in the ordinary course of business, the bankrupt is required to give notice to the trustee of any property acquired by or devolving upon him after the making of the bankruptcy order.[33] This notice must be given within 21 days of his becoming aware of the relevant facts.[34] The trustee then has 42 days to decide whether or not to claim the property for the estate. During that period the bankrupt must not dispose of it without the trustee's consent in writing.[35] If he does dispose of the property before giving the required notice to the trustee or within the 42 day period after the notice, he is required forthwith to give the trustee the name and address of the person to whom he has transferred it and to provide any other information which may be necessary to enable the trustee to trace it and recover it for the estate.[36]

12.18   Where the bankrupt disposes of after-acquired property other than property acquired in the ordinary course of his business without informing the trustee of its acquisition or within 42 days of giving notice to the trustee, the trustee may, within 28 days of his becoming aware of the identity and an address for service of the person to whom it has been disposed of, serve notice on him claiming the property for the bankrupt's estate.[37]

12.19   The requirement of notice of acquisition of property by a bankrupt does not apply to property acquired in the ordinary course of his business.[38] However, if the bankrupt does carry on a business, he must, not less than 6 monthly, furnish to the trustee information with respect to it, showing the total goods bought and sold or services supplied and the profit and loss from the business,[39] and the trustee may require the bankrupt to furnish fuller details (including accounts) of the business.[40] Such information should assist the trustee to determine whether any property has been acquired by the bankrupt otherwise than in the ordinary course of his business.

12.20   The trustee's right to claim after-acquired property does not apply to any property acquired by or devolving upon the bankrupt after his discharge;[41] but such property may be made available for the benefit of the creditors by a condition imposed by the Court when granting a discharge.[42]

12.21   Where, whether before or after service of a notice claiming after-acquired property, such property is acquired by a person in good faith, for value and without notice of the bankruptcy, or a banker enters into a transaction in good faith and without such notice, the trustee has no remedy against that person or banker or any person deriving title to the property from him.[43]

12.22 Subject to this protection of bona fide dealings by innocent third parties, the property specified in the notice vests in the trustee as part of the bankrupt's estate upon service of the notice and the trustee's title to it relates back to the time when it was acquired by or devolved upon the bankrupt.[44]

12.23 The provisions relating to after-acquired property do not extend to income of the bankrupt which may be the subject of an income payments order.[45]

12.24 Any expenses incurred by the trustee in acquiring title to after-acquired property are payable out of the estate, in the prescribed order of priority.[46]

Protection of estate pending appointment of trustee
12.25 Until the bankrupt's estate vests in a trustee it is protected in the interests of the creditors by the provisions of Articles 257 and 260 and, in respect of the bankrupt's land, by the provisions for registration contained in the Registration of Deeds Act, section 3A and the Land Registration Act, section 67A.

12.26 Under Article 257(3) the restrictions on dispositions by the bankrupt from the date of presentation of the bankruptcy petition continue until his estate vests in a trustee, although the protection given to bona fide purchasers without notice of the petition ceases to operate after the making of the bankruptcy order.[47]

12.27 By Article 260(1) the Official Receiver is the receiver of the bankrupt's estate during the period between the making of the bankruptcy order and the vesting of the bankrupt's estate in a trustee and, unless a special manager is appointed,[48] he is also the manager of the estate.

12.28 The Official Receiver's function is to protect the estate and for this purpose he has the same powers as if he were receiver or manager appointed by the High Court and he may sell or otherwise dispose of any perishable goods or any other goods the value of which is likely to diminish if not disposed of.[49] Whilst he must take such steps as he thinks fit for protecting any property which the trustee may claim for the estate, he is not required to incur expenditure except on the directions of the Department.[50] He must register the bankruptcy order promptly in the Registry of Deeds and (if appropriate) in the Land Registry.[51]

12.29 The bankrupt must deliver possession of his estate to the Official Receiver and hand over to him all books, papers and other records relating to his estate and affairs which are in his possession or under his control, including any documents privileged from disclosure in any proceedings.[52] The bankrupt must do all such things as may reasonably be required by the Official Receiver to protect any part of the estate of which possession cannot be delivered or property that may be claimed by the trustee (excluded property of excess value or after-acquired property).[53] If the bankrupt, without reasonable excuse, fails to carry out these obligations with regard to delivery up or protection of his estate or to comply with directions of the Court, he is guilty of a contempt of court.[54]

12.30   The Official Receiver is protected against liability for loss or damage caused by mistakenly seizing or disposing of any property which is not in fact comprised in the bankrupt's estate, provided that he had reasonable grounds for believing that he was entitled to do so and the loss or damage is not caused by his negligence.[55] He has a lien on such property or the proceeds of its sale, for expenses incurred in connection with the seizure or disposal.[56]

12.31   The Official Receiver as receiver has the same right as a trustee to require delivery up of books, papers and other records of the bankrupt in the possession of any person who claims a lien on them, except documents of title held as security[57] and to request the supply of electricity, water, telephone or other public telecommunication services, for the purpose of carrying on a business, upon giving a personal guarantee to pay any charges in respect of such supply, but without payment of any outstanding charges.[58]

12.32   If the Official Receiver thinks it advisable to consult creditors as to any proposed action whilst acting as receiver or manager he may summon a general meeting of creditors, and must do so if so directed by the Court.[59] He may also apply to the Court for directions with regard to the compliance by the bankrupt with any directions of the Court[60] or generally[61] and may apply for an order for an examination of the bankrupt either publicly[62] or privately.[63]

12.33   The Official Receiver's receivership obligations and the bankrupt's duty to deliver up possession of the estate to him as receiver do not arise in those cases where there is a trustee immediately the bankruptcy order is made, i.e. where at that time the Official Receiver becomes trustee by the issue by the Court of a certificate for summary administration or where the Court appoints as trustee the insolvency practitioner who reported to the Court under Article 248 or the supervisor of a voluntary arrangement.[64] In such cases the trustee takes immediate possession and control of the bankrupt's estate.[65]

12.34   If the Official Receiver cannot voluntarily obtain possession of the personal property comprised in the bankrupt's estate or books, papers or records relating to his affairs from the bankrupt or any other person required to hand them over, he may apply to the Court for the issue of a warrant of seizure under which forcible entry may be made by the person to whom the warrant is directed[66] into any premises where the bankrupt or anything seizable under the warrant is believed to be and to any receptacle of the bankrupt which contains or is believed to contain any such property or records.[67] Such a warrant is not, as formerly, issued in every case without application. He may also, if necessary, apply to the Court for the issue of a search warrant authorising a constable to search for and seize any such property or records on premises not belonging to the bankrupt.[68] Such a warrant may only be issued if the Court is satisfied that such property or records are concealed in such premises.[69]

12.35 The Official Receiver may apply to the Court for the issue of a warrant for the debtor's arrest and for the seizure of any books, papers, records, money or goods in his possession, in the circumstances set out in Article 335(2).[70]

Special manager
12.36 Before the appointment of a trustee the Official Receiver may apply to the Court for the appointment of a special manager of the estate or business of the bankrupt in any case where it appears to him that the nature of the estate or business, or the interests of the creditors generally, require the appointment of another person to manage the estate or business.[71]

12.37 The application must be accompanied by the Official Receiver's report setting out the reasons for the application and including an estimate of the value of the estate or business in respect of which the special manager is to be appointed.[72]

12.38 The Court may appoint a special manager to act for a specified period, or until further order, and the appointment may be renewed.[73]

12.39 The special manager has such powers as may be entrusted to him by the Court.[74] The Court may direct that any provision of the Order that has effect in relation to the Official Receiver shall have the like effect in relation to the special manager for the purposes of the carrying on by him of any of the functions of the Official Receiver.[75]

12.40 The special manager's remuneration is fixed from time to time by the Court[76] or, on its directions, by the Taxing Master.[77] Payments on account may be made by the Official Receiver.[78]

12.41 The Court's order must specify -
   (a) the special manager's responsibility over the bankrupt's estate,
   (b) he powers entrusted to him by the Court,
   (c) the period of his appointment,
   (d) the security to be given and within what time,
   (e) his remuneration.[79]

12.42 The appointment does not take effect until the special manager has given security to the Official Receiver or the Court accepts his undertaking to do so.[80] The amount of the security must be not less than the value put on the estate or business in the Official Receiver's report.[81] It may be given either specially for a particular bankruptcy or generally for any bankruptcy in relation to which the person appointed may be employed as special manager.[82] When the security has been given, the Official Receiver files in the Court a certificate of its adequacy.[83]

12.43   If the security is not given within the time required by the order appointing him or any allowed extension of time the Official Receiver must report the failure to the Court, which may thereupon discharge the order.[84] The Official Receiver must also report to the Court any subsequent failure by the special manager to keep up the security and the Court may remove the special manager and make an order for costs.[85] When discharging an order appointing a special manager or removing him the Court may give directions regarding the appointment of another person in his place.[86]

12.44   The special manager pays the cost of providing the security, but he is entitled to be reimbursed out of the estate in the prescribed order of priority.[87]

12.45   The special manager must keep accounts containing details of his receipts and payments in respect of each 3 month period of his appointment (or part of such period, if less) and produce them for approval of the trustee when appointed.[88] When the accounts have been approved, the receipts and payments from the special manager are added to those of the trustee.[89]

12.46   The acts of a special manager are valid notwithstanding any defect in his appointment or qualifications.[90]

12.47   If the Official Receiver is of the opinion that the employment of a special manager is no longer necessary or profitable for the estate or if the creditors at a general meeting resolve to request the termination of such appointment, he must apply to the Court for directions and the Court may order the termination of the appointment.[91]

Clients' account of bankrupt solicitor
12.48   Although property held by a bankrupt on trust for any other person does not form part of his estate,[92] where a solicitor is adjudged bankrupt the sum at credit of his clients' account with his bankers is divisible rateably amongst the clients on whose behalf money has been received by the solicitor and remains due to them.[93]

Footnotes

(1)   Para.12.06.
(2)   Hals 417.
(3)   Art.11: MH 3-151: Hals 204, fn.15.
(4)   Art.2(2).
(5)   Art.243(1)(a): paras. 7.049/050.
(6)   R.6.113: para.19.35.
(7)   Art.11(2).
(8)   Art.281(1).
(9)   Art.282(1)(b). See MH 3-373 as to extension of such time limits affecting interests both of the bankrupt and those dealing with him in respect of such property.
(10)   Art.281(2).
(11)   Art.281(3).
(12)   Art.281(4).
(13)   R.6.184.
(14)   R.6.185.
(15)   Art.276.
(16)   Art.288(4): para.14.074.
(17)   Art.257: para.7.022.
(18)   Art.279. See Hals 381 re vesting of foreign land and 383 re nature of title acquired.
(19)   Sch. 8, para.19.
(20)   Art.279(1).
(21)   Art.356(3).
(22)   JH 21.12/19.
(23)   LR Act s.59(1).
(24)   LR Act s.59A.
(25)   LR Rules 151, 151H.
(26)   LR Rules 151A, 151B(1).
(27)   LR Rules 151(2), 151B(2).
(28)   LR Rule 151H.
(29)   Art.280(1).
(30)   Art.280(2).
(31)   Hals 427.
(32)   Art.282(1). See fn.(9) above re extension of time.
(33)   Art.306(2). Failure to disclose after-acquired property is an offence, unless the bankrupt proves absence of intent to defraud or conceal the state of his affairs - Art.324, read with Arts.322 & 323.
(34)   R.6.197(1).
(35)   R.6.197(2).
(36)   R.6.197(3).
(37)   R.6.198.
(38)   R.6.197(4).
(39)   R.6.197(5).

(40)   R.6.197(6).
(41)   Art.280(2)(c).
(42)   *Ibid*: Art.254(2)(c): para. 21.28. Such an order should specify the dates on which accounts of after-acquired property or income are to be filed and sent to the trustee - Atkin Form 425.
(43)   Art.280(4).
(44)   Art.280(3).
(45)   Art.280(5): Ch.18.
(46)   RR.6.199, 6.222(1)(a).
(47)   Art.257(4).
(48)   Para.12.36.
(49)   Art.260(2).
(50)   Art.260(3).
(51)   Paras.9.07/08.
(52)   Art.264(1).
(53)   Art.264(2).
(54)   Arts.264(6), 334(4).
(55)   Art.260(4).
(56)   *Ibid*.
(57)   Art.320.
(58)   Art.343.
(59)   Art.260(3).
(60)   Art.334(3).
(61)   R.10.3.
(62)   Para.11.08.
(63)   Para.11.45.
(64)   Arts.260(5), 264(3).
(65)   Paras.14.021/027.
(66)   Usually an officer of the Official Receiver's office.
(67)   Art.336(1),(2): R.7.23: F.7.10: Atkin Forms 348, 349.
(68)   Art.336(3),(4): R.7.23: F.7.11: Atkin Form 350.
(69)   Art.336(3).
(70)   Para.7.036.
(71)   Art.341(1),(2): Atkin Form 202.
(72)   R.6.164(1),(2).
(73)   R.6.164(3),(4).
(74)   Art.341(3).
(75)   Art.341(4).
(76)   R.6.164(5).
(77)   R.7.31: paras.5.122/125.
(78)   R.7.30(3).
(79)   RR.6.164/5: F.6.57.
(80)   Art.341(5): R.6.165(1).
(81)   R.6.165(3).
(82)   R.6.165(2).
(83)   R.6.165(4).
(84)   R.6.166(1).

(85)   R.6.166(2).
(86)   R.6.166(3).
(87)   RR.6.165(5), 6.222(1)(e).
(88)   Art.341(5): R.6.167(1),(2).
(89)   R.6.167(3).
(90)   Art.345.
(91)   R.6.168(2),(3).
(92)   Para.12.01.
(93)   Solicitors (Northern Ireland) Order 1976, Art.41(3),(4).

Chapter 13

TRUSTEE IN BANKRUPTCY

Introduction
13.001 The administration of the bankrupt's estate is carried out by the trustee.[1]

13.002 Except where the Official Receiver becomes trustee,[2] the trustee is appointed by the creditors, the Department or the Court.[3]

Official name
13.003 The official name of the trustee, including the Official Receiver where he becomes trustee, is "the trustee of the estate of AB *(name of the bankrupt)*".[4] When he is a party to any document or in court proceedings, this description should follow his own name and address and, in the case of the Official Receiver, the phrase "an Official Receiver for Northern Ireland". The trustee may, however, be referred to as "the trustee in bankruptcy" of the particular bankrupt.[5]

I. OFFICIAL RECEIVER AS TRUSTEE

13.004 Where, on the hearing of a debtor's petition, the Court makes a bankruptcy order and issues a certificate for summary administration,[6] the Official Receiver is the trustee from the date of issue of that certificate, unless and until the Court appoints another person as trustee[7] or he is replaced by a trustee appointed by the Department on his application.[8]

13.005 The Official Receiver also becomes the trustee where he decides not to summon a meeting of creditors for the purpose of appointing a trustee,[9] where no appointment is made at such meeting[10] or during any vacancy in the office of trustee.[11] He does not become trustee by reason only of the making of a bankruptcy order.[12]

13.006 Where the Official Receiver becomes trustee he does so by the operation of the relevant provision of the Order. He may not be appointed trustee.

II. APPOINTMENT OF TRUSTEE

Qualifications of trustee
13.007 No person may be appointed as trustee unless he is, at the time of the appointment, qualified to act as an insolvency practitioner in relation to the bankrupt.[13]

Security by trustee

13.008   A trustee, other than the Official Receiver, is not qualified to act as such unless the requisite security is in force.[14]   Within 14 days of his appointment the trustee must file in the Court a certificate of specific penalty in respect of the security.[15]

Joint trustees

13.009   Two or more persons may be appointed as joint trustees.[16]   In such a case the appointment must provide for the circumstances in which the trustees must act together and the circumstances in which one or more of them may act for the others.[17]

Effective date of appointment

13.010   Where the trustee is appointed by a creditors' meeting or by the Department, his appointment takes effect at the time specified in his certificate of appointment[18] and where appointed by the Court, at the date of the order of appointment[19] provided that, in each case, the trustee has accepted the appointment.[20]

Notice of appointment

13.011   Where the trustee is appointed at a creditors' meeting he must, forthwith after receiving his certificate of appointment, give notice of his appointment in such newspaper as he thinks most appropriate for ensuring that it comes to the notice of the creditors.[21]

13.012   Where the appointment is made by the Department or by the Court the trustee must give notice of his appointment to the creditors or, if the Court so allows, advertise it in accordance with the directions of the Court.[22]   In the notice or advertisement he must state whether he proposes to summon a general meeting of creditors for the purpose of establishing a creditors' committee[23] and, if not, set out the power of the creditors to require him to do so.[24]

13.013   The expense of such notice or advertisement is borne in the first instance by the trustee, but he is entitled to be reimbursed by the estate, as an expense of the bankrupcy.[25]

Defects in appointment

13.014   The acts of a trustee are valid notwithstanding any defect in his appointment, election or qualification.[26]

Proof of trustee's authority

13.015   A sealed copy of the order of appointment or (as the case may be) a copy of his certificate of appointment may be adduced in any proceedings as proof that he is duly authorised to exercise the powers and perform the duties of trustee.[27]

A. APPOINTMENT BY CREDITORS

First meeting of creditors
(a) Decision to summon meeting
13.016   Where a bankruptcy order has been made and no certificate for summary administration has been issued and a trustee has not been appointed by the Court under Article 270(3) or (4) on the making of the order, [28] so that there is not already a trustee in office, the Official Receiver is required to decide whether to summon a general meeting of the bankrupt's creditors for the purpose of appointing a trustee (in the Rules and hereafter referred to as "the first meeting of creditors"). [29] This decision should be made as soon as practicable after the making of the bankruptcy order and in any case must be made within 12 weeks from that date, unless the decision is pre-empted by a requisition by creditors. [30] Clearly it is desirable that provision for the administration of the estate either by an insolvency practitioner or the Official Receiver as trustee should be made as quickly as possible, but before deciding whether to call a creditors' meeting the Official Receiver will require information as to the estimated value of the bankrupt's estate. If the value of the estate is likely to be small it is unlikely that an appointment would be made at a creditors' meeting unless creditors were prepared to indemnify the person proposed as trustee in respect of his fees and expenses.

(b) Requisition of meeting
13.017   Where the Official Receiver has decided not to summon a first meeting of creditors in circumstances where he is required to make such decision or before he has summoned such a meeting, he must summon it if requested by any creditor, with the concurrence of at least one-quarter, in value, of the creditors. [31]

13.018   The request must be accompanied by a statement of the purpose of the proposed meeting and, unless the requisitioning creditor's debt is alone at least the requisite one-quarter, in value, of the creditors, a list of the creditors concurring with the request and the amount of their respective claims in the bankruptcy, together with written confirmation from each supporting creditor. [32]

13.019   If the Official Receiver considers that the request is properly made with the concurrence of the requisite proportion of creditors, he is required to summon the meeting, [33] but not until the requisitioning creditor has deposited such sum as the Official Receiver determines for the expenses of summoning and holding the meeting. [34]

(c) No meeting summoned
13.020   If the Official Receiver decides not to summon a first meeting of creditors and no proper requisition for such a meeting is received from a creditor he must, within the 12 weeks from the date of the bankruptcy order allowed for his decision, give notice of that decision to the Court and to every

creditor known to him or identified in the bankrupt's statement of affairs.[35] The Official Receiver becomes the trustee from the date of giving such notice.[36] Proof of his status as trustee would be provided by production of an office copy of the notice filed in the Court. However, he is required to withdraw the notice upon receipt of a proper requisition for a meeting from a creditor.[37]

(d) Summoning of meeting

13.021 If the Official Receiver decides to summon a first meeting of creditors he must fix a venue for the meeting.[38] The date fixed must not be more than 4 months from the date of the bankruptcy order.[39] He must then give immediate notice of the meeting to the Court and, at least 21 days before the date fixed for it, give notice to every creditor known to him or identified in the bankrupt's statement of affairs and to the bankrupt.[40] The notice to the creditors must specify a time and date, not more than 4 days before the date fixed for the meeting, by which they must lodge proofs and (if applicable) proxies, in order to be entitled to vote at the meeting.[41] The notice to the bankrupt must state whether he is required to be present or in attendance.[42] Notice of the meeting must also be advertised.[43]

13.022 Where the meeting is requisitioned by a creditor it must be convened by the Official Receiver for not later than 3 months from receipt of the request.[44] Otherwise it is convened in accordance with the Rules governing a meeting which the Official Receiver decides to summon.[45]

(e) Business at meeting

13.023 The only resolutions which may be taken at the first meeting of creditors are-

    (i)   to appoint a named insolvency practitioner as trustee or two or more named insolvency practitioners as joint trustees;

    (ii) to establish a creditors' committee;[46]

    (iii) (unless it has been resolved to establish a creditors' committee) to specify the terms on which the trustee is to be remunerated,[47] or to defer consideration of that matter;

    (iv) if two or more persons are appointed as joint trustees, to specify whether acts are to be done by both or all of them or by only one;

    (v) where the meeting has been requisitioned, to authorise payment out of the estate as an expense of the bankruptcy of the cost of summoning and holding the meeting;

    (vi) to adjourn for not more than 3 weeks;

    (vii) any other resolution which the chairman thinks it right to allow for special reasons.[48]

No resolution may be proposed which has for its object the appointment of the Official Receiver as trustee.[49]

13.024 Subject to these provisions the first meeting is conducted in accordance with the general Rules regulating the conduct of meetings of creditors and the use of proxies.[50]

13.025   If on a resolution for the appointment of a trustee there is more than one nominee, the chairman may at any time propose a resolution for the joint appointment of two or more nominees.[51]   If no such resolution is passed, -
- (i)   if there are 2 nominees, the person obtaining the most support is appointed, but only if such support represents a majority in value of all those present (in person or by proxy) and entitled to vote;
- (ii)   if there are three or more nominees, and one of them has a clear majority over both or all the others together, that one is appointed; and
- (iii)   in any other case the chairman is required to continue to take votes (disregarding at each vote any nominee who has withdrawn and, if no nominee has withdrawn, the nominee who obtained the least support last time), until a clear majority is obtained for any one nominee.[52]

Thus, the winning candidate must have the support of the majority in value of the creditors present and entitled to vote at the meeting.

Certification of appointment
13.026   Where a trustee is appointed by resolution of a creditors' meeting the appointment is certified by the chairman of the meeting.[53] Before issuing a certificate he must procure from the appointee a written statement to the effect that he is an insolvency practitioner duly qualified under the Order to act as trustee in relation to the bankrupt and that he consents to act.[54]

13.027   The appointment is effective from the date on which the appointment is certified and that date must be endorsed on the certificate.[55]

13.028   The chairman of the meeting (if not the Official Receiver) must send the certificate to the Official Receiver.[56] The Official Receiver is then required to send it to the trustee and to file a copy in the Court.[57]

B. APPOINTMENT BY THE DEPARTMENT

13.029   The Order makes provision for the Department to appoint an in-solvency practitioner instead of or in place of the Official Receiver. Presumably the practitioner will be selected from a panel of insolvency practitioners willing to accept such an appointment.

13.030   A trustee may be appointed by the Department-
- (a)   where a first meeting of creditors is held, but no resolution to appoint a trustee is passed,
- (b)   where there is a vacancy in the office of trustee, or
- (c)   at any time when the Official Receiver is trustee.

Appointment on failure of creditors to appoint
13.031   If no appointment of a person as trustee is made at the first meeting of creditors or at any adjournment the Official Receiver must decide whether he wishes to act as trustee or, on a reference by him, give the Department an opportunity to consider appointing an insolvency practitioner instead.[58] On

such a reference the Department must either make such appointment or decline to do so.[59]

13.032   If the Official Receiver decides not to refer the matter to the Department or if the Department, on such reference, declines to make an appointment, he must give notice of his decision or, as the case may be, the decision of the Department, to the Court.[60]   From the giving of such notice the Official Receiver is the trustee.[61]   Proof of his status as trustee would be provided by production of an office copy of the notice filed in the Court.

Appointment to fill vacancy in office
13.033   Such an appointment is dealt with below.[62]

Appointment on application of Official Receiver
13.034   At any time when the Official Receiver is the trustee he may seek to divest himself of the office by applying to the Department for the appointment of an insolvency practitioner in his place.[63]   Such an application may be made even where the Department has declined to make an appointment on a previous application by the Official Receiver or on a reference following the failure of a creditors' meeting to appoint or on the occurrence of a vacancy in the office.[64]

Certificate of appointment
13.035   Where the Department appoints a trustee it must issue a certificate of appointment, specifying the date from which the appointment is to be effective, and send 2 copies to the Official Receiver, who must transmit one copy to the person appointed, and file the other copy in the Court.[65]

C. APPOINTMENT BY THE COURT

13.036   A trustee may be appointed by the Court-
   (a) where a bankruptcy order is made on a debtor's petition and -
      (i)   a certificate for summary administration is issued or is in force, in which case an insolvency practitioner may be appointed instead of the Official Receiver,[66] or
      (ii) such an appointment has been made, either by the Court or the Department,[67] a vacancy in the office subsequently occurs and the Official Receiver refers the need to fill the vacancy to the Court,[68] or
      (iii) an insolvency practitioner's report has been submitted to the Court under Article 248[69] and a bankruptcy order is made but no certificate for summary administration is issued, in which case the practitioner who made the report may be appointed;[70]
   (b) where a bankruptcy order is made on any petition at a time when there is a supervisor of an approved voluntary arrangement in relation to the bankrupt, in which case the supervisor of the arrangement may be appointed trustee.[71]

13.037 The order of the Court appointing a trustee[72] may not issue unless and until the appointee has filed in the Court a statement to the effect that he is an insolvency practitioner duly qualified under the Order to be the trustee and that he consents to act.[73]

13.038 Two copies of the order (one of which is to be sealed) when issued are sent by the Court to the Official Receiver, who is required to send the sealed copy to the trustee.[74] The trustee's appointment takes effect from the date of the order.[75] The sealed copy order constitutes proof of the trustee's title.

III. VACATION OF OFFICE OF TRUSTEE

A. DEATH

13.039 Where the Official Receiver is not the trustee and the trustee dies it is the duty of his personal representatives to notify the Official Receiver, specifying the date of death, unless the trustee was a partner in a firm and a surviving partner who is a qualified insolvency practitioner or a member of a body recognized by the Department for the authorisation of insolvency practitioners has done so, or unless some other person produces to the Official Receiver the certificate of the death of the trustee or a copy.[76]

13.040 When he receives notice of the death the Official Receiver must notify the Court.[77] This notice fixes the date of the deceased trustee's release.[78]

B. RESIGNATION

13.041 The trustee may, in the circumstances prescribed by the Rules, resign his office by giving notice of his resignation to the Court.[79]

13.042 The trustee may resign in the following circumstances only-
  (a) ill health,
  (b) he intends to cease to practice as an insolvency practitioner,
  (c) there is some conflict of interest or change of personal circumstances which precludes or makes impracticable the further discharge by him of the duties of the office, or
  (d) he is one of two or more joint trustees and in his opinion and that of the other or others, it is no longer expedient that there should continue to be the present number of joint trustees.[80]

13.043 The trustee wishing to resign is required to summon a meeting of creditors for the purpose of receiving his resignation.[81] The notice must indicate that this is the purpose, or one of the purposes, of the meeting and draw attention to the Rule with respect to the release of the trustee.[82] A copy of the notice must at the same time be sent to the Official Receiver.[83]

13.044 The notice to the creditors must be accompanied by an account of the trustee's administration of the bankrupt's estate, including summary of his receipts and payments and a statement by him that he has reconciled his account with that held by the Department.[84]

13.045 If no quorum[85] is present at the meeting, it is deemed to have been held, a resolution is deemed to have been passed that the trustee's resignation be accepted and the creditors are deemed not to have resolved against the trustee having his release.[86]

13.046 If the chairman of the meeting is not the Official Receiver and any of the following resolutions are passed-
    (a)   that the trustee's resignation be accepted,
    (b)   that a new trustee be appointed,
    (c)   that the resiging trustee be not given his release,
the chairman must, within 3 days, send to the Official Receiver a copy of the resolution and, if it has been resolved to accept the trustee's resignation, a certificate to that effect.[87] Where there is no quorum present, in place of a resolution to accept the trustee's resignation, the person who would otherwise have been chairman must send to the Official Receiver a signed statement that no quorum was present and that the trustee may resign.[88]

13.047 If the creditors resolve to appoint a new trustee the certificate of his appointment must also be sent to the Official Receiver within 3 days.[89]

13.048 Where a new trustee is appointed in place of one who has resigned the new trustee must, in the advertisement of his appointment, state that his predecessor has resigned and (if that be the case) that he has been given his release.[90]

13.049 If the trustee's resignation is accepted, he must forthwith after the meeting give notice of it to the Court, accompanied by a copy of the account sent to the creditors and send a copy of the notice to the Official Receiver.[91] The Official Receiver is required to file a copy of the notice in the Court.[92]

13.050 The trustee's resignation is effective as from the date on which the Official Receiver files the copy of the trustee's notice in the Court and that date must be endorsed on the copy notice.[93]

13.051 If at the creditors' meeting summoned to accept the trustee's resignation it is resolved that it be not accepted the trustee may apply to the Court for an order giving him leave to resign.[94] The Court's order giving such leave[95] may include such provision as it thinks fit with respect to matters arising in connection with the resignation, and must fix the date from which the trustee's release is effective.[96] The Court sends 2 sealed copies of the order to the trustee who is required to send one of the copies to the Official Receiver.[97] When given leave to resign by the Court the trustee must send notice of his resignation to the Court[98] and a copy of it to the Official Receiver.[99]

C. REMOVAL

13.052 A trustee appointed by the Department may be removed by a direction of the Department.[100] Otherwise, the trustee may be removed from office only by an order of the Court or by a general meeting of creditors summoned specially for that purpose in accordance with the Rules.[101]

Removal by the Court
13.053 An application may be made to the Court for the removal of the trustee or for an order directing him to summon a meeting of creditors for the purpose of removing him.[102]

13.054 If it thinks that sufficient cause is not shown for the application, the Court may dismiss it on an ex parte hearing of which the applicant has been given at least 7 days' notice; otherwise it fixes a venue for the hearing.[103]

13.055 At least 14 days before the hearing date the applicant must send to the trustee and the Official Receiver notice of the venue, together with a copy of the application and any evidence to be adduced in support of it.[104] Unless the Court otherwise orders, the costs of the application may not be charged to the estate.[105]

13.056 Where the Court removes a trustee it sends copies of the order of removal to the trustee and to the Official Receiver.[106] The order may include such provision as the Court thinks fit with respect to matters arising in connection with the removal.[107]

13.057 If the Court appoints a new trustee in place of the trustee removed the procedure following such an appointment must be complied with.[108]

Removal by creditors
13.058 The power of a general meeting of creditors to remove the trustee is subject to the following limitations -
  (a)   such a meeting may not be held at any time when a certificate for the summary administration of the estate is in force;[109]
  (b)   where the Official Receiver is trustee because he has decided not to summon a first meeting of creditors[110] or following the failure of a first meeting of creditors to appoint a trustee[111] or where the trustee is appointed by the Department or by the Court (other than a supervisor of a voluntary arrangement so appointed), such a meeting may be summoned only if the trustee thinks fit or the Court so directs or the meeting is requisitioned by a creditor, with the concurrence of not less that one-quarter, in value, of the creditors.[112]

13.059   The notice summoning a meeting of creditors to remove the trustee[113] must indicate that this is the purpose, or one of the purposes, of the meeting and draw the attention of the creditors to the provisions of Article 272(3) with respect to the trustee's release.[114] A copy of the notice must at the same time be sent to the Official Receiver.[115]

13.060   A person other than the trustee or his nominee may be elected to act as chairman of the meeting.[116] If the trustee or his nominee is chairman and a resolution for the trustee's removal is proposed, the chairman may not adjourn the meeting without the consent of at least one-half (in value) of the creditors present (in person or by proxy) and entitled to vote.[117]

13.061   Where the chairman of the meeting is not the Official Receiver and any of the following resolutions are passed-
  (a)   that the trustee be removed,
  (b)   that a new trustee be appointed,
  (c)   that the removed trustee be not given his release,
the chairman must, within 3 days, send to the Official Receiver a copy of the resolution[118] and, if it has been resolved to remove the trustee, a certificate to that effect.[119]

13.062   If the creditors resolve to appoint a new trustee the requirements regarding the issue of a certificate of his appointment must be complied with and the certificate sent to the Official Receiver within 3 days.[120]

13.063   Special directions with regard to the meeting may be given by the Court on the application of any creditor.[121]

13.064   Where the creditors have resolved that the trustee be removed, the Official Receiver must file the certificate of removal in the Court, but not until the Department has certified to him that the removed trustee has reconciled his account with that held by the Department.[122] The resolution is effective from the date of such filing, which is to be endorsed on the certificate.[123] A copy of the certificate, so endorsed, must be sent by the Official Receiver to the trustee who has been removed and, if a new trustee has been appointed, also to him.[124]

Removal by the Department
13.065   The trustee may be removed by a direction of the Department only if he was appointed by the Department.[125]

13.066   If the Department decides to remove the trustee it must notify him and the Official Receiver of its decision and the grounds of it and specify a period within which the trustee may make representations against his removal.[126]

13.067   Where the Department removes the trustee it must file notice of the decision in the Court and send notice of it to the trustee and the Official Receiver.[127]

13.068   Following the removal of the trustee by the Department the Court may make any necessary provision with respect to matters arising in connection with the removal.[128]

13.069   A trustee appointed by the Department may also be removed by the Court or, subject to the limitations mentioned above,[129] by a general meeting of creditors.[130]

Advertisement of removal

13.070   Where a new trustee is appointed in place of one who has been removed, the new trustee must, in the advertisment of his appointment,[131] state that his predecessor has been removed and (if it be the case) that he has been given his release.[132]

D. OTHER OCCASIONS

Disqualification of trustee

13.071   The trustee (not being the Official Receiver) must vacate office if he ceases to be qualified to act as an insolvency practitioner in relation to the bankrupt.[133]

13.072   On such an occurrence the trustee must forthwith give notice of vacation of office[134] to the Official Receiver, who is required to notify the Department and file a copy of the notice in the court.[135]

Completion of administration

13.073   The trustee vacates office by giving notice to the Court that a final meeting of creditors has been held[136] and of the decision (if any) of that meeting.[137]

Annulment of bankruptcy

13.074   The trustee vacates office if the bankruptcy order is annulled.[138]

E. TRUSTEE'S DUTIES ON VACATING OFFICE

13.075   Where the trustee intends to vacate office, for whatever reason, he must give notice of his intention to the Official Receiver, together with notice of any creditors' meeting to be held in respect of his vacation of office, including any meeting to receive his resignation.[139]   Such notice must be given at least 21 days before any such creditors' meeting.[140]

13.076   Where any property of the estate has not been fully dealt with, the trustee intending to vacate office must include details of it in his notice to the Official Receiver and state its value or the fact that it has no value, its location, any action he has taken to deal with it or any reason for not doing so and the current position in relation to it.[141]

13.077 Where the trustee ceases to be in office in consequence of removal, resignation or cesser of qualification as an insolvency practitioner, he must forthwith deliver up to his successor as trustee the assets of the estate (after deducting any expenses properly incurred and distributions made by him) and also the records of the bankruptcy (including correspondence, proofs etc.) and the bankrupt's books, papers and other records not destroyed or otherwise disposed of under the authorisation of the Official Receiver.[142]

13.078 When the administration of the bankrupt's estate is for practical purposes complete the trustee must forthwith file in the Court all proofs of debt which he holds.[143]

F. FILLING THE VACANCY

13.079 Where the appointment of any person as trustee fails to take effect or a vacancy in the office of trustee occurs the Official Receiver immediately becomes trustee and remains trustee unless and until another person is appointed in his place.[144] Any unrealised assets of the bankrupt's estate vest in him.[145]

13.080 Where a certificate for summary administration is in force in a case where an insolvency practitioner has been appointed trustee and a vacancy in the office of trustee occurs the Official Receiver may refer the need to fill the vacancy to the Court or, if the trustee had been appointed by the Department, either to the Court or to the Department and on such a reference the Department must either make the appointment or decline to do so.[146]

13.081 On becoming trustee in any other case the Official Receiver may summon a general meeting of creditors for the purpose of filling the vacancy, and he must do so if a creditor, with the concurrence of at least one-tenth, in value, of the creditors, so requests.[147]

13.082 If within 28 days of the vacancy coming to his attention the Official Receiver has not summoned such a general meeting of creditors and is not proposing to do so, he must refer the need for an appointment to the Department, who must either make an appointment or decline to do so.[148] If no appointment is made the Official Receiver continues to be the trustee, but he may make a further reference to the Department at any time if he later considers it appropriate that he should be replaced as trustee.[149]

G. REVIVAL OF TRUSTEESHIP

13.083 If the trusteeship has terminated because the administration of the bankrupt's estate is for practical purposes complete and either a final meeting of creditors has been held[150] or the Official Receiver has given notice to that effect[151] but it is necessary to revive the trusteeship in order to deal with property comprised in the estate, the Official Receiver may take steps to have an insolvency practitioner appointed trustee as if a vacancy in the office had occurred.[152]

IV. REMUNERATION OF TRUSTEE

Official Receiver

13.084   Where the Offical Receiver is trustee his remuneration is regulated by fees prescribed by the Insolvency Regulations.[153]

Other trustee

13.085   Where the trustee is other than the Official Receiver his general remuneration is fixed by the creditors' committee, if there is one.[154] If there is no such committee, or if the committee fails to fix the remuneration, it may be fixed by a resolution of a creditors' meeting called by the trustee.[155]. The Department may not fix the remuneration in exercise of the functions of a creditors' committee.[156]

13.086   The remuneration may be fixed -
  (a)   as a percentage of the value of the assets realised,
  (b)   as a percentage of the amount distributed to creditors,
  (c)   a combination of (a) and (b), or
  (d)   by reference to the time properly occupied by the trustee and his staff.[157]

13.087   In choosing between methods (a) to (d), the committee or meeting of creditors is required to have regard to certain prescribed factors-complexity (or otherwise), exceptional degree of responsibility falling on the trustee, effectiveness of carrying out of duties and value and nature of the assets.[158]

13.088   If the remuneration is not fixed by the committee or creditors' meeting by any of these methods the trustee is remunerated on the scale laid down for the fees of the Official Receiver.[159] The Court has no jurisdiction to fix the remuneration initially, nor may it direct that it be taxed by the Taxing Master.[160]

13.089   In addition to his general remuneration, where the trustee sells assets on behalf of a secured creditor he is entitled to deduct from the proceeds of sale a fee equivalent to the fee chargeable by the Official Receiver for such services.[161]

13.090   Where there are joint trustees any dispute between them as to the apportionment of remuneration may be referred to the Court, the creditors' committee or a meeting of creditors.[162]

13.091   Where the trustee is a solicitor, the profit costs of work done on behalf of the estate by his firm or a partner in it may not be paid unless authorised by the creditors' committee, the creditors or the Court.[163]

13.092   If the trustee considers that the rate or amount of his remuneration fixed by the creditors' committee is insufficient he may convene a meeting of creditors, who may by resolution increase it.[164] Alternatively, or if his remuneration is fixed by a meeting of creditors or determined by the Official Receiver's scale of charges, he may apply to the Court to have it increased.[165] Where there is a creditors' committee, he must give at least 14 days notice of such an application to the members of the committee and the committee may nominate one or more of its members to appear or be represented, and to be heard, on the application.[166] If there is no creditors' committee, notice of the application must be sent to such one or more of the bankrupt's creditors as the Court directs, which creditors may nominate one or more of their number to appear or be represented.[167] The Court may order the costs of the application, including the costs of any member of the creditors' committee or any creditor appearing or being represented, to be paid out of the estate.[168]

13.093   Any creditor who procures the concurrence of at least 25% in value of the creditors (including himself) may apply to the Court to have the trustee's remuneration reduced, on the grounds that it is, in all the circumstances, excessive.[169] If no prima facie case is shown by the applicant at an ex parte hearing of which he has been given at least 7 days' notice the Court may dismiss the application; otherwise a venue will be fixed for the hearing on at least 14 days' notice to the trustee, accompanied by a copy of the application and any evidence the applicant intends to adduce.[170] If the Court considers the application to be well-founded, it fixes the remuneration at a reduced amount or rate.[171] Unless the Court otherwise orders, the costs of the application are to be paid by the applicant and not out of the estate.[172]

13.094   It would appear that if on an application to the Court by the trustee to have his remuneration increased or by a creditor to have such remuneration reduced the Court considers that the amount of the remuneration should be reviewed it may either fix the amount to be allowed or direct that it be measured by the Taxing Master.[173]

13.095   Notwithstanding any provision of the Rules or any resolution of the creditors' committee or of the creditors, if the trustee or anyone on his behalf uses improper solicitation in obtaining proxies or procuring his appointment, the Court may order that he be allowed no remuneration out of the estate.[174]

V. RELEASE OF TRUSTEE

Effect of release
13.096   A trustee who is released under the Order is, from the effective date of the release, discharged from all liability both in respect of acts or omissions of his in the adminstration of the estate and otherwise in relation to his conduct as trustee.[175] However, notwithstanding his release, the trustee may still be liable to be ordered by the Court to account for money or other property of the estate misapplied or retained by him or to pay compensation for misfeasance

or breach of duty, but an application for such an order after release of the trustee requires the leave of the Court.[176]

Release on completion of adminstration
(a) Official Receiver
13.097   Where the Official Receiver is the trustee he may, on giving notice to the Department that the administration of the estate is for practical purposes complete, be released by the Department with effect from a date to be determined by it .[177] No meeting of creditors is required, but before giving notice to the Department the Official Receiver must send to all creditors who have proved their debts and to the bankrupt notice of his intention to do so, accompanied by a summary of his receipts and payments as trustee.[178]

13.098   When the Department has determined the date from which the Official Receiver is to have his release it must give notice to the Court that it has done so, together with the summary of receipts and payments.[179]

(b) Other trustee
13.099   Where a trustee other than the Official Receiver vacates office by giving notice to the Court of the result of the final meeting of creditors[180] the notice[181] must state whether or not the creditors have resolved against the release of the trustee.[182] A copy of the report laid before the final meeting must accompany the notice and the trustee must send a copy of the notice to the Official Receiver.[183]

13.100   The trustee is released from the time of filing the notice of the final meeting of creditors in the Court, unless the meeting resolves against his release, in which case he can only obtain a release by applying to the Department and the Department determines the time of his release.[184] When the release is thus given by the Department it must issue a certificate and send it to the Official Receiver to be filed in the Court and also send a copy to the former trustee.[185] In such a case the trustee's release is effective from the date of the certificate.[186]

Other occasions for release
(a) Official Receiver
13.101   Where a person is appointed trustee in place of the Official Receiver by a general meeting of creditors or by the Department the Official Receiver is released upon giving notice to the Court that he has been replaced.[187] Where the appointment of the new trustee is made by the Court the Official Receiver is released from such time as the Court may determine.[188]

(b) Other trustee
13.102   Where a trustee other than the Official Receiver dies, the date of the release of the deceased trustee is fixed by the date of the notice to the Court which the Official Receiver is required to give on receiving notice of the death.[189]

13.103   Where a trustee's resignation is accepted by a general meeting of creditors which has not resolved against his release he is released when his resignation is effective, i.e. from the date the Official Receiver files in Court the copy notice of resignation.[190]

13.104   Under Article 272(3)(a) where a trustee has been removed from office by a general meeting of creditors that has not resolved against his release he is released at the time notice is given to the Court "in accordance with the rules" that he has ceased to hold office. The Rules provide that in these circumstances the certificate of removal issued by the chairman of the meeting must state that the meeting has not resolved against his release.[191] This certificate is to be sent to the Official Receiver, who files it in the Court.[192] Presumably the filing of this certificate is a notice to the Court under Article 272(3)(a).

13.105   Where the trustee resigns but the general meeting of creditors called to receive his resignation resolves that he be not released or where he is removed from office by a general meeting of creditors which resolves against his release the trustee may only be released by applying to the Department and the Department determines the time of his release.[193] When the Department gives the release it must issue a certificate and send it to the Official Receiver, to be filed in the Court, and send a copy to the former trustee.[194] The release is effective from the date of the certificate.[195]

13.106   Where the trustee is removed by the Court or by the Department or where he vacates office by reason of ceasing to be qualified to act as an insolvency practitioner in relation to the bankrupt, he must apply to the Department for his release.[196] His release is effective from the date of the certificate of release issued by the Department.[197]

13.107   Where a new trustee is appointed in place of one who has resigned or been removed and the former trustee has been released, the advertisement of the new appointment must state this fact.[198]

13.108   Where a bankruptcy order is annulled, the Court fixes the date of the release of the trustee.[199]

VI. ACCOUNTS AND RECORDS

(A) ACCOUNTS

The Insolvency Account
13.109   Unless authorised to operate a local bank account [200] the trustee must pay all money received by him in the discharge of his functions, without any deduction, into the Insolvency Account kept by the Department with a bank agreed with the Department of Finance and Personnel.[201] The payment, accompanied by forms obtainable from the Department, must be made once every 14 days, or forthwith if £5,000 or more has been received. It is made direct to

the bank where the Insolvency Account is kept (currently the Bank of Ireland) by cheque drawn in favour of the "Insolvency Account" and crossed "A/C payee only". The Department must give the trustee a receipt for the payment, if required.

13.110 If the trustee fails to make any required payment into the Insolvency Account and is unable to explain such failure to the satisfaction of the Department, he must pay interest on the amount he has failed to pay into the account at the rate of 20% per annum and is liable to pay any expenses incurred by his default. [202]

13.111 All necessary disbursements made by the trustee and expenses properly incurred by him to the date of his vacation of office may, on application to the Department and on a form obtainable from it, on which the details of the disbursements and expenses claimed must be given, be repaid out of any money outstanding to the credit of the bankrupt's estate in the Insolvency Account. [203] Any such disbursements or expenses not repaid to the trustee before he vacates office must be repaid by any trustee appointed to suceed him, or if none by the Official Receiver, out of any available funds.

13.112 Other sums payable on account of the bankrupt's estate are made to the persons entitled by payment instrument obtainable by the trustee on application to the Department on a requisition form obtainable from the Department. [204]

13.113 The trustee may obtain a certificate of the balance standing to the credit of the bankrupt's estate in the Insolvency Account on written application to the Department. [205]

13.114 Whenever the cash balance standing to the credit of the bankrupt's estate in the Insolvency Account exceeds £2,000, the Department is required to pay into the Insolvency Account to the credit of the estate interest on the excess at the rate of 3 ½% per annum. [206]

13.115 Any moneys representing unclaimed dividends or unclaimed or undistributed assets of the bankrupt in the hands of the trustee at the date he vacates office or which come into the hands of any former trustee at any time after he vacates office must forthwith be paid by him into the Insolvency Account. [207]

13.116 On or before 31st March in each year the Department is required to pay into the Consolidated Fund the amount of any lodgment made into the Insolvency Account of unclaimed dividends and unapplied or undistributed balances, which has remained unclaimed for a period of at least 2 years from the date of the lodgment. [208]

13.117   Any person claiming to be entitled to any moneys paid into the Insolvency Account may apply to the Department for payment, supported by such evidence of the claim as the Department may require.[209] Any person dissatisfied with the decision of the Department in respect of such claim may appeal to the Court.[210]

Local bank account [211]

13.118   If the trustee intends to carry on the business of the bankrupt he may apply to the Department for authorisation to open a local bank account. On such an application the Department may authorise him to make his payments into and out of a specified bank, subject to a limit, instead of into and out of the Insolvency Account, if satisfied that an administrative advantage will be derived in having such an account.[212] Any surplus over any authorised limit must be paid without deduction into the Insolvency Account. The local bank account must be closed and any balance remitted to the Insolvency Account as soon as the trustee ceases to carry on the business of the bankrupt or vacates office or the Department's authorisation is withdrawn.

13.119   Where a local bank account is opened money received by the trustee for the purpose for which it was opened may be paid into the account to the credit of the bankrupt's estate.

13.120   The account must be in the bankrupt's name. Where money is provided for a specific purpose a separate account must be opened for it.

13.121   The trustee must keep proper records, including documentary evidence of all money paid into and out of such bank account. He must also obtain and keep bank statements relating thereto and these must accompany his account submitted to the Department.[213] Particulars of all transactions must be included in his trading account.[214]

Submission of accounts to Department [215]

13.122   Every year during his tenure of office the trustee must send to the Department either an account of his receipts and payments in relation to the bankrupt's estate in the prescibed form and accompanied by any bank statements relating to any local bank account in the bankrupt's name or, in respect of any period since the beginning of his tenure of office or since last sending an account to the Department during which he has not received or paid any money on account of the estate, a prescribed form of certificate of no receipts or payments. The prescribed forms contain a schedule requiring the trustee to report on the proceedings in and the position of the administration of the bankrupt's estate.

13.123   The first account or certificate sent to the Department must be accompanied by a copy of the bankrupt's statement of affairs (if any) or, where a statement of affairs has not been submitted, a summary of all known assets and liabilities.

13.124   The first account or certificate must be sent by the trustee within 30 days after the expiration of 12 months from the date of the bankruptcy order, unless he vacates office within that period, and subsequent accounts or certificates within 30 days after each suceeding 12 month period until he vacates office.

13.125   Within 14 days of vacating office the trustee must send to the Department an account of his receipts and payments since the date of the last account so sent or, if no such account has been sent, such an account for the whole period of his office.

Audit of accounts [216]

13.126   The Department may require any account sent to it to be audited, but whether or not it does so, the trustee must send to the Department on demand any vouchers, any bank statements and any information relating to the account.

Submission of accounts to bankrupt or creditors [217]

13.127   A copy of any account or certificate of no receipts or payments sent to the Department must be supplied by the trustee to the bankrupt or any creditor on request. Such copy must be sent free of charge within 14 days of the account or certificate being sent to the Department or on the receipt of the request, whichever is the later. The request may call for an account or certificate to be sent in respect of future periods.

(B) RECORDS

Administrative records

13.128   In addition to the records required to be maintained by him under the Insolvency Practitioners Regulations, [218] the trustee must keep records containing -

    (a)   minutes of any meetings of creditors or of the creditors' committee, including a record of every resolution passed at any such meeting and, where the agreement of members of a creditors' committee to a resolution has been obtained by post, a copy of such resolution and a note that the concurrence of the committee was obtained;

    (b)   any other matters necessary to give an accurate record of his administration. [219]

Financial records [220]

13.129   The trustee must keep separate financial records in respect of the bankrupt's estate and from day to day enter in those records all receipts and payments made by him. Where he carries on any business of the bankrupt he must keep a separate trading account and incorporate in his financial rewards the total weekly amount of receipts and payments recorded in such account. He must also keep such other financial records as are required to explain all receipts and payments and to give an explanation of the source of any receipts and the destination of any payments. Where he operates a local bank account he must obtain and keep bank statements relating to that account.

Retention and delivery of records

13.130   The trustee's records, including any received from a predecessor in office, must be retained by him for a period of 6 years following his vacation of office or, in the case of the Official Receiver, his release, unless he delivers them to a successor in office.[221]

13.131   Where the trustee is succeeded in office by another trustee, the records must be delivered to the successor forthwith following his appointment, unless the bankruptcy is for practical purposes complete and the successor is the Official Receiver, in which case the records are only to be delivered to the Official Receiver if he so requests.[222]

Disposal of records.[223]

13.132   The trustee, if not the Official Receiver, may destroy or otherwise dispose of the books, papers and other records of the bankrupt's estate if authorised to do so by the Official Receiver during his tenure of office or on vacating office. Where the Official Receiver is acting as trustee he may dispose of records at any time.

Production and inspection of records [224]

13.133   The trustee must submit his financial records to the creditors' committee, when required. If the committee is not satisfied with their content it may so inform the Department, giving the reasons for dissatisfaction, and request the Department to cause any account sent to the Department to be audited.

13.134   The trustee is obliged to produce to the Department on demand, and allow it to inspect, any accounts, books and other records kept by him and such production and inspection may be required at the trustee's premises. The demand may be made when any account or certificate of no receipts or payments is sent to the Department or at any time afterwards and whether or not the Department requires any account to be audited. When the purpose of the production and inspection is to ascertain whether the trustee has complied with the Insolvency Regulations relating to handling of moneys received by him it may be made at any time.

Transitional provisions

13.135   Certain provisions of the Insolvency Reguoations relating to accounta apply retrospectively to bankruptcies which commenced before 1st October 1991.[225]

13.136   The following Regulations so apply where any application is made under them-

(a)   Regulation 5(1),(2),(4) and (12) (payment out of the Insolvency Account and certification of balance [226]);

(b)   Regulation 6 (local bank account [227]).

13.137   Regulation 13 governing the submission of accounts to the Department and the audit of accounts applies to any account required to be sent to the Department, except an account due to be sent to it under the Bankruptcy Acts before 1st October 1991 or for a period which includes that day, or an account by the Official Assignee under the 1980 Order. [228]

Footnotes

(1)   Administration of the estate (including powers of trustee) is dealt with in Ch.14.

(2)   Paras.13.004/006.

(3)   Art.265(1).

(4)   Art.278(4).

(5)   *Ibid.*

(6)   Para.9.10.

(7)   Art.270(1),(2).

(8)   Art.269(1),(2).

(9)   Para.13.02.

(10)   Paras.13.031/032.

(11)   Para. 13.079. See paras.13.080/082 re replacement of Official Receiver as trustee.

(12)   Cf.Art.116(2) re Official Receiver as liquidator on the making of a winding-up order.

(13)   Art.265(2): Ch.4.

(14)   Art.349(3): para.4.12.

(15)   Para.4.13.

(16)   Art.265(3).

(17)   *Ibid.*

(18)   Art.265(4): para.13.027.

(19)   Para.13.038.

(20)   Art.265(4),(5): RR.6.117(2),(3), 6.118(2),(4).

(21)   R.6.121(1).

(22)   Arts.269(4), 270(6).

(23)   Para.15.10.

(24)   Arts.269(5), 270(7).

(25)   R.6.121(2),(3).

(26)   Art.345.

(27)   R.6.120.

(28)   Para.13.036.

(29)   Arts.266(1), 270(5): R.6.077(7).

(30)   Arts.266(1): paras. 13.017/019.

(31)   Art.267(1),(2).

(32)   R.6.081(1),(2): F.6.37. A creditor may inspect the file of proceedings to ascertain this information or it may be obtained from the Official Receiver.

(33)   Art.267(2).

(34)   R.6.085(2). A resolution at the meeting may provide for the expenses to be paid out of the estate - para.16-38.

(35)   Arts.266(2), 267(3).

(36)   Art.266(3).

(37)   R.6.077(6).

(38)   R.6.077(1).

(39) *Ibid*.
(40) RR.6.077(2),(3), 6.082(1).
(41) R.6.077(4).
(42) R.6.082(3): F.6.39.
(43) R.6.077(5).
(44) R.6.077(6).
(45) *Ibid*.
(46) Para.15.10.
(47) Paras.13.085/087.
(48) R.6.078(1).
(49) R.6.078(2).
(50) Chs.16, 17.
(51) R.6.086(3).
(52) R.6.086(2).
(53) R.6.117(2): FF.6.43, 6.44.
(54) Art.265(5): R.6.117(2).
(55) Art.265(4): R.6.117(3).
(56) R.6.117(4).
(57) R.6.117(5).
(58) Art.268(1).
(59) Art.268(2).
(60) Art.268(3).
(61) Art.268(4).
(62) Para.13.082.
(63) Art.269(1),(2).
(64) Art.269(3).
(65) R.6.119.
(66) Art.270(2).
(67) Para.13.030.
(68) Art.273(5).
(69) Paras.7.144/148.
(70) Art.270(3).
(71) Art.270(4).
(72) FF.6.45, 6.46.
(73) Art.265(5): R.6.118(2).
(74) R.6.118(3).
(75) R.6.118(4).
(76) R.6.140(1)-(4).
(77) R.6.140(5).
(78) Art.272(3)(a): para.13.102.
(79) Art.271(6).
(80) R.6.123(4),(5).
(81) R.6.123(1).
(82) *Ibid:* F.6.38.
(83) R.6.123(2).
(84) R.6.123(3).
(85) Para.16.16.

(86)   R.6.123(6).
(87)   R.6.124(1),(2),(3).
(88)   R.6.123(7).
(89)   R.6.124(4).
(90)   R.6.131.
(91)   Art.271(6): R.6.124(5),(6): F.6.47.
(92)   R.6.124(7).
(93)   R.6.124(8).
(94)   R.6.125(1).
(95)   F.6.48.
(96)   R.6.125(2).
(97)   R.6.125(3).
(98)   Art.271(6): F.6.49.
(99)   R.6.125(4).
(100)   Art.271(4).
(101)   Art.271(1). See *Re Keypak Homecare Ltd.* [1987] BCLC 409 where the court removed a liquidator in a company voluntary winding up for failure to carry out his duties with sufficient vigour, particularly in relation to investigation of disposals of stock by the company.
(102)   Art.271(1): R.6.129(1).
(103)   R.6.129(2),(3).
(104)   R.6.129(4).
(105)   R.6.129(5).
(106)   R.6.129(6).
(107)   *Ibid.*
(108)   *Ibid:* paras.13.037/038.
(109)   Art.271(2).
(110)   Para.13.016.
(111)   Para.13.032.
(112)   Art.271(3).
(113)   F.6.38.
(114)   R.6.126(1): para. 13.104.
(115)   R.6.126(2).
(116)   R.6.126(3).
(117)   *Ibid.*
(118)   R.6.126(4).
(119)   R.6.126(5): F.6.50.
(120)   R.6.126(6).
(121)   R.6.127. Thus, a direction may be given that the trustee or his nominee do not act as chairman - MH 3-190.
(122)   R.6.128(1),(4): F.6.50.
(123)   R.6.128(2).
(124)   R.6.128(3).
(125)   Art.271(4).
(126)   R.6.130(1).
(127)   R.6.130(2).
(128)   RR.6.129(6), 6.130(3).

(129) Para.13.058.
(130) Art.271(3).
(131) Paras.13.011/012.
(132) R.6.131: para.13.104.
(133) Art.271(5).
(134) F.6.54.
(135) R.6.141(1),(2),(3).
(136) Para.14.113.
(137) Art.271(7).
(138) Art.271(8): Ch.22.
(139) R.6.142(1).
(140) R.6.142(2).
(141) R.6.142(3).
(142) R.6.143(1): Ins Regs 16: para.13.132.
(143) R.6.143(2).
(144) Art.271(1),(2),(7).
(145) Art.279(1).
(146) Art.273(5),(6). A further reference to the Department may be made later
 - Art.273(7).
(147) Art.273(3).
(148) Art.273(4),(6).
(149) Art.273(7).
(150) Para.14.113.
(151) Art.272(2): para.13.097.
(152) Art.273(8).
(153) Ins Regs 22/24.
(154) R.6.135(3).
(155) RR.6.135(5), 6.079(1).
(156) Para.15.022.
(157) R.6.135(2). Assets realised by a mortgage are included, but not assets
 realised by the Official Receiver or sums paid into the estate by third
 parties - MH 7-336.
(158) R.6.135(4).
(159) R.6.135(6).
(160) R.7.30(7). See paras. 13.092/094 re increase or reduction of remuneration
 by the Court.
(161) R.6.136(1).
(162) R.6.136(2).
(163) R.6.136(3).
(164) RR.6.137, 6.079(1).
(165) R.6.138(1).
(166) R.6.138(2).
(167) R.6.138(3).
(168) R.6.138(4).
(169) R.6.139(1).
(170) R.6.139(2),(3),(4).
(171) R.6.139(5).

(172) R.6.139(6).
(173) R.7.31.
(174) R.6.145.
(175) Art.272(5).
(176) Arts.272(6), 277(4): paras.14.007/008.
(177) Art.272(2).
(178) R.6.133(1),(2).
(179) R.6.133(3).
(180) Art.271(7): para.14.117.
(181) F.6.53.
(182) R.6.134(4).
(183) *Ibid.*
(184) Art.272(3)(d): R.6.134(6).
(185) R.6.132(4),(5) as applied by R.6.134(6).
(186) R.6.132(5).
(187) Art.272(1).
(188) *Ibid.*
(189) Art.272(3)(a): R.6.140(5): para.13.040.
(190) Art.272(3)(c): RR.6.124(8), 6.132(1).
(191) R.6.132(2): F.6.50.
(192) R.6.128(1).
(193) Art.272(3)(b): R.6.132(3): F.6.52.
(194) R.6.132(4),(5).
(195) R.6.132(5).
(196) Art.272(3)(b): R.6.132.
(197) RR.6.141(4), 6.132(5).
(198) R.6.131.
(199) Art.272(4).
(200) Para.13.118.
(201) Art.358: Ins Regs 4.
(202) Ins Regs 7.
(203) Ins Regs 5.
(204) *Ibid.*
(205) Ins Regs 12.
(206) Ins Regs 21.
(207) Ins Regs 19.
(208) Art.358(5).
(209) Ins Regs 20(1): Atkin Forms 364, 365.
(210) Ins Regs 20(2).
(211) Ins Regs 6.
(212) See *Re PX Nuclear Ltd.* (1986) 8 NIJB 39, decided under previous law.
(213) Ins Regs 9(2), 13(2).
(214) Ins Regs 10.
(215) Ins Regs 13.
(216) *Ibid.*
(217) Ins Regs 15.
(218) Para.4.16.

(219) Ins Regs 8: R.6.159(5).
(220) Ins Regs 9, 10.
(221) Ins Regs 11(1). Records required to be kept under the Ins Pract Regs must be preserved for longer - see para.4.18.
(222) Ins Regs 11(2).
(223) Ins Regs 16.
(224) Ins Regs 9,14: R.6.149(5).
(225) Ins Regs 52.
(226) Paras.13.111/113.
(227) Paras.13.118/120.
(228) Paras.13.122/126.

Chapter 14

ADMINISTRATION OF BANKRUPT'S ESTATE

INTRODUCTION

14.001 The function of the trustee (whether a person so appointed or the Official Receiver when he is the trustee) is to get in, realise and distribute the bankrupt's estate.[1] For this purpose he is entitled to the assistance of the bankrupt and the Official Receiver, where the Official Receiver is not himself the trustee.[2]

I. CONTROL OF TRUSTEE

14.002 In the carrying out of this function and in the management of the bankrupt's estate the trustee must comply with the provisions of the Order, but subject to that he uses his own discretion in doing so.[3] Whilst he is entitled to apply to the Court for directions in relation to any particular matter,[4] he should only do so in a case of genuine difficulty. The Court will not relieve him of his statutory obligations and is not obliged to give directions.[5]

14.003 The trustee may only act within the restraints of his powers and duties as laid down in the Order, and the Rules and Regulations made thereunder and he is subject to control by the Court, the creditors and the Department. As an officer of the Court he must act as is just and right and he will not be permitted to take advantage of a mistake.[6]

14.004 The Court exercises general control of the bankruptcy.[7] The bankrupt, any creditor or any other person dissatisfied by any act, omission or decision of the trustee may apply to the Court and on such an application the Court may confirm, reverse or modify any such act or decision and may give the trustee directions or make such other order as it thinks fit.[8] Transactions by the trustee with associates of his may be set aside by the Court and the trustee ordered to compensate the estate for any loss.[9]

14.005 Certain powers of the trustee can only be exercised with the permission of the Court or the creditors' committee and the exercise of certain other powers must be notified to the committee.[10] The trustee must also submit financial records and periodic progress reports to the committee and comply with reasonable requests by the committee for information[11] and may be required to summon a general meeting of creditors.[12] The creditors are thus afforded opportunities to monitor the trustee's actions and obtain information so that, if dissatisfied, they may apply to the Court for directions or, if appropriate, to have the trustee made liable for the consequences of a breach of duty.[13]

14.006 The Department has numerous specific functions in relation to the trustee's funds and accounts, the distribution of the bankrupt's estate and the release of the trustee. In addition, it exercises most of the functions of the creditors' committee where the Official Receiver is the trustee and in other cases at any time when there is no creditors' committee.[14]

II. LIABILITY OF TRUSTEE

14.007 Where the trustee has misapplied or retained, or become accountable for, any money or other property comprised in the bankrupt's estate, or where the estate has suffered any loss in consequence of any misfeasance or breach of fiduciary or other duty by the trustee in the carrying out of his functions, the Court may order him to repay, restore or account for such money or other property, with interest, or to pay compensation for such consequences, without prejudice to any other liability.[15]

14.008 The application for such an order may be made by the Official Receiver, the Department or a creditor, but if made after the trustee has been released the prior leave of the Court is required.[16] The bankrupt may also apply, but only with leave of the Court, whether or not there is likely to be a surplus from the administration of the estate which he would be entitled to receive.[17]

14.009 If the trustee enters into any transaction with a person who is an associate of his,[18] the Court may, without prejudice to any other remedy, on the application of any person interested, set the transaction aside and order the trustee to compensate the estate for any loss suffered in consequence of it, unless;
   (a) the transaction was entered into with the prior consent of the Court, or
   (b) it is shown to the Court's satisfaction that the transaction was for value, and that it was entered into by the trustee without knowing, or having any reason to suppose, that the person concerned was an associate.[19]

14.010 The trustee is protected from liability for the seizure or disposal of property not comprised in the bankrupt's estate if at the time of seizure or disposal he believes, on reasonable grounds, that he is entitled to do so, except in respect of any loss or damage caused by his negligence, and he has a lien on such property, or the proceeds of its sale, for expenses incurred in connection with the seizure or disposal.[20]

14.011 The trustee is also protected against any action for refusal or neglect to pay a dividend, but he may be ordered to pay it and also to pay out of his own money, interest on the unpaid dividend and costs.[21]

III. POWERS OF TRUSTEE

14.012 The general powers of the trustee are set out in Article 287 and Schedule 3. These fall into three categories.

(a) Ancillary powers
14.013   In the exercise of his powers the trustee may, by his official name -
(i)   hold property of every description,
(ii)   make contracts,
(iii) sue and be sued,
(iv)   enter into engagements binding on himself and, in respect of the bankrupt's estate, on his successors in office,
(v)   employ an agent,
(vi)   execute any power of attorney, deed or other instrument; and he may do any other act which is necessary or expedient for the purposes of or in connection with the exercise of those powers. [22]

14.014   Where the trustee (not being the Official Receiver), in the exercise of his power to appoint an agent, appoints a solicitor, he must give notice of the appointment to the creditors' committee, if there is one. [23]

(b) Powers exercisable without sanction
14.015   The general powers which the trustee may exercise without requiring permission of the Court or the creditors' committee include power to sell any part of the bankrupt's estate (and, in the case of leaseholds or lands held in fee farm, to do so by sub-lease or sub-fee farm grant, where appropriate). [24] He may also, without sanction, at any time summon a general meeting of the bankrupt's creditors to ascertain their wishes in all matters relating to the bankruptcy. [25]

14.016   Where there is a creditors' committee, the trustee is required to notify it where he disposes of any part of the bankrupt's estate to an associate of the bankrupt. [26] It would appear that the notification of the exercise of this power (and of the employment of a solicitor) [27] must either precede the exercise of the power or be contemporaneous with it, so that the committee will have an early opportunity of challenging the trustee's action by applying to the Court. [28]

(c) Powers exercisable with sanction
14.017   The powers specified in Article 287(2) and Part I of Schedule 3 may only be exercised with the permission of the Court or of the committee of creditors (or the Department when exercising the functions of such committee). However, a person dealing with the trustee need not enquire whether any permission so required has been given. [29]
14.018   The powers exercisable with such permission include -
(i)   to appoint the bankrupt to superintend the management of his estate or any part of it, to carry on his business for the benefit of his creditors or in any other respect to assist in the administration of the estate under the directions of the trustee,
(ii)   to carry on any business [30] of the bankrupt (other than any business

by statute requiring specific qualifications), but only so far as necessary for winding it up beneficially.
(iii) to commence or defend any action or legal proceedings relating to the bankrupt's estate,[31]
(iv) to compromise claims by the bankrupt, or claims by creditors or others.

14.019   Neither the Court nor the creditors' committee may give the trustee general permission to exercise powers which require such sanction; each particular proposed exercise of the power must be sanctioned.[32] However, where the trustee acts without obtaining the necessary prior sanction, the Court or the creditors' committee may ratify his action, but only for the purpose of enabling him to meet his expenses out of the bankrupt's estate, and the committee may not give such ratification unless it is satisfied that the trustee has acted in a case of urgency and has sought its ratification without undue delay.[33] If these factors are not present, he can only obtain ratification from the Court.

IV. SPECIAL MANAGER

14.020   The trustee may apply to the Court for the appointment of a special manager of the bankrupt's estate or business in any case where it appears to him that the nature of the estate or business, or the interests of the creditors generally, require the appointment of another person to manage the estate or business. [34] The procedure relating to such an application and subsequent proceedings are similar to those in respect of an application by the Official Receiver whilst acting as receiver.[35] A special manager so appointed has such powers as may be entrusted to him by the Court and the Court may direct that any provision of the Order that has effect in relation to the trustee shall have like effect in relation to the special manager for the purposes of the carrying out by him of any of the functions of the trustee. [36] The acts of a special manager are valid notwithstanding any defect in his appointment or qualifications.[37]

V. ACQUISITION OF CONTROL OF ESTATE BY TRUSTEE

14.021   The trustee must take possession of all books, papers and other records relating to the bankrupt's estate or affairs belonging to the bankrupt or in his possession or under his control (including documents privileged from disclosure in any proceedings and documents held by any person subject to a lien, except documents of title held as security).[38]

14.022   To enable the trustee to require the delivery up to him of possession of the bankrupt's estate the following obligations, enforceable by contempt of court proceedings, are imposed on the bankrupt and others -
(a) the bankrupt must hand over to the trustee any property, books, papers or other records in his possession or under his control and of which the trustee is required to take possession,
(b) the Official Receiver, a person who has ceased to be trustee or a person who has been the supervisor of an approved voluntary arrangement

tary arrangement in relation to the bankrupt must hand over to the
trustee any such property, etc. in his possession,

(c) any banker or other agent of the bankrupt or any other person who
holds any property to the account of, or for, the bankrupt is required
to pay or deliver to the trustee all property in his possession or under
his control which forms part of the bankrupt's estate and which he is
not legally entitled to retain as against the bankrupt or the trustee. [39]

14.023 Where the bankrupt's estate vests in the trustee following a period
when the Official Receiver is receiver and manager of the estate under Article
260 or where the trustee is appointed in succession to the Official Receiver
acting as trustee, the Official Receiver is under a general obligation to do all that
is required for putting the trustee into possession of the bankrupt's estate,
subject to the trustee discharging or undertaking to discharge, any balance due
to the Official Receiver on account of expenses incurred by him and any
advances made by him in respect of the estate, with interest, for which balance
he has a charge on the estate. [40]

14.024 For the purposes of acquiring or retaining possession of the bankrupt's
estate the trustee is in the position of a receiver of property appointed by the
High Court and the Court may, on his application, enforce such acquisition or
retention. [41] He has the same power to transfer stocks and shares, etc. as the
bankrupt might have exercised if he had not become bankrupt. [42] Things in
action are deemed to have been assigned to the trustee and no notice of the
assignment is required, except where necessary for protecting his priority. [43]

14.025 Where the trustee cannot obtain possession of personal property voluntarily, the Court may, on his application, issue a warrant of seizure, as on the
application of the Official Receiver as receiver. [44] He may also apply to the
Court for a search warrant in the same circumstances as the Official Receiver.
[45]

14.026 To protect his title to any land of the bankrupt the trustee should verify
that the Official Receiver has registered the bankruptcy order in the Registry of
Deeds [46] and if at any time he ascertains that the bankrupt is the registered
owner of land he should notify the Registrar of Titles, if the Official Receiver
has not already done so, so that a bankruptcy inhibition may be entered against
the title of the registered owner. [47]

14.027 If the bankrupt fails to give up possession of land (other than his home,
for which special provisions are made by the Order [48]), the trustee may apply
to the Court, on notice to the bankrupt, for an order for possession. [49]

VI. INFORMATION AS TO BANKRUPT'S AFFAIRS

14.028 The primary responsibility for investigating the bankrupt's conduct
and affairs rests with the Official Receiver [50] and the trustee must give him

whatever assistance he reasonably requires for this purpose.[51] However, in order to carry out his duty to get in and distribute the bankrupt's estate the trustee must investigate the bankrupt's affairs to determine the admissible debts, to ascertain the location of any property remaining in the possession of the bankrupt or under his control, to identify any rights of action he may have against third parties and to be in a position to consider whether any gifts, payments to creditors or other disposals of assets by the bankrupt may be challenged under any provision of the Order relating to prior transactions, with a view to enhancement of the assets available for the benefit of the creditors. [52]

14.029　The trustee should invite creditors to bring to his notice any particular matters they consider require investigation and he should report the result of his inquiries to the creditors' committee, if there is one. He should also inform the committee if he is unable to pursue desirable investigations on account of lack of funds. Whilst it is not his responsibility to seek out offences by the bankrupt or others, if his investigations disclose possible offences he should pass on the information obtained to the Official Receiver.

14.030　The bankrupt must give the trustee such information as to his affairs, attend on him at such times and do all such other things as the trustee may reasonably require for the purposes of carrying out his functions.[53] Failure to do so, or to comply with any directions of the Court, without reasonable excuse, is a contempt of court.[54] These obligations continue after the bankrupt's discharge. [55]

14.031　If the trustee considers that there are grounds for having the bankrupt arrested and his records, money or goods seized under Article 335, he may apply to the Court for the issue of a warrant of arrest.[56]

14.032　The Official Receiver is required to give the trustee all such information relating to the bankrupt's affairs and the course of the bankruptcy as the Official Receiver considers to be reasonably required for the effective discharge by the trustee of his duties in relation to the estate and must send him a copy of any report which he has sent to creditors.[57]

14.033　The trustee may obtain further assistance in his investigations by examining the bankrupt at any public examination which may be ordered[58] or he may himself apply to the Court for a private examination of the bankrupt and others.[59] For the purposes of either of these examinations he may apply to the Court for an order for disclosure of documents by the Inland Revenue.[60] He may also apply to the Court for an order for the re-direction of the bankrupt's mail for a specified period.[61]

VII. SUPPLIES OF ELECTRICITY, WATER, ETC.

14.034　If the trustee requests the supply of electricity, water, telephone or other public telecommunication services (other than cable programme services) for the purpose of any business which is or has been carried on by or on behalf of the bankrupt or a firm or partnership of which the bankrupt is or was a member, the supplier may make it a condition of giving it that the trustee personally guarantees payment of any charges thereafter incurred, but is not permitted to require, as a condition of the giving of the supply, that any charges incurred before the making of the bankruptcy order be paid.[62]

VIII. BANKRUPT'S HOME [63]

14.035 Where an interest in a dwelling house is comprised in the bankrupt's estate, the realisation of such interest - often the most valuable asset of the estate - is subject to restrictions introduced by the Order, which give limited rights of occupation to the bankrupt's spouse and, in certain circumstances, to the bankrupt himself, which may delay, but will not prevent, such realisation. These is also provision in the Order designed to avoid the completion of the practical administration of the bankrupt's estate and the release of the trustee being indefinitely postponed by reason only of the fact that the bankrupt's home cannot be sold within a reasonable time.

14.036 A "dwelling house" is defined in Article 9(1) as including any building or part of a building which is occupied as a dwelling and any yard, garden, garage or outhouse belonging to the dwelling house and occupied with it.

(a) Restrictions on realisation
(i) Rights of bankrupt's spouse
14.037 Where the bankrupt has a beneficial interest in a dwelling house any charge on it acquired by his or her spouse by reason of registration of rights of occupation under the Family Law (Miscellaneous Provisions) (Northern Ireland) Order 1984 ("the 1984 Order") continues to subsist after the bankruptcy and binds the trustee and his successors in title.[64] This reverses the former position under Article 5(7) of the 1984 Order, repealed by Schedule 10 to the Insolvency Order. However, no such rights of occupation may be acquired by the spouse between the presentation of the petition and the vesting of the bankrupt's estate in the trustee.[65]

14.038 Where such registered rights are enjoyed by a spouse, the 1984 Order prevents the spouse being evicted or excluded from the dwelling house without an order of the Court.[66] Where the rights are against the bankrupt's estate any application for such an order must be made to the Bankruptcy Court.[67]

14.039 Where the bankrupt and his spouse or former spouse own the dwelling house jointly or as tenants in common it can only be sold by the trustee, in the absence of agreement with the bankrupt and such spouse or former spouse, by an order for sale in lieu of partition under the Partition Act 1868. An application by the trustee for such an order must be made to the Bankruptcy Court which, subject as mentioned in the next paragraph, may make such order as it thinks fit and is not restricted by the narrow discretion given by the Partition Act. [68]

14.040   On an application to the Bankruptcy Court for an order under Article 4 of the 1984 Order or under the Partition Act 1868 the Court must make such order as it thinks just and reasonable having regard to -
   (A)   the interests of the bankrupt's creditors,
   (B)   the conduct of the spouse or former spouse, so far as contributing to the bankruptcy,
   (C)   the needs and financial resources of the spouse or former spouse,
   (D)   the needs of any children, and
   (E)   all the circumstances of the case other than the needs of the bankrupt.[69]
On such an application an alternative claim for a charge on the home under Article 286 may be made. [70]

14.041   These restraints on the realisation of the bankrupt's dwelling house are materially reduced by the provision that, where the trustee's application to the Court is not made until after one year from the first vesting of the bankrupt's estate in a trustee, the Court is to assume, unless the circumstances of the case are exceptional, that the interests of the bankrupt's creditors outweigh all other considerations.[71] It is anticipated that it will be difficult for a spouse or former spouse to establish "exceptional circumstances" and, therefore, that the trustee's application after the expiration of the one year period will usually be successful.[72] The knowledge of the difficulty of defending such an application will greatly strengthen the hand of the trustee in negotiating with the bankrupt's spouse or former spouse with a view either to the purchase by such person of the bankrupt's interest in the dwelling house or the vacation of the house to enable it to be sold. In the meantime the trustee can make an arrangement with the bankrupt that the bankrupt and his family can remain in occupation of the dwelling house on condition of making payments under a mortgage or of paying other outgoings on the premises, without thereby risking the acquisition by the bankrupt of any interest in the premises. [73]

(ii) Rights of bankrupt
14.042   Where the bankrupt has a beneficial interest in a dwelling house and a person under the age of 18 with whom he had at some time occupied it had his home with the bankrupt at the time the petition was presented and when the bankruptcy order was made, the bankrupt is given certain rights of occupation in the house.[74] These rights apply whether or not the bankrupt's spouse (if any) has rights of occupation under the 1984 Order [75] and extend to the protection of the interests of minor children living with a single, divorced or separated bankrupt. The necessary qualification of having a home with the bankrupt must be satisfied both at the date of the petition and at the date of the bankruptcy order.

14.043   In such circumstances the bankrupt has the right against the trustee, if in occupation of the dwelling house, not to be evicted or excluded except with the leave of the Court and, if not in occupation, a right with the leave of the Court to enter and occupy it. [76]

14.044 The bankrupt's rights are a charge on the interest in the dwelling house vested in the trustee, having the like priority as an equitable interest created immediately before the making of the bankruptcy order. [77] Such rights should be protected by registrations in the Registry of Deeds or the Land Registry, as appropriate. [78]

14.045 The 1984 Order is applied to such rights of occupation of the bankrupt as if they were rights of occupation under that Order and as if the charge on the interest of the trustee were a charge on the interest of the spouse. [79] An application by the trustee to evict or exclude the bankrupt from the dwelling house or by the bankrupt to enter and occupy it is treated as an application under Article 4 of the 1984 Order and must be made to the Bankruptcy Court. [80]

14.046 On such an application the Court must make such order as it thinks just and reasonable having regard to the interests of the creditors, to the bankrupt's financial resources, to the needs of the children and to all the circumstances of the case other than the needs of the bankrupt. [81] The trustee may join in such an application an alternative claim for a charge on the home under Article 286. [82]

14.047 As in the case of an application by the trustee against the bankrupt's spouse, if it is made after the expiration of one year from the first vesting of the bankrupt's estate in a trustee the Court must assume, unless the circumstances of the case are exceptional, that the interests of the bankrupt's creditors outweigh all other considerations. [83] The observations made above [84] with regard to the operation of the similar provision in respect of a spouse's rights of occupation apply equally to this provision. Again, where the bankrupt remains in occupation of the dwelling house on condition that he makes payments towards satisfying any liability under a mortgage or pays other outgoings, the bankrupt does not, by virtue of those payments, acquire any interest in the premises. [85]

(b) Creation of charge
14.048 A provision has been included in the Order to enable the trustee to vacate his office and obtain a release when he has completed the administration of the bankrupt's estate except for the realisation of the bankrupt's home and where early realisation cannot be anticipated. Where a dwelling house is occupied by the bankrupt or by his or her spouse or former spouse and the trustee is, for any reason, unable for the time being to realise the interest in it comprised in the estate, the Court may, on the application of the trustee, impose a charge on the property. [86] The benefit of the charge is comprised in the bankrupt's estate and is enforceable, up to the value from time to time of the property secured, for the payment of any amount payable otherwise than to the bankrupt out of the estate and of interest at the judgment debt interest rate prevailing on the day the charge is imposed. [87] The charge has the like effect and is enforceable in the same courts and in the same manner as an equitable

charge created by the bankrupt by writing under his hand. [88] The application is by ordinary application [89] and may be made either as a sole claim or as alternative relief in an application for possession and/or sale. The bankrupt's spouse or former spouse must be made respondent and the Court may direct other persons to be made respondents also, in respect of any interest which they may have in the property. [90] Directions as to any such additional respondents should be sought when requesting a venue for the hearing.

14.049   The application must be supported by a report from the trustee stating the extent of the bankrupt's interest in the property and the amount remaining owing to unsecured creditors at the date of the application. [91]

14.050   The order of charge may be made absolutely or subject to conditions as to notifying the bankrupt or any person holding any interest in the property or as to the time when the charge is to become enforceable, or as to other matters. [92]

14.051   The trustee should endeavour to reach agreement with the bankrupt as to the terms of the charge. If not so agreed, the terms are settled by the Court. [93]

14.052   The order must -
   (i)   describe the property to be charged, state whether the title is registered and if so, specify the folio number;
   (ii)   set out the extent of the bankrupt's interest in the property which has vested in the trustee;
   (iii) indicate how the amount of the charge to be imposed is to be ascertained and state the rate of interest;
   (iv) set out any conditions imposed by the Court;
   (v)   provide that the property charged is to cease to be comprised in the bankrupt's estate and, subject to the charge (and any prior charge) to vest in the bankrupt, and identify when this is to occur. [94]

14.053   The date under (v) is to be the date of registration of the order of charge in the Registry of Deeds or the Land Registry, as the case may be. [95]

14.054   To secure the registration of the order of charge in the appropriate registry the trustee must, forthwith after the order of charge is made, send 2 sealed copies (one of which is required to be certified by the Master) to the Registrar of Deeds, in the case of unregistered land, or a sealed and certified copy to the Registrar of Titles, in the case of registered land. [96]

14.055   The Court may at any time, on the application of the bankrupt or of any person holding any interest in the property to which the charging order relates, make an order discharging or varying it and, if the order is discharged, directing the vacation of the entry in the Registry of Deeds or the Land Registry in respect of it. [97] When an order of discharge or variation is made and the

Court orders the vacation or amendment of any such entry the trustee must send 2 sealed copies (one of which must be certified by the Master) to the Registrar of Deeds if the order of charge has been registered in the Registry of Deeds, or send a sealed and certified copy to the Registrar of Titles if the order of charge has been registered in the Land Registry. [98]

IX. DISCLAIMER OF ONEROUS PROPERTY [99]

(a) Introduction

14.056 Where the bankrupt's estate vested in the trustee includes any contract or property which may give rise to a liability or other property which cannot be profitably disposed of, he may seek to avoid or diminish any potential loss to the creditors by disclaiming the contract or property. As mentioned in the next paragraph, the opportunity for disclaimer of onerous property has been considerably widened by the Order and the abolition of the doctrine of election in relation to land held under a lease or fee farm grant [100] will increase the instances where disclaimer of such land will require to be considered by the trustee.

(b) Property which may be disclaimed

14.057 The categories of property which may be disclaimed by the trustee have been significantly enlarged by the Order. "Onerous property" capable of being disclaimed is defined in Article 288 (2) of the Order as -
  (i)   any unprofitable contract, and
  (ii) any other property comprised in the bankrupt's estate which is unsaleable or not readily saleable, or is such that it may give rise to a liability to pay money or perform any other onerous act.

14.058 Thus, it is no longer necessary, as it was under section 97 of the 1872 Act, that land to be disclaimed must be "burdened with onerous covenants" or that other property must be unsaleable, or not readily saleable "by reason of its binding the possessor thereof to the performance of any onerous act, or to the payment of any sum of money". [101] Now the requirement of liability to pay money or to perform any other onerous act is no longer linked to unsalability but is a separate ground for disclaiming property.

14.059 The trustee may, as under the 1872 Act, disclaim any "onerous property" notwithstanding that he has taken possession of it, endeavoured to sell it or otherwise exercised rights of ownership in relation to it. [102]

(c) Effect of disclaimer

14.060 The effect of a disclaimer is to determine, as from the date of the disclaimer, [103] the rights, interests and liabilities of the bankrupt and his estate in or in respect of the property disclaimed, and to discharge the trustee from all personal liability in respect of that property as from the commencement of the trusteeship. [104] However, it does not affect the rights or liabilities of any other person, except so far as is necessary to release the bankrupt, the bankrupt's estate and the trustee from any liability.[105]

(d) Compensation of persons affected by disclaimer

14.061 Any person sustaining loss or damage in consequence of the operation of a disclaimer is deemed to be a creditor of the bankrupt to the extent of the loss or damage and accordingly may prove for the loss or damage as a bankruptcy debt.[106] Where the Court makes a vesting or delivery order in respect of disclaimed property [107] the effect of such an order is to be taken into account in assessing the extent of any such loss or damage. [108]

(e) Time for disclaimer

14.062 There is no time limit on the exercise of the trustee's right of disclaimer of onerous property except where a person interested in the property gives notice in writing requiring him to decide whether he will disclaim or not. [109]

(f) Mode of disclaimer

14.063 The disclaimer is effected by notice from the trustee. [110] Such notice may be given without leave of the Court except in respect of after-acquired property claimed for the estate or personal property of the bankrupt which would be excluded from his estate were it not that its value exceeds the amount of a reasonable replacement and which for that reason is claimed for the estate. [111] It is no longer necessary, as it was under the Bankruptcy Rules, for leave of the Court to be obtained in all cases where the property sought to be disclaimed is land.

14.064 There is a prescribed form of notice of disclaimer [112] which must contain such particulars of the property disclaimed as enable it to be easily identified.[113] It must be signed by the trustee and filed in the Court together with a copy.[114] The Court seals the notice and copy and endorses the date of filing on both.[115] This is the date from which the disclaimer operates. [116] The copy notice is returned by the Court to the trustee or his agent or, if it was sent to the Court by post, the Court sends the copy to the trustee by first class post. [117] The manner in which the copy notice was returned to the trustee must be endorsed on the original notice or otherwise recorded on the Court file. [118]

(g) Notice of disclaimer

14.065 Within 7 days of receiving the copy notice of disclaimer from the Court the trustee must send copies of the notice, showing the date of filing endorsed, to the following persons, if known to him -
  (i)   where the disclaimed property is leasehold or is held under a fee farm grant, to every person claiming under the bankrupt as underlessee or mortgagee,
  (ii) where the disclaimed property is a dwelling house, to every person to his knowledge in occupation or claiming a right to occupy it, or to the parent or guardian of any such person under the age of 18,

(iii) where the disclaimer is of an unprofitable contract, to all parties to the contract and any other persons having interests under it,

(iv) every other person claiming an interest in the disclaimed property or who is under a liability in respect of it which is not discharged by the disclaimer. [119]

The trustee may also at any time give notice of the disclaimer to any person who in his opinion ought, in the public interest or otherwise, to be informed of it. [120]

14.066 To assist the trustee in ascertaining to whom such notices should be sent the Rules provide that he may give notice to any person who, it appears to him, claims or may claim an interest in the property proposed to be disclaimed, calling upon such person to declare within 14 days whether he claims any such interest and, if so, the nature and extent of it. [121] Failing compliance with such a notice the trustee is entitled to assume that the person concerned has no such interest in the property that will prevent or impede its disclaimer. [122] If the trustee subsequently discovers that he has not sent a copy of the notice of a disclaimer to some person who would have been entitled to receive it, he must forthwith send him one, unless he is satisfied that such person is already aware of the disclaimer and of its date or he applies to the Court and obtains an order dispensing with such a requirement. [123]

14.067 The trustee must notify the Court as to the persons to whom he has sent copies of the notice of disclaimer, giving their names and addresses, and the nature of their respective interests. [124]

(h) Notice requiring trustee's decision
14.068 A person interested in property of a bankrupt who considers that the trustee may decide to disclaim it may wish to know whether he is going to do so or not, particularly if some time has elapsed since the bankruptcy order without a notice of disclaimer being issued. Such a person may force a decision by the trustee by serving on him personally or by registered post a notice to elect, requiring him to decide within 28 days of receiving the notice whether he will disclaim the property and to notify his decision accordingly. [125] If the trustee fails to give notice of disclaimer within that period he cannot do so thereafter and where the property in question is an unprofitable contract, the trustee is thereupon deemed to have adopted it. [126]

(i) Disclaimer of leaseholds, etc.
14.069 The disclaimer of leasehold property does not take effect unless a copy has been served on every person claiming under the bankrupt as underlessee or mortgagee of whose address he is aware and either no application is made for a vesting order in respect of the property [127] within 14 days thereafter or, where such an application has been made, the Court directs that the disclaimer is to take effect. [128] Where the Court makes such a direction it may also, instead of or in addition to a vesting order, make orders with respect to fixtures, tenant's improvements and other matters arising out of the lease. [129]

14.070 These provisions apply also to property held under a fee farm grant creating the relation of landlord and tenant and an under-lessee includes a person who holds a lease from a fee farm grantee. [130]

(j) Disclaimer of dwelling house

14.071 The disclaimer of any property in a dwelling house (defined in Article 9 (1)) does not take effect unless a copy of the disclaimer has been served on every person in occupation of or claiming a right to occupy the dwelling house, of whose address the trustee is aware, and either no application is made for a vesting order in respect of the property [131] within 14 days thereafter or, where such an application has been made, the Court directs that the disclaimer is to take effect. [132]

14.072 Any person who was in occupation of or entitled to occupy the dwelling house at the time the bankruptcy petition was filed may apply to the Court for an order vesting the property in him. [133] Thus, such an application may be made by a bankrupt's spouse who is in occupation but has no interest in the property. [134]

(k) Land subject to rent charge

14.073 Where, in consequence of a disclaimer of land subject to a rent charge, that land vests by operation of law in the Crown or any other person, the Crown or such person, and its or his successors in title, are not subject to any personal liability in respect of any sums becoming due under the rent charge, except sums becoming due after taking possession or control of the land or entering into occupation of it. [135]

(l) Leave to disclaim

14.074 In the limited circumstances in which the disclaimer requires the leave of the Court (property claimed for the estate as after-acquired or as exempt personal property of excess value)[136] the trustee may apply for such leave ex parte. [137] The application must be accompanied by a report identifying the property proposed to be disclaimed, giving reasons why, the property having been claimed for the estate, leave to disclaim is now applied for, and specifying the persons (if any) who have been informed of the trustee's intention to make the application. [138] If the report refers to any person's consent to the disclaimer having been given, a copy of that consent must be annexed.[139] The Court may either grant leave without a hearing or fix a venue for a hearing and order that notice be given to all such persons who, if the property is disclaimed, will be entitled to apply for a vesting or other order under Article 293. [140]

14.075 Where the trustee applies for leave to disclaim within 28 days from receiving a notice to elect, [141] the Court is required to extend the time allowed for giving notice of disclaimer to a date not earlier than the date fixed for hearing such application.[142]

(m) Vesting or delivery of disclaimed property

14.076 The Court may make an order on such terms as it thinks fit for the

vesting of disclaimed property in, or for its delivery to, -
(i)   a person entitled to it or a trustee for such a person,
(ii) a person subject to any liability in respect of the disclaimed property
      which is not discharged by the disclaimer, or a trustee for such a person,
      or
(iii) where the disclaimed property is property in a dwelling house, any
      person who at the time when the bankruptcy petition was presented
      was in occupation of or entitled to occupy the dwelling house. [143]
Such an order may only be made in favour of a person mentioned in (ii) above
where it appears to the Court that it would be just to do so for the purpose of
compensating the person subject to the liability in respect of the disclaimer. [144]

14.077   An application for such an order may be made by -
(i)   any person who claims an interest in the disclaimed property,
(ii) any person who is under any liability in respect of the disclaimed
      property which is not discharged by the disclaimer, or
(iii) where the disclaimed property is property in a dwelling house, any
      person who at the time when the bankruptcy petition is presented was
      in occupation of or entitled to occupy the dwelling house. [145]

14.078   The application must be made within 3 months of the applicant becoming aware of the disclaimer or of his receiving a copy of the trustee's notice of disclaimer, whichever is the earlier. [146]

14.079   The application must be supported by an affidavit stating the entitlement of the applicant to apply, the date on which he received a copy of the trustee's notice of disclaimer or otherwise became aware of the disclaimer, and specifying the grounds of the application and the order requested. [147]

14.080   When a venue for the hearing has been appointed by the Court the applicant must serve a copy of the application and supporting affidavit on the trustee at least 7 days before the hearing date. [148] On the hearing the Court may direct service of notice of the application and the grounds on which it is made on other persons. [149]

14.081   Where the effect of the disclaimer is suspended because the property is leasehold or is a dwelling house, [150] the Court's order must include a direction giving effect to the disclaimer, [151] unless at the time the order is issued other applications are pending in respect of the same property. [152]

14.082   Where the property is leasehold or held in fee farm any order vesting it in any person can only be made on terms of subjecting him to the same liabilities and obligations as the bankrupt was subject to under the lease or fee farm grant when the bankruptcy petition was presented or, if the Court thinks fit, as that person would be subject to if the lease or fee farm grant had been assigned or conveyed to him on that date. [153] A person who is unwilling to accept an order on these terms is excluded from all interest in the property [154] and in these circumstances the Court may vest the estate or interest of the bankrupt in the property in any person who is liable solely or jointly with the bankrupt to perform the lessee's or grantee's covenants, freed and discharged from all estates, incumbrances and interests created by the bankrupt. [155]

14.083 Where a vesting order is made the property vests in the person named in the order without any conveyance, assignment or transfer being required. [156]

14.084 Sealed copies of any order made on the application are sent by the Court to the applicant and the trustee. [157]

(n) Validity of disclaimer
14.085 Any disclaimer of property by the trustee is presumed valid and effective, unless it is proved that it has been given in breach of his duty to give notice or is otherwise in breach of the requirements of the Order or the Rules. [158]

X. CONTRACTS TO WHICH BANKRUPT IS A PARTY

14.086 Where a party to a contract made with a person who is subsequently adjudged bankrupt does not wish to proceed with the contract and the trustee has not disclaimed it as unprofitable, the non-bankrupt party may apply to the Court for an order discharging obligations under the contract. [159]   Such an order may be made on such terms as to payment by the applicant or the bankrupt of damages for non-performance or otherwise as appear to the Court to be equitable. [160] If the Court orders damages to be paid by the bankrupt, such damages are provable as a bankruptcy debt. [161] Where the bankrupt has entered into a contract jointly with any person, that person may sue or be sued in respect of the contract without the bankrupt having to be joined in the action. [162]

XI. ADJUSTMENT OF PRIOR TRANSACTIONS BY THE BANKRUPT

A. INTRODUCTION

14.087 The Order contains a number of provisions under which property not owned by the bankrupt at the date of the bankruptcy order may be recovered by the trustee and form part of the bankrupt's estate, or whereby liabilities incurred by the bankrupt may be reduced.

B. VOIDABLE DISPOSITIONS AFTER FILING OF BANKRUPTCY PETITION

14.088 Any payments made or property transferred by the bankrupt between the date of filing of the bankruptcy petition and the vesting of the bankrupt's estate in the trustee which is void under Article 257 form part of the bankrupt's estate and are recoverable by the trustee, except from a person who received the property or payment before the making of the bankruptcy order in good faith, for value and without notice of the petition, or a person deriving title from such person, and subject to the provisions of the Registration of Deeds Act or the Land Registration Act as to land. [163]

C. BANKRUPT'S INCOME

14.089 Where the bankrupt is in receipt of income which the trustee considers to be more than is necessary for meeting the reasonable domestic needs of the bankrupt and his family, the trustee may apply to the Court for an income payments order and any sums received by him under such an order form part of the bankrupt's estate. Such orders are dealt with in Chapter 18.

D. TRANSACTIONS AT AN UNDERVALUE [164]

14.090 Where the bankrupt has, within the relevant period prior to the filing of the bankruptcy petition, entered into a transaction with any person at an undervalue the Court may, on the application of the trustee, [165] make such order as it thinks fit to restore the position to what it would have been if the bankrupt had not entered into that transaction. [166]

14.091 A transaction is treated as having been entered into at an undervalue where the bankrupt -
  (a) makes a gift or enters into a transaction on terms under which he is to receive no consideration,
  (b) enters into a transaction in consideration of marriage, or
  (c) enters into a transaction for a consideration which is significantly less valuable than that provided by the other party. [167]

14.092 The fact that an undervalue transaction is made under a court order in a matrimonial cause (e.g. a property adjustment order) does not prevent it being adjusted under these provisions. [168]

14.093 The undervalue transaction may only be adjusted by the Court if it was entered into within 5 years of the presentation of the bankruptcy petition. [169] If the transaction was entered into less than 2 years before that date an order may be made whether or not the bankrupt was insolvent at the time of the transaction, but if it was entered into within 5 years of the presentation of the petition but more than 2 years before that date, an order can only be made if the bankrupt was insolvent at that time or became insolvent in consequence of the transaction. [170] However, where the other party to the transaction is an associate of the bankrupt, [171] otherwise than by reason only of being his employee, the trustee does not have to prove such insolvency. This is presumed unless the other party can prove the contrary. [172] For the purposes of these provisions insolvency means either that at the relevant time the bankrupt was unable to pay his debts as they fell due or that the value of his assets was less than the amount of his liabilities, taking into account his contingent and prospective liabilities.[173]

14.094 The Court's powers to adjust the undervalue transaction are set out in Article 315 and are very wide. Such an order may affect the property of or impose any obligation on not only the party with whom the bankrupt entered into the transaction but any other person. However, provision is made in Article 315(2) for the protection of bona fide purchasers.[174]

E. PREFERENCES [175]

14.095 Where the bankrupt has, within the relevant period prior to the presentation of the bankruptcy petition, given a preference to any person the Court may, on the application of the trustee [176] make such order as it thinks fit to restore the position to what it would have been if the bankrupt had not given that preference.[177]

14.096 The person preferred must at the relevant time have been a creditor or a surety or guarantor for any of the debts or other liabilities of the bankrupt. [178] The bankrupt must have done or have suffered to be done something which has the effect of putting the person preferred into a better position in the subsequent bankruptcy than he would otherwise have been, and in deciding to do so the bankrupt must have been influenced by a desire to produce that effect, although such a desire is presumed to exist, unless the contrary is shown, where the person preferred was an associate of the bankrupt,[179] otherwise than by reason only of being his employee. [180]

14.097 The fact that something has been done under an order of a court does not, without more, prevent the doing or suffering of that thing from constituting the giving of a preference[181] and, specifically, a settlement or transfer of property in compliance with a property adjustment order made under the Matrimonial Causes (Northern Ireland) Order 1978 does not prevent it being a voidable preference. [182]

14.98 The Court may only make an order in respect of the preference if it was given within certain periods preceding the presentation of the bankruptcy petition, namely -
    (a)   if it constituted a transaction at an undervalue, [183] 5 years,
    (b)   if not, but it was given to an associate of the bankrupt, [184] 2 years,
    (c)   otherwise, 6 months. [185]

14.099 Unless the preference constituted a transaction at an undervalue given within 2 years of the presentation of the bankruptcy petition (in which case an order may be made without proof of insolvency) the trustee must prove that the bankrupt was insolvent at the time he gave the preference or that he became insolvent in consequence of giving it. However, where the preference constituted a transaction at an undervalue (but not in other cases) and was given to a person who was an associate of the bankrupt, otherwise than by reason only of being his employee, such insolvency is presumed unless the contrary is shown. [186] Insolvency has the meaning stated above in relation to transactions at an undervalue. [187]

14.100 The specific orders which the Court may make are the same as in respect of transactions at an undervalue and the interests of bona fide third parties are similarly protected. [188]

F. TRANSACTIONS DEFRAUDING CREDITORS [189]

14.101 One of the former acts of bankruptcy was that the debtor had made a fraudulent conveyance, delivery or transfer of his property or any part thereof. This ground for upsetting pre-bankruptcy transactions by a bankrupt has been removed by the abolition of all acts of bankruptcy. Fraudulent transfers of land or goods could also be challenged by the assignees in bankruptcy under the former law by invoking section 10 of the Conveyancing Act (Ireland) 1634. [190] This old provision has been repealed by the Order and replaced by Articles 367-369 which contain a new code for setting aside transactions defrauding creditors and which (like the 1634 statute) is not limited to insolvency proceedings. Where the transferor is not a bankrupt or a company being wound up or in relation to which an administration order has been made, an application for relief under the new provision can be made by the "victim" of the transaction (i.e. any person who is, or is capable of being, prejudiced by it) [191] or where the victim is bound by a voluntary arrangement, by the supervisor of the voluntary arrangement. [192] In such a case the application is made to the Court by originating application. [193] Where the transferor is a bankrupt an application may be made by the Official Receiver or the trustee or, with the leave of the Court, by a victim of the transaction. [194]

14.102 The application is to be treated as made on behalf of every victim of the transaction [195]

14.103 Relief can be given in respect of a transaction which falls within Article 367 notwithstanding that it was entered into outside the time limits applying to applications in respect of transactions at an undervalue or preferences.

14.104 The transaction must have been entered into by the bankrupt at an undervalue, defined in Article 367(1) in similar terms as in the Article relating to the setting aside of transactions at an undervalue. In addition, the trustee must satisfy the Court that it was entered into by the bankrupt for the purpose of putting assets beyond the reach of a person who is making, or may at some time make, a claim against him, or of otherwise prejudicing the interests of such a person in relation to the claim which he is making or may make. [196] It is to be noted that the intent to withdraw assets from persons who may become creditors in the future is embraced. [197]

14.105 If these conditions are met the Court may make such order as it thinks fit to restore the position to what it would have been if the transaction had not been entered into and to protect the interests of the victims of the transaction.[198] The specific provisions which may be included in the order are set out in Article 369(1). The order may benefit not only the applicant but every victim of the transaction.

14.106 The interests of bona fide third parties are protected in terms similar to those relating to transactions at an undervalue and preferences.[199]

G. ASSIGNED BOOK DEBTS

14.107 Where the bankrupt was engaged in business and made a general assignment of existing or future book debts, such assignment is void against the trustee as regards any such debts not paid before the presentation of the petition, unless the assignment has been registered under the Bills of Sale (Ireland) Acts 1879 and 1883 as if it were a bill of sale given otherwise than by way of security. [200] An assignment may be invalidated under this provision whether or not it is by way of security or charge on book debts, but not if it is an assignment of book debts due at the date of assignment from specified debtors or of debts becoming due under specified contracts, nor if it is an assignment of book debts included either in a transfer of a business made in good faith and for value or in an assignment of assets for the benefit of creditors generally.

H. EXTORTIONATE CREDIT TRANSACTIONS

14.108 Article 316 makes provision for the Court to re-open certain credit transactions made by the bankrupt where the terms on which the credit was given to him were extortionate. This provision is in substitution for the provisions of the Consumer Credit Act 1974 under which extortionate credit bargains may be re-opened, and neither the trustee nor an undischarged bankrupt may apply under section 139(1)(a) of that Act. [201]

14.109 On the application of the trustee the Court may make certain orders with respect to a transaction for, or involving, the provision of credit to the bankrupt if the transaction is or was extortionate and was not entered into more than 3 years before the making of the bankruptcy order. [202]

14.110 A transaction is extortionate if, having regard to the risk accepted by the person providing credit, the terms of it required grossly exorbitant payments to be made or otherwise grossly contravened ordinary principles of fair dealing.[203] The onus of proof that the transaction is or was not extortionate lies with the other party to the transaction. [204]

14.111 An order of the Court under this provision may -
   (a) set aside the whole or part of any obligation,

    (b)   otherwise vary the terms of the transaction or of any security,

    (c)   order repayment to the trustee of any sums paid by the bankrupt,

    (d)   require the surrender of any security, or

    (e)   direct accounts to be taken. [205]

Any sums or property ordered to be paid or surrendered to the trustee become part of the bankrupt's estate. [206]

Ascertainment of liabilities and distribution of the estate

14.112 These aspects of the administration of the bankrupt's estate are dealt with in Chapters 19 and 20 respectively.

XII. CONCLUSION OF ADMINISTRATION

14.113 Where it appears to a trustee other than the Official Receiver that the administration of the bankrupt's estate is for practical purposes complete he is required to summon a final general meeting of creditors to receive his report on the administration of the estate and to determine whether he should be released. [207] At least 28 days notice of the meeting must be given to all creditors who have proved their debts, and to the bankrupt. [208] The notice may be given at the same time as notice of intention to declare a final dividend or that no dividend, or further dividend, will be declared, [209] but the final meeting cannot be concluded, and if necessary must be adjourned from time to time until any final distribution has been made and the trustee is able to report to the meeting that the administration of the estate is for practical purposes complete. [210]

14.114 If the only reason why the trustee cannot complete the administration is that he has been unable, for any reason, to realise an interest in a dwelling house comprised in the estate which is occupied by the bankrupt or his spouse or former spouse, he may still summon a final meeting of the creditors with a view, in particular, to obtaining his release, but only if one of the following conditions exist -

    (a)   the Court has either made an order imposing a charge on the bankrupt's interest in the dwelling house for the benefit of the estate, [211] or, on an application for such an order, has declined to make it, or

    (b)   the Department has issued a certificate to the trustee stating that it would be inappropriate or inexpedient for such an application to be made in the case in question. [212]

14.115 The trustee's report to be laid before the final meeting must include a summary of his receipts and payments and a statement by him that he has reconciled his account with that which is held by the Department in respect of the bankruptcy. [213]

14.116 At the meeting the creditors may question the trustee with respect to any matter contained in his report, and may resolve against his release. [214]

14.117 After the final meeting the trustee must give notice to the Court [215] that it has been held and the notice must state whether or not the creditors have resolved against his release. [216] A copy of the report laid before the meeting must accompany the notice to the Court and a copy of the notice must be sent by the trustee to the Official Receiver. [217]

14.118 If the final meeting was duly summoned but no quorum was present, the trustee must report to the Court accordingly. [218] When this has been done the meeting is deemed to have been held and the creditors not to have resolved against the trustee having his release. [219]

14.119 The trustee's release is effective from the time the Court is notified that the meeting has been held unless the meeting has resolved against the release. [220] It is not necessary for the meeting to resolve positively in favour of the release and the form of notice to the Court [221] does not envisage for any such resolution.

14.220 The trustee vacates office on giving notice to the Court that the final meeting has been held and of the decision (if any) of that meeting. [222]

Footnotes

(1)   Art.278(1),(2).
(2)   Paras.14.022/023, 14/032.
(3)   Art.278(2).
(4)   Art.276(2).
(5)   *Re Pilling* [1906] 2 KB 644.
(6)   This is the principle known as "The rule in *Ex parte James*". See Hals 447:
       MH 3-147: JH 19.07/10.
(7)   Art.334(1).
(8)   Art.276(1).
(9)   Para.14.009.
(10)   Paras.14.014, 14.016, 14.018.
(11)   RR.6.149, 6.160: Ins Regs 9(3): paras. 15.22/26.
(12)   Art.287(9): para.16.03.
(13)   Art.277: para.14.007.
(14)   Art.275: para.15.02.
(15)   Art.277(1),(2).
(16)   Art.277(3),(4).
(17)   Art.277(3).
(18)   Art.4.
(19)   R.6.144.
(20)   Art.277(5).
(21)   Art.298(2): para.20.20.
(22)   Sch.3, para.15.
(23)   Art.287(7)(b): Atkin Forms 392, 393.
(24)   Sch.3, paras 9, 10. See paras.14.035/047 re sale of bankrupt's home.
(25)   Art.287(8): R.6.079.
(26)   Art.287(7)(a).
(27)   Para.14.014.
(28)   M.H. 3-197.
(29)   Art.287(3).
(30)   Includes a trade or profession - Art 2(2).
(31)   For precedent of indemnity by creditors against costs of proceedings, see
       Atkin Form 323. A trustee may assign his right of action to the bankrupt
       - Hals 448, fn.4, JH 31-05.
(32)   Art.287(3).
(33)   Art.287(4),(5).
(34)   Art.341(1),(2).
(35)   Paras.12.36/47.
(36)   Art.341(3),(4).
(37)   Art.345.
(38)   Arts.284(1), 320.
(39)   Art.285.
(40)   R.6.122.
(41)   Art.284(2).

(42) Art.284(3).
(43) Art.284(4).
(44) Art.336(1),(2): para.12.34.
(45) Art.336(3): para.12.34.
(46) Para.9.04.
(47) Para.9.07.
(48) Paras.14.035/047.
(49) Atkin Forms 259/262.
(50) Art.262: para.11.01.
(51) Art.278(3).
(52) See *Re Keypak Homecare Ltd.* [1987] BCLC 409, where a liquidator in a voluntary winding up was held not to have discharged his investigatory duties with sufficient vigour.
(53) Art.306(1).
(54) Arts.306(4), 334(4).
(55) Art.306(3): para.21.41.
(56) Para.7.036.
(57) R.6.122(7),(8).
(58) Art.263(4): para.11.25.
(59) Art.337(1): para.11.45.
(60) Art:340: paras.11.80, 11.82.
(61) Art.342: para.11.93.
(62) Art.343. This provision applies, with adaptations, to debtors adjudicated under the Bankruptcy Acts or after 1st June 1990 - Insolvency (1989 Order) (Commencement No. 1) Order (Northern Ireland) 1990, Art.3, Sch.1.
(63) For a full discussion of the problems associated with the realisation of the bankrupt's home or former home see Roger Gregory, "Bankruptcy of Individuals and Partnerships" Ch.9 and MH 3-275, 3-282/289, Hals 390, 635/641.
(64) Art.309(2)(a).
(65) Art.309(1). E.g. when the bankrupt marries after presentation of the petition - MH 3-284.
(66) 1984 Order, Art 4.
(67) Art.309(2)(b): RSC O.1, rr.10(d), 15(d). The application is made by originating summons - RSC O.5, r.3.
(68) Art.309(3). This provision makes the decision in *Northern Bank Ltd. v. Beattie* [1982] 18 NIJB inapplicable on the trustee's application. The application is made by originating summons - RSC O.5, r.3. The prior consent of the creditors' committee (or the Department exercising the functions of the committee) or the Court must be obtained - Art.287(1)(a), Sch.3, para.2.
(69) Art.309(4).
(70) Paras.14.048/055.
(71) Art.309(5): Hals 637. In *Re Citro (a bankrupt)* [1991] Ch 142 at p.159 Nourse L.J. said that this reflected the previous law, which was still applicable

to unmarried couples. See S.M. Cretney "Women and children last" (1991) 4 Ins Int 78.

(72) MH 3-287. See also MH 3-373 where the author questions whether the Court has power to extend this one year period.

(73) Art.311: MH 3-290.

(74) Art.310(1).

(75) Art.310(2).

(76) *Ibid.*

(77) Art.310(2)(b).

(78) Ins R of D Regs 8; LR Rules 151E. The application is made by originating summons - RSC 0.5, r.3. See fn. (68) above re consent.

(79) Art.310(3)(a),(c).

(80) Art.310(3)(b), (4): RSC 0.1, rr.10(d), 15(d).

(81) Art.310(5).

(82) Paras.14.048/055.

(83) Art.310(6).

(84) Para.14.041.

(85) Art.311.

(86) Art.286(1).

(87) Art.286(2): R.6.229(5). For a discussion of the practical problems in securing such a charge see "Charge on bankrupt's home" by Steve Hill - *Insolvency Law and Practice* vol 6. No 1 (1990) p.12.

(88) Art.286(5).

(89) Atkin Form 407.

(90) R.6.229(2).

(91) R.6.229(3).

(92) Art.286(4).

(93) R.6.229(4).

(94) Art.286(3),(4): R.6.229(5),(6): Atkin Form 408.

(95) R.6.229(7).

(96) R.6.229(8): LR Rules 151D.

(97) Art.286(6),(7).

(98) R.6.229(9). Being an equitable charge, the order is registered in the Land Registry but the charge is not registered.

(99) For a commentary on the disclaimer provisions of the IA 1986. See MH 3-233/246 and re extension of statutory time-limits 3-373.

(100) Para.12.11.

(101) See *Re Potters Oils Ltd.* [1985] PCC 148 for an illustration of the restraints of such a provision.

(102) Art.288(1).

(103) Para.14.064.

(104) Art.288(3).

(105) *Ibid.* For the operation of disclaimer in relation to third parties, including guarantors, see MH 3-234 and also *Re Madeley Homecare Ltd.* [1983] NI 1. *Cf. Tempan v. Royal Liver Trustees Ltd.* [1984] ILRM 273, [1984] BCLC 568.

(106) Art.288(5).

(107) Para.14.076.

(108) Art.293(5).
(109) Para.14.068.
(110) Art.288(1).
(111) Art.288(4).
(112) F.6.64: Atkin Form 251 (notice of disclaimer with leave of court).
(113) R.6.175(1).
(114) R.6.175(2).
(115) *Ibid.*
(116) Art.288(3): R.6.175(5).
(117) R.6.175(3).
(118) R.6.175(4).
(119) R.6.176: MH 7-416.
(120) R.6.177: MH 7-418.
(121) R.6.181(1): F.6.66.
(122) R.6.181(2).
(123) R.6.176(6),(7).
(124) R.6.178: Atkin Form 247.
(125) Art.289(1): R.6.180(1),(2): F.6.65.
(126) Art.289(2).
(127) Para.14.076.
(128) Art.290(1). In line 4 "of" should clearly read "or".
(129) Art.290(2): MH 3-238.
(130) Art.290(3).
(131) Para.14.076.
(132) Art.291.
(133) Art.293(2)(c).
(134) MH 3-244.
(135) Art.292.
(136) Para.14.063.
(137) R.6.179(1): Atkin Form 248.
(138) R.6.179(2): Atkin Form 249.
(139) R.6.179(3).
(140) R.6.179(4). For form of notice of disclaimer with leave, see Atkin Form 251.
(141) Para.14.068: Atkin Forms 254, 255.
(142) R.6.180(3),(4).
(143) Art.293(1),(3).
(144) Art.293(4).
(145) Art.293(2).
(146) R.6.183(1),(2).
(147) R.6.183(3).
(148) R.6.183(4).
(149) R.6.183(5).
(150) Paras.14.069/072.
(151) Arts.290(1)(b), 291(b): R.6.183(7).
(152) R.6.183(8).
(153) Art.294(1),(6).

(154) Art.294(5).
(155) Art.294(3),(4),(6).
(156) Art.293(6).
(157) R.6.183(6).
(158) R.6.182.
(159) Art.318(1),(2).
(160) *Ibid.*
(161) Art.318(3).
(162) Art.318(4).
(163) Paras.7.022/032.
(164) For a full commentary on the provisions of the IA 1986 relating to transactions at an undervalue and preferences, see MH 3-292/301. Transactions entered into before the Order came into operation are not affected by Arts. 312/317 - Sch.8, para.14.
(165) Atkin Form 398.
(166) Art.312(1),(2). This provision binds the Crown - Art. 378(c). See Roger Gregory "Bankruptcy of Individual and Partnerships", para.1009 re "restoring the position".
(167) Art.312(3).
(168) Matrimonial Causes (Northern Ireland) Order 1978, Art. 41, as amended by Sch.9, para.91, of the Order.
(169) Art.314(1).
(170) Art.314(2).
(171) Defined in Art. 4 and including a husband or wife or former husband or wife.
(172) Art.314(2).
(173) Art.314(3). Cf. 1929 Act, s.12 where the only criterion is inability to pay debts.
(174) For title problem re gifts of land see para.28.76.
(175) See fn.164 above.
(176) Atkin Form 396.
(177) Art.313(1),(2). See fn.(166) above.
(178) Art.313(3)(a).
(179) Fn.171 above.
(180) Art.313(3)(b),(4),(5). For an analysis of the requirements for a voidable preference see *Re M C Bacon Ltd. v National Westminster Bank* (1990) 6 BCC 78, per Millet J. (pp 86/88).
(181) Art.313(6).
(182) Fn.168 above.
(183) Para.14.091 above.
(184) Fn.(171) above.
(185) Art.314(1).
(186) Art.314(2).
(187) Para.14.093.
(188) Art.315(2).
(189) MH 3-465/470 Hals 652/6.
(190) JH 24.01/12.

(191) Art.367(4).
(192) Art.368(1)(b),(c).
(193) Atkin Form 397.
(194) Art.368(1)(a).
(195) Art.368(2).
(196) Art.367(3). This purpose may not have been the only motive - *Chohan* v. *Saggar and anor.* [1991] TLR 452.
(197) MH 3-467/1.
(198) Art.367(2).
(199) Art.369(2).
(200) Art.317.
(201) Art.316(6).
(202) Art.316(1),(2).
(203) Art.316(3).
(204) *Ibid.*
(205) Art.316(4).
(206) Art.316(5).
(207) Art.304(1),(2). Cf. Art.272(2) re release of Official Receiver as trustee.
(208) R.6.134(1): F.6.38.
(209) Para.20.25.
(210) Art.304(3).
(211) Para.14.048.
(212) Art.305. In an article by Steve Hill in *Insolvency Law and Practice* vol 6 No 1 (1990) p 12, it is suggested that a ground for issuing such a certificate may be that there are no funds in the estate to enable the application to be made.
(213) R.6.134(2).
(214) R.6.134(3).
(215) F.6.53.
(216) R.6.134(4).
(217) *Ibid.*
(218) R.6.134(5)
(219) *Ibid.*
(220) R.6.134(6).
(221) F.6.53.
(222) Art.271(7).

Chapter 15

CREDITORS' COMMITTEE

Introduction

15.01 With a view to giving creditors an opportunity to participate more actively in the administration of the bankrupt's estate Article 274(1) provides for the establishment by a general meeting of creditors of a creditors' committee to exercise functions conferred on it by or under the Order. The most important of these functions is to give permission for the proposed exercise by the trustee of the powers as set out in Schedule 3, Part I of the Order,[1] the review from time to time of the adequacy of the trustee's security and the fixing of the trustee's remuneration.[2] Having regard in particular to the latter function a proposed trustee may only be prepared to act if a creditors' committee is to be established.

Committee's functions vested in Department

15.02 A creditors' committee may not be established nor may any functions be conferred on such a committee at any time when the Official Receiver is trustee, except in connection with an appointment made by a general meeting of creditors of a person to be trustee instead of the Official Receiver,[3] nor may the committee carry out its functions at any time when the Official Receiver is trustee.[4] At any such time, or when the trustee is a person other than the Official Receiver and there is for the time being no creditors' committee, the functions of such a committee are vested in the Department, except to the extent that the Rules otherwise provide.[5] Thus, for example, the Department cannot fix the remuneration of the trustee where there is no committee because in that event that function is by the Rules vested in a general meeting of creditors.[6]

15.03 Where the Official Receiver is not the trustee and the functions of a creditors' committee are vested in the Department because there is no creditors' committee, those functions may be exercised by the Official Receiver.[7] However, only the Department may exercise such functions when the Official Receiver is the trustee.

15.04 At any time when the functions of a creditors' committee are vested in the Department (whether or not the Official Receiver is the trustee) the requirements of the Order or the Rules about notices to be given or reports to be made to the committee by the trustee do not apply, except that where there is a committee it may require a report as to any matter.[8]

Membership of committee

15.05 There must be not less than 3 and not more than 5 members of the committee.[9] Each member must be a creditor of the bankrupt (other than a fully secured creditor) and have lodged a proof of debt which has neither been wholly disallowed for voting purposes nor wholly rejected for the purposes of

distribution or dividend.[10]   A body corporate may be a member, acting only
by a duly authorised representative.[11] No person may act as a member unless
and until he has agreed to do so.[12]   Such agreement may be given by his
proxy-holder present at the meeting establishing the committee, unless the
relevant proxy contains a statement to the contrary.[13]

15.06   A member may resign by delivering written notice to the trustee.[14] A
person's membership of the committee is also terminated if -
   (a)   he becomes bankrupt (in which case he is replaced by his trustee in
         bankruptcy) or compounds or arranges with his creditors, or
   (b)   he is neither present nor represented at 3 consecutive committee meet-
         ings, unless at the third meeting it is resolved to the contrary, or
   (c)   he ceases to be, or is found never to have been, a creditor.[15]

15.07   A member may be removed by a resolution of a meeting of creditors,
of which at least 14 days notice of the intention of moving the resolution has
been given.[16]

15.08   A vacancy in the membership need not be filled if there are still at least
3 members and the trustee and a majority of the remaining members so agree.[17]
If the vacancy is to be filled, this may be done by the trustee, with the agreement
of the majority of the remaining members, appointing a qualified creditor who
consents to act.[18] Alternatively, the vacancy may be filled by a resolution of a
meeting of creditors appointing a creditor, with his consent.[19] At least 14 days
notice of such a resolution must be given (whether or not the proposed appointee is named in the notice).[20] If the trustee is not present at such a meeting the
chairman must notify him of any appointment to the committee.[21]

Committee-members' representatives
15.09   A member of the committee may be represented by another person
(other than a body corporate, an undischarged bankrupt or a person subject to
a composition or arrangement with his creditors) duly authorised by him for
that purpose.[22] The representative must hold a letter of authority entitling him
to act generally or specially, signed by or on behalf of the committee-member,
which the Chairman at any meeting of the committee may call on him to
produce.[23] Any proxy in relation to any meeting of creditors is to be treated
as such a letter of authority, unless it contains a statement to the contrary.[24]
No person may represent more than one committee-member or act both as a
member and as representative of another member.[25] A representative signing
a document on behalf of a committee-member must so state below his signature.[26] A defect in the appointment or qualification of any representative will
not invalidate any act of the committee.[27]

Establishment of committee
15.10   If a first meeting of creditors is held it will consider whether or not to
resolve to establish a creditors' committee, but such a resolution may also be

passed at any general meeting of creditors and the trustee may be required by the creditors to summon such a meeting for this purpose.[28]

15.11   The committee does not come into being, and accordingly cannot act, until the trustee has issued a certificate of its due constitution.[29] Such a certificate cannot be issued until at least 3 persons have been elected to be members of the committee and have agreed to act.[30] If a resolution to establish a committee is made at a creditors' meeting where the trustee is not the chairman (e.g. the first meeting of creditors, where the Official Receiver or his nominee is chairman) the chairman must give notice of the resolution to the trustee or to the person appointed trustee at that same meeting and inform him of the names and addresses of the persons elected to be members of the committee.[31]

15.12   As and when other persons (if any) agree to act as members of the committee, the trustee must issue an amended certificate.[32]

15.13   The certificate, and any amended certificate, must be filed in the Court by the trustee and he is also required to report to the Court any change in the membership of the committee after its first establishment.[33]

15.14   The acts of the creditors' committee are valid notwithstanding any defect in the election or qualification of any member of it.[34]

Meetings
15.15   The trustee must call the first meeting of the committee to take place within 3 months of his appointment or of the committee's establishment (whichever is the later) and thereafter he must call a meeting within 21 days of receiving a request from a member of the committee or his representative or for the date on which the committee has previously resolved that a meeting be held.[35] Subject to these requirements, the trustee may call a meeting whenever he wishes.[36]

15.16   Seven days notice in writing of the venue of a meeting must be given to every member or his representative, unless this requirement has been waived by or on behalf of any member at or before the meeting.[37]

15.17   The chairman at each meeting is the trustee or a person appointed by him in writing to act, such nominee being either a person qualified to act as an insolvency practitioner in relation to the bankrupt or an employee of the trustee or his firm who is experienced in insolvency matters.[38]

Quorum
15.18   A creditors' committee is duly constituted if due notice of it has been given to all its members and at least 2 of them are present or represented.[39]

Voting rights and resolutions

15.19   Each member or his representative has one vote and a resolution is passed when a majority of the members present or represented have voted in favour of it.[40]

15.20   Every resolution passed must be recorded in writing, either as part of the minutes of the meeting or separately, and the record must be signed by the chairman and kept with the records of the bankruptcy.[41]

15.21   A resolution may be agreed by the members of the committee without a meeting under the following procedure:-

(a)   the trustee sends to each member of the committee or his representative designated for the purpose a copy of each proposed resolution set out so that agreement with or dissent from it may be indicated by the recipient on such copy;

(b)   unless any member, within 7 business days from the date the resolution is so sent, requires the trustee to summon a meeting of the committee to consider the matters raised by the resolution, the resolution is deemed to have been carried in the committee if and when the trustee is notified in writing by a majority of members that they concur with it.[42]

A copy of every resolution passed under this procedure, and a note that the concurrence of the committee was obtained, must be kept with the records of the bankruptcy.[43]

Trustee's obligations to the committee

15.22   The trustee must report to the committee any disposal by him of any part of the bankrupt's estate to an associate of the bankrupt or if he employs a solicitor.[44]

15.23   The trustee must, at intervals of not more than 6 months, send a written report to every member of the committee setting out the position generally as regards the progress of the bankruptcy and matters arising in connection with it, to which he considers the committee's attention should be drawn.[45] The committee may also require him to give such a report at more frequent intervals, but not more than once in every 2 months.[46]

15.24   Where the meeting has come into being more than 28 days after the appointment of the trustee, the trustee must report to the committee, in summary form, what action he has taken since his appointment and answer such questions as the members may put to him regarding his conduct of the bankruptcy hitherto.[47]

15.25   The trustee must report to the members of the committee all such matters as appear to him to be of concern to them with respect to the bankruptcy.[48] He must also furnish information at the request of the committee, unless it appears to him that the request is frivolous or unreasonable, or that the cost of doing so would be excessive, having regard to the relative importance of the information, or that the estate does not have sufficient funds to enable him to comply with the request.[49] However, a person who becomes a member of the committee after its first establishment is not entitled to require a report from the trustee otherwise than in summary form of any matter previously arising.[50]

15.26   Members of the committee have access to the trustee's records and may seek an explanation of any matter within the committee's responsibility.[51]

Dealing by committee-members and others

15.27   A member of the committee is subject to restrictions in respect on entering into any transaction whereby he receives out of the bankrupt's estate any payment for services given or goods supplied in connection with the estate's administration, obtains any profit from the administration or acquires any part of the estate. He may not enter into any such transaction unless -
  (a) he obtains the prior leave of the Court, or
  (b) he acts as a matter of urgency or in performance of a pre-bankruptcy contract and obtains the Court's leave, having applied for it without undue delay, or
  (c) he obtains the prior consent of the committee, obtained after full disclosure of the circumstances and where the committee is satisfied that he will be giving full value in the transaction.[52]

15.28   These restrictions apply also to -
  (a) any committee-member's representative,
  (b) any person who is an associate, or who has been an associate at any time in the last 12 months, of a member of the committee or of a committee-member's representative, and
  (c) any person who has been a member of the committee or a committee-member's representative at any time in the last 12 months or who is, or has been at any time in the last 12 months, an associate of such a person.[53]

15.29   The costs of any application for leave of the Court are not payable out of the estate unless the Court so orders.[54]

15.30   Where a resolution is proposed in the committee to sanction such a transaction, no member of the committee or a representative of a member may vote if he is to participate directly or indirectly in the transaction.[55]

15.31   The Court may, on the application of any person interested, set aside any such transaction entered into in contravention of these provisions and make any other order it thinks fit, including requiring a person to account for any profit obtained from the transaction and to compensate the estate for any resultant loss.[56] No such order may be made against an associate of a member of the committee or of a committee-member's representative if the Court is satisfied that he entered into the transaction without having any reason to suppose that in doing so he would contravene the provisions.[57]

Travelling expenses of members, etc.

15.32   Any reasonable travelling expenses directly incurred by members of the committee or their representatives in respect of their attendance at the committee's meetings, or otherwise on the committee's business, are payable out of the bankrupt's estate, in the prescribed order of priority.[58]

Footnotes

(1) Paras.14.017/019.
(2) Paras.4.15, 13.085.
(3) Art.274(2).
(4) Art.275(1).
(5) Art.275.
(6) R.6.135(5).
(7) R.6.163(2). The Department may by direction limit the excercise of such functions by the Official Receiver.
(8) R.6.163(1).
(9) R.6.147(1).
(10) R.6.147(2).
(11) R.6.147(3).
(12) R.6.148(3).
(13) *Ibid.*
(14) R.6.154.
(15) R.6.155.
(16) R.6.156.
(17) R.6.157(1),(2).
(18) R. 6.157(3).
(19) R.6.157(4).
(20) *Ibid.*
(21) R.6.157(5).
(22) R.6.153(1),(4).
(23) R.6.153(2),(3).
(24) R.6.153(2).
(25) R.6.153(5).
(26) R.6.153(6).
(27) R.6.153(7).
(28) Arts.274(1), 287(9): paras.16.03/05.
(29) R.6.148(1): F.6.55.
(30) R.6.148(4).
(31) R.6.148(2).
(32) R.6.148(5): F.6.55.
(33) R.6.148(6),(7): F.6.56.
(34) Art.345.
(35) R.6.150(2).
(36) R.6.150(1).
(37) R.6.150(3),(4).
(38) R.6.151.
(39) R.6.152.
(40) R.6.158(1).
(41) R.6.158(2): para.13.128.
(42) R.6.159(1)-(4).
(43) R.6.159(5): para.13.128.

(44) Art.287(7): paras.14.014, 14.016.
(45) R.6.160(1),(2).
(46) R.6.160(1).
(47) R.6.149(3).
(48) R.6.149(1).
(49) R.6.149(2).
(50) R.6.149(4).
(51) R.6.149(5).
(52) R.6.162(1)-(3).
(53) R.6.162(1). See Art. 4 for definition of "associate".
(54) R.6.162(7).
(55) R.6.162(4).
(56) R.6.162(5).
(57) R.6.162(6).
(58) RR.6.161, 6.222(1)(m).

Chapter 16

CREDITORS' MEETINGS IN BANKRUPTCY

Introduction
16.01   This Chapter deals with the provisions of the Order and the general Rules governing general meetings of creditors in bankruptcy. These provisions are subject to special rules relating to the first meeting of creditors, and to meetings to accept the resignation of, or to remove, a trustee, which are dealt with in Chapter 13. [1]

General power to convene meetings
16.02   In addition to specific provisions of the Order requiring or authorising the summoning of creditors' meetings, the Official Receiver or the trustee may summon such a meeting at any time for the purpose of ascertaining the wishes of the creditors in all matters relating to the bankruptcy. [2]

Meetings ordered or requisitioned
16.03   The Official Receiver or the trustee may be required to summon a meeting of creditors by an order of the Court under its general powers. [3] The trustee must also summon such a meeting if requested to do so by a creditor with the concurrence of not less than one-tenth, in value, of the creditors. [4]

16.04   A request by creditors for a meeting to be convened must be accompanied by-
    (a) (except where the requisitioning creditor's debt is alone at least one-tenth, in value, of the creditors) a list of the creditors concurring with the request and the amount of their respective claims in the bankruptcy,
    (b) written confirmation of concurrence from each creditor, and
    (c) a statement of the purpose of the proposed meeting. [5]

16.05   If the Official Receiver or the trustee considers that the request is properly made with the concurrence of the requisite proportion of creditors, and provided that the requisitioning creditor deposits with him such sum as he (the Official Receiver or the trustee) determines to be appropriate to cover the expenses of summoning and holding the meeting, he must fix the venue for the meeting to take place not more than 35 days from receipt of the request, and give 21 days notice of the meeting to creditors. [6].

16.06   A meeting summoned on the requisition of a creditor may vote that the expenses of summoning and holding it shall be payable out of the estate as an expense of the bankruptcy, and to the extent that the deposit is not required for the payment of such expenses it is repayable to the person who made it. [7]

Venue of meetings

16.07   In fixing the time, date and place for the meeting the convener must have regard to the convenience of the creditors and, unless the Court otherwise directs, the commencement time must be between 10.00 and 16.00 hours on a business day. [8]

Notice of meetings

16.08   Unless the Court orders notice by public advertisement only,[9], the convener must give at least 21 days notice of the meeting to every creditor who is known to him or is identified in the bankrupt's statement of affairs, and to the bankrupt.[10] The notice must specify the purpose of the meeting and a time and date (not more than 4 days before the meeting) by which creditors must lodge proxies and those who have not already lodged proofs must do so, in order to be entitled to vote at the meeting.[11] A form of proxy must accompany each notice.[12]

16.09   The convener may give additional notice of a meeting by public advertisement and must do so if ordered by the Court.[13] The Court may also order notice to be given by public advertisement and not by individual notice to the persons concerned.[14] In considering whether to adopt this course the Court is required to have regard to the cost of public advertisement, to the amount of the funds available in the estate and to the extent of the interest of creditors or any particular class of them.[15]

16.10   Where a meeting is summoned by notice in accordance with the Order or the Rules the meeting is presumed to have been duly summoned and held, notwithstanding that not all those to whom notice is required to be given have received it.[16]

Chairman

16.11   Where the convener is the Official Receiver he or a person nominated by him in writing is the chairman.[17] Otherwise the chairman is the convener or a person nominated by him in writing, being either a person who is qualified to act as an insolvency practitioner in relation to the bankrupt or an employee of the trustee or his firm who is experienced in insolvency matters. [18]

Attendance at meetings of bankrupt, etc.

16.12   The convener may require the bankrupt to be present or in attendance at a meeting of creditors by giving him notice to that effect. [19]

16.13   If the bankrupt is not present and it is desired to question him, the chairman may adjourn the meeting with a view to obtaining his attendance. [20] Where he is present, only such questions may be put to him as the chairman may in his discretion allow.[21]

16.14   A bankrupt who has not been required to attend, or any other person may, if he has given reasonable notice of his wish to be present, be admitted at the discretion of the chairman. [22]

16.15   The chairman's decision is final as to what (if any) intervention may be made by the bankrupt or by any other person admitted to the meeting. [23]

Quorum
16.16   One creditor entitled to vote, whether present in person or represented by proxy by any person (including the chairman) constitutes a quorum. [24] However, where the chairman alone, or one other person in addition constitutes the quorum and the chairman is aware, by virtue of proofs and proxies received or otherwise, that one or more additional creditors would, if attending, be entitled to vote, the meeting may not commence until after 15 minutes from the appointed time. [25]

Entitlement to vote
16.17   Subject as mentioned in the next paragraph, a creditor may vote at a creditors' meeting only if there has been lodged, by the time and date stated in the notice of the meeting, -

(a)   a proof of the debt claimed to be due to him from the bankrupt and the claim has been admitted by the chairman for the purpose of entitlement to vote, and

(b)   any proxy requisite for that entitlement. [26]

It is to be noted that the chairman at a meeting has no discretion to admit a late proof.

16.18   In exceptional circumstances the Court may by order declare the creditors, or any class of them, entitled to vote without being required to prove their debts. [27] Where a creditor is so entitled, the Court may, on the application of the trustee, make such consequential orders as it thinks fit (e.g. an order treating a creditor as having proved his debt for the purpose of dividend). [28]

16.19   A creditor may only vote in respect of a debt for an unliquidated amount or a debt whose value is not ascertained if the chairman agrees to put upon the debt an estimated value for the purpose of entitlement to vote and admits his proof for that purpose. [29]

16.20   A secured creditor may only vote in respect of the balance (if any) of his debt after deducting the value of his security as estimated by him. [30]

16.21   A creditor may not vote in respect of a debt on, or secured by, a current bill of exchange or promissory note, unless he is willing to treat the liability to him on the bill or note of every person who is liable on it antecedently to the bankrupt, and against whom a bankruptcy order has not been made (or, in the case of a company, which has not gone into liquidation), as a security in his hands, and to estimate the value of the security and (for the purpose of entitlement to vote, but not for dividend) to deduct it from his proof. [31]

Admission and rejection of proof for purpose of voting

16.22 The chairman of the meeting may admit or reject a creditor's proof, in whole or in part, for the purpose of entitlement to vote, subject to appeal to the Court by any creditor, or by the bankrupt. [32] Neither the Official Receiver nor his nominee as chairman is personally liable for costs in respect of such an appeal and no other chairman is so liable unless the Court so orders. [33]

16.23 If a proof is disputed and the evidence in support is insufficient, the chairman ought to reject it, but if he is in doubt as to the admission or rejection of any proof he is required to mark it as objected to and allow the creditor to vote, subject to his vote being subsequently declared invalid if the objection to the proof is sustained. [34] If, on appeal, the chairman's decision is reversed or varied, or a creditor's vote is declared invalid, the Court may order that another meeting be summoned, or make such other order as it think just. [35]

Resolutions

16.24 Subject as mentioned below, a resolution is passed when a majority (in value) of those present and voting, in person or by proxy, have voted in favour of it. [36]

16.25 Special provisions are made for a resolution for the appointment of a trustee where there is more than one nominee [37] and for a resolution which would place a proxy-holder or any associate of his in a position to receive any remuneration out of the estate. [38]

16.26 Where a resolution is proposed which affects a person in respect of his remuneration or conduct as trustee, or as proposed or former trustee (e.g. a proposal that a person be appointed trustee), the vote of that person and of any partner or employee of his must be excluded in calculating the majority required for passing such resolution. [39] This applies to a vote given by a person whether personally or on his behalf by a proxy-holder either as creditor or as proxy-holder for a creditor, [40] but subject to the restrictions on voting by proxy on a resolution relating to remuneration from the estate. [41]

16.27 Where a creditor has given the chairman at a meeting a proxy which requires him to vote for a particular resolution and no other person proposes that resolution he must himself propose it, unless he considers that there is good reason for not doing so and in that case he must, forthwith after the meeting, notify his principal what that reason was. [42]

Suspension and adjournment

16.28 The chairman has a discretion to suspend the meeting for any period up to one hour but he may only do this once in the course of the meeting. [43]

16.29   The chairman has a general discretion to adjourn the meeting for a period not exceeding 21 days and (subject to the restriction on adjournment where the trustee or his nominee is chairman and a resolution has been proposed for the trustee's removal [44]) he must do so if the meeting so resolves. [45]

16.30   If no quorum is present within 30 minutes from the time appointed for the commencement of the meeting, the chairman may at his discretion adjourn the meeting. [46] However, he should conclude the meeting if he considers that an adjournment would serve no useful purpose.

16.31   If the person entitled to act as chairman fails to attend the meeting, a creditor present who is entitled to vote may fix the adjournment of the meeting in the circumstances mentioned in the preceding paragraph, with the agreement of other creditors present who are entitled to vote, and if such agreement cannot be reached the meeting stands adjourned to the same time and place in the next following week, or if that is not a business day, to the business day immediately following. [47]

16.32   Any adjournment must be to a time and place appointed by the chairman having regard to the convenience of the creditors and the time appointed must be between 10.00 and 16.00 hours on a business day, unless the Court otherwise directs. [48] If the bankrupt was not present at the meeting the chairman must give him notice of the adjournment unless for any reason it appears to him to be unnecessary or impracticable. [49]

16.33   Proofs and proxies may be used at an adjourned meeting if they are lodged not later than midday on the business day immediately before the adjourned meeting. [50]

Inspection of documents at meetings
16.34   Any person attending a meeting of creditors is entitled, immediately before or in the course of the meeting, to inspect proxies and associated documents (including proofs) sent or given for the purpose of that meeting. [51] This is a more general right of inspection than is afforded in relation to inspection by creditors of proofs and proxies held by a trustee, in that a person attending the meeting whose proof has been wholly rejected is not precluded from exercising the right. [52]

Record of proceedings
16.35   The chairman must make up and keep a list of all the creditors who attended the meeting and have minutes of the proceedings drawn up, signed by him and retained as part of the records of the bankruptcy. [53]

16.36   The minutes must include a record of every resolution passed. [54] The chairman must ensure that particulars of all such resolutions, certified by him, [55] are filed in the Court not more than 21 days after the date of the meeting.

16.37   A minute of the meeting, signed by the chairman, is admissible in insolvency proceedings without further proof. [56] The minute is prima facie evidence that the meeting was duly convened and held, that all resolutions passed at the meeting were duly passed, and that all proceedings at the meeting duly took place. [57]

Expenses of meetings

16.38   The expenses of summoning and holding a meeting called by the Official Receiver or trustee are payable out of the estate. Otherwise the person at whose instance the meeting is convened is liable to pay such expenses and he is required to deposit security for their payment with the trustee or, if no trustee has been appointed, with the Official Receiver. [58] The amount of the deposit is determined by the trustee or the Official Receiver and neither may proceed to summon the meeting until it has been paid. [59] The deposit is repayable to the person who made it to the extent that it is not required for the payment of expenses of summoning and holding the meeting. [60] The meeting may resolve that the expenses be payable out of the estate as an expense of the bankruptcy. [61]

Footnotes

(1)   For procedure for creditors' meeting in voluntary arrangements see paras.26.062/079.
(2)   Art.287(8): R.6.079(1).
(3)   Arts.276, 334.
(4)   Art.287(9).
(5)   R.6.081(1),(2): F.6.37.
(6)   RR.6.081(3),(4), 6.085(1),(2). Cf. the first meeting of creditors, when 3 months is allowed for holding a requisitioned meeting - para.13.022.
(7)   R.6.085(3),(4).
(8)   R.6.084 (1),(2).
(9)   Para.16.09 below.
(10) RR.6.079(3),(4), 6.082(1): FF.6.38, 6.39.
(11) R.6.079(5).
(12) R.6.084(3): F.8.4.
(13) R.6.079(6).
(14) R.6.083(1).
(15) R.6.083(2).
(16) R.12.18.
(17) R.6.080(1): Atkin Form 170. The nomination need not be in writing if the nominee is another Official Receiver or a Deputy Official Receiver - R.6.080(2).
(18) R.6.080(3),(4).
(19) R.6.082(3): F.6.39.
(20) R.6.082(6).
(21) R.6.082(7).
(22) R.6.082(4).
(23) R.6.082(5).
(24) R.12.05(1)-(3). A creditor may not be represented at a creditors' meeting in individual insolvency proceedings by a person appointed under Art.383 of the Companies (Northern Ireland) Order 1986 - para.17.08.
(25) R.12.05(4).
(26) R.6.090(1).
(27) R.6.090(2).
(28) R.6.090(3).
(29) R.6.090(4).
(30) R.6.090(5). If a secured creditor votes in respect of the unsecured balance of his debt he may re-value his security only with leave of the Court - R.6.112(2).
(31) R.6.090(6).
(32) R.6.091(1),(2). An appeal to the Court lies in respect of any matter arising under R.6.090.
(33) R.6.091(5).
(34) R.6.091(3): *Re a Debtor (No 222 of 1990)* [1991] TLR 313 decided under rule corresponding to R.5.20(6).

(35)   R.6.091(4).
(36)   R.6.086(1).
(37)   Para.13.025.
(38)   Para.17.14.
(39)   R.6.086(4).
(40)   R.6.086(5).
(41)   Para.17.14.
(42)   R.6.087.
(43)   R.6.088.
(44)   Para.13.060.
(45)   R.6.089(1),(4): Atkin Form 172.
(46)   R.6.089(3).
(47)   R.6.089(5),(6).
(48)   RR.6.089(4), 6.084(1),(2).
(49)   R.6.082(2).
(50)   R.6.089(7).
(51)   R.8.5(4).
(52)   Cf. RR.6.101, 8.5(2).
(53)   R.6.092(1),(2): Atkin Forms 171, 174.
(54)   R.6.092(3).
(55)   *Ibid:* Atkin Form 173.
(56)   R.12.06(1).
(57)   R.12.06(2).
(58)   R.6.085(1).
(59)   R.6.085(2).
(60)   R.6.085(4).
(61)   R.6.085(3).

Chapter 17

PROXIES

Introduction
17.01 This Chapter deals with the general rules which apply to proxies at creditors' meetings summoned or called under the Order or the Rules in a bankruptcy or individual voluntary arrangement.

Definition
17.02 A proxy is defined for the purposes of the Rules as an authority given by a person ("the principal") to another person ("the proxy-holder") to attend a meeting and speak and vote as his representative. [1] This makes it clear that the proxy-holder may speak at a meeting on behalf of his principal as well as vote.

Authority of proxy-holder
17.03 A proxy-holder is required to give the principal's vote on matters arising for determination at the meeting, or to abstain or to propose, in the principal's name, a resolution to be voted on by the meeting. [2] He must vote in accordance with any specific directions given in the proxy, but if he holds a "general" proxy, he may vote in accordance with his own discretion, as he may do in respect of any resolution not dealt with in any specific direction [3] subject to the restrictions on the use of a proxy referred to in paragraph 17.14 below.

17.04 A proxy-holder may propose any resolution which, if proposed by another, he would have authority to support. [4]

17.05 A proxy directing a proxy-holder to vote for or against the appointment of a person as trustee or supervisor of a voluntary arrangement may, unless the proxy states otherwise, be used to support or oppose the appointment of that person jointly with another or others. [5]

Form
17.06 The Rules prescribe forms of proxy to be used in individual voluntary arrangements [6] and bankruptcy. [7] Only one proxy may be given by a person for any one meeting at which he desires to be represented. [8]

17.07 No name or description of any person may be inserted in the form of proxy required to be sent with the notice of a meeting, and only the forms so sent, or a substantially similar form, may be used. [9]

Signature
17.08 A form of proxy must be signed by the principal, or by some person authorised by him. [10] The authority given may be a general one or with reference to a particular meeting. [11] The authority of a person to sign a proxy on behalf of a principal which is a corporation does not require to be in the form

223

of a resolution of that corporation.[12] However, a representative appointed by resolution under Article 383 of the Companies (Northern Ireland) Order 1986 to represent the corporation at a meeting of creditors of a company may not, under that authority, act as proxy-holder at a meeting of creditors in individual insolvency proceedings. Only a person holding a duly executed proxy in proper form may do so. A proxy on behalf of a partnership firm signed in the firm name, or in any other manner showing an intention to bind the firm, by a person authorised to do so (who need not be a partner) is binding on the firm and all the partners of it. [13]

Who may hold
17.09   A proxy may only be given to one person, being an individual [14] aged 18 or over, but it may specify one or more individuals to be proxy-holder in the alternative in the order in which they are named in the proxy.[15]

17.10   A proxy may be given to whoever is to be the chairman of the meeting. [16] In bankruptcy (but not in individual voluntary arrangement proceedings) the proxy may be given to the Official Receiver.[17] The chairman of the meeting or the Official Receiver to whom a proxy is given may not decline to accept it. [18]

Use at meetings
17.11   A proxy given for a particular meeting may be used at any adjournment of that meeting.[19]

17.12   Where proxies are held by the Official Receiver, they may be used at a meeting by his deputy, or any other Official Receiver or another officer of the Department authorised by the Official Receiver in writing to act for him at the meeting and use the proxies.[20]

17.13   Where the responsible insolvency practitioner holds proxies to be used by him as chairman of a meeting, and some other person acts as chairman, that other person may use those proxies as if he were himself the proxy-holder.[21]

17.14   A proxy-holder may not vote in favour of any resolution which would directly or indirectly place him, or any associate[22] of his, in a position to receive any remuneration out of the estate (e.g. to be appointed trustee) unless the proxy specifically directs him to do so.[23] Where the proxy does so direct him the proxy-holder is nevertheless prohibited from voting in favour of such resolution where he himself has signed the proxy as being authorised to do so by his principal, unless he produces to the chairman of the meeting written authorisation from the principal sufficient to show that the proxy-holder was entitled to sign the proxy containing such a direction.[24]

17.15   These restrictions apply to any person acting as chairman of a meeting and using proxies in that capacity which have been given to the responsible insolvency practitioner,[25] and in such application the proxy-holder is deemed to be an associate of the person so using such proxies. [26]

Inspection

17.16   So long as proxies lodged with the trustee in a bankruptcy or the supervisor of a voluntary arrangement are in his hands he must allow them to be inspected by -

(a)   in bankruptcy, by the creditors who have proved their debts, or by the bankrupt,

(b)   in a voluntary arrangement, by persons who have submitted in writing a claim to be creditors of the debtor, or by the debtor himself,

but in neither case does a person whose proof or claim has been wholly rejected for purposes of voting or dividend have a right to inspect proxies. [27]

17.17   Proxies and associated documents (including proofs) may also be inspected by any person attending a meeting of creditors at or immediately before the meeting for which they have been sent.[28]

Retention

17.18   Proxies used for voting at a meeting must be retained by the chairman until the meeting is concluded, when, if he is not himself the trustee or supervisor, as the case may be, he must hand them over to that person. [29]

Footnotes

(1)   R.8.1(1),(2).
(2)   R.8.1(6).
(3)   RR.8.1(6), 8.3(6).
(4)   R.8.3(5).
(5)   R.8.3(4).
(6)   F.8.1.
(7)   F.8.4.
(8)   R.8.1(3).
(9)   RR.6.084(3), 8.2(1),(2).
(10) R.8.2(3). For this reason a facsimile is not acceptable - (1989)2 Ins Int 64.
(11) R.8.2(3).
(12) R.8.7(3).
(13) Partnership Act 1890, s.6.
(14) I.e. not a corporation or a firm.
(15) R.8.1(3).
(16) R.8.1(4).
(17) *Ibid*.
(18) R.8.1(5).
(19) R.8.3(1).
(20) R.8.3(2): Atkin Form 170.
(21) R.8.3(3).
(22) Art.4.
(23) R.8.6(1).
(24) R.8.6(2).
(25) Para.17.13 above.
(26) R.8.6(3).
(27) R.8.5(1)-(3).
(28) R.8.5(4): para.16.34.
(29) R.8.4.

Chapter 18

INCOME PAYMENTS ORDER

Introduction

18.01 Following a recommendation of the Insolvency Law Review Committee[1] that more emphasis be placed in future on the payment of debts by contributions from an insolvent's income, the categories of income which can be the subject of a Court order requiring such contributions from a bankrupt have been greatly widened and the bankrupt placed under an obligation to notify the trustee from time to time of any increase in his income since the commencement of the bankruptcy.

The order

18.02 Under Article 283(1) the Court may, on the application of the trustee, make an order, called "an income payments order" claiming for the bankrupt's estate so much of the income of the bankrupt as may be specified in the order during the period for which the order is in force. Such an order cannot be made after the bankrupt's discharge.[2] It can be made on representations made by the trustee at the hearing of an application by the bankrupt for leave to act as director etc. of a company. [3]

18.03 The bankrupt's income which may be made the subject of an income payments order comprises every payment in the nature of income which is from time to time made to him or to which he from time to time becomes entitled, including any payment in respect of the carrying on of any business or in respect of any office or employment.[4] This wide definition appears to avoid the problems associated with the former provisions for attachment of the earnings of a bankrupt.[5]

18.04 The bankrupt's income falling within Article 283 is not after-acquired property. [6] It may only be claimed for the bankrupt's estate under an income payments order. Sums received by the trustee under the order form part of the estate. [7]

18.05 No income payments order can be made which would have the effect of reducing the bankrupt's income below what appears to the Court to be necessary for meeting the reasonable domestic needs of the bankrupt and his family. [8]

18.06 The order will fix the period during which it is to have effect, but it will cease to operate on the bankrupt's discharge unless -
    (a) where the discharge is by order of the Court, the Court, when granting the discharge, imposes a condition that the income payments order should continue, [9] or

(b) in the case of an automatic discharge, the income payments order provides that it shall continue in force after the discharge for a period which cannot exceed 3 years after the making of such order. [10]

18.07 The order may either require the bankrupt himself to pay to the trustee the amount of the income ordered to be paid or require the person making the payment to pay such amount to the trustee instead of to the bankrupt. [11]

Information as to bankrupt's income

18.08 The Official Receiver's investigation of the bankrupt's affairs will include an enquiry as to his current income and the domestic needs of the bankrupt and his family, and such information will be passed by the Official Receiver to the trustee if another person is appointed trustee. [12] If necessary, the bankrupt can be examined about his income at a private or public examination. Thus, the trustee should be in a position at an early stage of the bankruptcy proceedings to decide whether the bankrupt is in a position to make payments from his income for the benefit of his creditors. If he considers that such payments should be made and if he cannot obtain the bankrupt's consent to make appropriate voluntary payments, he should apply to the Court for an income payments order.

18.09 Whether or not the bankrupt is making payments to the trustee out of his income either voluntarily or under an income payments order, the trustee will need to keep himself informed of the bankrupt's income at all times before the bankrupt's discharge so that he may consider whether payments out of income should be commenced or increased. To assist the trustee, the bankrupt is required to notify him of any increase in his income within 21 days of becoming aware of it. [13]

Procedure

(a) Application

18.10 The trustee applies for an income payments order by ordinary application. When the Court has fixed the venue for the hearing of the application the trustee must send a copy of it to the bankrupt, at least 28 days before the hearing date, together with a prescribed form of notice [14] informing him that unless, at least 7 days before the hearing date, he sends to the Court and to the trustee written consent to an order being made in the terms of the application, he is required to attend the hearing and that, if he attends, he will have an opportunity to object to any such order being made or to ask for an order in different terms. [15] The notice has attached to it a tear-off form on which the bankrupt can, if he wishes, intimate to the Court and the trustee his consent to the proposed order. A short statement of the grounds on which the application is made must accompany the notice. [16]

(b) Form of order

18.11 There are two alternative forms of order [17] depending on whether the bankrupt is required to make payment to the trustee or his employer or other payor is required to make payments to the trustee.

(c) Service of order
18.12   The trustee must forthwith send a sealed copy of the order to the bankrupt and if it is an order directing payments by a person other than the bankrupt, to that person.[18]

(d) Variation of order
18.13   It is anticipated that the initial order will usually be in the form requiring the bankrupt to make payments to the trustee. If the bankrupt does not comply with the order, the trustee may apply to the Court for it to be varied so as to take effect as an order directed to the payor of the income. [19]

18.14   Such an application may be made ex parte. [20] A sealed copy of any order made on the application [21] is sent by the Court to the trustee and the bankrupt. [22] The bankrupt may apply to have it set aside.[23] Where appropriate, an additional sealed copy is sent by the Court to the trustee, to be sent by him forthwith to the payor to which it is directed. [24]

18.15   An income payments order may be varied by the Court on representations made by the trustee on the hearing of an application by the bankrupt for leave to act as director etc. of a company. [25]

(e) Compliance by payor of income
18.16   The employer or other person to whom an income payments order is directed must, on receipt of the order, make arrangements to comply with it, unless he is then no longer liable to make any payment of income to the bankrupt, in which case he must forthwith give notice of that fact to the trustee. [26] If, having made payments in compliance with the order, he ceases to be liable to do so, he must forthwith notify the trustee.[27]

18.17   In making any payment to the trustee the payor may deduct the appropriate fee[28] towards the clerical and administrative cost of compliance with the order. [29] He must give the bankrupt a written statement of any such deductions made by him.[30]

Review of order
18.18   Either the bankrupt or the trustee may apply to the Court for an income payments order to be varied or discharged. [31]

18.19   If the trustee applies, he proceeds as in the case of an initial application. [32] Where the bankrupt applies, his application must be accompanied by a short statement of the grounds on which it is made. [33] If no sufficient cause is shown at an ex parte hearing, of which the applicant has been given at least 7 days notice of his right to attend, the application may be dismissed: otherwise a venue will be fixed for hearing, at least 28 days notice of which must be sent by the applicant to the trustee or the bankrupt (whichever of them is not himself the applicant) accompanied by a copy of the application and, when the bankrupt is the applicant, by a copy of the statement of the grounds of the application. (34)

18.20 The trustee may, if he thinks fit, appear and be heard on the application, and, whether or not he intends to appear, he may, not less than 7 days before the hearing date, file a written report of any matters he considers ought to be drawn to the Court's attention, a copy of which must be sent to the bankrupt. (35)

18.21 Sealed copies of any order made on the application are sent by the Court to the trustee, the bankrupt and the payor (if other than the bankrupt). (36)

Footnotes

(1)   Report, Cmd. 8558, paras.1155/1163.
(2)   Art.283(6). See para.18.06 below as to operation of order after discharge.
(3)   Para.28.10.
(4)   Art.283(7).
(5)   MH 3-221: JH 26.09.
(6)   Art.280(5): para12.15: Hals 437.
(7)   Art.283(5).
(8)   Art.283(2).
(9)   Para.21.28.
(10)   Art.283(6).
(11)   Art.283(3).
(12)   Para.14.032.
(13)   Art.306(2): R.6.197(1).
(14)   F.6.67.
(15)   R.6.186.
(16)   R.6.186(2): Atkin Form 266.
(17)   FF.6.68, 6.69.
(18)   R.6.187.
(19)   R.6.188(1).
(20)   R.6.188(2).
(21)   F.6.70.
(22)   R.6.188(3).
(23)   RSC. O.32, r.6: MH 7-440.
(24)   R.6.188(4).
(25)   Para.28.10.
(26)   R.6.189(1),(4).
(27)   R.6.189(4).
(28)   At present 50p - R.0.2.
(29)   R.6.189(2).
(30)   R.6.189(3).
(31)   R.6.190(1).
(32)   R.6.190(2): para.18.10 above: Atkin Form 272.
(33)   R.6.190(3).
(34)   R.6.190(4)-(7).
(35)   R.6.190(8),(9).
(36)   R.6.190(10): F.6.71.

Chapter 19

PROOF OF DEBTS IN BANKRUPTCY

Introduction

19.01   A creditor (defined in Article 9(1), in relation to a bankrupt, as a person to whom a bankruptcy debt is owed) who wishes to recover his debt in whole or in part from the bankrupt's estate must prove his debt by submitting a claim in writing (his "proof") to the Official Receiver, where acting as receiver and manager, or to the trustee, save in the exceptional case referred to in paragraph 19.11 below. [1] The manner of proving debts is prescribed by the Rules [2] and described below. [3]

Provable debts

19.02   The debts which are provable in bankruptcy are, with the limited exceptions referred to below, [4] those debts which are defined as "bankruptcy debts" [5] and other claims which, under provisions of the Order, are declared to be provable, although not due at the date of the bankruptcy order (e.g. loss or damage sustained in consequence of disclaimer of onerous property by the trustee, [6] damages payable under an order of the Court discharging obligations under contracts, [7] debts incurred by a banker or other person in the circumstances mentioned in Article 257(5). [8]

19.03   A bankruptcy debt is -
   (a)   any debt or liability to which the bankrupt is subject at the date of the bankruptcy order,
   (b)   any debt or liability to which he may become subject after the date of the bankruptcy order (including after his discharge from bankruptcy) by reason of any obligation incurred before that date, and
   (c)   any interest on any such debt which bears interest, up to, but not beyond, the date of the bankruptcy order. [9]

19.04   In the Order "liability" means a liability to pay money or money's worth, including any liability under a statutory provision, any liability for breach of trust, any liability in contract, tort or bailment and any liability arising out of an obligation to make restitution. [10] It is immaterial whether the debt or liability is present or future, whether it is certain or contingent or sounding only in damages or whether its amount is fixed or liquidated, or is capable of being ascertained by fixed criteria or as a matter of opinion. [11]

19.05   In determining whether any liability in tort is a bankruptcy debt, the bankrupt is deemed to become subject to that liability by reason of an obligation incurred at the time when the cause of action accrued. [12]

19.06   If, after the making of the bankruptcy order the bankrupt incurs a debt to a banker or other person by reason of making a payment which is void under Article 257 (restrictions on dispositions of property by debtor after the presentation of a bankruptcy petition against him,[13] (e.g. payment of a cheque drawn against an overdrawn account), the debt is deemed to have been incurred before the bankruptcy order was made (and therefore provable as a bankruptcy debt) unless -

(a)   the bank or other person had notice of the bankruptcy before the debt was incurred, or

(b)   it is not reasonably practicable for the banker or other person who made the payment to recover it from the payee.[14]

19.07   The following claims are not provable - [15]

(a)   any fine imposed for an offence [16] and any obligation arising under an order made in family or domestic proceedings; [17]

(b)   any obligation arising under a confiscation order made under Article 4 or 5 of the Criminal Justice (Confiscation) (Northern Ireland) Order 1990;

(c)   a debt which under any enactment or rule of law is not provable, whether on grounds of public policy or otherwise.

19.08   These categories of debts provable in bankruptcy under the Order are broadly the same as under Article 14 of the 1980 Order,[18] with the following variations -

(a)   unliquidated damages in tort are provable, provided that the cause of action has accrued before the date of the bankruptcy order,

(b)   liabilities under a statutory provision (e.g. damages for breach of statutory duty) are expressly included,

(c)   liabilities in bailment are included,

(d)   lump sum orders and orders for costs in matrimonial proceedings, as well as arrears of maintenance, are not provable.[19]

The rule against double proofs continues to apply. [20]

19.09   Of these changes the most significant is the opening up of claims for unliquidated damages in tort. Hitherto a claim based on a tort could only be proved if liquidated by judgment before the adjudication order.

Form of proof

19.10   A "proof of debt" must be in writing, either in the prescribed form or a substantially similar form, made out by or under the directions of the creditor and signed by him or someone authorised in that behalf, [21] except that -

(a)   the trustee may, if he thinks it necessary, require a claim to be verified by affidavit in the prescribed form, whether or not an unsworn proof has already been lodged, [22] and

(b)   a minister of the Crown or a Government Department may prove by any form which shows all such particulars of the debt as are required as are required in the prescribed form of proof of debt and as are relevant in the circumstances.[23]

19.11   There is one case in which a proof of debt is not required, namely where the Court, in exceptional circumstances, by order declares the creditors, or any class of them, entitled to vote at a creditors' meeting without being required to prove their debts and, on the application of the trustee, makes a consequential order treating a creditor as having proved his debt for the purpose of permitting payment of dividend.[24]

19.12   Unless the Court otherwise orders, forms of proof of debt must be sent by the Official Receiver or the trustee to every creditor of the bankrupt known to the sender or identified in the bankrupt's statement of affairs, at the same time as he sends the earliest of the following notices -
- (a)   notice to creditors of the Official Receiver's decision not to call a first meeting of creditors, or
- (b)   the first notice calling a meeting of creditors, or
- (c)   where a certificate of summary administration has been issued, the notice sent by the Official Receiver to creditors notifying them of the bankruptcy order, or
- (d)   where a trustee is appointed by the Court, the notice of his appointment sent by him to creditors.[25]

19.13   Where a trustee is appointed by the Court and the Court gives the trustee leave to advertise his appointment instead of sending notice of it to the creditors, the trustee is required to send proofs to the creditors within 4 months after the date of the bankruptcy order.[26]

19.14   A proof of debt must contain -
- (a)   the creditor's name and address;
- (b)   the total amount of his claim as at the date of the bankruptcy order, and whether or not it includes any outstanding uncapitalised interest;
- (c)   whether or not the claim includes value added tax;[27]
- (d)   whether the whole or any part of the debt falls within any (and if so which) of the categories of preferential debts;[28]
- (e)   particulars of how and when the debt was incurred by the bankrupt;
- (f)   particulars of any security held, the date when it was given and the value which the creditor puts on it;
- (g)   the name, address and authority of the person signing the proof (if not the creditor himself); and
- (h)   references to any documents by which the debt can be substantiated.[29]

19.15   Documents referred to in a proof as substantiating the debt need not be attached to the proof or submitted with it, but the trustee, or the convener or chairman of any meeting, may call for any document or other evidence to be produced to him for that purpose. [30]

19.16 Unless the trustee allows, the proof in respect of money owed on a negotiable instrument or security cannot be admitted without production of the instrument or security itself or a copy of it, certified by the creditor or his authorised representative to be a true copy. [31]

Time for proving debt
19.17 A proof for the purpose of voting at a meeting of creditors must be lodged within the time specified in the notice convening the meeting[32] or, if the meeting is adjourned, up to midday on the business day immediately before the adjourned meeting. [33]

19.18 For the debt proved to rank for dividend, the proof must be lodged by the last day for proving specified in the notice of intention to declare a dividend or a postponed date fixed by the Court on the application of any person, although the trustee may, if he thinks fit, deal with a proof lodged after that date. [34] A creditor who proves after a dividend has been paid is entitled to receive a dividend from any money available for the payment of any further dividend. [35]

Withdrawal or variation of proof
19.19 A proof may at any time, by agreement between the creditor and the trustee, be withdrawn or varied as to the amount claimed. [36]

Transmission of proofs to trustee
19.20 On the appointment of a trustee the Official Receiver must forthwith send him all proofs he has received, with an itemised list of them which the trustee signs by way of receipt and returns to the Official Receiver. [37] Thenceforth all proofs must be sent to the trustee and retained by him. [38]

Inspection of proofs
19.21 The trustee must allow the proofs in his hands to be inspected at all reasonable times on any business day by any creditor who has submitted his proof (unless it has been wholly rejected), the bankrupt and any person acting on behalf of such creditor or the bankrupt. [39] He cannot refuse inspection on the grounds of confidentiality. [40]

Quantification of certain claims
(a) Claims of uncertain value
19.22 Under Article 295(3) and (4) where the debt claimed does not bear a certain value, by reason of its being subject to any contingency or contingencies or for any other reason, its value is to be estimated by the trustee or (on an application under Article 276(2) [41]) by the Court, and the value of the estimate is the amount provable. In contrast to Article 14(7) of the 1980 Order, the new provisions do not permit the exclusion of any proof on the ground that the value

of the debt cannot be fairly estimated. The task of the trustee in estimating the value of some claims, particularly claims for unliquidated damages in tort, may be formidable. If he cannot reach agreement with the claimant, he may either make his own decision, leaving it to the creditor to appeal to the Court if dissatisfied,[42] or himself invite the Court to make the estimate.[43]

(b) Interest
19.23 Interest provided for in a contract, except in so far as it is payable in respect of any period after the date of the bankruptcy order, is provable as part of that debt.[44] The rate of interest is the rate stipulated in the contract, subject to any order made by the Court under Article 316 (extortionate credit transactions).[45]

19.24 Where a money judgment bears interest under Article 127 of the Judgments Enforcement Order such interest up to the date of the bankruptcy order or until the date of any enforcement application (including a preliminary application) may be proved.

19.25 Interest not otherwise payable may be proved as follows -
(i) if the debt is due by virtue of a written instrument and payable at a certain time, interest may be claimed from that time to the date of the bankruptcy order;[46]
(ii) if the debt is due otherwise, interest may be claimed only if, before the presentation of the bankruptcy petition, a written demand for payment was made by or on behalf of the creditor and notice given that interest would be payable from the date of the demand to the date of payment, in which case interest may be claimed for the period from the date of the demand to the date of the bankruptcy order.[47]
In either case the rate of interest is the rate payable on a money judgment of the High Court on the date of the bankruptcy order.[48]

(c) Debts payable after a bankruptcy order
19.26 A creditor may prove for a debt of which payment was not due at the date of the bankruptcy order, but any dividend paid before the date the debt becomes due is subject to a reduction for early payment, effected by a reduction of the amount of the proof admitted for dividend in accordance with a prescribed formula.[49] However, other creditors are not entitled to interest out of surplus funds[50] until the full amounts of any such debts are paid in full.[51]

(d) Periodical payments
19.27 The amount of any rent and other periodical payments (unless otherwise excluded[52]) due and unpaid up to the date of the bankruptcy order and the apportioned part of any payment accruing due at that date may be proved.[53]

(e) Discounts
19.28   The creditor must deduct from his claim all trade and other discounts, except any discount for immediate, early or cash settlement.[54]

(f) Debt in foreign currency
19.29   The amount of a debt incurred or payable in a currency other than sterling must be converted into sterling at the official exchange rate at the Bank of England as published for the date of the bankruptcy order or, in the absence of such published rate, at such rate as the Court determines. [55]

(g) Costs of legal proceedings [56]
19.30   With the exception of costs in matrimonial proceedings,[57] costs awarded against a person subsequently adjudged bankrupt are provable if the judgment or order under which they are payable is given or made before the date of the bankruptcy order, even if not then taxed. Otherwise the plaintiff's costs are not provable unless they are incurred in an action in respect of a claim which is provable and at the date of the bankruptcy order he was in a position to enter judgment as of right as a result of the defendant having failed to enter an appearance or serve a defence or having admitted liability by paying money into court. The defendant's costs of an action by a person subsequently adjudged bankrupt are not provable where neither judgment on the claim nor an order for costs is given or made before the date of the bankruptcy order.

Proof of debt by secured creditor
19.31   The rights of a secured creditor to realise his security are preserved by the Order,[58] subject to a minor restriction in relation to a security on goods held by any person by way of pledge, pawn or other security. Such security cannot be realised without leave of the Court where the Official Receiver has given notice that he intends to inspect the goods, unless the person holding the security has given the trustee a reasonable opportunity of inspecting them and of exercising the bankrupt's right of redemption.[59]

19.32   A secured creditor means a creditor holding a mortgage, charge, lien or other security over any property of the bankrupt, other than a lien on books, papers or other records, not being documents held as documents of title to property.[60]

19.33   A secured creditor may rely entirely on his security and refrain from proving in the bankruptcy. If, however, he is prepared to surrender his security voluntarily, for the general benefit of the creditors, he may prove for his whole debt, as if it were unsecured.[61]

19.34   If the creditor considers that his debt is not fully secured, he may value the security and prove for the unsecured balance. He may subsequently alter the value he has put upon his security in his proof, with the agreement of the trustee or with leave of the Court, unless he is the petitioning creditor and has valued his security in the petition or has voted in respect of the unsecured balance of his debt, in either of which cases he may re-value his security only with leave of the Court.[62] If he realises his security after he has valued it in his proof, the net amount realised is substituted for such value and treated as an amended valuation made by him.[63] If he realises the security before proving his debt, he may prove for the balance of the debt, after deducting the amount realised.[64]

19.35 If a secured creditor omits to disclose his security in his proof, he must surrender it for the general benefit of creditors unless, on his application, the Court relieves him on the ground that the omission was inadvertent or the result of honest mistake.[65] If the Court does grant such relief, it may require or allow the creditor's proof to be amended, on such terms as may be just.[66]

19.36 Where a creditor has valued his security in his proof the trustee may at any time give notice to him that he proposes, at the expiration of 28 days from the date of the notice, to redeem the security at the value put upon it in the proof.[67] The creditor may then exercise his right to re-value the security (with leave of the Court if required) within 21 days or such longer period as the trustee may allow, and if he does so the trustee can only redeem at the new value.[68] The creditor may at any time serve a written notice on the trustee calling upon him to elect whether he will or will not exercise his power to redeem the security at the value then placed on it; and the trustee then has 6 months in which to redeem or determine not to do so.[69] In any event the cost of redemption is borne by the estate.[70]

19.37 Unless the re-valuation of the security has been approved by the Court, the trustee, if he is dissatisfied with the value placed on it by the secured creditor in his proof or when re-valued in response to a notice to redeem, may require any property comprised in the security to be offered for sale on such terms as may be agreed, or as directed by the Court; and if the sale is by auction, the trustee on behalf of the estate and the creditor on his own behalf may appear and bid.[71]

19.38 Failure by a secured creditor to comply with the requirements of the Order or the Rules relating to the valuation of securities may result in his being wholly or partially disqualified from participating in any dividend.[72]

Admission and rejection of proofs
(a) For entitlement to vote
19.39 A creditor's proof for the purpose of his entitlement to vote at a meeting of creditors may be admitted or rejected by the chairman, subject to appeal to the Court against his decision.[73]

(b) For dividend
19.40 The trustee may admit a proof for dividend either for the whole amount claimed by the creditor, or for part of that amount.[74]

19.41   The trustee must deal with every proof, either by admitting or rejecting it in whole or in part or by making such provision as he thinks fit in respect of it, not later than 7 days from the last date for proving specified in his notice of intention to declare a dividend ("the final date"),[75] unless the Court, on the application of any person, postpones that date.[76]

19.42   Before making a decision as to the admission of a proof the trustee may require further evidence from the claimant.[77]

19.43   The trustee is not obliged to deal with a proof lodged after the final date, but he may do so if he thinks fit.[78]

19.44   After the final date the trustee is under an obligation, if he intends to declare a final dividend, to declare and distribute that dividend without regard to the claim of any person in respect of a debt which has not already been proved.[79]

19.45   If the trustee rejects a proof in whole or in part, he must forthwith send to the creditor a written statement of his reasons for doing so. [80]

19.46   If a creditor is dissatisfied with the trustee's decision with respect to his proof (including any decision on the question of preference) he may, within 21 days of receiving the written statement of the trustee's reasons for rejection, apply to the Court to have the decision reversed or varied.[81] The bankrupt or any other creditor dissatisfied with the trustee's decision on any proof, may make such an application within 21 days of becoming aware of the decision.[82]

19.47   Notice of the venue fixed by the Court for the hearing of the application must be sent by the applicant to the creditor who lodged the proof (if it is not himself) and to the trustee.[83] On receiving such notice the trustee is required to file in the Court the proof, together (if appropriate) with a copy of his statement of his reasons for rejecting it.[84]

19.48   After the application has been determined the proof must be returned by the Court to the trustee, unless it has been wholly disallowed.[85]

19.49   The Official Receiver is not personally liable for costs incurred by any person on such an application, and the trustee (if other than the Official Receiver) is not so liable unless the Court so orders.[86]

Expunging of proofs
19.50   Where the trustee considers that a proof has been improperly admitted or that the amount for which it has been admitted ought to be reduced, he will first endeavour to reach agreement with the creditor to have the proof withdrawn or varied.[87] If such agreement cannot be reached he may apply to the Court to expunge the proof or reduce the amount claimed. [88] A creditor may also apply for such an order if the trustee declines to interfere in the matter. [89]

19.51   Notice of the date fixed by the Court for hearing the application must be sent by the applicant, in the case of an application by the trustee, to the creditor who made the proof, and if the application is made by a creditor, to the trustee and to the creditor who made the proof (if not himself).[90]

Mutual dealing[91]

19.52   Where, before the date of the bankruptcy order, there have been mutual credits, mutual debts or other mutual dealings between the bankrupt and any creditor of the bankrupt proving or claiming to prove for a bankruptcy debt, an account is to be taken of what is due from each party to the other in respect of the dealings, and the sums due from one party are to be set off against the sums due from the other. [92] If the balance of the account is in favour of the creditor he may prove for that balance; if the account shows a balance due to the estate, this is to be paid to the trustee.[93]

19.53   In taking the account sums due from the bankrupt to another party who had notice at the time they became due that a bankruptcy petition relating to the bankrupt was pending must be excluded.[94]   This replaces Article 17(2) of the 1980 Order which was related to notice of an available act of bankruptcy committed by the bankrupt, but whereas under the 1980 Order the time at which notice was relevant was the time of giving credit to the bankrupt, under the Order the relevant time is the time the sums became due.

19.54   Where the creditor has both a preferential claim and a non-preferential claim against the bankrupt, the amount due from him to the bankrupt must be set off rateably against the non-preferential debt and the preferential debt in proportion to the respective amounts of those debts.[95]

19.55   A debt owed by a Government Department may be set off against a debt owed to another Government Department. [96]

Costs of proving debt
19.56   Unless the Court otherwise orders -
  (a)   a creditor must bear the cost of proving his debt, including the cost of providing documents or evidence called for by the trustee or the convener or chairman of any meeting,
  (b)   the trustee's costs of estimating the value of a bankruptcy debt which does not bear a certain value are payable as an expense of the bankruptcy.[97]

Footnotes

(1)   R.6.094(1),(2). For proof of debts, for purpose of voting at creditor's meetings, see paras.16.17/23.
(2)   Art.295(1), Sch.6, para.15.
(3)   Paras.19.10/16.
(4)   Para.19.07.
(5)   Arts.9(1), 295(1).
(6)   Para.14.061.
(7)   Para.14.086.
(8)   Para.19.06.
(9)   Arts.9(1), 295(2): R.6.110(1).
(10)   Art.2(2).
(11)   Art.2(4):R.12.03(1).
(12)   Art.2(3).
(13)   Para.7.022.
(14)   Art.257(5): MH 3-158: Paget, Law of Banking, 10th edn.p.310.
(15)   R.12.03(2)-(5): MH 7-710: Hals 485, 488, 490.
(16)   Thus revering the previous law as declared in Re Pascoe (No 2) [1944] Ch 310.
(17)   As defined in Art.255(8) - R.12.03(3). Penalties under ss. 93 and 95 of the Taxes Management Act 1970 are provable - Re Harren [1983] 1 WLR 183.
(18)   JH Ch.29.
(19)   MH 3-388.
(20)   Hals 483: JH 29.013.
(21)   R.6.094(3): F.6.40. A facsimile proof is not acceptable - (1989) Ins Int 64.
(22)   RR.6.094(6), 6.097(1),(2): F.6.42. The affidavit may be sworn before an Official Receiver or a Deputy Official Receiver or any authorised officer of the Department or of the Court - R.6.097(3), or before the creditor's own solicitor - R.7.52(4).
(23)   R.6.094(4).
(24)   R.6.090(2),(3): para.16.18.
(25)   R.6.095(1),(2),(4).
(26)   R.6.095(3).
(27)   See paras.28.55/58 re V.A.T. bad debt relief.
(28)   Paras.28.08/09.
(29)   R.6.096(1),(2).
(30)   R.6.096(2),(3).
(31)   R.6.105.
(32)   R.6.077(4).
(33)   R.6.089(7).
(34)   Art.303: RR.11.02(3), 11.03(2): paras 20.22/24.
(35)   Art.298(1).
(36)   R.6.103: Atkin Form 156.
(37)   R.6.100.
(38)   Ibid.

(39)   R.6.099. See para.16.34 re inspection of proofs at creditor's meetings.
(40)   R.12.14(4).
(41)   Para.14.004.
(42)   *Ibid.*
(43)   Art.276(2).
(44)   Art.295(2).
(45)   Paras.14.108/111.
(46)   R.6.110(2).
(47)   R.6.110(3),(4).
(48)   R.6.110(5).
(49)   RR.6.111, 11.13(1),(2).
(50)   Para.20.17.
(51)   R.11.13(3).
(52)   Para.19.07.
(53)   R.6.109.
(54)   R.6.107.
(55)   R.6.108.
(56)   Hals 489.
(57)   Fn.19 above.
(58)   Art.258(5).
(59)   Art.258(6),(7).
(60)   Art.10(1),(3).
(61)   R.6.106(2).
(62)   R.6.112.
(63)   R.6.116.
(64)   R.6.106(1).
(65)   R.6.113(1).
(66)   R.6.113(2).
(67)   R.6.114(1).
(68)   R.6.114(2),(3). See para.20.41 re re-valuation of security after declaration of dividend.
(69)   R.6.114(5).
(70)   R.6.114(4).
(71)   R.6.115.
(72)   Para.20.42.
(73)   R.6.091(1),(2): paras.16.22/23.
(74)   R.6.101(1).
(75)   R.11.03(1): para.20.23.
(76)   Art.303(3).
(77)   Atkin Form 155.
(78)   R.11.03(2).
(79)   Art.303(4).
(80)   R.6.101(2): Atkin Form 154.
(81)   R.6.102(1),(2): Atkin Forms 428, 429. As to extension of time for such application, see *Re Vanbergen* [1955] WLR 20, MH 3-373, JH 29.079, but note change of wording from former rule.
(82)   R.6.102(3).

(83) R.6.102(4).
(84) R.6.102(5).
(85) R.6.102(6).
(86) R.6.102(7).
(87) Para.19.19.
(88) R.6.104(1): Atkin Forms 163, 165, 166.
(89) *Ibid.*
(90) R.6.104(2).
(91) MH 3-251/3-254/2: Hals 535/547: Paget, Law of Banking, 10th edn. pp.513/7 re set off in company winding up.
(92) Art.296(1),(2). A creditor is not required to set off a secured debt - *Re Norman (Holdings) Co. Ltd.* [1991] 1 WLR 10.
(93) Art.296(4).
(94) Art.296(3).
(95) *Re Unit 2 Windows Ltd.* [1985] 1 WLR 1383.
(96) *Re D.H. Curtis (Builders) Ltd.* [1978] Ch.162, *Re Cushla Ltd.* [1979] 3 All ER 415.
(97) R.6.098.

Chapter 20

DISTRIBUTION OF BANKRUPT'S ESTATE

I. ORDER OF PAYMENTS

Introduction
20.01 The bankrupt's estate must be applied by the trustee in an order of priority fixed by the Order and the Rules, but subject to any other statutory provisions under which the payment of any debt or the making of any other payment is, in the event of bankruptc y, to have a particular priority or to be postponed.[1]

A. EXPENSES

Priority of expenses
20.02 Certain expenses are a first charge on the estate, namely -
  (a) costs properly incurred in the administration of a voluntary arrangement where a bankruptcy order is made against the arranging debtor on the petition of the supervisor or a person bound by the arrangement.[2]
  (b) expenses properly incurred in the administration of a voluntary arrangement where a bankruptcy order is made on a debtor's petition presented at a time when the voluntary arrangement is in force, [3]
  (c) trustee's expenses of purchasing items to replace exempt property of excess value,[4]
  (d) in the case of a subsequent bankruptcy of an undischarged bankrupt, in respect of property acquired since the earlier bankruptcy, the expenses incurred by the trustee in the earlier bankruptcy,[5]
  (e) expenses properly incurred by the trustee under a deed of arrangement where the deed is avoided by reason of the bankruptcy of the debtor.[6]

20.03 If, after allowing for any such charges, and subject to any order of the Court for the payment out of the estate of costs of proceedings against the trustee,[7] the property comprised in the bankrupt's estate is insufficient to pay all proper expenses, such expenses[8] must be discharged strictly in the order of priority prescribed by the Rules, unless the Court otherwise orders. [9]

20.04 When all prior charges and expenses have been paid or provided for any balance of funds available from the bankrupt's estate must be applied by the trustee firstly in payment of the bankrupt's debts in the priority mentioned below. Such distribution may be made without providing for the costs of any person payable out of the estate which have been required to be taxed if the bill has not been delivered for taxation within the time allowed under the Rules. [10]

B. DEBTS

Debts payable in priority to preferential debts

20.05 Where, under Article 319, the trustee repays fees to an apprentice or articled clerk of the bankrupt, such payment has priority over the trustee's obligation to distribute the bankrupt's estate.[11]

20.06 If the debtor dies after the presentation of a bankruptcy petition by or against him reasonable funeral and testamentary expenses have priority over preferential debts.[12]

20.07 Money or property of a registered friendly society or branch in the possession of an officer who becomes bankrupt must be paid or delivered to the trustees of the society or branch on demand, in preference to any other debt or claim against the officer's estate.[13]

Preferential debts

20.08 Subject to the pre-preferential debts mentioned above and to any other statutory provision giving special priority to any other payments, the debts to which preference is given by the Order must be paid in priority to the debts of other unsecured creditors.[14] Where the estate is insufficient, after payment of the expenses of the bankruptcy, for meeting such preferential debts in full, they abate in equal proportions between themselves.[15]

20.09 The preferential debts are listed in Schedule 4 to the Order.[16] The relevant date for their determination is the date of the making of the bankruptcy order (or the date of appointment of an interim receiver, if applicable). Rates and assessed income tax are no longer preferential. Value added tax preference has been reduced to a period of 6 months before the relevant date. Any outstanding sum advanced to make payments of remuneration to employees which, if they had not been paid, would have been preferential debts, is now categorised as such a debt.[17]

20.10 In the case of a bankruptcy where the adjudication order was made between 1st June 1990 and 1st October 1991, revised categories of preferential debts, identical to those in Schedule 4 to the Order, are applicable.[18]

20.11 Preferential creditors are not distinguished from other creditors with regard to voting at meetings of creditors. There is no provision in the Order or the Rules corresponding to Article 21 of the 1980 Order, under which a preferential creditor who voted for or against the acceptance of a bankrupt's offer of composition thereby lost his preferential rights unless the Court, on application, was satisfied that his so voting had arisen from inadvertence.

Debts of ordinary creditors

20.12 After the pre-preferential and preferential debts have been paid in full, the debts of all other unsecured creditors, except those whose debts are postponed[19](usually referred to as "ordinary creditors"), are payable in full, unless the estate is insufficient for meeting them, in which case they abate to equal proportions between themselves.[20]

Interest on debts

20.13 If there is a surplus after payment of all unsecured debts, other than postponed debts, interest is payable out of such surplus on the debts of ordinary creditors and preferential creditors equally in respect of the period during which they have been outstanding since the date of the bankruptcy order.[21] The rate of interest is the greater of the following -

(a) the rate applicable to a money judgment of the High Court at the date of the bankruptcy order, and

(b) the rate applicable to that debt apart from the bankruptcy[22]

20.14 Such interest is not payable until any proved debt the payment of which is not due until after declaration of a dividend, has been paid in full.[23]

Postponed debts
(a) Under the Order
20.15 Two categories of postponed debts are created by the Order, namely debts to a spouse and unsatisfied debts arising in an earlier bankruptcy.

<u>(i) Debts to spouse</u>
Debts in respect of credit provided by a person who (whether or not the bankrupt's spouse at the time the credit was provided) was the bankrupt's spouse at the date of the bankruptcy order rank in priority after the debts of ordinary creditors and interest on such debts.[24] Interest is payable on debts due to a spouse in respect of the period during which they have been outstanding since the date of the bankruptcy order at the same rate as in respect of debts of ordinary creditors, and such interest has the same priority as the debts on which it is payable[25]

<u>(ii) Debts in earlier bankruptcy</u>
If a bankruptcy order is made against an undischarged bankrupt, the trustee in the earlier bankruptcy may prove in the later bankruptcy for the unsatisfied balance of the debts provable in the earlier bankruptcy, any interest payable on that balance and any unpaid expenses of the earlier bankruptcy, but any amount so provable ranks in priority after all the other debts provable in the later bankruptcy and interest on such debts.[26]

(b) Under other statutory provisions
20.16 Under the provisions mentioned below the payment of certain debts in bankruptcy is postponed until other creditors of the bankrupt have been paid in full (with statutory interest, where applicable).

(i) Partnership Act 1890

Where a loan is made to a person engaged or about to be engaged in business under a contract that the lender is to receive a rate of interest varying with the profits or a share of the profits of the business, or where a person sells the goodwill of his business in consideration of a share of the profits of the business, then if the borrower or buyer is adjudged bankrupt or makes an arrangement to pay his creditors less than one hundred pence in the pound, or dies insolvent, the lender is not entitled to recover anything in respect of his loan, or even to prove his debt[27] until the claims of the other creditors of the borrower for valuable consideration have been satisfied.[28]

(ii) Financial Services Act 1986 and Banking Act 1987

The following are not provable until all other claims of creditors have been paid in full, with statutory interest, namely any claim arising by virtue of -

(A) section 6(3)(a) of the Financial Services Act 1986 (sums ordered by the court to be paid by a person carrying on investment business without due authorisation), not being a claim also arising by virtue of section 6(3)(b), where one or more investors have suffered loss or been otherwise adversely affected as a result or that person's contravention of the statutory provisions;

(B) section 61(3)(a) of the said Act (sums ordered by the court to be paid by a person carrying on investment business who contravenes any provision or condition mentioned in sub-section (1)(a)), not being a claim also arising by virtue of section 61(3)(b), where one or more investors have suffered loss or been otherwise adversely affected as a result of that person's contravention of the investment rules and regulations;

(C) section 49 of the Banking Act 1987 (sums ordered by the court to be paid by a person accepting deposits whilst unauthorised). [29]

C. SURPLUS

General

20.17 If a surplus remains after payment of expenses[30] of the bankruptcy and the payment in full and with interest, of all the bankrupt's creditors the bankrupt is entitled to the surplus.[31]

Re-vesting in bankrupt

20.18 If the surplus includes any unrealised land vested in the trustee, it will usually be necessary for him to re-vest title in the bankrupt by conveyance, assignment or Land Registry transfer, as appropriate. Similarly, any other unrealised property vested in the trustee which cannot be transferred by delivery will usually be re-vested in the bankrupt by the appropriate means of transfer. Any such conveyance or other requisite mode of transfer will be at the expense of the bankrupt. There is no provision in the Order, as there was in the

1980 Order[32]for the Court, on the application of the bankrupt, to make a vesting order in relation to surplus property. Presumably, in an appropriate case, a vesting order could be made under section 41 (1) or 51 (1) of the Trustee Act (Northern Ireland) 1958, but this would require an application to the Chancery Division by originating summons, which would be more expensive than the execution by the trustee of the appropriate transfer document.

II. DIVIDENDS

General
20.19 Whenever the trustee has sufficient funds in hand, after retaining such sums as are necessary for the expenses[33]of the bankruptcy, (including the costs of the final meeting of creditors[34]) to make payments to creditors, he is required to declare and distribute dividends among the creditors in respect of the bankruptcy debts they have proved.[35]

20.20 No action lies against the trustee for a dividend, but if he refuses to pay a dividend the Court may order him to pay it and also to pay, out of his own money, interest on the dividend from the time it was withheld, at the rate applicable to a money judgment of the High Court at that time and the costs of the proceedings in which the order to pay is made.[36]

20.21 Except as mentioned below,[37]the Rules governing the declaration and payment of dividends apply to any distribution made to preferential creditors, with such adaptations as are appropriate to creditors of a limited class.[38]

Notice of intended dividend
20.22 The trustee must give notice of his intention to declare and distribute a dividend.[39] Such notice must be given to all creditors whose addresses are known to him and who have not proved their debts, except that notice of a dividend to preferential creditors need only be given to those creditors whose debts he believes to be preferential.[40] A notice of an intended dividend must also be given by public advertisement before a first dividend is declared, unless the trustee has previously, by public advertisement, invited creditors to prove their debts or where a dividend is to be declared for preferential creditors, in which case public advertisement of the intended dividend is only to be given if the insolvency practitioner thinks fit.[41]

20.23 The notice must specify the last date for proving, which must be the same for all creditors and not less than 21 days from the date of the notice.[42] It must also specify whether the dividend is interim or final and state the trustee's intention to declare the dividend within 4 months from the last date for proving.[43]

20.24 The trustee must deal with any outstanding creditor's proof within 7 days from the date he has specified as the last date for proving.[44]

20.25   When the trustee has realised all the bankrupt's estate or so much as can, in his opinion, be realised without needlessly protracting the trustee-ship,[45] he must give notice of his intention to declare a final dividend, or if no dividend or no further dividend will be declared, notice to that effect.[46] Such notice must specify the final date for the establishment of claims against the estate.[47] Such date may be postponed by the Court, on the application of any person.[48]

20.26   A notice that no dividend or no further dividend is to be declared must contain a statement to the effect either that no funds have been realised or that the funds realised have already been distributed or used or allocated for defraying the expenses of administration.[49]

20.27   Notice of intention to declare a final dividend may be given at the same time as notice of the final meeting of creditors.[50]

20.28   The trustee is under an obligation to declare a dividend within the period stated in the notice of intended dividend unless, within that period, he has rejected a proof in whole or in part and there is a pending application for this decision to be reversed or varied,[51] or for any decision of his on a proof to be reversed or varied, or for a proof to be expunged or for a reduction in the amount claimed; in any such case he may postpone or cancel the dividend and may not, without leave of the Court, declare the dividend.[52] If such leave is given, the trustee must make such provision in respect of the proof in question as the Court directs.[53]

Calculation of dividend
20.29   In the calculation and distribution of a dividend, the trustee must make provision -
   (a)   for any bankruptcy debts which appear to him to be due to persons who, by reason of the distance of their place of residence, may not have had sufficient time to tender and establish their proofs,
   (b)   for any bankruptcy debts which are the subject of claims which have not yet been determined, and
   (c)   for disputed proofs and claims.[54]

Notice of dividend
20.30   Where the trustee has declared a dividend, he must give notice of the dividend and how it is proposed to distribute it to all creditors who have proved their debts, and the notice must include the following particulars of the bankruptcy and the administration of the bankrupt's estate -
   (a)   amounts realised from the sale of assets, indicating (so far as practicable) amounts raised by the sale of particular assets;
   (b)   payments made by the trustee in the administration of the estate;
   (c)   provision (if any) made for unsettled claims, and funds (if any) retained for particular purposes;
   (d)   the total amount to be distributed, and the rate of dividend;

(e) whether, and if so when, any further dividend is expected to be declared. [55]

Payment of dividend

20.31   Dividends are paid by payment instruments (payable orders or cheques) issued by the Department on the application of the trustee. [56] The application [57] must be accompanied by a certified list of all proofs admitted for dividend and if requested by the Department, by the proofs themselves. [58]

20.32   The trustee must enter the total amount of every dividend which he desires to pay in his financial records in respect of the estate in one sum. [59] The date and the amount in the pound of each dividend is also required to be recorded. [60]

20.33   The dividend may be distributed simultaneously with the notice declaring it. [61] The payable order or cheque in payment of the dividend may be posted or arrangements made with any creditor for the dividend to be paid to him in another way, or held for his collection. [62]

20.34   Where a dividend is paid on a negotiable instrument, the amount of the dividend must be endorsed on the instrument, or on a certified copy of it, if required to be produced by the holder for that purpose. [63]

20.35   On the expiration of 6 months from the last day of the month of issue, any lapsed payable orders and any cheques which have not been delivered, must be destroyed by the trustee after first preparing a list of their numbers, names of payees and amounts, which list is to be sent to the Department. [64]

20.36   If a creditor entitled to a dividend has assigned his entitlement to another person or wishes it to be paid to another person and gives notice to the trustee to that effect, specifying the name and address of the person to whom payment is to be made, the trustee must pay the dividend to that other. [65]

20.37   Where a creditor has proved for a debt of which payment is not due at the date of the declaration of dividend, he is entitled to be paid a dividend equally with other creditors, but subject to a reduction for early payment, effected by a reduction of the amount of the admitted proof in accordance with a prescribed formula. [66] However, the full amount of any such debt must be paid in full before other creditors are entitled to interest out of surplus funds. [67]

20.38   A creditor who has not proved his debt before a dividend is declared may not, by reason that he has not participated in it, disturb the distribution of that dividend or any other dividend declared earlier, but when he has proved his debt he is entitled to be paid any dividend or dividends he has failed to receive out of any money available for the payment of any further dividend before such further dividend is paid. [68]

20.39   After the final date for proof of debts specified in the notice of intention to declare a dividend[69] the trustee must defray any outstanding expenses of the bankruptcy out of the bankrupt's estate and, if he intends to declare a final dividend, declare and distribute that dividend without regard to the claim of any person in respect of a debt which has not already been proved.[70]

Alteration of proof after payment of dividend
20.40   If the amount claimed by a creditor in his proof is increased after payment of dividend, the creditor is not entitled to disturb the distribution of the dividend; but he is entitled to be paid any dividend or dividends he has failed to receive out of any money available for the payment of any further dividend before such further dividend is paid.[71]

20.41   If a creditor's proof is withdrawn or expunged after it has been admitted, or if the amount admitted is reduced, the creditor must repay to the trustee any amount of dividend overpaid.[72]

20.42   Similar consequences follow where a secured creditor re-values his security after payment of a dividend and as a consequence the amount of his unsecured claim ranking for dividend is increased or reduced.[73]

20.43   If a creditor contravenes any provision of the Order or the Rules relating to the valuation of securities, the Court may, on the application of the trustee, order that the creditor be wholly or partly disqualified from participation in any dividend.[74]

Unclaimed dividends etc.
20.44   Any moneys representing unclaimed dividends or unclaimed or undistributed assets in the hands of the trustee at the date he vacates office or which come into the hands of any former trustee at any time after he vacates office, must forthwith be paid by him into the Insolvency Account.[75]

20.45   Any person claiming to be entitled to any money paid into the Insolvency Account may apply to the Department for payment, supported by such evidence of the claim as the Department may require.[76] Any person dissatisfied with the decision of the Department in respect of such claim may appeal to the Court.[77]

20.46   If at the time of vacating office the trustee has in his hands any valid unclaimed payable orders for dividends or cheques for dividends which have not been delivered, he must send to the Department such payable orders after defacing them by cutting off the bottom right hand corner and such cheques after endorsing them with the word "cancelled".[78]

Distribution of property in specie
20.47   Where any property cannot be readily or advantageously sold because of its peculiar nature or other specified circumstances, the trustee may, without

prejudice to his power of disclaimer, with the permission of the creditors' committee, distribute it among the bankrupt's creditors in specie, as dividends, according to its estimated value.[79] Where prior permission of the creditors' committee is not obtained, the action of the trustee may be ratified by the Court or the committee, for the purpose of enabling him to meet his expenses out of the bankrupt's estate.[80] Any permission must relate to a particular proposed exercise of the power in question and cannot be a general permission; but a person dealing with the trustee in good faith and for value is not concerned to enquire whether the required permission has been given.[81]

Footnotes

(1) Art 300(6).
(2) Art 250(2).
(3) R.6.044.
(4) Art.281(3): para.12.07.
(5) Art.308(3): R.6.226: para.23.11.
(6) Art.220: para.27.45.
(7) Under the Court's general discretion in relation to costs - Judicature (Northern Ireland) Act 1978, s.59(1): para.5.112.
(8) "Expenses" includes all costs incurred in the course of bankruptcy proceedings R.12.02.
(9) R.6.222: MH 7-504. The N.I. Rule preserves the Court's discretion - cf. Insolvency Rules 1986, Rule 6.224(1).
(10) R.7.32(4): para.5.130.
(11) Art.319(4). If the fee is repaid by the Department out of the Northern Ireland Redundancy Fund the rights and remedies of the apprentice are transferred to the Department - Industrial Relations (Northern Ireland) Order 1976, Arts 42, 45.
(12) DIEO, Art 5(1),(2).
(13) Friendly Societies Act (Northern Ireland) 1970, s.50.
(14) Art.300(1),(6).
(15) Art.300(2). See para.28.41 re payment of preferential debts from proceeds of distress levied within 3 months prior to bankruptcy order.
(16) Arts.346, 347. These provisions bind the Crown - Art 378(b).
(17) Sch.4, para 11.
(18) Sch.9, Pt. III, brought into operation by Insolvency (1989 Order) (Commencement No. 1) Order (Northern Ireland) 1990.
(19) Paras.20.15/16.
(20) Art.300(3).
(21) Art.300(4).
(22) Art.300(5).
(23) R.11.13(3): para.20.37.
(24) Art.302.
(25) *Ibid.*
(26) Art.308(5),(6): para.23.10.
(27) *Ex p. Taylor* (1879) 12 Ch D 366.
(28) Partnership Act 1890, s.2(3)(d), 3: Hals. 575: IPO Art 10(2). A claim is not "satisfied" until paid in full, with statutory interest -*Re Baughan* [1947] Ch 313, 327.
(29) R.12.03(4).
(30) Fn.(8) above.
(31) Art.303(5).
(32) 1980 Order, Art.26(2).
(33) Fn.(8) above.
(34) Art.304(4): para.14.113.

(35)   Art.297(1). See para.16.18 re exceptional order under which debts not proved may be admitted for dividend.

(36)   Art.298(2): Atkin Form 362.

(37)   Para.20.22.

(38)   R.11.12(1).

(39)   Art.297(2).

(40)   RR.11.02(1), 11.12(2).

(41)   RR.11.02(2), 11.12(2). Such an invitation will often be included in the advertisement of the appointment of the trustee.

(42)   R.11.02(3). See para.20.25 re postponement of this date.

(43)   R.11.02(4).

(44)   R.11.03(1): para.19.18.

(45)   See para.14.114 re unrealised dwelling house.

(46)   Art.303(1).

(47)   Art.303(2). This provision also requires the notice to contain prescribed particulars, but no such particulars have been prescribed for the notice of intention to declare a dividend, although prescribed for notice of declaration of dividend - para 20.30.

(48)   Art.303(3).

(49)   R.11.07.

(50)   Art.304(3): para.14.113.

(51)   Para.19.46.

(52)   RR.11.04, 11.05.

(53)   R.11.05(3).

(54)   Art.297(4).

(55)   Art.297(3): R.11.06(1),(2): Atkin Forms 357, 358.

(56)   Ins Regs 17(1). This provision and Reg 17(2) apply retrospectively to applications made in a bankruptcy which commenced before 1st October 1991 - Ins Regs 52(1).

(57)   Ins Regs, Sch.Form 3.

(58)   Ins Regs 17(2): Atkin Form 360. See fn.(56) above re retrospection.

(59)   Ins Regs 17(4).

(60)   Ins Pract Regs 15, Sch.3.

(61)   R.11.06(3).

(62)   R.11.06(4).

(63)   R.11.06(5).

(64)   Ins Regs 17(5),(6).

(65)   R.11.11: Atkin Form 361.

(66)   R.11.13(1),(2).

(67)   R.11.13(3).

(68)   Art.298(1).

(69)   Para.20.23.

(70)   Art.303(4).

(71)   R.11.08(1),(2).

(72)   R.11.08(3).

(73)   R.11.09: para. 19.34.

(74)   R.11.10.

(75) Ins Regs 19.
(76) Ins Regs 20(1): paras.13.109/117: Atkin Forms 364, 365.
(77) Ins Regs 20(2).
(78) Ins Regs 17(7).
(79) Art.299(1).
(80) Art.299(3).
(81) Art.299(2).

Chapter 21

DISCHARGE

Introduction
21.01 The Order introduces significant changes in the law governing the discharge of bankrupts. New provisions are made for the discharge of individuals adjudged bankrupt on petitions presented on or after 1st October 1991.[1] In this Chapter such bankrupts are referred to as "new bankrupts". The discharge of an individual adjudged bankrupt before that date (or on or after that date on a petition presented before that date) remains governed by the provisions of the 1980 Order, but with significant modifications contained in the transitional provisions of Schedule 8, Part II, under which he may be discharged under the new provisions in certain circumstances, where not discharged earlier under the 1980 Order. [2]

21.02 The discharge of new bankrupts is dealt with in Part I of this Chapter and the discharge of other bankrupts in Part II.

I. DISCHARGE OF "NEW BANKRUPTS"

Automatic discharge
(a) The relevant period
21.03 Any new bankrupt who has not been an undischarged bankrupt during a period of 15 years before the bankruptcy order, unless he is a solicitor, will be discharged automatically at the expiration of the relevant period of time without any application to the Court by the bankrupt or the Official Receiver. Unless extended by order of the Court, the relevant period is 3 years or, where a certificate for summary administration is in operation at the expiration of the period, 2 years, from the date of the bankruptcy order.[3]

21.04 A bankrupt entitled to automatic discharge under the 1980 Order could apply to the Court for an earlier discharge. Such a course is not open to a new bankrupt in a similar position. He may only get released from bankruptcy before the expiration of the relevant period if he obtains an order annulling the bankruptcy order on payment of the creditors in full or following acceptance by the requisite majority of creditors of a proposal for a voluntary arrangement or on the ground that the order ought not to have been made.[4]

21.05 Whilst an order of discharge may be rescinded or varied,[5] once a bankrupt is discharged automatically at the expiration of the relevant period or such period as extended by the Court, the discharge cannot be revoked.

(b) Where automatic discharge does not operate
21.06 The following bankrupts are ineligible for automatic discharge -

257

(i)   any individual who had been adjudged bankrupt in Northern Ireland previously and remained undischarged from that bankruptcy at any time within the 15 years immediately preceding the date of the bankruptcy order, unless the order under which he was so adjudged bankrupt has been annulled;

(ii)   a solicitor.[6]

In either of these cases a discharge can only be obtained by an order of the Court.[7]

(c) Suspension of automatic discharge
<u>(i) Application for suspension</u>
21.07   In order to provide a sanction to help to enforce the bankrupt's obligation to co-operate with the Official Receiver and the trustee in the conduct of his bankruptcy the Court is given power, on the application of the Official Receiver, to order that the relevant period for automatic discharge shall cease to run (i.e. that the duration of his bankruptcy shall be extended) for such period, or until the fulfilment of such conditions, as may be specified in the order, if it is satisfied that an undischarged bankrupt who qualifies for automatic discharge has failed or is failing to comply with any of his obligations under the bankruptcy.[8]

21.08   Usually the Official Receiver will request an order suspending the discharge until the bankrupt fulfils stated conditions. Such an application may be made orally at a public examination of the bankrupt without any formal application or report, where such examination is adjourned generally.[9] Otherwise a formal application must be made, and with it the Official Receiver must file a report setting out the reasons why it appears to him that an order suspending the discharge should be made.[10] Where a trustee (not being the Official Receiver) encounters non-co-operation by the bankrupt, he should consider requesting the Official Receiver to apply for suspension of discharge.

21.09   When the Court has fixed a venue for the hearing of the application it serves a sealed copy of the application, with venue endorsed, on the Official Receiver, the trustee and the bankrupt.[11]

21.10   The Official Receiver must send copies of his report to the trustee and the bankrupt so as to reach them at least 21 days before the hearing date.[12]

21.11   If the bankrupt wishes to deny or dispute any statements in the Official Receiver's report he may, not later than 7 days before the hearing date, file a notice specifying such statements.[13] If he does so, he must send copies of his notice to the Official Receiver and the trustee not less than 4 days before the hearing date.[14]

21.12   Copies of any order suspending discharge[15] are sent by the Court to the Official Receiver, the trustee and the bankrupt .[16]

(ii) Lifting of suspension

21.13   Where an order suspending discharge has been made, the bankrupt may apply to the Court for such order to be discharged.[17] Unless it is evident from the Court file that the bankrupt has fulfilled his obligations, the application should be supported by an affidavit giving reasons why the suspension of discharge should cease.

21.14   When the Court has fixed a venue for the hearing, the bankrupt must serve a copy of the application, with the venue endorsed, on the Official Receiver and the trustee not less than 28 days before the hearing date.[18]

21.15   The Official Receiver may file in the Court a report of any matters which he considers ought to be drawn to the Court's attention[19] and if the suspension order provided for the relevant period to cease to run until the fulfilment of specified conditions, the Court may request a report from him as to whether those conditions have or have not been fulfilled.[20] The Official Receiver must send a copy of any such report filed by him to the bankrupt and the trustee not less than 14 days before the hearing date.[21]

21.16   If the bankrupt wishes to deny or dispute any statements in the Official Receiver's report he may, not later than 7 days before the hearing date, file a notice specifying such statements.[22] If he does so, he must send copies of his notice to the Official Receiver and the trustee not less than 4 days before the hearing date.[23]

21.17   The application is heard by the Master in chambers, unless it is opposed, when it is heard in open court.[24] The Official Receiver and the trustee may appear and be heard.[25] Usually the Official Receiver will appear, but he may rely on his report without appearing. If the Court is satisfied that the relevant period should begin to run again, it makes an order discharging the suspension order and issues to the bankrupt a certificate that it has done so with effect from a specified date.[26]

Discharge by order of the Court
(a) Introduction

21.18   A bankrupt who does not qualify for an automatic discharge[27] may only be discharged by an order of the Court.[28] If the disqualification is by reason of a previous bankruptcy, the bankrupt may not apply to the Court for his discharge until after 5 years from the date of the bankruptcy order.[29] There is no provision for abridging this 5 year period. If the bankrupt is a solicitor, but is not disqualified from automatic discharge because of a previous bankruptcy, he may apply for his discharge at any time,[30] although it is anticipated that the Court will be reluctant to grant the discharge to a bankrupt solicitor earlier than the date when the applicant would have qualified for automatic discharge had he not been a solicitor, in view of the fact that a bankrupt who is not a solicitor cannot apply to the Court to be discharged before that date.[31]

(b) Application

21.19   A bankrupt intending to apply to the Court for an order of discharge must notify the Official Receiver accordingly and deposit with him such sum as he may require to cover the costs of the application.[32]

21.20   The bankrupt's application to the Court[33] must be accompanied by the Official Receiver's receipt for the deposit. The Court serves a sealed copy of the application, with venue endorsed, on the Official Receiver and the bankrupt at least 42 days before the hearing date.[34]

21.21   The Official Receiver must, not later than 14 days before the hearing date, give notice of the application to the trustee, to every creditor who, to the Official Receiver's knowledge, has a claim outstanding against the estate which has not been satisfied and, where the bankrupt is a solicitor, to the Law Society of Northern Ireland.[35]

21.22   At least 21 days before the hearing date the Official Receiver is required to file in the Court a report containing the following information with respect to the bankrupt -
  (i)   any failure by him to comply with his obligations under the Order;
  (ii) the circumstances surrounding the present bankruptcy, and those surrounding any previous bankruptcy of his;
  (iii) the extent to which, in the present and in any previous bankruptcy, his liabilities have exceeded his assets;
  (iv) particulars of any distribution which has been, or is expected to be, made to creditors in the present bankruptcy or, if such is the case, that there has been and is to be no distribution; and
  (v)   any other matters which in his opinion ought to be brought to the Court's attention.[36]

21.23   Where the Official Receiver is not himself the trustee he will require information from the trustee to enable him to prepare his report.

21.24   The Official Receiver's report is, in any proceedings, prima facie evidence of the facts stated in it.[37] Consequently, he must be careful not to include any facts which he is not satisfied are correct.

21.25   The Official Receiver must send a copy of the report to the bankrupt and the trustee so as to reach them at least 14 days before the date of the hearing.[38]

21.26   If the bankrupt wishes to deny or dispute any statements in the Official Receiver's report he may, not later than 7 days before the hearing date, file a notice specifying such statements.[39] If he does so, he must send copies of his notice to the Official Receiver and the trustee not less than 4 days before the hearing date.[40]

21.27 The application is heard by the Master in chambers, unless it is opposed, when it is heard in open court.[41] The Official Receiver, the trustee, any creditor and, where the bankrupt is a solicitor, the Law Society of Northern Ireland may appear on the hearing and may make representations and put to the bankrupt such questions as the Court may allow.[42] In practice the Official Receiver will always appear.

(c) Order

21.28 On the hearing of the application the Court may refuse to discharge the bankrupt, make an order discharging him absolutely, or make an order discharging him subject to such conditions with respect to any income which may subsequently become due to him, or with respect to property devolving upon him, or acquired by him, after his discharge, as may be specified in the order.[43] Copies of any order made on the application must be sent by the Court to the bankrupt, the trustee and the Official Receiver.[44]

21.29 An order discharging the bankrupt, whether absolutely or subject to conditions, may be made either to have immediate effect or to have its effect suspended for a specified period or until the fulfilment of specified conditions.[45]

21.30 Where the discharge is made subject to conditions as to income or property, the dates on which accounts of such income or property are to be filed in the Court and sent to the Official Receiver should be included in the order.[46]

21.31 The Court's discretion is no longer restricted, as it was under Article 28(5) of the 1980 Order, where the bankrupt had been convicted of any offence connected with his bankruptcy or where statutory "facts" were proved. However, the Official Receiver will usually include in his report any circumstances giving rise to such "facts" which are relevant and material.[47]

21.32 An order of discharge bears the date on which it is made, but does not take effect until drawn up by the Court, when it has effect retrospectively to the date on which it was made.[48] It may not be issued, except for the purpose of an appeal, nor advertised, until the time allowed for appealing has expired or, if an appeal is entered, until the appeal has been determined.[49]

21.33 An order of discharge may be rescinded or varied on an application to review under Article 371.[50] The bankrupt may wish to apply for such a review if he is unable to comply with conditions imposed by the order. The Official Receiver may consider making such an application where the bankrupt has failed to comply with such conditions or where facts which have come to light since the order was made would have caused him to oppose the discharge had he been aware of them at the time of the hearing. If the order of discharge is rescinded on a review the debtor becomes an undischarged bankrupt again.

21.34 The Department may appeal against an order of discharge.[51]

Certificate of discharge

21.35 When the bankrupt's discharge has become effective he may apply to the Court for a certificate of discharge.[52] If on considering such an application it appears to the Court that the applicant has been discharged, whether by expiration of time or by order of the Court, it will issue such a certificate, which will state the date from which the discharge is effective.[53] Before issuing a certificate to a bankrupt on the ground that he has been discharged by affluxion of time the Court must be satisfied that he is not a person ineligible for such automatic discharge[54] and if not, that the appropriate period for such discharge has expired, having regard to any order of suspension. Where the discharge is by an order of the Court, the time for appealing must have expired or any appeal have been determined, and where the discharge was suspended by the order the Court will require to be satisfied that the discharge has taken effect and on what date. Where the order provided for suspension until the fulfilment of conditions the Court will require a report from the Official Receiver that such conditions have been complied with.

21.36 In many cases the Court will have sufficient information on the file of proceedings and from a search in the register of bankruptcies[55] to verify that the applicant's discharge has become effective, but if in doubt it will call for appropriate evidence to be furnished by the applicant.

Advertisement of discharge

21.37 A bankrupt who has been discharged is entitled, upon a request in writing, to require the Department to advertise the discharge in the Belfast Gazette or in any newspaper in which the bankruptcy was advertised or in both, upon payment of the cost of such advertisement as notified by the Department.[56] Where the former bankrupt has died or is a person incapable of managing his affairs, the request may be made by his personal representative or, as the case may be, a person appointed by the Court to represent or act for him.[57]

21.38 Where the discharge is by order of the Court, it may not be advertised until the time allowed for appealing has expired or, if an appeal is entered, until the appeal has been determined.[58]

Effect of discharge
(a) General

21.39 The bankruptcy of an individual terminates on his discharge,[59] but the bankruptcy itself does not terminate.[60] Only an annulment has the effect of setting aside the bankruptcy.

21.40 In particular, a discharge has no effect on any function of the trustee which remains to be carried out or on the operation, for the purposes of the carrying out of those functions, of the provisions of the Order, nor does it affect the right of any creditor to prove in the bankruptcy for any debt from which the bankrupt is released.[61]

21.41   Discharge does not remove the obligation of the former bankrupt to give the Official Receiver such information and to attend on him at such times as the Official Receiver may reasonably require to carry out his functions,[62] and the bankrupt's similar obligation to the trustee and his general obligation to do anything required by the trustee in the discharge of the trustee's functions continues.[63]

21.42   Whilst any part of the bankrupt's estate is still being administered by a trustee the former bankrupt remains liable to arrest in the circumstances mentioned in Article 335.[64]

21.43   Discharge does not release any person other than the bankrupt from any liability (whether as partner or co-trustee of the bankrupt or otherwise) from which the bankrupt is released by the discharge, or from any liability as surety for the bankrupt or as a person in the nature of such a surety.[65]

(b) Effect on bankrupt's property and income
21.44   Discharge does not effect a re-vesting in the bankrupt of any part of his estate which is unrealised. Such property remains vested in the trustee.

21.45   Discharge does not affect the right of any secured creditor to enforce his security for the payment of a debt from which the bankrupt is released.[66]

21.46   Property which is acquired by or devolves upon the bankrupt after his discharge may not be claimed by the trustee as after-acquired property.[67] However, where the bankrupt is discharged by order of the Court, such an order may be made subject to conditions with regard to such after-acquired property.[68]

21.47   An income payments order[69] may not be made after the bankrupt's discharge and such an order made earlier ceases to have effect after his discharge, except -
   (i)   in the case of a discharge by order of the Court, where the discharge is made subject to conditions with respect to the bankrupt's income after discharge, or
   (ii)   where the income payments order provides for payments to continue for a period ending after the date on which an automatic discharge operates, such period not to exceed 3 years after the making of the order.[70]

(c) Release from disabilities and disqualifications
21.48   A bankrupt is, on his discharge, released from the disabilities and disqualifications of bankruptcy,[71] with two exceptions -

(i)   a solicitor applying for a practising certificate after his discharge may be refused by the Registrar of Solicitors,[72]

(ii)   unless his bankruptcy has been annulled, a discharged bankrupt remains ineligible for appointment as Justice of the Peace until he obtains from the Court a certificate that, in the opinion of the Court, his bankruptcy was caused by misfortune without any misconduct on his part.[73]

(d) Release of debts

21.49   The discharge of the bankrupt releases him from personal liability for all debts which come within the definition of "bankruptcy debts" in the Order,[74] with the following exceptions -

(i)   a debt incurred by the bankrupt in respect of, or forbearance in respect of which was secured by means of, any fraud or fraudulent breach of trust to which he was a party,

(ii)   a liability in respect of a fine imposed for any offence or a liability under a recognisance, unless in the case of a penalty for a public revenue offence or a recognisance, the Treasury consents to the bankrupt being released,

(iii) except to such extent and on such conditions as the Court may direct, liability to pay damages in respect of personal injuries to any person resulting from negligence, nuisance, breach of statutory, contractual or other duty or under Part II of the Consumer Protection (Northern Ireland) Order 1987, or a debt arising under any order made in family or domestic proceedings,

(iv) an obligation arising under a confiscation order made under Article 4 or 5 of the Criminal Justice (Confiscation) (Northern Ireland) Order 1990. [75]

21.50   It will be noted that, although unliquidated damages in tort is now a provable debt,[76] the bankrupt remains liable after discharge for damages in respect of personal injuries arising under most causes of action, unless the Court relieves him from such liability, wholly or partially, with or without conditions. An application for such relief should be made by the bankrupt on notice to the creditor entitled to claim the damages.

(e) Criminal Offences

21.51   A former bankrupt may be prosecuted after his discharge in respect of an offence under the Order committed before his discharge but, unless he is subsequently adjudicated again, he may not be convicted of any offence in respect of anything done after his discharge.[77]

II . DISCHARGE OF OTHER BANKRUPTS

Discharge under the 1980 Order

21.52   Since 1st January 1984 and until 1st October 1991 the discharge of bankrupts was governed by Articles 28-32 of the 1980 Order.[78] By the operation of those provisions all persons adjudged bankrupt before 1st January 1979 and remaining undischarged on 1st January 1984 have since been discharged automatically without a Court order.[79] A person adjudged bankrupt on or after 1st January 1979 is discharged -

(a) where, on his own application, he has obtained an order of discharge, on the date such discharge becomes effective;[80]

(b) where, on the application of the Official Assignee for a review of the adjudication, the Court makes a discharge order, on the date such discharge becomes effective;[81]

(c) if he was adjudged bankrupt after 1st January 1984 where, following an order declaring that his public examination has been concluded or dispensing with his examination, the Court makes an order under Article 29(1) of the 1980 Order, on the 5th anniversary of his adjudication.

Transitional provisions of the Insolvency Order

21.53 Under the transitional provisions of the Insolvency Order a person adjudged bankrupt before 1st October 1991 (or on or after that date on a petition presented earlier) may be discharged earlier than he would be under the 1980 Order unless he was an undischarged bankrupt at any time in the period of 15 years before his adjudication and such earlier adjudication has not been annulled.[82] The effect of these provisions is set out in the following paragraphs.

21.54 A bankrupt to whom these transitional provisions apply, if not discharged earlier under the 1980 Order, will be discharged automatically on 1st October 1994 (or 3 years after his adjudication if adjudged bankrupt on or after 1st October 1991 on a petition presented earlier), but subject to the power of the Court, on the application of the Official Receiver, to suspend the discharge in the same way and on the same grounds of non co-operation as in the case of new bankrupts.[83] A bankrupt solicitor qualifies for automatic discharge under these provisions in the same way as other bankrupts.

21.55 Automatic discharge under the transitional provisions of the Insolvency Order takes effect notwithstanding the fact that under the terms of an order of discharge made under the 1980 Order the discharge may take effect at a later date.

21.56 Whilst the Court retains the power to make a discharge order under the 1980 Order where the bankrupt was adjudicated before 1st October 1991 (or on or after that date on a petition presented earlier), no order made under Article 29(1) of that Order will be effective in respect of any person adjudged bankrupt on or after 1st October 1989 who is not excluded from the operation of the transitional provisions of the Insolvency Order, nor will any order usually be made by the Court on any review of the adjudication of such a person under Article 30 of the 1980 Order, as in most cases he will be discharged before any such review is made or if not, his discharge will be the subject of a suspension order made under those transitional provisions.

21.57   A bankrupt to whom the 1980 Order continues to apply who does not wish to wait for discharge under Article 29 or 30 of that Order or the transitional provisions of the Insolvency Order may apply to the Court for an earlier discharge under Article 28 of the 1980 Order.

Footnotes

(1) These provisions bind the Crown - Art 378(e).
(2) Paras.21.52/57.
(3) Art.253(1),(2).
(4) Ch.22.
(5) Para.21.33.
(6) Arts.253(1),256(5). Category (i) above includes not only persons adjudged bankrupt within the 15 year period but also anyone adjudicated earlier but who remained undischarged at the commencement of the period.
(7) Art.253(1). paras.21.18/34.
(8) Art.253(3).
(9) RR.6.173(4), 6.213(1): para.11.34.
(10) R.6.213(1),(2): Atkin Form 409.
(11) RR.6.213(3), 0.3(4).
(12) R.6.213(4).
(13) R.6.213(5): Atkin Form 410.
(14) R.6.213(6).
(15) F.6.75.
(16) R.6.213(7).
(17) R.6.214(1): Atkin Form 412.
(18) RR.6.214(2), 0.3(4).
(19) R.6.214(3).
(20) R.6.214(4).
(21) R.6.214(5).
(22) R.6.214(6).
(23) R.6.214(7).
(24) R.7.02(1).
(25) R.6.214(3).
(26) R.6.214(8): FF. 6.76, 6.77.
(27) Para.21.06.
(28) Art.253(1)(a),(b).
(29) Art.254(1)(a).
(30) Art.254(1)(b).
(31) Para.21.04 above.
(32) R.6.215(1).
(33) Atkin Form 415.
(34) RR.6.215(2), 0.3(4).
(35) R.6.215(3),(4): Atkin Form 418.
(36) Art.262(2): R.6.216(1).
(37) Art.262(3).
(38) R.6.216(2).
(39) R.6.216(3): F.6.78.
(40) R.6.216(4).
(41) R.7.02(1).

268   Northern Ireland Personal Insolvency

(42) R.6.216(5).
(43) Art.254(2): F.6.79.
(44) R.6.217(3).
(45) Art.254(3).
(46) Atkin Form 425.
(47) MH 3-131, 7-493.
(48) R.6.217(1),(2).
(49) R.6.219.
(50) Atkin Forms 426, 427. For procedural guide see Atkin supplement pp. 179/180.
(51) R.7.43.
(52) R.6.218(1): F.6.80.
(53) *Ibid.*
(54) Para.21.06.
(55) Such a search should not be restricted to a period of 15 years preceding the bankruptcy order - see fn. (6) above.
(56) R.6.218(2),(3).
(57) R.6.218(4).
(58) R.6.219.
(59) Art.252(b).
(60) MH 3-126.
(61) Art.255(1).
(62) Art.264(4),(5).
(63) Art.306(1),(3).
(64) Para.7.036.
(65) Art.255(7).
(66) Art.255(2).
(67) Art.280(2)(c).
(68) Art.254(2)(c): para.21.28.
(69) Ch.18.
(70) Art.283(6).
(71) Paras.9.21/37.
(72) Solicitors (Northern Ireland) Order 1976, Art 13(1)(h).
(73) Magistrates' Courts Act (Northern Ireland) 1964 s.6(2),(3). Such a certificate is not required in England and Wales in respect of any disqualification nor is it required in Northern Ireland in respect of any other disqualification.
(74) Art.9(1): para.19.03.
(75) Art.255(1),(3)-(6),(8): R.6.221.
(76) Para.19.08.
(77) Art.321(3).
(78) JH Ch.13.
(79) 1980 Order, Art.29(4).
(80) 1980 Order, Art.28.
(81) 1980 Order, Art. 30.
(82) Sch.8, paras.9(2),11.
(83) Sch.8, para. 11(3): paras.21.07/17.

Chapter 22

ANNULMENT OF BANKRUPTCY ORDER

Introduction
22.01 Under the Bankruptcy Acts the only statutory provisions for annulling an adjudication order were on a successful application by the bankrupt to show cause against such an order made on a creditor's petition (which was not served on the debtor) and on the acceptance by the requisite majority of creditors of a bankrupt's offer of composition. However, the Court for long exercised a wide discretion to annul bankruptcy, formerly under inherent jurisdiction, later under section 6 of the 1872 Act and more recently under Article 36 of the 1980 Order, in exercise of the statutory power to review, rescind or vary any order.[1]

22.02 Under the Order the annulment of a bankruptcy order is based exclusively on specific statutory provisions. The Court will no longer exercise a discretionary power to annul an adjudication order on the consent of the creditors or on any ground other than those provided for in the Order. However, a bankruptcy order may be rescinded under the Court's general power under Article 371 to rescind any order. This power may be exercised where, for example, the bankruptcy order was made by mistake, where there have been serious procedural irregularities[2] or where the presentation of the bankruptcy petition was an abuse of process.[3] Where a bankruptcy order made against a solicitor is rescinded, a copy of the order of rescission must be sent by the Court to the Law Society of Northern Ireland.[4] The Department may appeal against an order made on an application for rescission of a bankruptcy order.[5]

Grounds of annulment
22.03 The Court has a discretionary power to annul a bankruptcy order on the following grounds -
  (a) that on any grounds existing at the time the order was made, the order ought not to have been made;[6]
  (b) that the bankruptcy debts and the expenses of the bankruptcy have either been paid or secured for to the satisfaction of the Court to the extent required by the Rules;[7]
  - (c) that a proposal by the bankrupt for a voluntary arrangement has been approved by the requisite majority of creditors at a creditors' meeting.[8]

22.04 A bankruptcy order made on the petition of the Law Society of Northern Ireland under Article 238(1)(d)[9] must be annulled if at any time the order appointing the Society as attorney for the bankrupt solicitor has been rescinded on appeal.[10]

269

Bankruptcy order ought not to have been made
22.05   On the hearing of an application to annul a bankruptcy order on this
ground the Court is limited to a consideration of the facts existing at the time
the order was made, although such facts need not have been before the Court
on the application for the bankruptcy order.[11]

Payment of debts in full
22.06   Under the former law it was established that a bankrupt who had been
guilty of serious misconduct may not be permitted to rid himself of his status
as a bankrupt by procuring the payment of his debts, i.e. to buy himself out of
bankruptcy[12] and it is anticipated that considerations of public interest will be
similarly applied to the new provisions.[13]

22.07   There cannot be an annulment on this ground until all the bankruptcy
debts have been proved and paid or secured.[14] If the bankrupt intends to
discharge such debts subsequently under a scheme of arrangement he must
proceed by the voluntary arrangement procedure and seek to obtain an annulment order on the next mentioned ground.[15]

Approved voluntary arrangement
22.08   A bankruptcy order may not be annulled on this ground within 28 days
of the date on which the report of the creditors' meeting is filed in the Court or
at any time when an application to challenge the decision of the meeting or an
appeal in respect of such an application is pending or during the period within
which such an appeal may be brought.[16]

Procedure for annulment and consequent proceedings
(a) Application
22.09   The application[17] must specify the provision of the Order under which
it is made and be supported by an affidavit stating the grounds on which it is
made. [18] Where the ground is that all debts and expenses of the bankruptcy
have been paid or secured the affidavit must set out all the facts by reference to
which the Court is required to be satisfied before annulling the bankruptcy
order.[19]

(b) Notice of application
22.10   When the application and supporting affidavit have been filed in the
Court and notice of the venue fixed by the Court for the hearing notified to the
applicant, he must serve copies of the application, with the venue endorsed,
and the supporting affidavit on the Official Receiver and (if other) the trustee.
[20] If the application is made on the ground that the bankruptcy order ought
not to have been made the applicant must also serve these documents on the
petitioner.[21]

22.11   Where the application is on the ground that all the bankruptcy debts
and expenses of the bankruptcy have been paid or secured, service must be
effected not less than 28 days before the hearing date.[22] In other cases the notice

parties must be served in sufficient time to enable them to be present at the hearing.[23]

(c) Stay of proceedings

22.12   The Court has power before the hearing of the annulment application to make an interim order staying any proceedings, i.e. not only proceedings in the bankruptcy but proceedings in any court, e.g. proceedings by the trustee to claim property for the estate.[24]

22.13   Notice of an application to stay proceedings in the bankruptcy must be given to the Official Receiver and (if other) the trustee in sufficient time to enable them to be present at the hearing of the application to stay and (if they wish to do so) to make representations, but an application to stay other proceedings may be made ex parte.[25]

22.14   The Rules governing an application for annulment or other matters in connection with the annulment continue to apply notwithstanding an order staying proceedings in the bankruptcy.[26]

22.15   Copies of any order made on the application staying proceedings is sent by the Court to the applicant, the Official Receiver and (if other) the trustee.[27]

(d) Report by trustee

22.16   Where the application is on the ground that all the bankruptcy debts and expenses of the bankruptcy have been paid or secured the trustee, or if no trustee has been appointed, the Official Receiver, is required, not less than 21 days before the hearing date, to file in the Court a report stating -
- (i)   the circumstances leading to the bankruptcy;
- (ii)   a summary of the bankrupt's assets and liabilities at the date of the bankruptcy order and at the date of the annulment application;
- (iii) details of any creditors known to him to have claims, but who have not proved;
- (iv)   particulars of the extent (if any) to which, and the manner in which, the debts and expenses of the bankruptcy have been paid or secured, and where unpaid but secured, whether and to what extent he considers the security to be satisfactory;
- (v)   such other matters as he considers to be, in the circumstances, necessary for the information of the Court.[28]

22.17   The report should include, under (v) above, observations on the bankrupt's conduct during the proceedings.[29]

22.18   The trustee (if not the Official Receiver) must send a copy of his report to the Official Receiver at least 21 days before the hearing date and the Official Receiver may file an additional report, a copy of which must be sent to the applicant 7 days before the hearing date.[30]

22.19 A copy of the report must be sent to the applicant at least 14 days before the hearing date, and he may file further affidavits in answer to statements in it.[31] Copies of any such further affidavits must be sent by the applicant to the Official Receiver and (if other) the trustee.[32]

(e) Notice to non-proving creditors
22.20 Where the application is on the ground that all the bankruptcy debts and expenses of the bankruptcy have been paid or secured and the report to the Court by the trustee or the Official Receiver states that there are known creditors of the bankrupt who have not proved, the Court may direct the trustee (or the Official Receiver if no trustee has been appointed) to give notice of the application to such of the creditors as it thinks ought to be informed of it, with a view to their having an opportunity to prove their debts within 21 days and to advertise the fact that the application has been made, so that creditors who have not proved may do so within a specified time.[33] If such directions are given, the application must be adjourned meanwhile for a period of not less than 35 days.[34]

(f) Hearing
22.21 The trustee must attend the hearing of the application.[35] The Official Receiver, if he is not the trustee, may attend, but is not required to do so unless he has filed a report on an application made on the ground that all the bankruptcy debts and expenses of the bankruptcy have been paid or secured.[36]

22.22 Where the application is on the ground that all the bankruptcy debts and expenses of the bankruptcy have been paid or secured the bankrupt must either satisfy the Court that all such debts which have been proved have been paid in full or, in respect of a disputed debt or a proved debt where the creditor can no longer be traced, give such security (by money paid into court or by bond) as the Court considers adequate to satisfy any sum that may subsequently be proved to be due to the creditor concerned and (if the Court thinks fit)costs.[37] Where security is given in the case of an untraced creditor, the Court may direct advertisement of particulars of the alleged debt and the security.[38] Where such advertisement is ordered and no claim on the security is made within 12 months from the date of the advertisement (or the first advertisement, if more than one), the Court must, on application, order the security to be released.[39]

(g) The order
22.23 An order annulling the bankruptcy order provides for the dismissal of the petition on which it was made.[40] It may include a provision for vesting in a person appointed by the Court any of the bankrupt's estate which remains vested in the trustee.[41] It must include provision permitting the vacation of the registration of the bankruptcy petition and of the bankruptcy order in the Registry of Deeds and, where appropriate, cancellation of any entry in the Land Registry of notice of the petition or of any bankruptcy inhibition against the

title of the bankrupt as the registered owner of land. [42] It must also include any directions with regard to creditors. [43]

22.24 The Court must send copies of the order to the Official Receiver and (if other) the trustee. [44] Two sealed copies of the order must also be sent by the Court to the former bankrupt, together with the certificate required by section 3(4) of the Registration of Deeds Act, as applied by section 3B(3) of that Act, signed by the Master. [45] Upon lodgment of this certificate in the Registry of Deeds, together with the certificate required to vacate the registration of the petition, the registration of the petition and the bankruptcy order will be vacated. [46]

22.25 The Court must also give notice of the making of the order to the Department, the Enforcement of Judgments Office and, where the bankruptcy order was made against a solicitor, to the Law Society of Northern Ireland. [47]

22.26 Where the Official Receiver has notified creditors of the debtor's bankruptcy he must notify them of the annulment. [48] The expenses of giving such notice are a charge in favour of the Official Receiver on the property of the former bankrupt, whether or not actually in his hands, and this charge is valid where any property is in the hands of a trustee or any person other than the former bankrupt, subject only to any costs that may be incurred by the trustee or that other person in realising the property for the purpose of satisfying the charge.

22.27 The former bankrupt (or if he has died, or is a person incapable of managing his affairs, his personal representative or, as the case may be, a person appointed by the Court to represent or act for him) may in writing require the Department to give notice of the making of the order by advertisement in the Belfast Gazette or in any newspaper in which the bankruptcy order was advertised or in both, upon payment of the costs of the advertisement, to be notified by the Department. [49]

22.28 The Department may appeal any order of the Court made on an application for annulment of a bankruptcy order. [50]

22.29 Where an annulment order has been made on the ground that all the bankruptcy debts and expenses of the bankruptcy have been paid or secured, a creditor who has not in fact received payment may apply for rescission of the order. [51]

(h) Trustee's release
22.30 Notwithstanding the making of an order annulling a bankruptcy order, the trustee remains liable to account for all his transactions in connection with the former bankrupt's estate. [52]

22.31   As soon as practicable after the making of the order the trustee must submit a copy of his final account to the Department and file a copy in the Court.[53] This account must include a summary of the trustee's receipts and payments in the administration, and contain a statement to the effect that he has reconciled his account with that which is held by the Department in respect of the bankruptcy.[54]

22.32   The time of the trustee's release will be determined by the Court on his application, having regard to whether he has complied with his obligations regarding the final account and whether any security given in respect of disputed debts or untraced proving creditors has been, or will be, released.[55]

Effect of annulment
(a) On the bankrupt personally
22.33   An order annulling a bankruptcy order restores the former bankrupt to his pre-bankruptcy status as if the bankruptcy order had not been made. Unless and until he obtains his discharge he remains fully liable for all his debts, except those which have been proved in the bankruptcy.[56] A claim proved but rejected by the trustee cannot be enforced after annulment.[57]

22.34   The bankruptcy order may be annulled after the bankrupt is discharged.[58]

22.35   Where a bankruptcy order is annulled, that bankruptcy is disregarded in determining whether the bankrupt is entitled to automatic discharge in any subsequent bankruptcy (i.e. it does not prevent him from being regarded as a first-time bankrupt on the occasion of the subsequent bankruptcy).[59] This applies to an annulment order made under the Bankruptcy Acts as well as to such orders made under the Order.[60]

22.36   On annulment of the bankruptcy order the bankrupt is released from the disabilities and disqualifications of a bankrupt.[61]

22.37   A former bankrupt may be convicted of an offence under the Order notwithstanding the annulment of the bankruptcy order against him, but a prosecution for such an offence may not be commenced after the annulment.[62]

(b) On the bankrupt's estate
22.38   Notwithstanding the annulment of the bankruptcy order, any sale or other disposition of property, payment made or other thing duly done under the Order by or on behalf of the Official Receiver or a trustee or by the Court, is valid.[63]

22.39   If at the time the annulment order is made any of the bankrupt's estate remains vested in the trustee it vests in such person as the Court may appoint or, in default of any such appointment, reverts to the bankrupt on such terms (if any) as the Court may direct.[64] Thus it appears that such estate will re-vest in the bankrupt without any conveyance or transfer from the trustee where the annulment order contains no vesting provision,[65] but this is not free from doubt and a former bankrupt should request that the order should provide for re-vesting.

Footnotes

(1) JH Ch.12.
(2) See *Re Calmex* Ltd. [1989] 1 All ER 485 re rescission of company winding-up order made by mistake and when company was not served with the petition and had no knowledge of it; also *Re Virgo Systems Ltd.* [1990] BCLC 34.
(3) Hals 185.
(4) R.6.227.
(5) R.7.43.
(6) Art.256(1)(a): Hals 599.
(7) Art.256(1)(b): MH 3-140/2, 7-336: Hals 600.
(8) Art.235.
(9) Paras.7.168/172.
(10) Art.256(3).
(11) *Re Van Engel* (1989) The Independent, 21 August, (1989) 2 Ins Int 79.
(12) MH 3-139, JH 12.16/18, Hals 458.
(13) *Re Robertson* [1989] 1 WLR 1139, 1143.
(14) R.6.208(1)-(3): *Re Robertson, supra:* MH 7-336.
(15) *Re Robertson, supra,* per Warner J. at p.1142.
(16) Art.235(2).
(17) Atkin Form 285.
(18) RR.6.203(1),(2), 6.210: Atkin Forms 286, 287.
(19) R.6.203(2).
(20) RR.6.203(3),(4), 0.3(4).
(21) R.6.203(5).
(22) R.6.203(4).
(23) RR.6.203(4), 6.210.
(24) R.6.205(1).
(25) R.6.205(2),(3). See MH 7-473 for criticism of this Rule.
(26) R.6.205(4).
(27) R.6.205(5).
(28) R.6.204(1)-(4).
(29) MH 7-471: para.22.06.
(30) R.6.204(7).
(31) R.6.204(5).
(32) R.6.204(6).
(33) R.6.206: MH 7-474.
(34) *Ibid.*
(35) R.6.207(1).
(36) R.6.207(2).
(37) R.6.208(1)-(3).
(38) R.6.208(4).
(39) R.6.208(5).
(40) F.6.74.
(41) Art.256(4)(b): para.22.39.

(42)   R.6.211(1).
(43)   Paras.22.20, 22.22.
(44)   R.6.211(2).
(45)   *Ibid.*
(46)   Ins R of D Regs 4,5.
(47)   R.6.211(2).
(48)   R.6.209.
(49)   R.6.211(3)-(5).
(50)   R.7.43.
(51)   Art.371: Atkin Forms 243, 289.
(52)   R.6.212(1).
(53)   R.6.212(2).
(54)   R.6.212(3).
(55)   Art.272(4): R.6.212(4).
(56)   *More v More* [1962] Ch 424.
(57)   *Brandon v McHenry* [1891] 1 QB 538.
(58)   Arts.253(4), 256(2).
(59)   Art.256(5). para.21.06.
(60)   Sch.8, para.9(2).
(61)   Paras.9.21/37.
(62)   Art.321(2).
(63)   Art.256(4).
(64)   *Ibid.*
(65)   Hals 612. Cf.former law, JH 12.32.

Chapter 23

SUCCESSIVE BANKRUPTCIES [1]

Introduction

23.01 If a bankrupt who is undischarged incurs debts he may be adjudged bankrupt again on a petition presented by or against him or, if he dies insolvent before obtaining his discharge from bankruptcy, an order may be made for the administration of his estate in bankruptcy. The Order and the Rules make provision to regulate the respective interests of the creditors of the earlier bankruptcy and the later bankruptcy or administration in bankruptcy of the insolvent estate of the deceased, as the case may be. [2]

23.02 In this Chapter "the earlier bankruptcy" means the bankruptcy (or, as the case may be, the most recent bankruptcy) from which the bankrupt remains undischarged when the later bankruptcy order or order for administration of the bankrupt's estate in bankruptcy is made, "the later bankruptcy" means the bankruptcy or administration in bankruptcy arising from that order and "the existing trustee" means the trustee acting in the earlier bankruptcy or, where the earlier bankruptcy was under the Bankruptcy Acts, the Official Receiver.

23.03 The scheme of the Order is that any property acquired by the bankrupt since the commencement of the earlier bankruptcy which remains undistributed or undisposed of when the existing trustee receives notice of the presentation of the petition for the later bankruptcy or administration in bankruptcy of the insolvent estate of the deceased bankrupt must be applied first to meet the liabilities in the later bankruptcy and only if there is a surplus available after those liabilities (with interest) have been discharged can such property be applied to meet the liabilities of the earlier bankruptcy. [3] This deferment of the unsatisfied claims of the creditors in the earlier bankruptcy represents a significant change from the previous law. [4]

23.04 Where the earlier bankruptcy was under the Bankruptcy Acts and the later bankruptcy is under the Order the provisions of the Order relating to successive bankruptcies apply and not section 11 of the 1929 Act. [5]

Stay of distribution

23.05 If the existing trustee is given notice of the presentation of the petition for the later bankruptcy, any subsequent distribution or other disposition of -

(a) any property vested in the existing trustee as after acquired property (i.e. property claimed for the estate under Article 280 [6]) or, if the earlier bankruptcy was a bankruptcy under the Bankruptcy Acts, after-acquired property under those Acts, [7]

(b) any money paid to the existing trustee pursuant to an income payments order [8] or, if the earlier bankruptcy was a bankruptcy under the

279

Bankruptcy Acts, an order for payment from the bankrupt's income under those Acts,[9] or
(c)   any property or money which is, or represents, the proceeds of sale or application of such after-acquired property or income,
is void in the event of a bankruptcy order being made on that petition, unless the disposition was made with the consent of the Court or is or was subsequently ratified by the Court.[10]

23.06   The distribution or other disposition is only avoided if made after the existing trustee has been given notice in the prescribed form.[11] Presumably the notice will be given by the person who presents the petition against the bankrupt.

Property to be comprised in later bankruptcy
23.07   Any property and money within the categories referred to in paragraph 23.05 above is, from the date of the later bankruptcy order, to be treated as comprised in the bankrupt's estate in the later bankruptcy.[12] Any sums payable after that date to the existing trustee under an income payments order made in the earlier bankruptcy form part of the estate in the later bankruptcy and the Court may modify the order accordingly.[13] However, all other money or property comprised in the bankrupt's estate in the earlier bankruptcy or in any bankruptcy prior to that, including items of exempt property subsequently claimed by the existing trustee on the ground of excess value,[14] will remain part of that estate.[15]

Duties of existing trustee
23.08   It is the duty of the existing trustee to deal with property or money comprised in the bankrupt's estate in the later bankruptcy under these provisions until there is a trustee in the later bankruptcy.[16]

23.09   The existing trustee is required to take any after-acquired property into his custody or under his control in so far as he has not already done so, but he has the power to sell or otherwise dispose of any perishable goods, or goods the value of which is likely to diminish if they are not disposed of.[17] The proceeds of any such sale or disposal are to be held under the existing trustee's control, with the rest of the bankrupt's estate.[18] As and when requested by the trustee acting in the later bankruptcy, the existing trustee must deliver up to him any after-acquired property or such proceeds of sale or disposal in his custody or control.[19]

Proof in later bankruptcy for debts in earlier bankruptcy
23.10   Whilst creditors in the earlier bankruptcy are not to be creditors in the later bankruptcy in respect of the same debts, the existing trustee may claim in a later bankruptcy for -
(a)   the unsatisfied balance of the debts provable in the earlier bankruptcy,
(b)   any interest payable on that balance, and
(c)   any unpaid expense of the earlier bankruptcy.[20]

However, any amount so provable ranks in priority after all the other debts provable in the later bankruptcy and after interest on those debts and, accordingly, may not be paid unless those debts and that interest have first been paid in full.[21]

Expenses of existing trustee

23.11   The existing trustee has a first charge on any property or money comprised in the bankrupt's estate in the later bankruptcy under these provisions for any bankruptcy expenses incurred in compliance with the provisions of the Order or the Rules relating thereto, whether in the hands of the existing trustee or the trustee in the later bankruptcy.[22]

Deceased insolvent estate

23.12   The provisions apply when an undischarged bankrupt dies insolvent and an order is made for the administration in bankruptcy of his estate.[23]

Footnotes

(1)   MH 3-278/281, 7-505/511.
(2)   Arts.307, 308: DIEO Sch.1, Part II, para.31: RR 6.223/226.
(3)   MH 3-274.
(4)   JH, Ch.14.
(5)   Sch.8, para.13(2).
(6)   Para.12.15.
(7)   Sch.8, para.13(1).
(8)   Ch.18.
(9)   Sch.8, para.13(1).
(10)   Art.307.
(11)   F.6.81.
(12)   Art.308(1).
(13)   Art.308(2).
(14)   Para.12.06.
(15)   Art.308(4).
(16)   Art.308(1).
(17)   R.6.224(1),(2).
(18)   R.6.224(3).
(19)   R.6.225.
(20)   Art.308(5): R.6.094(5): F.6.41.
(21)   Art.308(6).
(22)   Art.308(3): R.6.226.
(23)   DIEO Sch.1, Part II, para.31.

Chapter 24

BANKRUPTCY OF PARTNERS

INTRODUCTION

24.001 The Order applies to the insolvency of companies and individuals but not to insolvent partnerships. However, by Article 364 the Lord Chancellor is empowered, with the concurrence of the Department, to make an order applying to insolvent partnerships such provisions of the Order, Part VI of the Judgments Enforcement Order, the Land Registration Act or the Registration of Deeds Acts as may be specified, with such modifications as may be specified. This power has been exercised in respect of provisions of the Order by the Insolvent Partnerships Order (Northern Ireland) 1991 ("the IPO").[1]

24.002 The IPO does not apply to any case in which a winding up petition against a partnership or a bankruptcy petition against a member of a partnership was presented or an adjudication in bankruptcy was made against such a member or in which any bankruptcy proceedings (including service of a debtor's summons) against him were pending before 1st October 1991, and such cases continue to be governed by the law in operation before that date.[2]

24.003 The relevant provisions of the Rules, the Insolvency Regulations, the Insolvency (Fees) Order (Northern Ireland) 1991 and the Insolvency (Deposits) Order (Northern Ireland) 1991 apply, with the necessary modifications, for the purpose of giving effect to the provisions of the Order which are applied to insolvent partnerships and in the case of any conflict between any provision of the Rules and any provision of the IPO, the latter provision is to prevail.[3]

24.004 The IPO follows closely the corresponding Insolvent Partnerships Order 1986 applying to England and Wales which, by what is perhaps a judicial understatement, has been described as "somewhat tortuously drafted provisions".[4]

24.005 The effect of the last mentioned Order in relation to a creditor to whom a partnership debt is owing has been summarised by Nicholls L.J. as follows -
"The Insolvent Partnerships Order 1986 has extended the remedy available to a partnership creditor. First, a creditor may still present an insolvency petition or petitions against one or more members of a partnership. An insolvency petition is a petition seeking either a bankruptcy order against an individual member or a winding-up order in respect of a corporate member. Secondly, a creditor may still present a petition for the winding up of an insolvent partnership as an unregistered company, without at the same time presenting an insolvency petition against an insolvent member, but now he may do

so regardless of the number of members. In this event, Part V of the Act of 1986, which is concerned with the winding up of unregistered companies, applies subject to certain modifications. Thirdly, a new remedy is provided whereby a creditor can bring, hand in hand, proceedings for the winding up of a partnership and for the bankruptcy or winding up of two or more of its insolvent members."

24.006 The IPO, like the corresponding English Order, also provides for all the members of a partnership firm presenting a joint bankruptcy petition not involving the winding up of the partnership as an unregistered company.

24.007 This Chapter contains an outline of the several procedures referred to above. The procedure for winding up an insolvent partnership as an unregistered company is dealt with only in so far as modified by the IPO. The general procedure for such a winding up is outside the scope of this book, as is the procedure for winding up a corporate member of the partnership, for which provision is made in the IPO. For a fuller treatment of partnership insolvency reference should be made to text books on the corresponding law in England and Wales.[5] Procedures in respect of the bankruptcy of an individual member of any insolvent partnership are only referred to where they differ from corresponding procedures in the bankruptcy of any individual debtor.

I. BANKRUPTCY PETITION(S) BY OR AGAINST ONE OR MORE PARTNERS

24.008 The IPO expressly preserves the right of a creditor to whom one or more debts is owed by an insolvent partnership ("a partnership creditor") to present a bankruptcy petition under the Order against one or more individual members of the partnership without including the others and without presenting a petition for the winding up of the partnership as an unregistered company and provides that in such a case the debt or debts shall be treated as a debt or debts of the member in question.[6]

24.009 Separate petitions must be presented against each partner.[7]

24.010 Where a debt is based on a judgment against a firm it would appear that it would be prudent (but probably not essential) for the creditor to apply for leave to enforce the judgment against the property of each partner against whom it is desired to present a bankruptcy petition, before serving a statutory demand on him.[8]

24.011 Nothing in the IPO affects the right of an individual partner to present a debtor's bankruptcy petition against himself or the rights of the supervisor of, or any person bound by a voluntary arrangement, or the Law Society of Northern Ireland to present a bankruptcy petition against such an individual under the Order.

24.012 The IPO contains the following useful provisions to assist the administration of partnership property where separate bankruptcy orders are made against partners.

24.013 Where at any time after a bankruptcy petition has been presented against an individual member the attention of the Court is drawn to the fact that the person in question is a member of an insolvent partnership, the Court may make an order as to the future conduct of the insolvency proceedings and any such order may apply any provisions of the IPO with any necessary modifications.[9]

24.014 Where in such a case bankruptcy petitions have been presented against two or more individuals the Court may give such directions for consolidating the proceedings, or any of them, as it thinks just.[10]

24.015 Such an order or direction may be made or given on the application of the Official Receiver, any responsible insolvency practitioner or any other interested person and may include provisions as to the administration of the estate of the partnership and in particular as to the joint estate of the partnership and any separate estate of any member.[11]

24.016 It has been stated that these provisions mean that by the presentation of separate bankruptcy petitions against partners all the benefits of winding up the partnership as an unregistered company may be attained without the complications of the other options available under the IPO.[12]

24.017 Where bankruptcy petitions have been presented against all the members of a partnership firm and a direction for consolidation is obtained, careful attention should be given to what further orders or directions are required for the effective administration of the partnership assets, bearing in mind that, subject thereto, each bankruptcy must be administered in accordance with the law governing the bankruptcy of an individual debtor. Examples of such orders and directions which may be sought are -

(a) the summoning of a single meeting of all the creditors of the partnership and of each bankrupt for the purpose of appointing an authorised insolvency practitioner to act as trustee of the estate of each of the bankrupts and to establish a creditors' committee for each bankruptcy composed of the same persons;

(b) the submission of a statement of the affairs of the partnership, as well as statements of the affairs of each bankrupt;

(c) to order any member or former member of the partnership or any other person who has or has had control or management of the partnership business to deliver up any partnership property which he holds to the trustee for the purpose of the exercise of his functions as trustee;[13]

(d) to provide for the priority of payment of expenses and debts as between the joint estate of the partnership and the separate estate of each partner.[14]

24.018   Where not all the partners have been adjudged bankrupt the Court should be asked to include, in addition to directions such as those suggested in the preceding paragraph, an order giving the trustee (or the trustees jointly if the same person is not appointed trustee of each bankrupt's estate) power to realise the partnership property.

24.019   The disqualification implications of Article 3(a) of the IPO do not apply, as the partnership is not being wound up as an unregistered company.

II. BANKRUPTCY PETITION BY ALL MEMBERS OF INSOLVENT PARTNERSHIP NOT INVOLVING THE WINDING UP OF THE PARTNERSHIP AS AN UNREGISTERED COMPANY

(a) Introduction
24.020   Article 13 of the IPO provides for a joint bankruptcy petition by all the members of a partnership where no member is a company or a limited partner and which will secure the administration of the separate estate of each member and also the winding up of the partnership without any winding up order being made.

(b) Petition
24.021   The petition is a joint debtor's petition in the prescribed form[15] signed by a member of the partnership, requesting the making of bankruptcy orders against all the partners, presented on the ground that the partnership is unable to pay its debts.[16] It must contain a request that the trustee of the partners' estates wind up the partnership business and administer the partnership property.[17]

24.022   The petition must be accompanied by an affidavit made by the partner who signs it showing that all the partners concur in the presentation of the petition.[18] The consent of each of the other partners should be exhibited to this affidavit. Unlike other debtor's petitions, the petitioners are not required to produce statements of affairs at the time of presenting the petition.[19]

(c) Bankruptcy orders
24.023   A separate bankruptcy order is made against each partner.[20]

24.024   The provisions of the Order providing for the appointment of an insolvency practitioner to consider a voluntary arrangement and for the issue of a certificate for summary administration are excluded.[21]

(d) Effect of bankruptcy orders
24.025   Where bankruptcy orders are made on the petition all the provisions of the Order about bankruptcy of individuals apply in relation to the bankruptcy of each partner, with the modifications specified in IPO, Schedule 2, Part III.[22]

24.026   A partner must deliver up to the trustee possession of any partnership property which he holds.[23]

24.027   The priority of expenses and debts as between the joint estate of the partnership and the separate estates of the bankrupt members is governed by Articles 9 and 10 of the IPO.

24.028   The bankrupt partners may propose a voluntary arrangement, which must include the partnership debts.[24]

24.029   The disqualification implications of the IPO[25] do not apply where bankruptcy orders are made on the petition of the members without an order being made for the winding up of the partnership as an unregistered company. Partners who fear such disqualification have therefore an incentive to present a joint bankruptcy petition before a creditor proceeds under the other provisions of the IPO.

(e) Statement of affairs
24.030   Each bankrupt must submit a statement of his affairs to the Official Receiver within 21 days of the making of the bankruptcy order against him and this must specify his interest in the partnership assets and the debts and liabilities of the partnership as well as his separate debts and liabilities.[26] An additional statement of the affairs of the partnership must also be submitted.[27]

(f) Appointment of trustee
24.031   Articles 266 and 267 of the Order (summoning of meeting of creditors to appoint trustee) do not apply.[28] Instead the Official Receiver must, within 4 months of the making of the bankruptcy orders, summon a meeting of all the creditors of the individual members for the purpose of appointing a trustee.[29] He has no power to refuse to summon such a meeting.

24.032   If the meeting fails to appoint a trustee the Official Receiver decides whether to act as trustee himself or to refer the need for an appointment to the Department.[30]

(g) Creditors' committee
24.033   The single meeting of creditors summoned by the Official Receiver may establish a creditors' committee for each bankruptcy, composed of the same persons.[31]

(h) Other modifications of the Order
24.034   Other modifications of the Order specified in Part III of Schedule 2 to the IPO[32] are referred to below.

III. WINDING UP OF INSOLVENT PARTNERSHIP ONLY

Introduction

24.035   An insolvent partnership may be wound up by the Court as an unregistered company under Part VI of the Order.[33] It may be wound up in any of
the circumstances specified in Article 185(4). There must be a partnership
within the definition in section 1 of the Partnership Act 1890. A mere holding
out as a partner under section 14 of that Act is not enough.[34] A partnership is
insolvent for the purposes of being wound up under the IPO if as an entity it is
unable to pay its debts as they fall due or if its assets when realised would be
insufficient to discharge its liabilities: it is not sufficient that one or more of the
members is or are individually insolvent, even though the partnership itself is
able to pay its debts or has assets exceeding its liabilities.[35]

24.036   A partnership which has a principal place of business in Great Britain
may not be wound up by the Court unless it also has a principal place of
business in Northern Ireland,[36] but the requirement of having carried on
business in Northern Ireland within 3 years of the presentation of the petition,
which applies to a petition to wind up a partnership in conjunction with
insolvency petitions against the members,[37] does not apply.

24.037   Part VI of the Order applies subject to the modifications specified in
IPO, Schedule 1, summarised below.[38]

Petition

24.038   A petition for winding up an insolvent partnership may be presented
by the liquidator of a corporate partner (or of a former corporate partner) or the
trustee of a bankrupt partner (or of a former bankrupt partner's estate) and if a
winding-up order is made on such petition the Court may appoint the liquidator or trustee presenting the petition as liquidator of the partnership.[39]

24.039   If the partnership assets are insufficient to satisfy the costs of such a
petition, the costs may be paid out of the assets of the member as part of the
expenses of the liquidation or bankruptcy, in the same order of priority as
expenses properly chargeable or incurred by the liquidator or trustee in getting
in any of the assets of the member.[40]

24.040   A winding-up petition may be presented by the partnership itself if it
consists of not less than 8 members.[41]

24.041   Where a demand in the prescribed form[42] has been served on the
partnership by a creditor in respect of a joint debt or debts exceeding £750 then
due by the partnership but paid by a member of the partnership other than out
of partnership assets that member may, with the leave of the Court, present a
petition to wind up the partnership.[43] Leave may only be given if the Court is
satisfied that the petitioner has obtained a judgment of a court against the
partnership for reimbursement to him of the amount of the joint debt or debts

so paid and that he has taken all reasonable steps (other than insolvency proceedings) to enforce that judgment.[44]

24.042   A form of petition is prescribed by the IPO where the petitioner is the liquidator of a corporate member or the trustee of a bankrupt partner's estate.[45] In other cases the form of company winding-up petition prescribed by the Rules, with appropriate modifications, should be used. The heading and title should follow the IPO prescribed form and not that of a company winding-up petition. The verifying affidavit must include the names in full and addresses of all members of the partnership so far as known to the petitioner.[46]

Liability of partners as contributories
24.043   The partners of an insolvent partnership being wound up by the Court are liable as contributories for the liabilities of the partnership not discharged from the partnership assets.[47]

24.044   If the liquidator wishes to seek to recover any deficiency from the partners he must settle a list of contributories and make calls in accordance with the Rules [48] If a call is made on an individual partner and he does not pay up, the liquidator may institute proceedings against him for recovery and/or petition for his bankruptcy.

Disqualification of partners
24.045   Where an insolvent partnership is being wound up as an unregistered company any member or former member of the partnership or any other person who has or has had control or management of the partnership business is deemed for the purpose of the disqualification provisions of the Companies (Northern Ireland) Order 1989 to be an officer and director of the company and those provisions apply as if the partnership were a company which may be wound up under the Order.[49]

IV. PETITION TO WIND UP PARTNERSHIP IN CONJUNCTION WITH INSOLVENCY PETITIONS AGAINST TWO OR MORE INSOLVENT MEMBERS

INTRODUCTION

24.046   The IPO provides for an insolvent partnership to be wound up as an unregistered company in conjunction with insolvency petitions (winding-up petition in the case of a corporate member and bankruptcy petition in the case of an individual member) presented by the petitioner against two or more insolvent members.

24.047   There will always be at least 3 petitions - one to wind up the partnership and at least two others against members of the partnership.

A. PARTNERSHIP WINDING-UP PROCEEDINGS

24.048   The provisions of the Order relating to the winding up of unregistered companies govern the winding up of the partnership subject to the provisions of the IPO.[50] The significant modifications are referred to below. References in the footnotes to an Article of the Order modified by the IPO are to such an Article as modified by Article 8 and Part I of Schedule 2 to the IPO.

Jurisdiction
24.049   The Court may only wind up an insolvent partnership in conjunction with insolvency petitions against the members if the partnership has a principal place of business in Northern Ireland and has carried on business in Northern Ireland at any time in the period of 3 years ending with the day on which the petition for winding it up was presented.[51] It may not be wound up by the Court if it has a principal place of business in Great Britain unless it also has a principal place of business in Northern Ireland.[52]

Petition
(a) The petitioner
24.050   The petition may be presented by all the members of the partnership or by any creditor or creditors to whom the partnership is indebted in respect of a liquidated sum payable immediately.[53]

(b) Grounds
24.051   The only ground on which an insolvent partnership may be wound up is that it is unable to pay its debts.[54]

24.052   For the purposes of this provision the partnership is deemed to be unable to pay its debts if a creditor to whom the partnership owes a joint debt exceeding £750 has served on the partnership a written demand in the prescribed form[55] and has also served on any two or more insolvent members demands in the same form requiring the partnership and its members to pay the sum due to the creditor and the sum has not been paid or compounded for to the reasonable satisfaction of the creditor within 3 weeks after service of the demands or the last of them if served at different times.[56] Service of the demand on the partnership is effected by leaving it at its principal place of business in Northern Ireland or by delivery to a partner or any person having at the time of service control or management of the partnership business there, or otherwise as the Court approves or directs.[57]

(c) Form and verification
24.053   The petition must be in the prescribed form.[58] It must contain particulars of the other petitions being presented in relation to the partnership against insolvent members, identifying the members concerned.[59]

24.054   The verifying affidavit must include the names in full and addresses of all members of the partnership so far as known to the petitioner.[60]

(d) Presentation
24.055 The petition must be presented at the same time as the insolvency petitions against the members.[61]

(e) Addition of other partners
24.056 At any time after the presentation of the petition the Court may, on application, give leave for other partners to be added as parties to the proceedings in relation to the insolvent partnership on such terms as it thinks just.[62]

24.057 The application should be for leave to issue a separate winding-up petition against a corporate member or a bankruptcy petition against an individual member. Such leave may only be given before the making of a winding-up order against the partnership. If an additional partner is ascertained after the making of such winding-up order and the liquidator presents a winding-up or bankruptcy petition against that partner, he may apply for directions for consolidation and other directions under Article 14 of the IPO.

(f) Advertisement
24.058 The advertisement of the petition must be in the prescribed form.[63]

(g) Withdrawal of petition
24.059 The petitioner may only withdraw the winding-up petition if he withdraws at the same time every petition which he has presented against any insolvent member and gives notice to the Court of his intention to withdraw at least 3 days before the hearing date.[64]

(h) Hearing
24.060 The hearing must be fixed for a time in advance of the hearing of the petitions against the insolvent members.[65] It is advisable that the interval between the hearing of the winding-up petition and petitions against the partners should be as short as possible and preferably the latter petitions should be heard immediately after the former.

24.061 Any partner or person against whom a winding-up or bankruptcy petition has been presented in relation to the insolvent partnership may appear and be heard on the petition for the winding up of the partnership.[66]

24.062 At the hearing the Court may give directions as to the future conduct of the proceedings against an insolvent member against whom a bankruptcy order or a company winding-up order has been made.[67]

(i) Substitution of petitioner
24.063 Where notice of withdrawal of the petition is given the Court may, on such terms as it thinks just, substitute as petitioner any creditor of the partnership who in its opinion would have a right to present a petition and at the same time substitute him as petitioner in respect of every petition which the peti-

tioner has presented against an insolvent member, and if such a substitution is made the petition in question will not be withdrawn.[68]

Appointment of liquidator etc.

24.064 The Official Receiver must, within 4 months of the making of the winding-up order against the partnership, summon and hold a single meeting of the partnership creditors and of the creditors of each insolvent member against whom a bankruptcy or company winding-up order has been made, for the purpose of choosing a person to be liquidator of the partnership in place of the Official Receiver and a liquidator of any such corporate insolvent member and/or a trustee of any such individual insolvent member.[69] Such single meeting is to be conducted as if the creditors of the partnership and of any such insolvent member were a single set of creditors.[70] At the meeting the creditors of the partnership and of the insolvent members may nominate a person to be liquidator of the partnership and liquidator or trustee (as the case may be) of any insolvent member.[71] If at any time the liquidator of the partnership considers that there is a conflict of interest between his functions as such liquidator and as liquidator or trustee of any individual member he may apply to the Court for directions and the Court may replace him in one or other or both of such offices.[72]

24.065 If no person is chosen as liquidator at the meeting of creditors the Official Receiver may either remain as liquidator or invite the Department to appoint an authorised insolvency practitioner to replace him.[73]

Creditors' meetings

24.066 In the application of other provisions of the Order relating to meetings of creditors the liquidator is given a discretion to summon either a single meeting of the creditors of the partnership and of the insolvent members or separate meetings of each class.[74] He has a similar discretion with regard to meetings of contributories of the partnership (i.e. the partners) and of any corporate members.

Liquidation committee

24.067 The single meeting of creditors summoned for the appointment of a liquidator etc. may establish a liquidation committee consisting of creditors of the partnership or of an insolvent member or of both.[75] Such a single meeting of creditors may also be summoned at any time by the Official Receiver for the purpose of establishing such a committee and must be so summoned on a requisition by the requisite majority of creditors in accordance with the Rules.[76] The Court may, on the application of a creditor of the partnership or of any insolvent member, increase the number of members of the committee beyond the number prescribed by the Rules.[77]

Public examination

24.068 At a public examination the person examined may be questioned about the promotion, formation or management of the partnership or of an insolvent member or both or as to the conduct of their business and affairs, or of his conduct or dealings in relation to the partnership or any insolvent member.[78] However, the Court has a discretion to refuse to hold a public examination of a person where such an examination has previously been directed in proceedings in relation to an insolvent member.[79]

Joint and separate estates

24.069   In distributing the assets of the partnership the liquidator must observe the requirements of Articles 9 and 10 of the IPO with regard to the priority of payment of expenses and debts between those of the partnership and of the insolvent members.[80] These Articles contain detailed rules designed to ensure that the assets of the partnership are used first to pay the expenses of the partnership winding up and the partnership creditors and only if there is any surplus is it divided among the separate estates of the partners, and similarly that the individual partner's assets are used first to pay the expenses of that partner's bankruptcy and his personal creditors.[81]

24.070   In adjusting the rights of the partners as contributories the Court must also have regard to Articles 9 and 10 of the IPO.[82] Thus, where a partner has paid more than his proper share of the partnership debts the Court should require an appropriate contribution from the other partners.

Interest on debts

24.071   The provisions of Article 160 regarding payment of interest on debts out of any surplus is subject to Article 10 of the IPO (priority of debts between joint and separate estates).[83]

Directions to liquidator

24.072   The liquidator's power to apply to the Court for directions is extended to directions in relation to insolvency proceedings in respect of an insolvent member.[84]

Removal and resignation of liquidator

24.073   The liquidator may only be removed by the Court or, if appointed by the Department, by the Department.[85]

24.074   The liquidator may resign, with the leave of the Court or, if appointed by the Department, of the Department, by giving notice of his resignation to the Court.[86]

Release of liquidator

24.075   A liquidator who has been removed from office by the Court or the Department or has vacated office on ceasing to be an authorised insolvency practitioner may be released by the Department on his application.[87]

24.076   A liquidator who has resigned may be released by the Court or, if he was appointed by the Department, by the Department.[88]

Disqualifications of partners
24.077 See paragraph 24.045 above.

B. BANKRUPTCY PROCEEDINGS BY OR AGAINST INDIVIDUAL MEMBERS

24.078 The provisions of the Order about bankruptcy apply in relation to the bankruptcy of an individual member, with the modifications specified in Part III of Schedule 2 to the IPO[89] and subject to the other provisions of Part III of the IPO. The significant modifications and additions to the general bankruptcy law are summarised below. References in the footnotes to an Article of the Order modified by the IPO are to such an Article as so modified.

Jurisdiction
24.079 A bankruptcy petition may not be presented unless the Court has jurisdiction to wind up the partnership.[90]

Petition
(a) Creditor's petition
24.080 A bankruptcy petition may be presented against an individual member by one or more of his creditors.[91] No bankruptcy petition may be presented by a creditor against a partnership or the partners in the name of the firm.[92]

(i) Grounds
24.081 The petition must be in respect of one or more joint debts owed by the insolvent partnership and the debt or each of the debts must be for a liquidated sum payable immediately.[93]

24.082 The inability of the debtor to pay the debt, required by Article 241(2)(c), may be established only in either of two ways -
    (A) if the petitioning creditor has served a statutory demand on the member in the prescribed form[94] and also a written demand on the partnership in the same form requiring the member and the partnership to pay the debt or to secure or compound for it to the reasonable satisfaction of the creditor and both demands have not been complied with within 3 weeks of service of the relevant demand or within the same period the demand against the member has not been set aside in accordance with the Rules, or
    (B) if the Court has made a winding-up order against the partnership.[95]

24.083 It is to be noted that inability to pay may not be proved by the granting of a certificate of unenforceability in respect of a judgment.

24.084 Where the petitioning creditor has obtained a judgment, decree or order against the individual member or against the partnership and he is entitled to enforce the judgment etc. against the property of the member or of the partnership,[96] the statutory demand may be served at the principal place of business of the partnership in Northern Ireland on the individual member or on any partner or any other person having at the time of service control or management of the partnership business there.[97] This is an addition to the provisions of the Rules regarding service of a statutory demand.

24.085 Article 243 relating to security held by the petitioning creditor does not apply.[98]

(ii) Form
24.086 The petition must be in the prescribed form.[99] It must contain particulars of other petitions being presented in relation to the partnership, identifying the partnership and members concerned.[100]

(iii) Presentation
24.087 The petition must be presented at the same time as the petition for the winding up of the partnership.[101]

24.088 Article 244 permitting the expedition of the presentation of a bankruptcy petition on grounds of jeopardy is omitted.[102]

(iv) Addition of other partners
24.089 At any time after presentation of the petition the Court may, on application, give leave for other partners to be added as parties to the proceedings in relation to the insolvent partnership on such terms as it thinks just.[103] See paragraph 24.057 above as to the operation of this provision.

(v) Withdrawal
24.090 The petitioner may withdraw the petition without leave if he notifies the Court not less than 3 days before the hearing date of his intention to do so and withdraws at the same time every other petition which he has presented against the partnership and any other insolvent member.[104] However, the Court may, on application by the petitioner, allow him to withdraw the petition in respect of which the application is made without withdrawing such other petitions if satisfied that, because of difficulties in serving the first mentioned petition or for any other reason, the continuation of that petition would be likely to prejudice or delay the proceedings on any of the other petitions.[105]

(vi) Hearing
24.091 The hearing must be fixed for a date or time after the hearing of the petition against the partnership.[106]

24.092 On the hearing the petitioner must draw the Court's attention to the result of the hearing of the winding-up petition against the partnership.[107] If no winding-up order has been made on that petition the Court may dismiss the petition against the member.[108] If such a winding-up order has been made against the partnership the Court is required to make a bankruptcy order against the individual member on the petition against him (except in the case of a limited partner, in respect of whom special provision is made) unless the petitioning creditor's debt has been paid.[109]

(vii) Substitution of petitioner
24.093 Where the petitioner has given notice of withdrawal of the petition the Court may, on such terms as it thinks just, substitute as petitioner any creditor of the partnership who in its opinion would have a right to present the petition and who has already been substituted by the Court as petitioner in respect of the winding-up petition against the partnership, and if such a substitution is made the petition in question will not be withdrawn.[110] If such a substitution is made the Court must also substitute such person as petitioner in respect of every petition which the petitioner has presented against other individual members. [111] Only a creditor who has served the required demands on the partnership and the individual members would qualify for substitution.[112]

(b) Debtor's petition
24.094 A debtor's petition in the prescribed from[113] may be presented to the High Court by an individual member of an insolvent partnership only on the ground that the partnership is unable to pay its debts and if -
  (i)   petitions are at the same time presented for a winding-up order against the partnership and for insolvency orders (i.e. a winding-up order in respect of any corporate member and a bankruptcy order in respect of any individual member) against every other member; and
  (ii) each member is willing for an insolvency order to be made against him and the petition contains a statement to this effect.[114]

24.095 No statement of affairs is required to accompany the petition.

24.096 No certificate for summary administration may be issued nor may the Court appoint an insolvency practitioner to report on the possibility of a voluntary arrangement.[115]

Appointment of trustee
24.097 As mentioned in paragraph 24.064 above, the single meeting of creditors summoned by the Official Receiver may appoint an authorised insolvency practitioner as liquidator of the partnership and as trustee in relation to an insolvent individual member. If no such appointment is made the Official Receiver must decide whether to act as such trustee or to invite the Department to appoint an authorised insolvency practitioner as trustee.[116]

Statement of affairs
24.098 The bankrupt member must submit a statement of his affairs to the Official Receiver within 21 days of the making of the bankruptcy order against him and this must specify his interest in the partnership assets and the debts and liabilities of the partnership as well as his separate debts and liabilities.[117]

Creditors' committee

24.099 The single meeting of creditors summoned by the Official Receiver for the appointment of a liquidator of the partnership and a trustee of an individual insolvent member's estate may establish a creditors' committee for the bankruptcy of each member, composed of the same persons as the liquidation committee established for the partnership.[118]

Bankrupt's property

24.100 The exclusion from the definition of "the bankrupt's estate" of tools, vehicles etc. necessary for the bankrupt's employment, business or vocation and of clothing, furniture etc. necessary for the basic domestic needs of the bankrupt and his family does not apply to any such items as are partnership property.[119]

24.101 The restrictions on dispositions of property made by a debtor after presentation of a bankruptcy petition by or against him apply to any property held by an insolvent partner on trust for the partnership.[120]

Public examination

24.102 At a public examination the bankrupt member may be examined not only as to his own affairs, dealings and property but also as to those of the partnership or of another insolvent member or both.[121] However, the Court has a discretion to refuse to hold a further public examination of a bankrupt member where such an examination has already been directed in proceedings relating to the partnership or another insolvent member.[122]

Joint and separate estates

24.103 The provisions of the Order with regard to the priority of debts, dealing with any surplus and distribution of the estate are subject to the provisions of Articles 9 and 10 of the IPO relating to the priority of expenses and debts between the joint estate of the partnership and the separate estates of the insolvent members.[123]

Removal and resignation of trustee

24.104 The trustee may only be removed by the Court or, if appointed by the Department, by the Department.[124]

24.105 The trustee may resign, with the leave of the Court or, if appointed by the Department, of the Department, by giving notice of his resignation to the Court.[125]

Release of trustee

24.106 A trustee who has been removed from office by the Court or who has vacated office on ceasing to be an authorised insolvency practitioner may be released by the Department.[126]

24.107   A trustee who has resigned may be released by the Court or, if appointed by the Department, by the Department.[127]

Vacancy in office of trustee

24.108   A vacancy in the office of trustee may be filled by the Department at the request of the Official Receiver, who remains trustee until the vacancy is filled.[128]

Voluntary arrangement

24.109   A bankrupt partner may propose a voluntary arrangement, which must include the partnership debts.[129]

Footnotes

(1) The IPO contains no application of the other legislation referred to in Art.364.

(2) IPO Art.15(1),(2).

(3) IPO Art.5(1),(2).

(4) Re Marr (bankrupts) [1990] Ch773, 780.

(5) E.g.MH 4-001/020, Hals 799/808, Roger Gregory "Bankruptcy of Individuals and Partnerships",Part III. See also a useful flow chart in (1991) 4 Ins Int 31.

(6) IPO Art.15(3).

(7) Para.7.042.

(8) MH 4-002/1: RSC O.81, r.5: County Court Rules (Northern Ireland) 1981, O.39, r.6.

(9) IPO Art.14(1).

(10) IPO Art.14(2).

(11) IPO Art.14(3).

(12) Stuart J Frith "Avoiding the Insolvent Partnership Order",(1991) 4 Ins Int 9.

(13) By application of IPO Art 3(b).

(14) IPO Arts.9 and 10 may be applied, with appropriate modifications.

(15) IPO Sch.3, Form 8.

(16) Art.246 as substituted by IPO Art.13(5).

(17) IPO Art.13(2).

(18) Ibid.

(19) Art.246 as substituted by IPO Art 13(5) omits para.(2).

(20) Atkin Form 331.

(21) IPO Sch.2, Pt.III, para.10, applied by IPO Arts.8(2),13(3).

(22) IPO Art.8(2),applied by IPO Art.13(3).

(23) IPO Art.3(b),applied by IPO Art.13(3).

(24) IPO Art.11, applied by IPO Art.13(3).

(25) IPO Art 3(a).

(26) Art.261 as modified by IPO Sch.2, Pt.III, applied by IPO Arts.8(2), 13(3).

(27) IPO Art.13(6).

(28) IPO Sch.2, Pt.III, para.15, applied by IPO Arts.8(2), 13(6).

(29) Art.116(4) as substituted by IPO, Sch.2, Pt I applied by IPO Art. 13(4). Query validity of this application having regard to wording of IPO Art.8(2).

(30) Art.268 as modified by IPO Sch.2, Pt.III and IPO Art.13(4), applied by IPO Arts.8(2), 13(3),(4).

(31) Art.274 as modified by IPO Sch.2,Pt.III and IPO Art.13(4),applied by IPO Arts.8(2), 13(3),(4).

(32) Applied by IPO Arts.8(2), 13(3). See Pt. IV B below.

(33) Art.104 as substitued by IPO Sch.2, Pt.I, applied by IPO Art.7.

(34) Re C & M Ashberg [1990] TLR 542.

(35) Re Hough (a bankrupt) (1990) The Independent, 23 April.

(36) Art.185(2).
(37) Para.24.049.
(38) IPO Art.7.
(39) Art 185 as modified by IPO Sch.1.
(40) *Ibid.*
(41) *Ibid.*
(42) IPO Sch.3, Form 2.
(43) Art.185 as modified by IPO Sch.1.
(44) *Ibid.*
(45) IPO Sch.3, Form 1.
(46) IPO Art.4.
(47) Art.190.
(48) RR.4.205/215.
(49) IPO Arts.3, 6.
(50) IPO Art.8(1), Sch.2, Pt.I.
(51) Art.185(1),(3A).
(52) Art.185(2).
(53) Art.104(1).
(54) Art.185(4).
(55) IPO, Sch.3, Form 3.
(56) Art.186(1).
(57) *Ibid.*
(58) Art.104(1):IPO, Sch.3 Form 4.
(59) Art.104(6).
(60) IPO Art.4.
(61) Art.104(2).
(62) Art.104(4).
(63) Art.104(3):IPO, Sch.3, Form 5.
(64) Art.104(8).
(65) Art.104(7).
(66) Art.104(5).
(67) Art.105(2).
(68) Art.104(9).
(69) Art.116(4).
(70) Art.116(4A).
(71) Art.118(1),(2).
(72) Art.118(3).
(73) Art.117.
(74) IPO, Sch.2, Pt.I, para.6.
(75) Art.120(1).
(76) Art.120(2).
(77) Art.120(3).
(78) Art.113(3).
(79) Art.113(5).
(80) Art.121(1A).
(81) For summary of rules, see Roger Gregory "Bankruptcy of Individuals and Partnerships", para.1606.

(82) Art.132.
(83) Art.160(5).
(84) Art.143(3).
(85) Art.146(2),(4).
(86) Art.146(6).
(87) Art.148(4)(b).
(88) Art.148(4)(c).
(89) IPO Art.8(2).
(90) Art.239: para.24.049 above.
(91) Art.238(1). The Law Society of Northern Ireland may only petition if it is a qualified creditor. A petition by the supervisor of or creditor bound by an approved voluntary arrangement is excluded.
(92) Art.238(1).
(93) Art.241.
(94) IPO Sch.3, Form 3.
(95) Art.242(1),(2): MH 3-083.
(96) I.e. that the judgment etc. is not subject to a stay of enforcement and that in the case of a judgment etc. against a firm leave to enforce it against the partner has been obtained under RSC 0.81, r.5 or County Court Rules (Northern Ireland) 1981, 0.39. r.6.
(97) Art.242(3),(4).
(98) IPO Sch.2, Pt.III, para.7.
(99) Art.238(1): IPO Sch.3, Form 7.
(100) Art.238(1C).
(101) Art.238(1A).
(102) IPO Sch.2, Pt.III, para.7.
(103) Art.238(1B).
(104) Art.238(1D).
(105) Ibid.
(106) Para.24.060 above.
(107) Art.245(2A).
(108) Art.245(2).
(109) Art.245(2A), as interpreted by English Court of Appeal in Re Marr (bankrupts)[1990] Ch 773. See MH 3-093, 3-097/1.
(110) Art.238(1E).
(111) Ibid.
(112) MH 4-043.
(113) IPO Sch.3, Form 7.
(114) Art.246.
(115) Arts.247/249 are omitted.
(116) Art.268.
(117) Art.261.
(118) Art.274.
(119) Art.11(2) is excluded in respect of partnership property.
(120) Art.257(6).
(121) Art.263(3).
(122) Art.263(4A).

(123) Arts.278(2A), 300(7), 303(5).
(124) Art.271(1),(4).
(125) Art.271(6).
(126) Art.272(3)(b).
(127) Art.272(3)(c).
(128) Art.273.
(129) IPO Art.11.

Chapter 25

ADMINISTRATION OF ESTATE OF DECEASED INSOLVENT [1]

Introduction

25.01 Where a person against whom a bankruptcy petition has not been presented dies and his estate is insolvent it may be administered by the personal representative without any court intervention unless an order for administration has been made in the Chancery Division of the High Court or in a County Court or an order is made for administration in bankruptcy under the provisions dealt with in this Chapter.

25.02 By Article 365 of the Order the Lord Chancellor is empowered, with the concurrence of the Department, to make an order applying to the administration of the insolvent estates of deceased persons such provisions of the Order, the Land Registration Act, the Registration of Deeds Acts and Part VI of the Judgments Enforcement Order as may be specified, with such modifications as may be specified. This power has been exercised by the Administration of Insolvent Estates of Deceased Persons Order (Northern Ireland) 1991 ("the DIEO").

25.03 Where the estate is being administered otherwise than under an insolvency administration order made by the Court under the DIEO the provisions of the bankruptcy law apply with respect to the respective rights of secured and unsecured creditors, to debts and liabilities provable, to the valuation of future and contingent liabilities and to the priorities of debts and other payments, except that the reasonable funeral, testamentary and administration expenses have priority over the preferential debts. [2] The person administering an estate otherwise than under an insolvency administration order is not required to be an authorised insolvency practitioner. [3]

25.04 The consequences of the death of a debtor by or against whom a bankruptcy petition has been presented are referred to in Chapter 7. [4] The remainder of this Chapter deals with the administration of the estate of a deceased person against whom no bankruptcy petition has been presented and references to a deceased insolvent are to such a person.

Application of Insolvency Order etc. [5]

25.05 The provisions of the Order and the related legislation mentioned above which are applied, with or without modification, to the administration in bankruptcy of the estate of a deceased insolvent are contained in Schedule I to the DIEO.

25.06   For the purpose of giving effect to the applied provisions of the primary legislation the relevant provisions of the Rules, the Insolvency Regulations, the Insolvency (Deposits) Order (Northern Ireland) 1991, the Insolvency (Fees) Order (Northern Ireland) 1991, the Land Registration Rules and the Insolvency (Registration of Deeds) Regulations apply and in the case of any conflict between any provision of the Rules and any provision of the DIEO, the latter provision is to prevail.

25.07   Parts II and III of Schedule 1 to the DIEO list the provisions of the primary legislation which are applied and the modifications to some of those provisions. All of the listed provisions and the relevant subordinate legislation are also to be applied with any further modification necessary to render them applicable to the estate of a deceased insolvent, and references to the expressions specified in *column (1)* of the following table are to be read as references to the substituted expressions in *column (2)* except in so far as the context otherwise requires.[6] Any provision of the Order not expressly applied must be disregarded in relation to the administration in bankruptcy of the estate of a deceased insolvent.

TABLE

Reference in provision of the Order, the Land Registration Act, the Registration of Deeds Act and the Judgments Enforcement Order specified in Part II	Substituted references
(1)	(2)
bankrupt;debtor	deceased debtor or his personal representative (or if there is no personal representative such person as the Court may order) as the case may require
bankruptcy	insolvency administration
the bankrupt's estate	the deceased debtor's estate
the commencement of the bankruptcy	the date of the insolvency administration order
a bankruptcy order	an insolvency administration order
a bankruptcy petition	an insolvency administration petition

Reference in provision of the order, the Land Registration Act, the Registration of Deeds Act and the Judgements Enforcement Order specified in Part II	Substituted references
(1)	(2)
an individual being adjudged bankrupt	an insolvency administration order being made
a debtor's petition	a petition by the personal representative of a deceased debtor for an insolvency administration order.

25.08   In this Chapter (including the footnotes) a reference to an Article of the Order modified in its application to the estate of a deceased insolvent by Schedule 1 to the DIEO is to that Article as so modified.

25.09   The general interpretation provisions of Article 2 are applied, together with Articles 3 and 4 defining the meaning of "acting as an insolvency practitioner" and "associate". Article 9 containing interpretation provisions governing individual insolvency is applied, subject to the modifications in the definition of "bankruptcy debt" referred to below.[7] Article 10 (security etc.) is applied.

Commencement of administration proceedings
25.10   The administration of a deceased insolvent's estate in bankruptcy is carried out under an insolvency administration order made by the Court. A petition for such an order ("an insolvency administration petition") may be presented by a creditor, the personal representative of the deceased debtor or the supervisor of or a person bound by a voluntary arrangement.[8] The Law Society of Northern Ireland may not present an insolvency administration petition except as a creditor. [9]

25.11   No such petition may be presented after proceedings for the administration of the deceased debtor's estate have been commenced in the Chancery Division of the High Court or in a County Court.[10] If the court in which such an administration is proceeding is satisfied that the estate is insolvent[11] it may transfer the proceedings to the Court (the Bankruptcy Court) which may then make an insolvency administration order as if a petition for such an order had been presented.[12] The jurisdictional requirements of Article 239 governing a bankruptcy petition by a creditor or by a debtor do not apply to an insolvency administration petition.

25.12   Although an insolvency administration order may not be made until a grant of probate or administration has been made in respect of the deceased insolvent's estate,[13] a petitioner who wishes to present an insolvency administration petition before such grant is available (e.g. so as to have the property of the deceased insolvent safeguarded by the appointment of an interim receiver) may do so. In such a case the prescribed forms of petition will require to be modified accordingly and to refer to the executor(s) named in the will or, if there is not known to be a will, name other persons on whom leave to serve the petition will be sought.[14]

25.13   The provisions of the Registration of Deeds Act and the Land Registration Act governing registration of bankruptcy petitions and bankruptcy orders apply in respect of an insolvency administration petition and an insolvency administration order, with the necessary adaptation.[15]

25.14   An insolvency administration petition may not be withdrawn without leave of the Court.[16] The Court may dismiss or stay proceedings on such petition in the same circumstances as in respect of a bankruptcy petition.[17]

Creditor's petition

25.15   A creditor to whom one or more debts were owed by the deceased may present a petition[18] if, had the debtor been alive at the time of the petition, -

(a)   the amount of the debt, or the aggregate amount of the debts, would have been sufficient to ground a creditor's bankruptcy petition,

(b)   the debt, or each of the debts, would have been for a liquidated sum payable immediately or at some certain future time, and would have been unsecured.[19]

25.16   A petition in respect of a secured debt is subject to the same requirements as govern a bankruptcy petition.[20]

25.17   The petitioning creditor's debt is not required to have been the subject of a statutory demand or of a certificate of unenforceability.

25.18   At the hearing of the petition the Court may make an insolvency administration order if it is satisfied -

(a)   that the debt, or one of the debts, in respect of which the petition was presented is a debt which,

   having been payable at the date of the petition or having since become payable, has neither been paid nor secured or compounded for; or

   has no reasonable prospect of being able to be paid when it falls due; and

(b)   that there is a reasonable probability that the estate will be insolvent.[21]

25.19   The estate is insolvent if, when realised, it will be insufficient to meet in full all debts and other liabilities to which it is subject.[22]

25.20 Unreasonable refusal by the petitioning creditor to accept an offer from the debtor or his personal representative to secure or compound for the debt is not a ground for dismissal of the petition.

25.21 The petition must be served on the personal representative of the deceased debtor, unless the Court otherwise directs, and the Court may direct service on other persons.[23]

Petition by personal representative
25.22 A petition[24] may be presented by the personal representative on the ground that the estate of the deceased debtor is insolvent.[25] Unlike a petition by a living debtor, a statement of affairs is not required to accompany the petition. There is no provision for the Court to appoint an insolvency practitioner to consider a voluntary arrangement with creditors.

25.23 At the hearing of the petition the Court is required to make an insolvency administration order if it is satisfied that the deceased debtor's estate is insolvent.[26]

25.24 Article 249 providing for the issue of a certificate for the summary administration of a bankrupt's estate in certain circumstances is not applied.

Petition by supervisor of, or person bound by, a voluntary arrangement
25.25 The form of petition by the supervisor of, or person bound by, a voluntary arrangement [27] does not include any allegation of failure by the deceased insolvent to comply with his obligations or that he gave false or misleading information or failed to do what the supervisor required him to do. This is because Article 250(1) is not applied.

25.26 It appears that the Court may make an administration order on such a petition if it is satisfied that there is a reasonable probability that the estate will be insolvent.[28]

25.27 Article 250(2) is applied, so that where an administration order is made, any costs properly incurred as costs of the administration of the voluntary arrangement are a first charge on the deceased insolvent's estate.

Consequences of insolvency administration order
25.28 The insolvency administration of a deceased insolvent's estate commences with the day on which the insolvency administration order in respect of the estate is made.[29]

25.29 Articles 257 (restrictions on dispositions of property) [30] and 258 (restrictions on proceedings and remedies) [31] are applied, with the modification that they have effect as if the petition had been presented and the insolvency administration order made on the date of death of the deceased debtor.

25.30   The effect of this modification of Article 257 appears to be that the trustee may challenge any disposition of the property of the deceased insolvent made since the date of his death otherwise than with the consent of or ratification by the Court. The provision of protection in respect of bona fide transactions by the personal representative before the date of the insolvency administration order contained in the substituted Article 245(5) is not related to this Article and indeed its effectiveness is doubtful.[32] Moreover, the effect of the modification on the position of third parties under paragraph (4) of the Article is obscure.[33]

Protection of property of deceased debtor
25.31   After the presentation of an insolvency administration petition and before the making of an insolvency administration order the Court may appoint an interim receiver if necessary for the protection of the property of the deceased debtor.[34]

25.32   Between the making of the insolvency administration order and the vesting of the estate of the deceased insolvent in a trustee the Official Receiver is receiver and (unless and until a special manager is appointed) manager of the deceased insolvent's estate, as in bankruptcy.[35]

Statement of affairs
25.33   Where an insolvency administration order has been made, the personal representative, or if there is no personal representative such person as the Court may on the application of the Official Receiver direct, must submit to the Official Receiver a statement of the affairs of the deceased insolvent as at the date of the insolvency administration order.[36] It must be in Form 6 set out in Schedule 3 to the DIEO or as the Official Receiver may require.[37]

25.34   The statement of affairs must be submitted within 56 days after it has been requested by the Official Receiver or such longer period as he or the Court may allow.[38]

25.35   The Official Receiver may release the personal representative or other person directed to submit a statement of affairs from the obligation to do so, but if not so released the person so obliged is guilty of a contempt of court if, without reasonable excuse, he fails to submit the statement of affairs within the time allowed or submits a statement of affairs which does not comply with the prescribed requirements.[39]

25.36   Article 375 (admissibility in evidence of statement of affairs etc.) is applied.

Investigation of deceased insolvent's affairs
25.37   The personal representative is under the same obligation as a bankrupt to give information to the Official Receiver and to attend on him.[40]

25.38 The Official Receiver is not obliged to investigate the conduct and affairs of the deceased insolvent unless he thinks fit but may make such report (if any) to the Court as he thinks fit.[41]

25.39 The Court may direct a private examination of the personal representative and others, as in a bankruptcy.[42] The bankruptcy provisions relating to production of documents by the Inland Revenue and re-direction of mail also apply.[43]

Deceased insolvent's estate
25.40 References in the Order to the bankrupt's estate are to be read as references to the deceased debtor's estate.[44] Article 11 defining such estate has effect as if the petition had been presented and the insolvency administration order had been made on the date of death of the deceased debtor and with modifications, of which the most significant are -
  (a) the exclusion of necessary tools etc. does not apply,
  (b) such clothing, bedding, furniture, household equipment and provisions as are necessary for satisfying the basic domestic needs of the family of the deceased debtor are excluded.

25.41 Any property acquired by or devolving upon the personal representative since the date of death of the deceased debtor may be claimed for the estate by the trustee as after-acquired property.[45]

25.42 Where an insolvency administration order has been made the duties of a bankrupt to deliver up possession of his estate to the Official Receiver, to deliver up to the Official Receiver his books, papers and other records and to carry out the instructions of the Official Receiver as regards safeguarding any part of his estate which consists of things possession of which cannot be so delivered apply to the personal representative or, if there is no personal representative, to such other person as the Court may direct.[46]

25.43 The provisions of the Order in respect of the issue of a warrant of seizure of the property of a bankrupt, the making of orders following a private examination and supplies of water, electricity etc. are applied.[47]

25.44 A special manager may be appointed in the same circumstances as in a bankruptcy.[48]

The trustee
25.45 The provisions of the Order providing for the appointment, removal and release of a trustee in bankruptcy and for the Official Receiver to act as trustee during any vacancy in the office of trustee apply, with the necessary modifications resulting from the fact that there can be no summary administration of a deceased insolvent's estate and no insolvency practitioner's report under Article 248.[49] Also applied are the provisions of the Order relating to the general control of the trustee by the Court and the liability of a trustee.[50]

25.46   As in bankruptcy, a creditors' committee may be appointed and in the absence of such a committee the Department may exercise its functions.[51] Where a meeting of creditors is summoned for the purposes of any provision in Articles 265-275, the rules regarding the trustee in bankruptcy and the creditors' committee apply.[52]

Administration of deceased insolvent's estate
25.47   The deceased insolvent's estate is administered and distributed to creditors in accordance with the provisions of Article 278-320 of the Order applying to bankruptcy, with the following modifications -
   (a)   any property acquired by or devolving upon the personal repre-
          sentative since the date of death of the deceased debtor may be claimed
          by the trustee as after-acquired property;[53]
   (b)   the claim of the personal representative to payment of reasonable
          funeral, testamentary and administration expenses incurred by him in
          respect of the deceased debtor's estate must be paid in priority to
          preferential debts;[54]
   (c)   the relevant date for proof of debts, the payment of interest on debts
          from any surplus after payment of debts, the determination of the
          existence and the amounts of preferential debts is the date of death of
          the deceased debtor and not the date of the insolvency administration
          order;[55]
   (d)   any surplus after payment of debts, with interest and the expenses of
          the administration, is payable to the personal representative unless the
          Court otherwise orders;[56]
   (e)   transactions at an undervalue may be re-opened if entered into within
          5 years of the date of death of the deceased debtor.[57]

25.48   The categories of preferential debts are the same as in bankruptcy.[58]

25.49   The provisions of Articles 367-369 with regard to transactions defrauding creditors are applied.

Annulment of insolvency administration order
25.50   An insolvency administration order may be annulled in the same circumstances as a bankruptcy order [59] and Article 256(4) (validation of dispositions prior to annulment, vesting of any of the estate remaining vested in trustee, etc.) applies.

Other applied provisions of the Order
25.51   Other provisions of the Order which are applied include -
   (a)   Article 334 (general control of the Court);
   (b)   Articles 344 (time-limits) and 345 (formal defects);
   (c)   Articles 348-354 (insolvency practitioners and their qualification);
   (d)   Articles 355-357 (Official Receivers);
   (e)   Article 358 (Insolvency Account);

(f)   Articles 359-361 (Insolvency Rules and fees and deposits Orders);
(g)   Article 362 (monetary limits);
(h)   Article 363 (regulations for insolvency practitioners);
(i)   Article 364 (insolvent partnerships);
(j)   Article 371 (review of orders of the Court);
(k)   Article 372 (annual report);
(l)   Article 378 (Crown application);
(m)   Parts II and III of Schedule 8 (transitional provisions), except para-
      graphs 11 (discharge from old bankruptcy), 17 (deeds of arrangement)
      and 20 (transitional effect of Articles 367-369).

Voluntary arrangements
25.52   The application of the provisions of the Order relating to voluntary
arrangements is dealt with in Chapter 26.[60]

Footnotes

(1)   MH 5-001/5-085: Hals 809/812.
(2)   DIEO Art.4(1),(2).
(3)   DIEO Art.4(3).
(4)   Paras.7.077, 7.140.
(5)   DIEO Art.3.
(6)   DIEO, Sch.1, Pt.I.
(7)   Para.25.47(c).
(8)   Arts.238, 246.
(9)   Art.238(1)(d) is omitted.
(10)   Art.245(2).
(11)   Para.25.19.
(12)   Art.245(3),(4).
(13)   *Re a Debtor* [1939] Ch 594.
(14)   Para.25.21.
(15)   DIEO, Sch.1, Pt.II, paras.39/41.
(16)   Art.240(2).
(17)   Art.240(3).
(18)   DIEO, Sch.3, Form 1.
(19)   Art.241.
(20)   Arts.10, 243.
(21)   Art.245(1).
(22)   Art.365(3).
(23)   Art. 240(1).
(24)   DIEO, Sch.3, Form 5.
(25)   Art.246.
(26)   Art.247.
(27)   DIEO, Sch.3, Form 2.
(28)   Art.245(1)(b) and Form 2 above. Art.245(1)(a) is not applicable to such a petition.
(29)   Art.252.
(30)   Para.7.022.
(31)   Para.28.26/28.
(32)   MH 5-022.
(33)   MH 5-035.
(34)   Art.259.
(35)   Art.260.
(36)   Art.261(1).
(37)   *Ibid.*
(38)   Art.261(2).
(39)   Art.261(3),(4).
(40)   Art.264(4).
(41)   Art.262.
(42)   Art.337.
(43)   Art.340, 342.

(44) See Table at para.25.07.
(45) Art.280.
(46) Art.264(1),(2).
(47) Arts.336/339, 343.
(48) Art.341.
(49) Arts.265/273.
(50) Arts.276, 277.
(51) Arts.274, 275.
(52) DIEO, Sch.1, Pt.II, para.21.
(53) Art.280.
(54) Art.278(5).
(55) Arts.9, 295, 300, 302, 347.
(56) Art.303.
(57) Art.314.
(58) Art.346, Sch.4.
(59) Art.256(1).
(60) Paras.26.138/141.

Chapter 26

VOLUNTARY ARRANGEMENTS [1]

INTRODUCTION

26.001   The Bankruptcy Acts included provisions whereby a debtor could make an arrangement with his creditors under the control of the Bankruptcy Court without becoming a bankrupt.[2] The debtor's proposal, if assented to by the requisite majority of his creditors and confirmed by the Court, was binding on all creditors who had notice of the proceedings. Whilst the arrangement proceedings were pending the debtor was protected by a Court order from enforcement proceedings by creditors and against service of a debtor's summons as a prelude to bankruptcy. If so provided in the resolution of the creditors accepting the debtor's proposal, the debtor's property vested in the Official Assignee for realisation and distribution among his creditors as in bankruptcy. Under the Bankruptcy Acts and the Bankruptcy Rules the Official Assignee was responsible for administering the arrangement, including the admission of debts and the payment of a composition or dividends to creditors.

26.002   By the Order the Court-controlled arrangement procedure of the Bankruptcy Acts is replaced by the new "voluntary arrangement" provided for in Chapter II of Part VIII. This follows the corresponding provisions of Part VIII of the Insolvency Act 1986.

26.003   The object of the new procedure has been expressed as being to provide machinery whereby an insolvent debtor can arrive at an agreement with his creditors which, unless revoked by the court, is binding on all of them, while affording protection for dissenting creditors, and maintaining a due regard for the interests of creditors generally and for the public interest.[3]

26.004   The Official Receiver has no functions under the new procedure except were the arrangement is made by an undischarged bankrupt, where he has certain limited functions, but is not responsible for administering the arrangement. It can only be operated if the debtor secures the services of an authorised insolvency practitioner. An arrangement approved by the creditors does not require the approval of the Court.

26.005   The new arrangement procedure may be initiated by a debtor at any time. There are no minimum or maximum levels of assets or debts required by the Order or the Rules. Neither pending enforcement proceedings nor a pending bankruptcy petition by a creditor is a bar. The procedure may be employed even if the debtor is an undischarged bankrupt, with a view to the arrangement superceding the bankruptcy. It thus replaces the provisions of the Bankruptcy Acts enabling an   undischarged bankrupt to make a composition with his creditors.[4] A discharged bankrupt may make a voluntary arrangement under the Order in respect of debts from which he is not discharged.[5]

26.006   A voluntary arrangement may follow on a debtor's bankruptcy petition in certain circumstances.[6]

26.007   An approved voluntary arrangement is not subject to the provisions of the Order governing deeds of arrangement.[7]

26.008   Part I of this Chapter deals with an arrangement by a debtor who is not a bankrupt and Part II indicates the variation in procedure applicable where the debtor is an undischarged bankrupt.

I. ARRANGEMENT BY NON-BANKRUPT DEBTOR

INTRODUCTION

26.009   A voluntary arrangement is only appropriate where there is no requirement for an investigation into the affairs of the debtor such as would be made in bankruptcy and where the debtor is in a position to make a proposal which will be of benefit to his creditors. Thus, he must either have adequate unsecured assets which will realise sufficient funds to discharge the costs of the arrangement, to pay any preferential debts and to provide a dividend to the ordinary creditors, or be in a position to procure funds from a third party or from his own income over the period of the arrangement to enable this to be done.

A. THE NOMINEE

26.010   A debtor wishing to consider making a voluntary arrangement must first consult a person who is for the time being qualified to act as an insolvency practitioner in relation to him and who is willing to act as trustee or otherwise to supervise the implementation of the arrangement.[8] Until the debtor's proposal is accepted at a meeting of his creditors such person is referred to as "the nominee" and thereafter as "the supervisor".[9]

B. THE PROPOSAL

(a) Contents of proposal
26.011   The debtor's proposal to his creditors may be either a composition in satisfaction of his debts or a scheme of arrangement of his affairs, in either case referred to in the Order as a "voluntary arrangement". The distinction between a composition and a scheme of arrangement was expressed by Cave J. in *Re Griffith* [10] thus -

> "Where the debtor makes over his assets to be administered by a trustee there is no doubt that that is a scheme. Where the debtor keeps his assets

and undertakes to pay over to the creditors a certain sum, that is a composition."

26.012   An important feature of the voluntary arrangement is its flexibility. Provided that the debtor's proposal is for such a composition or scheme of arrangement the legislation imposes only two limitations as to the kind of arrangement which may be proposed (as distinct from the information which the proposal must contain, which is dealt with in the following paragraph). No proposal, whether as initially framed or as subsequently modified, may be approved which would affect the right of a secured creditor to enforce his security or deprive a creditor of rights which he would enjoy as a preferential creditor in bankruptcy, unless the creditor concerned consents to such proposal or modification.[11] Subject to this, the terms of the arrangement are essentially a contract between the debtor and his creditors. In formulating the terms of the proposal the debtor's adviser should bear in mind the right of a creditor to challenge the arrangement, particularly the right to challenge on the ground of unfair prejudice.[12] It should be framed to avoid inequality of treatment amongst creditors.[13]

26.013   The proposal must name the qualified nominee.[14] It must provide a short explanation why, in the debtor's opinion, a voluntary arrangement is desirable, and give reasons why his creditors may be expected to concur with such an arrangement.[15] The Rules also require that a long list of specified information must be stated, or otherwise dealt with, in the proposal.[16] Significantly, this includes whether there are circumstances which would give rise to the possibility, in the event of the debtor being adjudged bankrupt, of claims arising under the provisions of the Order relating to transactions at an undervalue, preferences or extortionate credit transactions (which do not apply to voluntary arrangements) and, where any such circumstances are present, whether, and if so how, it is proposed to provide for wholly or partly indemnifying the debtor's estate in respect of such claims. The functions which are to be undertaken by the supervisor must be set out.[17]

26.014   To facilitate the checking of the proposal by the creditors and the Court it is desirable that these specified matters should be dealt with in separate paragraphs lettered to correspond with the provisions of the Rule. Care must be taken that the proposal does not contain any materially false or misleading information or omission, as this might provide grounds for a petition for a bankruptcy order against the debtor,[18] or constitute an offence.[19]

26.015   The listed requirements must be supplemented by whatever further provisions are necessary for the satisfactory administration of the arrangement proposed, bearing in mind that the provisions of the Order relating to bankruptcy will not apply except in so far as incorporated directly or by reference in the terms of the proposal.[20] Thus, for example, provision should be made for safeguarding the debtor's assets, for the continuation of the debtor's business (if appropriate), for payment of any tax liabilities and for the proof and admission of debts and payment of composition or dividends. If a creditors' committee is to be established, its constitution, functions and meetings should be dealt with. The consequences of failure by the debtor to fulfil his obligations under the proposed arrangement should also be stated.[21]

26.016   The debtor's proposal may, with the agreement in writing of the nominee, be amended at any time before the nominee's report to the Court is filed.[22]

(b) Notice of proposal
26.017   Although in practice the debtor's proposal will usually be drawn up by the intended nominee on the instructions of the debtor, the obligation to prepare it for the nominee is placed on the debtor and he is required to give written notice of it to the intended nominee, accompanied by a copy of the proposal, by delivery either to the nominee himself or to a person authorised to take delivery of documents on his behalf.[23] If the intended nominee agrees to act, a copy of the notice must be endorsed to that effect and with the date of receipt.[24] This date determines the date to which the debtor's statement of affairs must be made up and the date it is required to be delivered to the nominee.[25] The copy of the notice, so endorsed, must be returned by the nominee to the debtor forthwith at an address to be specified in the notice.[26]

C. THE INTERIM ORDER

26.018   When he has notified his proposal to the intended nominee the debtor or his solicitor should at once apply to the Court for an interim order.[27] The arrangement cannot proceed without such an application. Mr. Muir Hunter Q.C. has suggested that in an appropriate case the court may be prepared to combine the hearing of the application for an interim order with two of the subsequent stages of the procedure, referred to below, namely the submission by the nominee of his report to the Court and the consideration by the Court of such report.[28]

(a) Restriction on application
26.019   An application may not be made while a bankruptcy petition presented by the debtor is pending if the Court has, on the hearing of the petition, appointed an insolvency practitioner to inquire into the debtor's affairs and report to the Court.[29] However, the Court may make an interim order without any application, on consideration of such report.[30]

(b) Mode of application
26.020   The application is made by originating application.[31] The application and sufficient copies for service are filed in the Court, accompanied by an affidavit by the debtor deposing to the following matters-[32]
    (i)   the reasons for making the application;
    (ii)   particulars of any execution or other legal process which, to the debtor's knowledge, has been commenced against him;

(iii) that he is able to petition for his own bankruptcy;
(iv) that no previous application for an interim order hasbeen made by or
       in respect of the debtor in the period of 12 months ending with the date
       of the affidavit; and
(v)   that the nominee under the proposal (naming him) is a person who is
       qualified to act as an insolvency practitioner in relation to the debtor,
       and is willing to act in relation to the proposal.

There must be exhibited to the affidavit a copy of the notice to the intended
nominee, endorsed with his agreement to act, and a copy of the debtor's
proposal given to the nominee.[33] Where an immediate stay of actions or
execution against the debtor is required,[34] the necessary evidence to support
an application for a stay should be included in this affidavit.

(c) Notice of hearing
26.021   On receipt of the application and supporting affidavit the Court fixes
the venue for the hearing.[35]

26.022   At least 2 days notice of the hearing date must be given by the debtor
to any person who is known to him to have presented a bankruptcy petition
against him [36] and to the nominee who has agreed to act in relation to his
proposal.[37] The nominee will usually waive the requirement of notice to him
and if there are no other persons required to be served this would enable the
application to be heard as soon as a hearing can be arranged.

(d) Stay of proceedings pending hearing
26.023   Once the application for an interim order is filed the debtor may apply
for an immediate stay of any action, execution or other legal process against
him or his property.[38] Such an application is made by ordinary application.[39]
Where the necessary evidence has not been included in the affidavit supporting
the application for the interim order, a further affidavit will be required.

26.024   If a stay is ordered the debtor should immediately serve the order [40]
on the plaintiff in the action, the Enforcement of Judgments Office or the
authority levying distress, as appropriate.

26.025   Where there are pending proceedings against the debtor he may,
instead of applying to the Bankruptcy Court, apply to the court in which the
proceedings are pending. Such court may, on proof that an application for an
interim order is pending, either stay the proceedings or allow them to continue
on such terms as it thinks fit.[41]

(e) Proceedings on first hearing
26.026   Any person served with notice of the application for the interim order
may appear at the hearing and the Court must take into account any representations made by or on his behalf.[42]

26.027   The Court may only make an interim order if it thinks that such an order would be appropriate for the purpose of facilitating the consideration and implementation of the debtor's proposal.[43] Before making an order it must be satisfied that -

(i)   the debtor genuinely intends to make a proposal for a voluntary arrangement and, for example, is not using the procedure to delay his creditors in pursuing their legitimate remedies;

(ii)   at the date of the application he was in a position to petition for his own bankruptcy (i.e. that he satisfies the jurisdictional requirements relating to a bankruptcy petition and that he is unable to pay his debts [44]);

(iii)   he has not applied for an interim order within the preceding 12 months; and

(iv)   the intended nominee is qualified to act as an insolvency practitioner in relation to the debtor and is willing to act in relation to the proposal.[45]

(f) Effect of order
26.028   Whilst an interim order is in force -

(i)   no bankruptcy petition relating to the debtor may be presented or proceeded with, and

(ii)   no other proceedings, and no execution or other legal process may be commenced or continued against the debtor or his property except with the leave of the Court.[46]

26.029   Thus, even a secured creditor may not commence or continue proceedings against the debtor or his property to enforce his security during the period of operation of an interim order, without leave of the Court, although the Court would, presumably, readily give such leave, as a debtor's proposal may not affect the rights of a secured creditor without his consent.[47]

26.030   An interim order does not, as did a protection order made in an arrangement under the control of the Court under the Bankruptcy Acts, prohibit a debtor from disposing of his assets pending the consideration of his proposal. However, if he were to misapply his assets the nominee could apply for the discharge of the order, which, if granted, would leave a creditor free to present a bankruptcy petition against the debtor.[48] The nominee, unlike a supervisor, does not have power to seek directions from the Court.[49]

(g) Duration and discharge of order
26.031   An interim order made on the application of the debtor ceases to have effect 14 days after the day it is made, unless this period is extended by the Court, on the application of the nominee, to enable him to have more time to prepare his report.[50] It also ceases to have effect 28 days after the chairman of the creditors' meeting reports to the Court that the meeting has accepted the debtor's proposal, if still in force on that date, unless extended by the Court on an application to challenge the decision of the meeting.[51]

26.032 The initial duration of the interim order being so short, it is anticipated that the Court will be prepared to grant extensions of time for any properly constructed proposal.[52] However, a proper case for such an extension of time must be made out. In *Re a Debtor (No. 83 of 1988)* [53] Scott J. said -

"It will have been noticed, from the time limits prescribed by section 255(6), that the statutory provisions contemplate that the creditors' meeting will be summoned within a short time and that a decision will be taken expeditiously as to whether or not a voluntary arrangement will be brought into effect."

And later in his judgment he said -

"It is prima facie the right of an unpaid creditor, having first served a statutory demand, to institute bankruptcy proceedings. That right of an unpaid creditor has been interfered with by statute - the interim order provisions so interfere. But the evident intention of the legislature was that the resolution of issues arising in regard to an interim order would be dealt with speedily and expeditiously, see, for example, the initial period of 14 days prescribed under section 255(6)."

26.033 If the extension of time is asked for at the time of the hearing of the application for the interim order, any extension granted will be included in the order. The Court also has power to extend the operation of the order where the nominee is replaced.[54] Where the Court decides that a meeting of creditors to consider the debtor's proposal is to be summoned, the operation of the order will be extended until after that meeting [55] and such an extension may be granted where the decision of the meeting is challenged.[56]

26.034 If an order is made extending the period for which an interim order has effect, the Court must send to the Enforcement of Judgments Office notice of the making of the order and of the date to which the operation of the interim order has been extended.[57]

26.035 The interim order may be discharged by the Court if it is satisfied, on the application of the nominee, that -

(i) the debtor has failed to give the nominee a document setting out the terms of the arrangement he proposes or the prescribed statement of his affairs, or

(ii) for any other reason it would be inappropriate for a meeting of the debtor's creditors to be summoned to consider the debtor's proposal.[58]

26.036 The Court may also discharge the interim order where the chairman of the creditors' meeting reports that the meeting has declined to approve the debtor's proposal.[59]

26.037 The Court must send notice of the making of an order discharging an interim order to the Enforcement of Judgments Office.[60]

(h) Contents of order
26.038   The interim order includes a statement of its effect, specifies a date for
the filing of the nominee's report and fixes a venue for the consideration of the
report, the date being not later than the date the order will cease to have effect
(i.e. 14 days from its date or at the expiration of an extended period granted on
the nominee's application).[61]

(i) Service and notice of order
26.039   When an interim order is made the Court must forthwith -
   (i)   send at least 2 sealed copies to the debtor (who is required to serve one
          of them on the nominee),
   (ii)   send to the Enforcement of Judgments Office notice of the making of
          the order and of the date it ceases to have effect, and
   (iii) give notice of the making of the order to any person who has been given
          notice of the hearing and who was not present or represented at it.[62]

D. THE NOMINEE'S REPORT

26.040   Before the interim order ceases to have effect the nominee must report
to the Court his opinion as to whether a meeting of creditors should be
summoned to consider the debtor's proposal and if so, the proposed date, time
and place of such meeting.[63] It is from the information in this report that the
Court determines whether or not the arrangement proceedings should continue.

26.041   No form of nominee's report is prescribed, but it must contain his
opinion as to the desirability of convening a meeting of creditors. If he recommends such a meeting the report must have annexed to it his comments on the
debtor's proposal or, if he recommends otherwise, his reasons for that opinion.
[64] In the event of a meeting being summoned these comments will be sent to
the creditors.[65]

(a) Information for report
(i) Statement of affairs
26.042   To enable the nominee to prepare his report to the Court the debtor is
required to give him, in addition to the terms of the proposed arrangement, a
statement of the debtor's affairs containing such particulars of his creditors and
of his debts and other liabilities and of his assets as may be prescribed and such
other information as may be prescribed.[66] There is no prescribed form for this
statement, but the information it must contain is prescribed and this includes a
requirement to include any particulars required in writing by the nominee.[67]
The statement is to be made up to a date not earlier than 2 weeks before the date
of the notice of the proposal to the nominee, but the nominee may allow it to
be prepared to the nearest practicable date within 2 months before the date of
the notice, and if he does so he must give reasons in his report.[68] Unlike a
bankrupt's statement of affairs it is not required to be verified by affidavit, but
it must be certified by the debtor as correct, to the best of his knowledge and

belief.[69] Any information contained in it which is false or misleading in any material particular would be a ground for adjudicating the debtor bankrupt on a petition by the supervisor or any creditor bound by the arrangement and any false representation in it, if made for the purpose of obtaining the approval of the debtor's creditors to the proposal, is an offence.[70]

26.043 The debtor must deliver the statement of affairs to the nominee within 7 days of the delivery of the notice of the proposal, but the nominee may extend this time.[71]

26.044 The statement of affairs is admissible in evidence against the debtor in any proceedings, whether under the Order or otherwise.[72]

(ii) Other information
26.045 The debtor must give the nominee access to his accounts and records.[73] If the debtor's proposal and the statement of affairs do not provide the nominee with sufficient information to prepare his report he may require the debtor to furnish further particulars as to the circumstances in which and the reason why he is insolvent or threatened with insolvency, particulars of any previous voluntary arrangement proposals made by him, whether and in what circumstances he has at any time been concerned in the affairs of any insolvent company, been adjudged bankrupt or made an arrangement with his creditors, and any further information he thinks necessary.[74]

(iii) Failure to provide information
26.046 If the debtor fails to deliver a statement of affairs within the required time or to provide further information required by the nominee the Court may, on the nominee's application, discharge the interim order,[75] bringing the arrangement procedures to an end and removing the debtor's protection against bankruptcy or other proceedings.

(b) Filing report
26.047 The nominee's report must be filed in the Court not less than 2 days before the interim order ceases to have effect and the date of filing is endorsed on the report.[76] This date affects the date of the creditors' meeting, if called.[77] If the nominee requires more time to prepare his report he may apply to the Court for an extension of the period for which the interim order has effect.[78] Such an application should be grounded on a report in lieu of an affidavit.[79] If such an extension of time is granted, the order will extend the time for filing the report to a date not less than 2 days before the expiration of the extended period and fix the new date when the interim order ceases to have effect as the new date for consideration of the report.[80] The nominee must give at least 2 days' notice of such an order to the debtor and to any other person notified of the application for the interim order.[81]

26.048 The nominee must file with his report a copy of the debtor's proposal (with any amendments agreed in writing by the nominee[82]) and a copy or summary of any statement of affairs provided by the debtor.[83]

26.049 The Court file of proceedings, including the report, may be inspected by any creditor of the debtor at all reasonable times on any business day.[84]

(c) Service of report etc.

26.050 The nominee must send a copy of the debtor's proposal, his report and any accompanying comments and a copy or summary of the debtor's statement of affairs to any person who has presented a bankruptcy petition against the debtor.[85]

(d) Replacement of nominee

26.051 If the nominee fails to file his report within the required time the debtor may apply to the Court for an order directing the replacement of the nominee by another authorised insolvency practitioner and for the continuance or (if it has ceased to have effect) the renewal of the interim order.[86] On such an application the Court may alternatively make an order continuing or renewing the interim order without replacing the nominee, thus giving him further time to submit his report, even though he has not himself applied for such an order.[87]

26.052 The debtor must give at least 7 days notice of an application to replace the nominee, together with a copy of the supporting affidavit, to the nominee and the proposed replacement nominee.[88]

26.053 The consent of the proposed replacement nominee to act in that capacity should be exhibited to the supporting affidavit.

(e) Consideration of report (second hearing)

26.054 At the hearing by the Court to consider the nominee's report any of the persons given notice of the application for the interim order may appear or be represented.[89]

26.055 If the debtor has failed to deliver a statement of affairs to the nominee within the required time or to furnish further information required by him, or if for any other reason the nominee recommends against the summoning of a creditors' meeting, he should apply for the discharge of the interim order.[90]

26.056 If the nominee requires more time to prepare his report, he should apply for an extension of the operation of the interim order and the fixing of a new date for the filing of his report and its consideration by the court.[91]

26.057 Where the nominee reports to the Court that a meeting of creditors should be summoned he is required to do so unless the Court, after hearing any representations by persons having notice of the hearing, otherwise directs.[92]

26.058 The Court may give a direction against summoning a creditors' meeting if it is satisfied that such a meeting will serve no useful purpose because there is a strong probability that the debtor will be unable to obtain a majority vote in favour of his proposal.[93]

26.059 Where a meeting is to be summoned the Court will extend the period of the operation of the interim order to an appropriate date on which the chairman's report of the result of the meeting will be considered by the Court.[94]

26.060 If the nominee fails to file his report and the debtor wishes to apply to have him replaced, he may apply for an extension of the operation of the interim order to allow time for an application for his replacement to be made.[95]

26.061 At least 2 sealed copies of any order made at the hearing will be sent by the Court to the applicant, who is required to serve one copy on the nominee and forthwith to give notice of the making of the order to any person who was given notice of the application for the interim order and was not present or represented at the hearing, and also to the Enforcement of Judgments Office.[96]

E. THE CREDITORS' MEETING

Summoning of meeting

26.062 If the nominee reports to the Court that a meeting of creditors should be summoned he must, subject to any directions of the Court, summon that meeting for the time, date and place proposed in his report.[97]

26.063 If a meeting is to be held the date must be not less than 14 days from the date of filing the nominee's report nor more than 28 days from that on which the report is considered by the Court.[98] In fixing the time, date and place for the meeting the nominee must have regard to the convenience of creditors and, unless the Court otherwise directs, the commencement time must be between 10.00 and 16.00 hours on a business day.[99]

26.064 At least 14 days notice of the meeting must be sent by the nominee to all creditors specified in the debtor's statement of affairs and any other creditors of whom the nominee is otherwise aware.[100] The notice is required to state that the nominee's report has been filed in the Court and the effect of the Rules governing the requisite majority required to pass a resolution approving the debtor's proposal or any modification of it,[101] and be accompanied by -
  (a) a copy of the proposal,
  (b) a copy of the statement of affairs (or a summary of it, which must include a list of creditors and the amounts of their debts),
  (c) the nominee's comments on the proposal, and
  (d) a form of proxy.[102]

No form of notice has been prescribed. A precedent is to be found in the Appendix.

Proceedings at meeting

(a) Attendance of debtor

26.065　Although the attendance of the debtor at the meeting of creditors is not required by any provision of the Order or the Rules the nominee should ensure that he is available to attend if the creditors so wish.

(b) Decisions

26.066　The meeting must decide whether to approve the debtor's proposal as circulated with the notice of the meeting or any permissible modification to which the debtor consents.[103] Such modification may include a substitution for the nominee named in the proposal of another authorised insolvency practitioner.[104] If such a modification is proposed there must be produced to the chairman of the meeting at or before the meeting the written consent of the person being substituted to act as supervisor (unless such person is present and signifies his consent) and his written confirmation that he is qualified to act as an insolvency practitioner in relation to the debtor.[105]

26.067　A modification which would result in the proposal ceasing to be a voluntary arrangement within the meaning of the Order (i.e. a composition in satisfaction of the debtor's debts or a scheme of arrangement of his affairs) is not permitted.[106]

26.068　There is no provision for separate meetings of classes of creditors. All creditors meet and vote together. However, the rights of secured and preferential creditors are protected. Without the concurrence of the creditor concerned no proposal or modification may be approved at the meeting if it affects the right of a secured creditor to enforce his security [107] or provides for any preferential debt [108] to be paid otherwise than in priority to non-preferential debts or otherwise than pari passu with other preferential debts.[109] Preferential creditors do not, as under the Bankruptcy Acts, lose their preferential rights by voting.

(c) Chairman

26.069　The chairman will be the nominee unless he is unable to attend, in which case he may nominate as chairman another authorised insolvency practitioner or an employee of the nominee or his firm, provided that such employee is experienced in insolvency matters.[110]

(d) Who may vote

26.070　As a general rule a creditor given notice of the meeting may vote in respect of the amount of his debt at the date of the meeting.[111] However, a creditor may not vote in respect of a debt for an unliquidated amount or a debt whose value is not ascertained, unless the chairman agrees to put upon the debt an estimated minimum value for the purpose of entitlement to vote.[112]

(e) Disputed debts

26.071 The chairman may admit or reject the whole or any part of a creditor's claim for the purpose of voting.[113] If he is in doubt he must mark the claim as objected to and allow the creditor to vote, subject to his vote being subsequently declared invalid if the objection to the claim is sustained on appeal.[114] His decision on entitlement to vote is subject to appeal to the Court by any creditor or the debtor within 28 days of the filing of his report to the Court of the result of the meeting.[115] Appeal is by ordinary application. If on an appeal the chairman's decision is reversed or varied or a creditor's vote is declared invalid, the Court may, but only if it considers that there has been unfair prejudice or a material irregularity, order another meeting or make such other order as it thinks just.[116] The chairman is not personally liable for any costs incurred on such an appeal.[117]

(f) Requisite majorities

26.072 A resolution to approve the debtor's proposal or any modification of it must be supported by a majority exceeding three-quarters in value of the creditors (calculated as mentioned in the succeeding paragraph) present in person or by proxy and voting on the resolution; any other resolution requires a simple majority in value of such creditors.[118]

26.073 The following rules govern the calculation of the required majorities -
  (i) there is to be left out of account a creditor's vote in respect of -
      (A) any claim or part of a claim not notified in writing to the chairman or the nominee at the meeting or before it,
      (B) any claim or part of a claim which is secured, or
      (C) any claim or part of a claim in respect of a debt wholly or partly on, or secured by, a current bill of exchange or promissory note, unless the creditor is willing to treat the liability to him on the bill or note of every person who is liable on it antecedently to the debtor, and against whom a bankruptcy order has not been made (or, in the case of a company, which has not gone into liquidation), as a security in his hands, and to estimate the value of the security and (for the purpose of entitlement to vote but not of any distribution under the arrangement) to deduct it from his claim;[119]
  (ii) any resolution is invalid if those voting against it include more than half in value of the creditors to whom notice of the meeting was sent, other than creditors left out of account under (i) above and associates [120] of the debtor. [121]

26.074 These provisions for ascertaining the required majority for the approval of a voluntary arrangement are somewhat obscure. Broadly stated they appear to mean that the arrangement is not approved unless the resolution of the creditors to approve it -
  (i) is supported by the votes of more than three-quarters in value of the unsecured creditors present or represented at the meeting, and

(ii) is not opposed by the votes of more than one-half in value of all the unsecured creditors to whom notice of the meeting was sent and who have duly notified their claims, other than associates of the debtor.

26.075 It is for the chairman to decide whether a vote is to be left out of account or whether a person is an associate of the debtor.[122] The rules governing the action of the chairman if in doubt about admitting a claim and an appeal against his decision, mentioned in paragraph 26.071 above, apply.[123]

26.076 The rejection by a creditor of the debtor's proposal does not constitute refusal of an offer by the debtor which could be a ground for dismissal of a bankruptcy petition under Article 245(3).[124]

26.077 If, following any final adjournment of the meeting, the debtor's proposal (with or without modifications) is not agreed to, it is deemed rejected.[125]

(g) The chairman as proxy-holder
26.078 The chairman may not use any proxy held by him to vote to increase or reduce the amount of remuneration or expenses of the nominee or supervisor of a proposed voluntary arrangement, unless the proxy specifically directs him to do so.[126] If he does so, his vote with that proxy does not count towards any majority required to pass a resolution.[127]

(h) Adjournment of meeting
26.079 The meeting may from time to time be adjourned.[128] If the majority required for approval of the arrangement (with or without modifications) is not obtained the chairman may adjourn the meeting for not more than 14 days and he must do so if the creditors so resolve (by a simple majority, in value)[129] If there are subsequently further adjournments the final adjournment must not be to a day later than 14 days after the first meeting.[130] If the meeting is adjourned because of the absence of the requisite majority, the chairman must forthwith give notice of the adjournment to the Court.[131]

F. EFFECT OF APPROVAL OF ARRANGEMENT

(a) Creditors who are bound
26.080 Where the meeting of creditors approves the arrangement (with or without modifications) it takes immediate effect as if made by the debtor at the meeting.[132] No order of the Court is required for this purpose; any orders which may be made on consideration of the chairman's report or on subsequent applications will be to give any necessary further directions or on an application to challenge the decision of the meeting.[133]

26.081 An approved arrangement binds every person who, in accordance with the Rules, had notice of and was entitled to vote at the meeting (whether or not he was present or represented at it) as if he were a party to the arrangement.[134] Consequently, it is of the utmost importance to the debtor that a notice of the meeting is sent to every person entitled to receive notice of it.[135]

(b) The interim order
26.082   The interim order is not required to continue to have effect in order to protect the debtor against proceedings by creditors bound by the arrangement. However, it may remain in operation after the date of the meeting under an order of the Court. If it remains in force 28 days after the chairman has filed his report to the Court it will automatically cease to have effect on that day, unless its operation has been extended by the Court in connection with an application to challenge the decision of the meeting.[136]

(c) The supervisor
26.083   When the arrangement is approved the person who carries out the functions conferred on the nominee by virtue of such approval (or his replacement) is known as the supervisor of the voluntary arrangement.[137]

26.084   The person appointed as a supervisor, whether in the first instance or by way of replacement, must forthwith give written notice of his appointment to the Department and he must also give such notice if he vacates office.[138]

26.085   Where an arrangement is approved under which two or more insolvency practitioners are appointed to act as supervisor the creditors may resolve (by a simple majority, in value) whether they must act jointly or whether any of them may act alone.[139]

G. REPORT OF CREDITORS' MEETING

(a) Report to the Court
26.086   Within 4 days after the conclusion of the meeting of creditors the chairman must file in the Court a report of the result of the meeting.[140] The date of filing, to be endorsed by the Court on the copy of the report filed, governs the period allowed for an appeal from a decision of the chairman on entitlement to vote and for an application to challenge the decision of the meeting.[141] It also fixes the period on the expiry of which any interim order then current will expire.[142].

26.087   The report must -
   (i)   state whether the debtor's proposal was approved (and if approved with modifications, set out such modifications) or rejected;
   (ii)   set out the resolutions taken at the meeting and the decision on each one;
   (iii) list the creditors (with their respective values) who were present or represented at the meeting and how they voted on each resolution; and
   (iv)   include such further information (if any) as the chairman thinks it appropriate to make known to the Court (e.g. any decision with regard

to a creditor's entitlement to vote or whether a vote is not to be reckoned for calculation of majorities).[143]

(b) Consideration of report by the Court (third hearing)
26.088 Pursuant to the terms of the order made at the second hearing the matter will be listed for consideration by the Court of the chairman's report. If the report has not been filed before the date fixed for this hearing the chairman may ask the Court to accept it at the hearing and to extend the time for filing accordingly or, if it is not ready, request an adjournment to enable an application to be made for an extension of time to file.[144] The hearing may also be adjourned, where necessary, to await the outcome of any pending appeal against a decision of the chairman of the meeting as to entitlement to vote or of an application to challenge the decision of the meeting.

26.089 If the report is that the debtor's proposal has been approved the Court's order will record this and make no further order unless required in relation to a pending bankruptcy petition.

26.090 If there is a pending bankruptcy petition against the debtor (which is subject to a stay by the operation of the interim order) it is necessary for the petition to be dismissed as a consequence of the approval of the arrangement. Where the interim order ceases to have effect automatically under the provisions referred to in paragraph 26.082 above such petition is deemed to have been dismissed, unless the court otherwise orders.[145] In such circumstances the Court's order on consideration of the report of the chairman of the meeting must provide for the vacating of the registration of the petition in the Registry of Deeds and, if applicable, cancellation of the registration of notice of the petition in the Land Registry.[146] If the interim order had ceased to have effect prior to the date referred to in paragraph 26.082 above and therefore the "deemed dismissal" provision does not operate, it will be necessary for an application to be made in the bankruptcy proceedings for an order dismissing the petition and for the vacating of such Registry of Deeds registration and, if applicable, for the cancellation of such Land Registry registration.[147]

26.091 If the chairman reports that the meeting has declined to approve the debtor's proposal, the Court may discharge any interim order which remains in operation [148] and presumably would do so unless there is a pending application to challenge the meeting's decision. Such discharge removes the stay on proceedings, including bankruptcy proceedings against the debtor, but bankruptcy can only follow on a petition by a person qualified to present it. The Court has no power to make a bankruptcy order of its own motion following a refusal of the creditors' meeting to approve the debtor's proposal.

(c) Notice of result of meeting
26.092 The chairman must, immediately after filing his report in the Court, give notice of the result of the meeting to all creditors to whom notice of the meeting was sent.[149]

(d) Report to Department

26.093 If the chairman has reported to the Court that the arrangement has been approved he must immediately report the following details to the Department-
  (i)   the name and address of the debtor;
  (ii)   the date of approval of the arrangement by the creditors;
  (iii) the name and address of the supervisor.[150]
This information is recorded in the register of voluntary arrangements kept by the Department.[151]

H. CHALLENGE OF DECISION OF CREDITORS' MEETING [152]

26.094 The debtor, a creditor entitled to vote at the creditors' meeting or the nominee may apply to the Court within 28 days from the filing of the chairman's report of the meeting to challenge the decision of the meeting on one or both of the following grounds only -
  (a)   that the arrangement approved by the meeting unfairly prejudices the interests of a creditor;
  (b)   that there has been some material irregularity at or in relation to the meeting.[153]

26.095 A challenge to the approval of the arrangement would usually be by a dissenting creditor, whilst the debtor is the most likely applicant where the arrangement was not approved.[154]

26.096 A creditor alleging unfair prejudice has not merely to show a prima facie case that he has been prejudiced but to prove on a balance of probability that he has in fact suffered prejudice. Consequently, it is open to the applicant to seek discovery of documents to ascertain details of the facts of the transaction which he alleges to be unfair.[155]

26.097 It has been held by Hoffman J. that a voluntary arrangement is intended to bind the creditors only as creditors and does not affect any proprietary rights such as that of a landlord to forfeit a lease (subject to the court's discretion to grant relief). He held that since the effect of the arrangement in question was to modify the claims of all the creditors there would be no unfairness to the landlord, as a creditor, in the modification of his claim for rent arrears.[156] Moreover, the judge expressed the view that on an application by the lessee or an assignee for relief against forfeiture it is unlikely that, after the landlord's right to arrears of rent has been extinguished and replaced by its rights in the arrangement, the court in the exercise of its discretion, would impose any condition of full repayment before granting relief.

26.098 Where the Court is satisfied as to either of the permitted grounds of challenge of the decision of the creditors' meeting it may revoke or suspend any approval given by the meeting and/or direct the summoning of a further meeting to consider any revised proposal by the debtor or, where it has found an irregularity at or in relation to the meeting, to reconsider his original proposal.[157]

26.099   If a further meeting is directed the operation of the interim order may be continued, or if it has already ceased to have effect, be renewed for a specified period.[158] Where such a meeting has been directed and the Court is subsequently satisfied that the debtor does not in fact intend to submit a proposal to the further meeting, it must revoke the direction and revoke or suspend any approval given at the previous meeting.[159].

26.100   Where the Court directs a further meeting or revokes or suspends the approval of the arrangement it may give supplemental directions with respect to any acts done since such approval and such other directions as it thinks fit.[160].

26.101   No irregularity at or in relation to the meeting of creditors will invalidate the approval of the arrangement by the meeting unless the decision of the meeting is successfully challenged under this procedure.[161]

26.102
If an order is made revoking or suspending the approval of the arrangement-
   (a)   the applicant must -
        (i)   serve sealed copies of it on the debtor and the supervisor,
        (ii)   within 7 days give written notice of it to the Department, and
        (iii)   where a further meeting of creditors is directed, give notice to the person directed to summon the meeting;
   (b)   upon receipt of a copy of the order the debtor must -
        (i)   forthwith give notice of it to all persons to whom notice of the creditors' meeting which approved the arrangement was sent and to any other person who appears to be affected by the order, and
        (ii)   within 7 days (or such longer period as the Court may allow) give notice to the Court whether it is intended to make a revised proposal to creditors or to invite reconsideration of the original proposal.[162]

I. PROCEEDINGS AFTER APPROVAL OF ARRANGEMENT

(a) Possession of assets
26.103   Forthwith after approval of the arrangement the debtor must do all that is required for putting the supervisor into possession of the assets included in the arrangement.[163] The supervisor has the right to request the supply of electricity, water or public telecommunication services for the purposes of carrying on the debtor's business upon the same terms as a trustee in bankruptcy.[164].

26.104   None of the provisions of Chapter V of Part IX of the Order (rights of occupation of dwelling house, adjustment of prior transactions, unenforceability of liens on books etc.) are applicable to a voluntary arrangement. However, where a victim of a transaction defrauding creditors is bound by an approved voluntary arrangement the supervisor may apply for an order under Article 367 and the victim himself may apply, whether or not so bound.[165]

(b) Security by supervisor

26.105 The supervisor may not act unless there is in force the security required under the Insolvency Practitioners Regulations.[166] He must file in the Court a certificate of specific penalty required by those Regulations within 14 days of receipt.[167]

(c) Challenge of actions of supervisor

26.106 If the debtor, any of his creditors or any other person is dissatisfied by any act, omission or decision of the supervisor he may apply to the Court; and on such application the Court may -

    (i)   confirm, reverse or modify any act or decision of the supervisor,

    (ii) give him directions, or

    (iii) make such other order as it thinks fit.[168]

(d) Assistance of court

26.107 The supervisor may apply to the Court for directions in relation to any particular matter arising under the arrangement,[169] and he has the same rights as a trustee in bankruptcy under section 426 of the Insolvency Act 1986 to seek the assistance of courts outside Northern Ireland.[170]

(e) Replacement or appointment of additional supervisor

26.108 The Court has power to appoint a person who is qualified to act as an insolvency practitioner in relation to the debtor as supervisor in substitution for the existing supervisor (or for one of them if there are more than one), to fill a vacancy or as an additional supervisor, but this power is not to be exercised unless it is inexpedient, difficult or impracticable for an appointment to be made without the assistance of the Court.[171] This appears to imply that the debtor's proposal may provide for such replacement or appointment of an additional supervisor.

(f) Supervisor's accounts, records and reports

26.109 Where the arrangement authorises or requires the supervisor -

    (i)   to carry on the debtor's business or to trade on his behalf or in his name, or

    (ii) to realise assets of the debtor, or

    (iii) otherwise to administer or dispose of any funds of the debtor,

he must keep accounts and records of his acts and dealings in and in connection with the arrangement, including in particular records of all receipts and payments of money.[172]

26.110 The supervisor must also, at least once in every 12 months beginning with the date of his appointment, prepare an abstract of such receipts and payments and send copies of it, together with his report on the progress and efficacy of the arrangement to -

(i)   the Court,
(ii) the debtor, and
(iii) all creditors bound by the arrangement.[173]
Such abstract is to relate to a period from the supervisor's appointment or (as the case may be) the day following the end of the last period for which an abstract was prepared, and the copies must be sent out within 2 months following the end of the period to which the abstract relates.[174] Where there have been no receipts or payments within any period of 12 months, a statement to that effect is to accompany the report.[175]

26.111   The obligation to keep accounts will apply in almost any likely form of arrangement and the report will be sent to creditors with the abstract of receipts and payments or statement of no receipts or payments. Where, exceptionally, the obligation does not arise, i.e. where the supervisor does not handle any funds, he must still send a report on the progress and efficacy of the arrangement at least once in every 12 months to the Court, the debtor and the creditors bound by the arrangement.[176]

26.112   The dates on which the obligation to send abstracts of receipts and payments or reports arises may be varied by the Court on the application of the supervisor.[177]

26.113   The annual report by the supervisor will assist in providing a means of monitoring his actions and keeping the debtor and creditors informed of the progress of the arrangement.

26.114   The supervisor must also comply with the obligations of all insolvency practitioners with regard to the maintenance and preservation of prescribed records of his administration and the production of those records for inspection.[178]

(g) Role of Department
26.115   The supervisor is not required to make payments into the Insolvency Account, but the Department does have certain powers which may be invoked to control the exercise of his functions. It may at any time during the course of the arrangement or after its completion require the supervisor to produce either at his own premises or elsewhere, his records and accounts in respect of the arrangement and copies of abstracts of receipts and payments and progress reports.[179] The Department may audit any accounts and records so produced and the supervisor is required to give it such further information and assistance as is required for that purpose.[180] It is anticipated that intervention by the Department will normally only be at the instigation of a creditor or the debtor.

(h) Report of completion of arrangement
26.116   Within 28 days after the final completion of the arrangement, or within such extended time as the Court, on the application of the supervisor, may allow the supervisor must -

(i)   send to each creditor bound by the arrangement and to the debtor a
      notice that the arrangement has been fully implemented, accompanied
      by a copy of a report by him summarising all receipts and payments
      made under the arrangement and explaining any difference in the
      actual implementation of it as compared with the proposal as approved
      by the creditors' meeting, and

(ii) send a copy of the notice and report to the Department and to the Court.
      (181)

J. DEFAULT IN CONNECTION WITH THE ARRANGEMENT

26.117 The supervisor or a creditor bound by an approved voluntary arrangement may present a petition to the Court for a bankruptcy order to be made
against the arranging debtor and on such a petition a bankruptcy order may be
made if the Court is satisfied -

(a) that the debtor has failed to comply with his obligations under the
     arrangement, or

(b) that information which was false or misleading in any material particu-
     lar or which contained material omissions -

> (i) was contained in any statement of affairs or other document
> supplied by the debtor to any person, or
>
> (ii) was otherwise made available by the debtor to his creditors at or
> in connection with the creditors' meeting, or

(c) that the debtor has failed to do all such things as may for the purposes
     of the arrangement have been reasonably required of him by the
     supervisor. (182)

26.118 There is no statutory provision as to the effect on a voluntary arrangement of a bankruptcy order being made against the arranging debtor, except
that any costs properly incurred as costs of the administration of the arrangement are a first charge on the bankrupt's estate. (183) Whilst this seems to imply
that the arrangement ceases to be operative, there is no provision for revoking
or avoiding an approved arrangement, except on a successful challenge of the
decision of the creditors' meeting. (184) It would appear, therefore, that any
disposition of the debtor's property already effected under the terms of the
arrangement (e.g. a declaration of trust by the debtor or a transfer of assets to
the supervisor as trustee) would remain effective unless invalidated by the
Court as a transaction at an undervalue, avoidable preference or a transaction
in fraud of creditors. (185)

26.119 Apart from the provision for adjudging a debtor bankrupt on a petition
under Article 238(1)(c), the legislation makes no other provision for the consequences of a failure by him to fulfil his obligations under the arrangement. It is
desirable therefore for provision to be made for this in the terms of the arrangement. In particular, the supervisor should be required to notify significant
defaults to the creditors and the point of time when the creditors are to cease to

be bound by the arrangement and to be free to pursue remedies against the debtor should be determined.

False representations etc.
26.120 The debtor commits an offence if he makes any false representation or commits any other fraud for the purpose of obtaining the approval of his creditors to a proposal for an arrangement.[186]

K. ASCERTAINMENT AND PAYMENT OF CREDITORS' CLAIMS

26.121 Whilst a "bankruptcy debt" is defined in Article 9(1), there is no corresponding definition of a debt in relation to a debtor who is not a bankrupt and who makes a voluntary arrangement with his creditors although, under Article 2(4), for the purposes of any references in the Order to a debt or liability it is immaterial whether the debt or liability is present or future, whether it is certain or contingent or whether its amount is fixed or liquidated or is capable of being ascertained by fixed criteria or as a matter of opinion and references in any such provision to owing a debt are to be read accordingly. The wide definition of "liability" in Article 2(2) applies to all Parts of the Order and by Article 230(2)(b)(i) the debtor's statement of affairs must include particulars not only of his debts but of his "other liabilities". Presumably, therefore, liabilities which are not debts may be included in a voluntary arrangement. Preferential debts are determined by reference to the date of the interim order.[187] If the debtor's proposal is for payment to his creditors of less than 100 pence in the pound, the debt postponement provision of the Partnership Act, 1890, s.2(3)(d) operates.[188]

26.122 Although the Rules deal with the admission of creditors' claims for the purpose of voting at a creditors' meeting there are no provisions corresponding to those regulating the proof of bankruptcy debts, the determination of disputed claims by creditors and the declaration and payment of dividends in a bankruptcy. Accordingly, provision should be made for these matters in the terms of the arrangement, either directly or by reference to the bankruptcy provisions and the amount for which a claim may be admitted should be related to the amount owing on the day the creditors' meeting approves the debtor's proposal.

26.123 Interest accruing due to creditors after the date of approval of the arrangement will not be payable unless provided for in the terms of the arrangement, either expressly or by the application of the bankruptcy provisions.

26.124 The bankruptcy provisions relating to mutual credit and set off should be applied to the arrangement, otherwise the general law of set off will apply.

26.125 A creditor who has not been notified of the creditors' meeting and is therefore not bound by the arrangement may nevertheless wish to participate when he becomes aware of it. There would appear to be no objection to this provided that the debtor consents and the other creditors will not be prejudiced by the addition to the debtor's total liabilities (e.g. if the proposal is for a composition). If the amount payable to the other creditors will thereby be materially reduced the supervisor should consider applying to the Court for directions[189] and on such an application the Court may order the supervisor to convene a further creditors' meeting to reconsider the approval of the debtor's proposal. Similar directions may be advisable where the supervisor admits a creditor's claim for an amount materially in excess of that stated in the debtor's statement of affairs, if such increase will materially reduce the dividend payable to the other creditors.

26.126   In the absence of any provision in the arrangement for the determination of disputed claims by creditors a creditor dissatisfied with the decision of the supervisor on the admissibility of his claim may have the dispute determined by the Court on an application under Article 237(3).[190]

L. VALUE ADDED TAX BAD DEBT RELIEF

26.127   Bad debt relief in respect of value added tax on debts due to creditors in the voluntary arrangement is governed by the same provisions as apply to bankruptcy.[191]

M. COSTS

26.128   The remuneration and expenses of the insolvency practitioner appointed by the debtor to perform the functions of the nominee as such (i.e. up to the time of approval of the proposal by the creditors when the nominee becomes the supervisor) must be agreed before the intended nominee agrees to act, because the resolution must state the amount proposed to be paid in respect of such charges and expenses.[192]

26.129   The proposal must also state how the supervisor is to be remunerated and his expenses defrayed.[193] If a creditors' committee is constituted under the arrangement it would be appropriate to provide for such remuneration to be fixed by such committee. Otherwise the fixing of the remuneration may be entrusted to a general meeting of creditors.

26.130   The costs that may be incurred for any purposes of the arrangement are limited to -
  (a)   any disbursements made by the nominee prior to the approval of the arrangement and the remuneration of the nominee for that period agreed between himself and the debtor,
  (b)   any costs which are sanctioned by the terms of the arrangement or would be payable, or correspond to those which would be payable, in the debtor's bankruptcy.[194]

N. REGISTER OF VOLUNTARY ARRANGEMENTS

26.131   The Department is required to maintain a register of voluntary arrangements in which is to be entered the information reported to the Department under the Rules (i.e. report by the chairman of the meeting of creditors, notice of an order of revocation or suspension of approval of arrangement and notice of completion of arrangement).[195] The register is open to public inspection.[196]

O. INSOLVENT PARTNERSHIPS

26.132   The Order applies to an insolvent partnership only to the extent specified in the Insolvent Partnerships Order.[197] The provisions of the Order governing voluntary arrangements by non-corporate debtors are not capable of being applied to an arrangement by a partnership firm; the debtor is required to be an individual.[198] The Insolvent Partnerships Order does permit a voluntary arrangement by an individual member of such a firm, but only after he has been adjudged bankrupt under that Order.[199] There is no provision for an arrangement by a non-bankrupt member.

26.133   However, a voluntary arrangement in respect of a partnership can be achieved if the creditors, both partnership and personal, approve separate proposals for each individual partner, providing for the payment of both partnership and personal debts. For convenience each proposal could incorporate one document dealing with the partnership liabilities. The provisions of the Insolvent Partnerships Order governing the payment of costs and debts as between the joint state of the partnership and the separate estates of each partner should be applied.[200]

26.134   The Department of Trade and Industry has expressed the view (subject to ultimate interpretation of the legislation by the court) that two or more debtors who had been in partnership may apply to the court jointly for interim orders to be made against each debtor and that one creditors' meeting could be convened to deal with the proposals of the partners.[201]

26.135   To overcome practical problems all partners would require to join in the scheme. Statements of affairs of the partnership and of each partner would be required.

P. ARRANGEMENT BY SOLICITOR

26.136   A solicitor who has entered into a voluntary arrangement may be refused a practising certificate and the Law Society of Northern Ireland may exercise its powers under Schedule 1 to the Solicitors (Northern Ireland) Order 1976 in respect of him.[202]

26.137   The provisions of that Order whereby the sum at credit of a bankrupt solicitor's clients' account with his bankers is divisible rateably among the clients on whose behalf money has been received by the solicitor and remains due to them, which applied to certain arrangements under the Bankruptcy Acts, do not apply to a voluntary arrangement under the Order, although they continue to apply to a deed of arrangement.[203]

Q. EFFECT OF DEATH OF DEBTOR

26.138 The application of the individual voluntary arrangement provisions of the Order to the insolvent estate of a deceased debtor is governed by Part III of Schedule 1 to the Deceased Insolvent Estates Order.

26.139 Articles 226 to 229 do not apply and consequently an application for an interim order cannot proceed if the debtor dies before the order is made. Where the debtor dies after an interim order has been made the remaining Articles of Chapter II of Part VIII of the Order apply, with such modifications as may be necessary to make them applicable to the estate of a deceased person and with certain specific modifications, the effect of which is stated below.

26.140 Where the debtor dies before submitting the terms of the proposed arrangement and a statement of his affairs the nominee must, after he becomes aware of the death, give notice of it to the Court and on receiving such notice the Court must discharge the interim order.[204] Where the debtor dies after the nominee has reported to the Court that a creditors' meeting should be summoned but before the meeting has been held, no such meeting may be held.[205]

26.141 If the debtor dies after approval of the arrangement, the arrangement continues to operate. The supervisor is required to give notice of the death to the Court and the personal representative of the debtor, in addition to any of the deceased debtor's creditors and any other person dissatisfied by any act, omission or decision of the supervisor, may apply to the Court for redress under Article 237(3).[206]

R. DISQUALIFICATION OF DEBTOR

26.142 Under section 4(1)(b) of the Local Government Act (Northern Ireland) 1972 a person is disqualified for being elected to or being a member of a District Council if he has been adjudged bankrupt or has made any composition or arrangement with his creditors. The approval by creditors of a voluntary arrangement will therefore disqualify the debtor making the arrangement under this provision. Section 5(2) of the Act provides that the disqualification under section 4(1)(b) ceases on the date of payment of the debts in full and in any other case 5 years from the date on which the terms of the *deed* of composition or arrangement have been fully implemented. Thus there is no provision for the cesser of disqualification in the case of a debtor who enters into a voluntary arrangement under the Order and who does not pay his creditors in full. Even if the reference to a deed were removed, it would be anomalous that

a bankrupt (whose disqualification ceases on discharge) would in most cases
be disqualified for a shorter period than such a debtor.

II. ARRANGEMENT BY UNDISCHARGED BANKRUPT

INTRODUCTION

26.143   The provisions governing a voluntary arrangement by an individual
debtor who is not a bankrupt are generally applicable to an arrangement with
his creditors by an undischarged bankrupt, but some necessary modifications
are provided for by the Order and the Rules. This Part of this Chapter sets out
the variations to the text in Part I which are necessary in the case of an
arrangement by an undischarged bankrupt.

A. THE PROPOSAL

(a) Contents of proposal [207]
26.144   The proposal must include a statement as to whether, to the bankrupt's
knowledge, claims have been made in his bankruptcy under the provisions of
the Order relating to transactions at an undervalue, preferences or extortionate
credit transactions or whether there are circumstances giving rise to the possibility of such claims, and where any such circumstances are present, whether
and if so how, it is proposed to make provision under the arrangement for
wholly or partly indemnifying his estate in respect of such claims.[208]

(b) Notice of proposal [209]
26.145   The bankrupt must give notice of his proposal and the name and
address of the nominee to the Official Receiver and, if there is one, to the trustee
of his estate.[210]

B. THE INTERIM ORDER

(a) Application [211]
26.146   Not only the bankrupt but also the trustee of his estate or the Official
Receiver may apply for an interim order.[212] However, the proposal must be
prepared by the bankrupt [213] and it is unlikely that either the trustee or the
Official Receiver would wish to apply. The language of most of the Rules is
consistent only with applications in respect of a proposal by a bankrupt being
made by the bankrupt himself.[214]

26.147   The affidavit supporting the application must include a statement that
the debtor is an undischarged bankrupt.[215]

(b) Notice of hearing [216]
26.148   If the bankrupt is the applicant he must give notice of the hearing date
to the trustee (if any) and the Official Receiver; if the trustee or the Official

Receiver is the applicant notice must be given by him to the bankrupt and to the Official Receiver or trustee, as the case may be.[217]

(c) The hearing [218]

26.149 The Court must be satisfied that at the date of the application the debtor was an undischarged bankrupt.[219]

(d) Contents of order [220]

26.150 The interim order may contain provision as to the conduct of the bankruptcy, and the administration of the bankrupt's estate, during the period for which the order is in force, including provision staying proceedings in the bankruptcy or modifying any provision in Parts VIII to X of the Order and any provision of the Rules in their application to the bankruptcy.[221] The Court is required to take into account in particular any representations made by or on behalf of persons given notice of the hearing as to whether the interim order should contain any such provisions.[222] No requirement of any provision of the Order or the Rules may be relaxed or removed unless the Court is satisfied that it is unlikely that any significant diminution in, or in the value of, the bankrupt's estate will result.[223]

C. THE NOMINEE'S REPORT

(a) Information for report: statement of affairs [224]

26.151 If the bankrupt has already delivered a statement of affairs in the bankruptcy proceedings he need not deliver a further statement unless required to do so by the nominee with a view to supplementing or amplifying the earlier one.[225] He should, however, prepare a supplementary statement of affairs where he has incurred post-bankruptcy debts to new creditors to ensure that such creditors are given notice of the meeting of creditors; otherwise they will not be bound by the arrangement.[226]

(b) Service of report [227]

26.152 The nominee must send to the Official Receiver and (if any) the trustee a copy of the bankrupt's proposal, a copy of his report and any accompanying comments and a copy or summary of the bankrupt's statement of affairs.[228]

D. THE CREDITORS' MEETING

(a) Summoning of meeting [229]

26.153 The creditors to be summoned to the meeting are every person of whose claim and address the nominee is aware who is a creditor of the bankrupt in respect of a bankruptcy debt and every person who would be such a creditor if the bankruptcy had commenced on the day on which notice of the meeting is given.[230] Thus, post-bankruptcy creditors are included.

(b) Proceedings at meeting: who may vote [231]

26.154 The votes of creditors are calculated according to the amount of the creditor's debt at the date of the bankruptcy order.[232]

E. REPORT OF CREDITORS' MEETING

(a) Consideration of report by the Court [233]
26.155 Where the chairman reports that the bankrupt's proposal has been approved by the creditors' meeting (with or without modifications) the order will record such approval. The Court may annul the bankruptcy order and/or give such directions with respect to the conduct of the bankruptcy and the administration of the bankrupt's estate as it thinks appropriate for facilitating the implementation of the arrangement. [234] The procedure for an annulment is the same as for an annulment on the ground that a bankruptcy order ought not to have been made. [235] The bankruptcy order may not be annulled at a time during which the decision of the meeting is open to challenge. Thus, an annulment order may not be made before the expiration of 28 days from the filing of the chairman's report of the meeting [236] or at any time when an application to challenge the decision of the meeting or an appeal in respect of such an application is pending or may be brought. [237] If the time within which the decision of the creditors' meeting may be challenged has not yet expired the matter will be adjourned generally with liberty to restore. [238]

(b) Notice of result of meeting [239]
26.156 In addition to notifying the creditors to whom the notice of the meeting was given the chairman must give notice of the result of the meeting to the Official Receiver and (if any) the trustee. [240]

F. CHALLENGE OF DECISION OF CREDITORS' MEETING [241]

26.157 In addition to the persons mentioned in paragraph 26.094 above an application to challenge the decision of the creditors' meeting may be made by the trustee or the Official Receiver. [242]

26.158 If an order is made revoking or suspending the approval of the arrangement the applicant must serve sealed copies of the order on the bankrupt, the supervisor, the Official Receiver and the trustee (if any). [243] Upon receipt of the copy order the trustee, or if there is not a trustee, the Official Receiver must give the notices mentioned in paragraph 26.102 above. [244]

G. PROCEEDINGS AFTER APPROVAL OF ARRANGEMENT

Possession of assets [245]
26.159 Forthwith after approval of the arrangement the Official Receiver or trustee must do all that is required for putting the supervisor into possession of the assets included in the arrangement. [246]

26.160 The supervisor must either -
  (a) when taking possession of the assets discharge any balance due to the Official Receiver and (if other) the trustee by way of remuneration or on account of costs properly incurred and payable under the Order or

the Rules and any advances made in respect of the insolvent estate, with interest on such advances at the rate payable on judgment debts at the date of the bankruptcy order;[247] or

   (b) before taking possession of the assets, give the Official Receiver or the trustee a written undertaking to discharge any such balance out of the first realisation of assets.[248]

26.161 The Official Receiver and (if other) the trustee has a charge on the assets included in the arrangement in respect of any such sums due to him until they have been discharged, subject only to the deduction from realisations by the supervisor of the proper costs of realisation.[249] Any sums due to the Official Receiver take priority over those due to the trustee.[250].

26.162 The supervisor must, out of the realisation of assets, discharge all guarantee properly given by the Official Receiver or trustee for the benefit of the estate and pay all their expenses.[251]

Supervisor's accounts and records [252]

26.163 The supervisor's obligation to keep accounts and records arises, inter alia, where the arrangement authorises or requires him to realise assets of the bankrupt's estate.[253]

H. DEFAULT IN CONNECTION WITH THE ARRANGEMENT [254]

26.164 If the bankruptcy order was annulled following the approval of the arrangement by the creditors' meeting and the debtor fails to comply with his obligations under the arrangement or is guilty of any other default within Article 250(1), a petition to have him adjudged bankrupt again may be presented by the supervisor or a creditor bound by the arrangement.[255] Alternatively, an application may be made for an order rescinding the annulment order under Article 371. Such an order may be more advantageous to the creditors at the date of the bankruptcy order (e.g. if there are suspected voidable preferences made when they would be vulnerable under the bankruptcy order but not under a new adjudication), but in deciding whether or not to accede to the application to rescind the Court will have regard also to the interests of any subsequent bona fide creditors who might thereby be prejudiced.

I. ASCERTAINMENT OF CREDITORS' CLAIMS [256]

26.165 The persons to be admitted as creditors under the arrangement are those who were required to be summoned to the creditors' meeting, i.e. creditors in respect of bankruptcy debts at the date of the bankruptcy order and those who would be such creditors if the bankruptcy order had been made on the day on which notice of the meeting was given.[257] Preferential debts are determined by reference to the date of the bankruptcy order or, if an interim receiver had been appointed, the date of such appointment.[258].

J. COSTS [259]

26.166   The remuneration and expenses of the nominee prior to the approval of the arrangement must be agreed between himself and the Official Receiver or trustee (if any).[260]

K. INSOLVENT PARTNERSHIPS [261]

26.167   The Insolvent Partnerships Order applies the provisions of the Insolvency Order relating to individual voluntary arrangements to an individual member of an insolvent partnership where, under the first mentioned Order, either a winding-up order is made against the partnership and a bankruptcy order is made against the member or bankruptcy orders are made against all the members of the partnership on a joint petition by such members without the partnership being wound up.[262] In such application any reference to the creditors of the debtor includes a reference to the creditors of the partnership.[263] Consequently, an arrangement by a bankrupt partner must provide for the debts of the partnership as well as his personal debts.

L. EFFECT OF DEATH OF BANKRUPT [264]

26.168   If the bankrupt dies before a creditors' meeting is held, no such meeting is held and the personal representative must give notice of the death to the trustee of the bankrupt's estate and to the Official Receiver.[265]

Footnotes

(1) For a useful review of the initial operation of individual voluntary arrangements under IA 1986, see Keith Pond's articles in Insolvency Law and Practice, vol. 4, pp. 66 and 104. See also Richard Setchim and Keith Jewitt "Tax Aspects of Voluntary Arrangements" (1991) 4 Ins Int 25 and Flow chart at (1991) 4 Ins Int 39.

(2) JH Ch.17.

(3) MH 3-003.

(4) JH Ch.11.

(5) MH 3-012.

(6) Paras.7.160.

(7) Art.234(3).

(8) Arts.227(2), 229(1)(d).

(9) Arts.227(2), 237(2).

(10) (1886) 3 Morr. 111, 116.

(11) Art.232(5),(6),(7).

(12) Para.26.094.

(13) MH 3-049.

(14) Art.227(2).

(15) R.5.04(1). See article by Keith Pond in Insolvency Law and Practice, vol.4, p.104 for reasons cited in cases surveyed. The most popular was that the arrangement would achieve a better realisation of assets than a bankruptcy.

(16) R.5.04(2). The nominee's report to the Court should indicate the extent of compliance with these requirements - *Re a Debtor (No.222 of 1990)* [1991] TLR 313.

(17) See article by Keith Otter, "Responsibilities of Supervisors", (1989) 2 Ins Int 73.

(18) Art.250(1)(b).

(19) R.5.33.

(20) If bankruptcy provisions are applied, the date of the approval of the proposal should be substituted for the commencement of the bankruptcy.

(21) Para.26.119.

(22) R.5.04(3).

(23) RR.5.03, 5.05(1),(2).

(24) R.5.05(3).

(25) Paras.26.042/3.

(26) R.5.05(4).

(27) Arts.226(1), 227(1).

(28) MH 3-003.

(29) Arts.227(5), 247(2): paras.7.144/148.

(30) Art.248(3)(a): para.7.160.

(31) Atkin Form 1.

(32)   R.5.06(1).
(33)   R.5.06(2).
(34)   Para.26.023.
(35)   R.5.06(3).
(36)   There is no obligation to notify creditors who have commenced other proceedings against the debtor.
(37)   R.5.06(4).
(38)   Art.228(1). See also JEO, Art 14 for power of Enforcement of Judgments Office to stay enforcement in cases of insolvency.
(39)   Atkin Form 3.
(40)   F.5.1.
(41)   Art.228(2).
(42)   R.5.07(1),(2).
(43)   Art.229(2).
(44)   Arts.239, 246(1).
(45)   Art.229(1): F.5.2.
(46)   Art.226(2). Pending actions are stayed without an order staying specific proceedings, as is required following a bankruptcy order -para.28.16. Goods seized by the Enforcement of Judgments Office are liable to be returned to the supervisor of the arrangement subsequently approved - *Re Peake* (1987) CL Year Book para 215.
(47)   Art.232(5): MH 3-007.
(48)   Art.230(6): MH 3-020.
(49)   MH 3-020.
(50)   Arts.229(6), 230(4).
(51)   Art.234(4),(5): para.26.082.
(52)   MH 3-025.
(53)   [1990] 1 WLR 708,712,718. Also reported as *Re Cove (a debtor)* [1990] 1 All ER 949,952,957.
(54)   Art.230(3): para.26.051.
(55)   Art.230(5): para.26.059.
(56)   Art.236(6): para.26.099.
(57)   R.5.09. See para.26.039 re service of interim order on EJO.
(58)   Art.230(6).
(59)   Art.233(2): para.26.091.
(60)   R.5.10.
(61)   R.5.07(3): F.5.2.
(62)   R.5.08.
(63)   Art.230(1).
(64)   R.5.13(3),(4). See MH 3-022 and *Re a Debtor (No 222 of 1990,)* [1991] TLR 313 as to what the report should contain and liability of nominee to an order for costs for failure to provide adequate report.
(65)   R.5.16(3).
(66)   Art.230(2). See para.26.121 as to meaning of "debt" and "liability".
(67)   R.5.11(3).
(68)   R.5.11(4),(5).
(69)   R.5.11(6).

(70) Art.250(1): R.5.33.
(71) R.5.11(2).
(72) Art.375.
(73) R.5.12(3).
(74) R.5.12(1),(2).
(75) Art.230(6).
(76) R.5.13(1),(5).
(77) Para.26.063.
(78) Art.230(4).
(79) R.7.12(1).
(80) R.5.07(4).
(81) R.5.07(5).
(82) R.5.04(3).
(83) R.5.13(2).
(84) R.5.13(5).
(85) R.5.13(7).
(86) Art.230(3).
(87) *Ibid.*
(88) R.5.14.
(89) R.5.15(1).
(90) Art.230(6).
(91) Art.230(4): para.26.047.
(92) Art.231(1).
(93) *Re a Debtor (No.83 of 1988)* [1990] 1 WLR 708, 717, also reported as *Re Cove (a debtor)* [1990] 1 All ER 949, 956.
(94) Art.230(5).
(95) Para.26.051.
(96) RR.5.08, 5.15.
(97) Art.231(1).
(98) R.5.16(1).
(99) R.5.17(1),(2).
(100) R.5.16(2). Only creditors whose claims and addresses are known are required to be notified - Art.231(2). Failure to notify an associate of the debtor is not a material irregularity - *Re a Debtor (No. 259 of 1990)* [1992] 1 WLR 226
(101) Paras.26.072/074.
(102) RR.5.16(3), 5.17(3).
(103) Art.232(1),(2).
(104) Art.232(3).
(105) R.5.23(2).
(106) Art.232(4).
(107) Art.232(5).
(108) Listed in Sch. 4 (Art 232(9)). The existence and amounts of preferential debts are determined by the date of the interim order -Art.347(5).
(109) Art.232(6).
(110) R.5.18.
(111) R.5.20(1),(2): para.26.121.

(112) R.5.20(3).
(113) R.5.20(4).
(114) R.5.20(6): *Re a Debtor (No 222 of 1990)* [1991] TLR 313.
(115) R.5.20(5),(9).
(116) R.5.20(7),(8).
(117) R.5.20(10). Note omission of power of Court to order otherwise, found in R.6.091(5) (para.16.22), but in the case cited in fn.(114) above it was held that the chairman could be ordered to pay costs where the appeal was joined, with an application to challenge the decision of the creditors' meeting on the ground of material irregularity (para.26.094).
(118) R.5.21(1),(2). See paras.26.080/081 re effect of approval of arrangement.
(119) R.5.21(3).
(120) Art.4.
(121) R.5.21(4).
(122) R.5.21(5).
(123) R.5.21(7).
(124) Para.7.124: MH 3-095.
(125) R.5.22(5).
(126) R.5.19.
(127) R.5.21(6).
(128) R.5.22(1).
(129) R.5.22(2).
(130) R.5.22(3).
(131) R.5.22(4).
(132) Art.234(2)(a). An approved voluntary arrangement binds the Crown - Art.378(d).
(133) Paras.26.090, 26.098/100.
(134) Art.234(2)(b): MH 3-040.
(135) See MH 3-040 as to the consequences of failure to bind a creditor by the arrangement.
(136) Art.234(4),(5).
(137) Art.237(2).
(138) R.5.27(2),(3).
(139) R.5.23(1).
(140) Art.233(1): R.5.25(1),(3).
(141) Paras.26.071, 26.094.
(142) Para.26.082 above.
(143) R.5.25(2).
(144) F.5.4.
(145) Art.234(6). See MH 3-043 re costs of such petition and its revival in the event of a successful challenge to the decision of the meeting.
(146) RR.6.024(3), 6.040(3).
(147) Atkin, Table 5, para.32 (p.110).
(148) Art.233(2).
(149) Art.233(1): R.5.25(4),(5).
(150) R.5.27(1).

(151) Para.26.131 below. A fee is payable to the Department - (currently £35) - Insolvency (Fees) Order (Northern Ireland) 1991, Sch. Pt.II Fee No.9.
(152) MH 3-048/056.
(153) Art.236(1)-(3). A creditor may challenge an arrangement on the ground of unfair prejudice even if other creditors in the same position have accepted it - *Re Primlaks (UK) Ltd. (No. 2)* [1990] BCLC 234, 237. Prejudice to creditor must have been brought about by unfairness steming from actual terms of arrangement itself - *Re a Debtor (No.250 of 1990)* [1992] 1 WLR 226. Failure to notify an associate of the debtor is not a material irregularity - *ibid*.
(154) MH 3-037.
(155) *Re Primlaks (UK) Ltd. (No. 2)* [1990] BCLC 234, 237.
(156) *Re Naeem (a bankrupt)* [1990] 1 WLR 48, 50.
(157) Art.236(4).
(158) Art.236(6).
(159) Art.236(5).
(160) Art.236(7).
(161) Art.236(8).
(162) R.5.28.
(163) R.5.24(1).
(164) Art.343: para.14.034.
(165) Art.368: para.14.101.
(166) Arts.3(2)(c), 349(3): para.4.13.
(167) Ins Pract Regs 13(4).
(168) Art.237(3): MH 3-069.
(169) Art.237(4).
(170) Paras.28.45/50.
(171) Art.237(5),(6).
(172) R.5.29(1).
(173) R.5.29(2).
(174) R.5.29(4).
(175) R.5.29(3).
(176) R.5.29(5).
(177) R.5.29(6).
(178) Ins Pract Regs 14/18.
(179) R.5.30(1),(2).
(180) R.5.30(3).
(181) R.5.32.
(182) Arts.238(1)(c), 250(1): paras.7.164/5: MH 3-118.
(183) Art.250(2). See para. 7.073 re notice of petition to supervisor.
(184) MH 3-118.
(185) MH 3-118, 3-040, Keith Otter "Effect of Bankruptcy on Voluntary Arrangements", (1991) 4 Ins Int 51, 58.
(186) R.5.33.
(187) Art.347(5).
(188) Para.20.16.
(189) Para.26.107 above.

(190) Para.26.106 above.
(191) Paras.28.55/58.
(192) R.5.04(2)(g).
(193) R.5.04(2)(h). See para.26.078 above as to use of proxy by chairman to increase or reduce remuneration or expenses of nominee or supervisor.
(194) R.5.31.
(195) R.5.26(1).
(196) R.5.26(2).
(197) Art.364.
(198) Arts.9(1), 226(1).
(199) Para.26.167.
(200) Stuart J. Frith "Avoiding the Insolvency Partnerships Order " (1991) 4 Ins Int 11.
(201) (1988) 1 Ins Int 38, 39.
(202) Solicitors (Northern Ireland) Order 1976, Arts.13(1)(k), 36(2)(a).
(203) *Ibid*. Art.41(3),(4), as amended by Sch.10 to the Insolvency Order: para.12.48.
(204) Art.230 as modified by DIEO Sch.I, Pt.III, para.1.
(205) Art.231 as modified by DIEO Sch.I, Pt.III, para.2.
(206) Art.237 as modified by DIEO Sch.I, Pt.III, para.5.
(207) Para.26.01 above.
(208) R.5.04(2)(c).
(209) Para.26.017.
(210) Art.227(4): R.5.05(5).
(211) Paras.26.018/020.
(212) Art.227(3)(a).
(213) R.5.03.
(214) MH 7-004.
(215) R.5.06(1)(c): Atkin Form 2.
(216) Para.26.022.
(217) R.5.06(4)(a).
(218) Para.26.027.
(219) Art.229(1)(b).
(220) Para.26.038.
(221) Art.229(3),(4).
(222) R.5.07(2).
(223) Art. 229(5).
(224) Para.26.042.
(225) R.5.11(1).
(226) MH 3-029.
(227) Para.26.050.
(228) R.5.13(6).
(229) Para.26.064.
(230) Art.231(2),(3): paras.19.02/070.
(231) Para.26.070.
(232) R.5.20(2).
(233) Paras.26.088/091.

(234) Art.235(1): MH 3-045.
(235) R.6.210.
(236) Art.235(2)(a).
(237) Art.235(2)(b).
(238) Atkin, Table 5, para.32 (p.111).
(239) Para.26.092.
(240) R.5.25(4).
(241) Paras.26.094/102.
(242) Art.236(2).
(243) R.5.28(2).
(244) R.5.28(4).
(245) Para.26.103.
(246) R.5.24(1).
(247) R.5.24(2).
(248) R.5.24(3).
(249) R.5.24(4).
(250) R.5.24(5).
(251) R.5.24(6).
(252) Para.26.109.
(253) R.5.29(1)(b).
(254) Paras.26.117/119.
(255) Art.238(1)(c).
(256) Para.26.122.
(257) Art.231(2),(3).
(258) Art 347(6).
(259) Paras.26.128/130.
(260) R.5.31.
(261) Para.26.132.
(262) IPO Arts.11, 13(3).
(263) Ibid.
(264) Para.26.140.
(265) DIEO, Sch.1, Pt.III, para.2.

Chapter 27

DEEDS OF ARRANGEMENT [(1)]

Introduction

27.01 Chapter I of Part VIII of the Order replaces the Deeds of Arrangement Act 1887 in relation to any deed of arrangement between a debtor and his creditors registered under the Order on or after 1st October 1991.[(2)] It follows closely the provisions of the Deeds of Arrangement Act 1914, as amended, applying to England and Wales. A bankrupt may enter into a deed of arrangement.[(3)]

27.02 Chapter I of Part VIII of the Order applies, to specified categories of instrument (whether under seal or not) made by, for or in respect of the affairs of a debtor for the benefit of his creditors generally, otherwise than in pursuance of the voluntary arrangement or bankruptcy provisions of the Order.[(4)] By a significant extension of the 1887 Act, certain of its provisions (but not those requiring the trustee to provide security,[(5)] to send accounts to creditors every 6 months [(6)] or those creating offences where the trustee acts when a deed of arrangement is void [(7)] or makes unauthorised preferential payments to a creditor[(8)]) apply also to an instrument made by, for or in respect of the affairs of a debtor who was insolvent at the date of its execution for the benefit of any 3 or more of his creditors.[(9)] For this purpose any 2 or more of his joint creditors are treated as a single creditor.[(10)]

27.03 The instruments specified remain as under the 1887 Act.[(11)] The two principal categories are -
(a) an assignment of property;
(b) a deed of or agreement for a composition.[(12)]
In this Chapter "deed of arrangement" means a deed of arrangement to which Chapter 1 of Part VIII of the Order applies.

27.04 Where unregistered land is conveyed or assigned to the trustee by the deed it should, in addition to the registration required by the Order,[(13)] be registered in the Registry of Deeds. Where registered land is transferred to the trustee by the deed, a caution may be entered in the register to protect the title of the trustee, pending his registration as owner.

27.05 Although with the abolition of acts of bankruptcy the execution by a debtor of a deed of arrangement can no longer be relied upon to ground a bankruptcy petition, it is only binding on those creditors who execute it or expressly assent to it or who by their conduct put themselves in the same situation as if they had executed it [(14)] and a dissenting creditor may pursue any remedies available to him and, if and when he is in a position to do so, he may present a bankruptcy petition against the debtor.

27.06   The previous serious disadvantage of the non-availability of value added tax bad debt relief [15] to a creditor claiming under a deed of arrangement has now been removed.

27.07   Although there is no requirement to hold a meeting of creditors before a deed of arrangement is executed, an informal meeting is usually held in order to ascertain the views of the creditors on the proposed arrangement, unless the creditors are few in number and can be conveniently consulted without a meeting. The creditors should be invited to submit claims to enable a statement of affairs to be drawn up for consideration at the meeting. [16]

Registration
(a) Effect of non-registration
27.08   A deed of arrangement is void unless it is registered within the time prescribed by the Order and bears the proper Revenue stamp. [17]

(b) The register
27.09   The register is held at the Department and not, as heretofore, at the High Court. An officer of the Department is appointed Registrar and a deputy may also be appointed. [18] The Registrar must record specified information extracted from the deed. [19] Where there has been an omission or mis-statement of the name, residential address, place of business or occupation of any person the Court may, on the application of any party interested, and if satisfied that it was accidental, or due to inadvertence, or to some cause beyond the control of the debtor and not imputable to any negligence on his part, rectify the register under such terms and conditions as are just and expedient. [20]

27.10   Any person may, on payment of the requisite fee, at all reasonable times search the register, inspect any registered deed of arrangement and obtain certified copies or extracts from the deed. [21] The same rights apply to all documents filed with the Registrar or the Department. [22]

27.11   Any copy of or extract from a deed of arrangement purporting to be a certified copy or extract is admissible as prima facie evidence thereof and of the fact and date of registration as shown thereon. [23]

(c) Mode of registration
27.12   A deed of arrangement is registered by producing to the Registrar the original deed duly stamped with the Revenue duty [24] and presenting and filing with him -
(i)   such number of copies of the deed and of every schedule or inventory annexed to or referred to in it as the Registrar may determine;
(ii)   an affidavit (made by some person other than the debtor) verifying the time of execution and containing the name, residential address and occupation of the debtor and the address of the place or places where his business is carried on; and

(iii) an affidavit by the debtor stating the total estimated amount of property and liabilities included under the deed, the total amount of the composition (if any) payable under the deed and the names and addresses of his creditors.[25]

27.13 The person who presents the deed to the Registrar for filing must endorse on it the name of the debtor, the date of the deed, the date of filing of the deed, the total amount of Revenue duty with which it is stamped and a certificate signed by the solicitor of the debtor or the person who presents the copy for filing certifying that the copy is a correct copy of the deed.[26]

27.14 Before registering an assignment by a debtor to a trustee or assignee for the benefit of his creditors the Registrar must satisfy himself that the assignment purports to have been duly executed (if made by deed) or signed by the trustee or assignee.[27]

27.15 When a deed is registered a certificate, sealed with the seal of the Registrar, stating that it has been duly registered and the date of registration, must be endorsed on the original deed.[28]

(d) Time for registration
27.16 A deed is void unless it is registered within 7 clear days from its first execution by the debtor or any creditor, or if it is executed out of Northern Ireland, within 7 clear days from the time at which it would, in the ordinary course of post, arrive in Northern Ireland if posted within one week after its execution.[29] If this period expires on a Sunday or a public holiday, registration may be effected on the following day.[30]

27.17 The general power of the Court to extend time-limits under the Order does not apply to time-limits in relation to deeds of arrangement.[31] The Court may, however, on such terms and conditions as are just and expedient, extend the time for registration if, on the application of any party interested, it is satisfied that the omission to register within the required time was accidental, or due to inadvertence, or to some cause beyond the control of the debtor and not attributable to any negligence on his part.[32]

Assent of creditors
27.18 Where a deed of arrangement either is expressed to be or is in fact for the benefit of a debtor's creditors generally, it is void unless, within 21 days from its registration, or within such extended time as the Court may allow, it has received the assent of the majority in number and value of the debtor's creditors.[33] In calculating such majority a creditor holding security upon the debtor's property is reckoned as a creditor only in respect of the balance (if any) due to him after deducting the value of such security, and creditors whose debts amount to £100 or less are reckoned in the majority in value but not in the majority in number.[34]

27.19   The list of creditors annexed to the debtor's affidavit filed on the registration of the deed is prima facie evidence of the names of the creditors and the amounts of their claims.[35]

27.20   The assent of a creditor must be given either by his executing the deed or sending to the trustee his assent in writing attested by a witness.[36]

27.21   The trustee must file with the Registrar at the time of the registration of the deed, or, if the deed is assented to after registration, within 28 days from registration or within such extended time as the Court may allow, a statutory declaration by himself that the requisite assents have been obtained.[37] Such declaration is, in favour of a purchaser for value, conclusive evidence of the fact declared and in other cases is prima facie evidence thereof.[38]

27.22   Because of the short period allowed to obtain the necessary assents from creditors, particularly if there are a considerable number of relatively small creditors, it may be advisable to obtain such assents before the deed is registered.

Trustee
(a) Appointment
27.23   Where the deed of arrangement provides for administration by a trustee, the trustee will be named in and be a party to the deed. He must be a person qualified to act as an insolvency practitioner in relation to the debtor.[39]

27.24   The deed should provide for the removal of the trustee from office, the appointment of a replacement and by whom the power of appointing a new trustee under section 35 of the Trustee Act (Northern Ireland) 1958 is to be exercised. In the circumstances mentioned in section 40 of that Act a new trustee may be appointed by the court having jurisdiction under that Act.[40] Where a new trustee is appointed he must forthwith send to the Registrar for filing a notice of his appointment, giving his full name and address and showing how and when the appointment has been made.[41]

(b) Security
27.25   Except where a deed of arrangement is not for the benefit of creditors generally,[42] the trustee under the deed must, within 7 days from the date on which the statutory declaration certifying the assent of the creditors is filed, give security with respect to the proper administration of the deed and to account fully for the assets which come to his hands, unless a majority in number and value of the creditors, either by resolution passed at a meeting convened by notice to all the creditors, or by writing addressed to the trustee, dispense with giving such security.[43]

27.26   The security requirements are those applying to all insolvency practitioners.[44]

27.27 When the creditors dispense with the giving of security the trustee must forthwith make and file with the Registrar a certificate to that effect.[45] Such certificate is in favour of a purchaser for value conclusive evidence and in other cases prima facie evidence, of the facts certified.[46]

27.28 If the trustee fails to comply with the requirements of the Order regarding security, the Court may, on the application of any creditor and after hearing such persons as it may think fit, declare the deed of arrangement to be void or make an order appointing another trustee in the place of the trustee appointed by the deed.[47] Such an application must be served on the trustee named in the deed.[48] Where, on such an application an order is made declaring the deed to be void, the creditor must forthwith send a copy of the order to the Registrar.[49] It is an offence for the trustee to act after he has failed to give security within the permitted time, unless he provides that the contravention was due to inadvertence or that his action has been confined to taking such steps as were necessary for the protection of the estate.[50]

(c) Records and accounts
<u>(i) Records</u>
27.29 The trustee must maintain the records required by the Insolvency Practitioners Regulations.[51] He must also keep the same financial records as a trustee in bankruptcy is required to keep and submit them to any creditor when required.[52]

27.30 The trustee must produce on demand to the Department, and allow it to inspect, any accounts, books and other records kept by him and such production and inspection may be required at the trustee's premises.[53] The demand may be made when any account or certificate of no receipts or payments is sent to the Department under the provision for audit of the trustee's accounts[54] or at any time afterwards, whether or not the Department requires any account to be audited.[55]

<u>(ii) Accounts</u>
27.31 The provisions relating to the Insolvency Account do not apply to deeds of arrangement. The deed should provide for all money received by the trustee to be paid into a separate bank account in the name of the debtor's estate.

27.32 Every 6 months during his tenure of office the trustee must send to the Department either an account of his receipts and payments as trustee or, in respect of any period since the beginning of his tenure of office or since the last time his accounts have been sent to the Department during which he has not received or paid any money under the deed, a certificate of no receipts or payments.[56]

27.33 The first account or certificate of no receipts or payments so sent to the Department must be accompanied by a copy of the debtor's affidavit filed on the registration of the deed of arrangement.[57]

27.34   The first account must be sent within 30 days after the expiration of 6 months from the date of registration of the deed of arrangement, unless the trustee vacates office or completes his administration of the deed within that period, and subsequent accounts within 30 days after each succeeding 6 months period until he vacates office or until the estate has been finally wound up.[58]

27.35   After the trustee has vacated office or has distributed a final dividend or final instalment of composition, or in any other case has completely fulfilled the trusts of the deed of arrangement and his obligations, he must send to the Department an account of his receipts and payments in respect of the period since the date of the last account so sent or, if no such account has been sent, an account of his receipts and payments in respect of the whole period of his office, accompanied by a copy of the debtor's affidavit filed on registration of the deed.[59]

27.36   The Department may require any account sent to it to be audited but, whether or not it does so, the trustee must send to the Department on demand, any vouchers, any bank statements and any information relating to the account.[60]

27.37   Where a deed of arrangement has been made by a firm of debtors in partnership, the trustee must send to the Department a distinct account of, or certificate of no receipts or payments in relation to, the joint estate and each of the separate estates.[61]

27.38   Where the trustee pays dividends or instalments of composition under the deed of arrangement, he must enter the total amount of each dividend or instalment of composition in his accounts as one sum and forward to the Department with each account in which a charge in respect of dividend or composition appears a statement showing the amount of the claim of each creditor and the amount of dividend or composition payable to each creditor, distinguishing in such statement the dividends or instalments of composition paid and those remaining unpaid, and with his final account forward a complete statement in similar form showing the amount of the claim and the full amount of dividend or composition paid to or reserved for each creditor.[62]

27.39   Except where the deed of arrangement is not for the benefit of creditors generally,[63] the trustee must, at the expiration of 6 months from the date of registration of the deed and thereafter at 6 monthly intervals until the estate has been finally wound up, send to each creditor who has assented to the deed a prescribed form of account and a statement showing the amount of estimated assets and liabilities at the date of execution of the deed, a general description and estimated value of any outstanding assets, the causes which delay the completion of the proceedings and the period within which the final dividend may probably be paid.[64] In the certificate verifying the accounts or the certificate of no receipts or payments sent to the Department[65] the trustee must state whether or not he has duly sent such statements and the dates on which they were sent.[66]

27.40   Contravention by the trustee of his obligations to transmit accounts to the Department and the creditors is an offence.[67]

27.41   The debtor or any creditor or other person interested may, on payment of the requisite fee, inspect or obtain copies of the accounts transmitted by the trustee to the Department.[68]

Consequences of deed becoming void

27.42   When a deed of arrangement is void for any reason other than that it is for the benefit of creditors generally and has not been registered within the permitted time, the trustee must, as soon as practicable after becoming aware that it is void, give written notice thereof to each creditor whose name and address he knows and file a copy of the notice with the Registrar.[69] Failure to do so is an offence.[70]

27.43   It is also an offence for the trustee to act under a deed of arrangement for the benefit of creditors generally after it has to his knowledge become void by reason of non-compliance with any of the requirements of Chapter 1 of Part VIII of the Order or of the previous legislation, unless he proves that the contravention was due to inadvertence or that his action has been confined to taking such steps as were necessary for the protection of the estate.[71]

27.44   Where a deed of arrangement is void by reason of the requisite majority of creditors not having assented to it or, in the case of a deed for the benefit of 3 or more creditors, by reason that the debtor was insolvent at the time of the execution of the deed and that the deed was not duly registered, but is not void for any other reason, and a bankruptcy order is made against the debtor upon a petition presented after the expiration of 3 months from the execution of the deed, the trustee is not liable to account to the trustee in the bankruptcy for any dealings with or payments made out of the debtor's property which would have been proper if the deed had been valid, if he proves that at the time of such dealings or payments he did not know, and had no reason to suspect, that the deed was void.[72]

27.45   Where a deed of arrangement is avoided by reason of the bankruptcy of the debtor, any expenses properly incurred by the trustee in the performance of any of the duties imposed on him by the Order are payable to him by the trustee in bankruptcy as a first charge on the estate.[73]

Administration of the estate

27.46   The trustee must administer the estate in accordance with the terms of the deed, which should include, for example, provisions for the admission of creditors' claims, the powers exercisable by the trustee and his remuneration.

27.47   The provisions of the Order relating to the adjustment of transactions at an undervalue, preferences, extortionate credit transactions or disclaimer of onerous property do not apply.

27.48   Unless he is acting under a deed of arrangement which is not for the benefit of the creditors generally,[74] it is an offence for the trustee to pay any creditor in priority to others unless the deed authorises him to do so or the payment is made to a creditor entitled to enforce his claim by distress or would be lawful in an individual voluntary arrangement or a bankruptcy.[75] He may not pay interest on a debt out of any surplus, unless the deed provides for such interest.[76]

27.49   The postponement of certain debts under the Partnership Act 1890[77] applies to any arrangement by a debtor to pay his creditors less than 100 pence in the pound.

27.50   The provisions of the Solicitors (Northern Ireland) Order 1976 whereby the sum at credit of a bankrupt solicitor's clients' account with his bankers is divisible rateably amongst the clients on whose behalf money has been received by the solicitor and remains due to them, applies to deeds of arrangement.[78]

27.51   The trustee under a deed or arrangement has the right to request the supply of electricity, water or public telecommunication services for the purposes of carrying on the debtor's business upon the same terms as a trustee in bankruptcy.[79]

27.52   There is no provision in the Order or the Insolvency Regulations for dealing with unclaimed dividends arising under the administration of a deed of arrangement. Money representing such dividends may be paid into court under section 63 of the Trustee Act (Northern Ireland) 1958.

Disqualification of debtor etc.
27.53   A debtor who makes any composition or arrangement with his creditors is disqualified for being elected to or being a member of a District Council.[80] The disqualification ceases, if the debtor pays his debts in full, on the date on which the payment is completed, and in any other case, on the expiration of 5 years from the date on which the terms of the deed of composition or arrangement have been fully implemented.[81]

27.54   A solicitor who has entered into a deed of arrangement may be refused a practising certificate and the Law Society of Northern Ireland may exercise its powers under Schedule 1 to the Solicitors (Northern Ireland) Order 1976 in respect of him.[82]

Applications to the Court under deed of arrangement
27.55   Where a deed of arrangement is expressed to be or is in fact for the benefit of the debtor's creditors generally the trustee, the debtor or any creditor

entitled to the benefit of the deed may apply to the Court for the enforcement of the trusts or the determination of questions under it.[83] Such an application must be served -
  (a) if made by the trustee, on the debtor and any creditor or other person to be affected thereby;
  (b) if made by the debtor, on the trustee and any creditor or other person to be affected thereby; and
  (c) if made by a creditor, on the trustee and the debtor.[84]

Assistance of other courts
27.56   The trustee has the same rights as a trustee in bankruptcy under section 426 of the Insolvency Act 1986 to seek the assistance of courts outside Northern Ireland.[85]

Footnotes

(1) MH 2-001/2-067: Hals 829/862. For a useful guide to deeds of arrangement procedure, see Grier & Floyd "Personal Insolvency: A Practical Guide" pp 59/63. For precedents of deeds of arrangement, see Encyclopedia of Forms and Precedents 5th edn. Vol.3, and supplement. (2) Sch.8, para.17.

(3) Atkin Form 437.

(4) Art.209(1)(a).

(5) Para.27.25.

(6) Para.27.39.

(7) Para.27.43.

(8) Para.27.48.

(9) Art.209(1)(b).

(10) Art.209(4).

(11) Art.209(2).

(12) Hals 831/833.

(13) Paras.27.08/17.

(14) Hals 855.

(15) Paras.28.55/58.

(16) For precedents of statement of affairs and notice of creditors meeting see Encyclopedia of Forms and Precedents, 5th edn. Vol.3.

(17) Art.214.

(18) Art.210.

(19) Art.212: Ins Regs Sch.Form 10.

(20) Art.213.

(21) Art.225(1).

(22) Ins Regs 43.

(23) Art.225(3).

(24) Art.211(2).

(25) Art.211(1): Ins Regs Sch. Forms 7, 8, 9.

(26) Ins Regs 38.

(27) Ins Regs 39.

(28) Ins Regs 40.

(29) Art.214(a).

(30) Interpretation Act (Northern Ireland) 1954, s.39(4).

(31) Art.344.

(32) Art.213.

(33) Art.215(1). The majority required is a majority of all existing creditors, and not merely of those disclosed by the debtor - MH 2-010. For application for extension of time see Atkin Form 437.

(34) Art.215(5): Hals 835 fn.4.

(35) Art.215(2).

(36) Art.215(3): Ins Regs Sch. Form 11.

(37) Art.215(4): Ins Regs Sch. Form 12.

(38) Art.215(4).

(39) Art.3(2)(b). This requirement applies to any deed of arrangement for the benefit of the creditors of an individual debtor, whether or not within Art 209.
(40) Atkin Form 443.
(41) Ins Regs 41.
(42) Art.209(3).
(43) Art.221(1).
(44) Ins Pract Regs 10, 11, 13(3): paras. 4.12/13. Certificate of specific penalty must be filed with the Registry within 14 days of receipt.
(45) Art.221(2): Ins Regs Sch. Form 13.
(46) Art.221(2).
(47) Art.221(3): Atkin Forms 438/440.
(48) R.5.01(1).
(49) Ins Regs 42.
(50) Art.218.
(51) Para.4.16.
(52) Ins Regs 44, 45: para.13.129.
(53) Ins Regs 50.
(54) Paras.27.32/35.
(55) Ins Regs 50.
(56) Art.222(2): Ins Regs 47(1),(2),(7), Sch. Forms 5, 6.
(57) Ins Regs 47(3).
(58) Ins Regs 47(4).
(59) Ins Regs 47(5).
(60) Ins Regs 47(6).
(61) Ins Regs 49.
(62) Ins Regs 48.
(63) Art.209(3).
(64) Art.222(1)(a): Ins Regs 46, Sch. Form 4.
(65) Paras.27.32/35.
(66) Art.222(1)(b): Ins Regs Sch. Forms 5, 6.
(67) Art.222(3).
(68) Art.225(2).
(69) Art.217(1).
(70) Art.217(2).
(71) Arts.218, 209(3).
(72) Art.219.
(73) Art.220.
(74) Art.209(3).
(75) Art.223.
(76) *Re Rissick* [1936] Ch 68.
(77) Para.20.16.
(78) Solicitors (Northern Ireland) Order 1976, Art.41(3),(4): para.12.48.
(79) Art.343.
(80) Local Government Act (Northern Ireland) 1972, s.4(1).
(81) *Ibid*, s.5(2).
(82) Solicitors (Northern Ireland) Order 1976, Arts. 13(1)(k), 36(2)(a).

(83)   Art.224: Atkin Forms 438, 439, 447, 450.
(84)   R.5.01(2).
(85)   Paras.28.45/50.

Chapter 28

MISCELLANEOUS

I. LEAVE TO ACT AS DIRECTOR ETC.

Introduction
28.01 An undischarged bankrupt is prohibited from acting as director of, or directly or indirectly taking part in or being concerned in the promotion, formation or management of a company except with the leave of the Court.[1]

Application for leave
28.02 The application[2] must be supported by an affidavit identifying the company concerned and specifying -
  (a) if the company is already in existence, the date of its incorporation and the amount of its nominal and issued share capital or, if not already in existence, the amount, or approximate amount, of its proposed commencing share capital, and the sources from which that capital is to be obtained,
  (b) the nature of its business or intended business and the place or places where the business is, or is to be, carried on,
  (c) whether it is, or is to be, a private or a public company,
  (d) the persons who are, or are to be, principally responsible for the conduct of its affairs (whether as directors, shadow directors, managers, or otherwise),
  (e) the manner and capacity in which the applicant proposes to take part or be concerned in the promotion or formation of the company or, as the case may be, its management, and
  (f) the emoluments and other benefits to be obtained from the directorship.[3]

28.03 Where the bankrupt intends to take part or be concerned in the promotion or formation of a company, the affidavit must contain an undertaking by him that he will, within 7 days of the company being incorporated, file in the Court a copy of its memorandum of association and certificate of incorporation.[4]

28.04 It is the practice in England to file also an affidavit sworn on behalf of the company, confirming the bankrupt's statements and its own intention.[5]

28.05 The Court will fix a venue for the hearing and notify the bankrupt accordingly.[6]

28.06   The bankrupt must, not less than 28 days before the hearing date, send to the Official Receiver and the trustee a copy of the application, with the venue endorsed, accompanied by a copy of the supporting affidavit.[7]

Official Receiver's report
28.07   The Official Receiver may, not less than 14 days before the hearing date, file in the Court a report of any matters which he considers ought to be drawn to the Court's attention.[8] Such a report should always be filed if the Official Receiver intends to oppose the application.

28.08   A copy of any report made by the Official Receiver must be sent by him to the bankrupt and the trustee immediately it is filed and the bankrupt may, not less than 7 days before the hearing date, file a notice specifying any statement in the report which he intends to deny or dispute.[9] He must send copies of any such notice to the Official Receiver and the trustee not less than 4 days before the hearing date.[10]

Hearing
28.09   The hearing is in open court.[11] The Official Receiver and the trustee may appear and make representations and put to the bankrupt such questions as the Court may allow.[12] Where the Official Receiver is of opinion that it is contrary to the public interest that the application should be granted he is required to attend and oppose it.[13]

The order
28.10   At the hearing the trustee may in an appropriate case point out that if the leave requested is granted the bankrupt may henceforth be in receipt of an increased income. In such a case the Court may make an income payments order if no such order is in force or, if it is, vary the amount of the payments under the order.[14]

28.11   If leave is granted, the order must specify which of the relevant functions in relation to the company the bankrupt has leave to perform.[15]

28.12   Whether or not the application is granted, the Court sends copies of the order to the bankrupt, the trustee and the Official Receiver.[16]

II. EFFECT OF BANKRUPTCY ON ACTIONS AND ENFORCEMENT OF JUDGMENTS

A. ACTIONS

Actions pending by or against bankrupt
28.13   Where a party to an action becomes bankrupt but the cause of action survives, the action does not abate by reason of the bankruptcy.[17]

(a) Bankruptcy of plaintiff

28.14 If the bankrupt's right of action is of a category which vests in the trustee, i.e. is not one which is personal to the bankrupt [18] or is one which the trustee is entitled to enforce for the benefit of the creditors, the trustee may be made a party to the proceedings in place of the bankrupt or as co-plaintiff.[19] Alternatively, the trustee may assign the right of action for a consideration and, subject to appropriate terms, he may make such an assignment to the bankrupt himself.[20] Where the cause of action has occurred after the bankruptcy order an undischarged bankrupt may sue in his own name until the trustee intervenes.[21]

28.15 If the bankrupt is a joint contractor the other joint contractor may sue in respect of the contract without the joinder of the bankrupt.[22]

(b) Bankruptcy of defendant

28.16 At any time when proceedings on a bankruptcy petition are pending or after the making of a bankruptcy order the Court may stay any action against the property or person of the debtor or bankrupt and any court in which the action is proceeding may, on proof of the presentation of a bankruptcy petition against the defendant or that he is an undischarged bankrupt, either stay the proceedings or allow them to continue on such terms as it thinks fit.[23] Such a stay, although discretionary, will usually be granted if the action is in respect of a provable debt.

28.17 An order staying proceedings may be served by sending a sealed copy to whatever is the address for service of the plaintiff or other party having the carriage of the proceedings to be stayed.[24]

28.18 Until an order staying proceedings is made, an action against a bankrupt defendant continues.[25]

28.19 If the plaintiff elects to have the action stayed and to prove in the bankruptcy, he cannot include in his proof the costs of the action incurred before the bankruptcy order, unless a judgment or order for payment of such costs has been made.[26]

28.20 If the pending action is not stayed, the trustee may be made a party as defendant on his application or on the application of another party to the action.[27]

28.21 If the bankrupt is a joint contractor, the other joint contractor may be sued in respect of the contract without the joinder of the bankrupt.[28]

28.22 If the defendant is discharged from bankruptcy the discharge may be pleaded as a defence to an action in respect of a debt from which he is released by his discharge.[29]

Commencement of action against undischarged bankrupt

28.23 No action may be commenced against the bankrupt before he is discharged except with the leave of the Court and on such terms as the Court may impose.[30]

Actions by or against trustee

28.24 The trustee may, with the permission of the creditors' committee (or of the Department when exercising the functions of the committee) or the Court, bring, institute or defend any action or legal proceedings relating to the property comprised in the bankrupt's estate and may compromise any action brought against him.(31) Failure to obtain the necessary prior consent does not affect the validity of the proceedings, but the trustee loses his right to be paid any costs or expenses incurred in the proceedings out of the bankrupt's estate, unless his action is subsequently ratified.(32)

28.25 The trustee should sue and be sued as "the trustee of the estate of AB, a bankrupt".(33)

B. ENFORCEMENT OF JUDGMENTS

Effect of bankruptcy of judgment debtor

(a) Commencement of enforcement after bankruptcy

28.26 If the judgment is in respect of a debt provable in the bankruptcy no proceedings to enforce that judgment may be instituted after the making of the bankruptcy order, other than proceedings by way of distress, if applicable.[34]

28.27 If the judgment is in respect of a security held by a creditor, it may be enforced against the secured property notwithstanding the bankruptcy order subject, in the case of goods, to a right of inspection by the Official Receiver and to restraint on realisation without leave of the Court unless, following notice by the Official Receiver of intention to inspect, the trustee gives him a reasonable opportunity to inspect and to exercise the bankrupt's right of redemption.[35]

28.28 At any time when proceedings on a bankruptcy petition are pending or after the making of a bankruptcy order the enforcement of any judgment against the property or person of a debtor or bankrupt may be stayed by the Court.[36] Such an order may be served in the same way as an order staying an action.[37] Enforcement by the Enforcement of Judgments Office may also be stayed by that Office.[38]

28.29 Subject to any such stay, the enforcement of any judgment in respect of a debt which is not provable in bankruptcy may be commenced after the bankruptcy of the defendant but, except where he has been discharged from the bankruptcy and has acquired assets or income after discharge which may not be claimed by the trustee or where there is a surplus in the bankruptcy, such enforcement proceedings are unlikely to be fruitful. Where there is a surplus which remains in the hands of the trustee a judgment creditor who has commenced enforcement proceeding under the Judgments Enforcement Order may apply to the Enforcement of Judgments Office for the appointment of a receiver in respect of such surplus.[39]

(b) Enforcement pending or threatened before bankruptcy
28.30   The provisions governing the effect of bankruptcy on enforcement proceedings pending or threatened before the date of a bankruptcy order against the judgment debtor are contained in Articles 88 to 94 of the Judgments Enforcement Order, as amended by the Insolvency Order.

28.31   Subject to the power of the Court to restrain enforcement proceedings and to the provisions of the Judgments Enforcement Order mentioned below, a judgment creditor who has obtained a money judgment against a debtor who is subsequently adjudged bankrupt is entitled as against the Official Receiver or the trustee to any money paid by or on behalf of the debtor either to avoid enforcement of the judgment or in full or part satisfaction thereof, or to any proceeds of the enforcement, including any charge on the property of the debtor (except a charge on land, in respect of which separate provisions apply[40]), unless -
　(i)　the money is paid to avoid enforcement of the judgment or in full or part satisfaction thereof or, where enforcement is proceeded with, the enforcement producing the proceeds is completed before the date of the bankruptcy order; and
　(ii)　neither the creditor nor the Enforcement of Judgments Office received notice of the bankruptcy order or of the bankruptcy petition on which the bankruptcy order was made, within 21 days after the receipt of the money or, in the case of proceeds of enforcement, of the completion of the enforcement.[41]

28.32   A charge on land created by the Enforcement of Judgments Office under Article 46 of the Judgments Enforcement Order is void as against the trustee in the bankruptcy of the judgment debtor if, within 28 days after the date of registration of the order charging the land, or of notice of the charge, or of the charge, as the case may be, the debtor is adjudged bankrupt or notice is served on the creditor of a bankruptcy petition presented by or against the debtor on which a bankruptcy order is made.[42]

28.33   The Enforcement of Judgments Office is required to hold any money received to avoid enforcement or in full or partial satisfaction of the enforcement or as proceeds of the enforcement for a period of 21 days after the receipt of the money paid to avoid enforcement or the completion of the enforcement, as the case may be.[43] If within that period the Enforcement of Judgments Office receives notice of a bankruptcy order against the debtor, the money must be paid to the Official Receiver or, as the case may be, the trustee.[44] If within the same period that Office receives notice of a bankruptcy petition it must hold the money pending the disposal of the petition and pay it to the Official Receiver or the trustee if a bankruptcy order is made on the petition.[45]

28.34　Where at the time a bankruptcy order is made any money or other property of the debtor is under seizure by the Enforcement of Judgments Office, that Office or any person having custody of it must pay or deliver such money or property to the Official Receiver or trustee, as the case may be, on demand, and it becomes comprised in the bankrupt's estate.[46] Where at the time the Enforcement of Judgments Office becomes liable to pay or deliver money or property to the Official Receiver or trustee under these provisions an inter-pleader application is pending in relation to that money or property, the Enforcement of Judgments Office must hold the money or property until that application has been finally determined.[47]

28.35　Any money or property so paid or delivered to the Official Receiver or trustee is subject to a first charge for approved costs and expenses of enforcement, and the Official Receiver or trustee is empowered to realise such property or an adequate part for the purpose of satisfying the charge.[48]

28.36　The obligation to make such payments to the Official Receiver or trustee does not, however, apply to after-acquired property unless at the time the money is received or before completion of the enforcement the money has been or is claimed for the bankrupt's estate [49] and a copy of the notice claiming it has been or is served upon the Enforcement of Judgments Office.[50]

28.37　The rights of the Official Receiver or trustee to the payment of money or delivery of property under the provisions mentioned in paragraphs 28.31 28.33 and 28.34 above may, to such extent and on such terms as it thinks fit, be set aside by the Court in favour of the creditor.[51] Such an application is made to the Court by originating summons.[52]

28.38　Three species of continuing enforcement order made by the Enforcement of Judgments Office, namely an instalment order, a restraining order in respect of shares in a private company incorporated in Northern Ireland and an attachment of earning order, cease to have effect on the making of a bankruptcy order against the judgment debtor.[53]

28.39　Costs of enforcement which have not been recovered at the date of the bankruptcy order are not provable.[54]

Effect of bankruptcy of judgment creditor
28.40　If the judgment is in respect of a right of action which vests in the trustee, he may only commence or continue enforcement proceedings after such a vesting has taken effect. Such vesting constitutes a change in the parties entitled to enforce the judgment and, accordingly, the leave of the court giving the judgment is required before an application for enforcement may be accepted by the Enforcement of Judgments Office.[55] If the judgment is in respect of a

right of action which continues to belong to the bankrupt, he may proceed with enforcement.

C. DISTRESS

28.41 Where distress is levied upon the goods or effects of a person who is adjudged bankrupt within 3 months from the distraint, those goods or effects or the proceeds of their sale, are charged for the benefit of the bankrupt's estate with the preferential debts of the bankrupt to the extent that such estate is for the time being insufficient for meeting them.[56] Where by virtue of such charge such goods or effects are surrendered to the trustee or a payment is made to the trustee, the person making the surrender or payment ranks as a preferential creditor in respect of the amount of the proceeds of sale of such goods or effects by the trustee or (as the case may be) to the amount of the payment, but not against the part of the bankrupt's estate which represents the surrender or payment.[57]

III. CO-OPERATION BETWEEN INSOLVENCY COURTS [58]

Introduction
28.42 Section 426 of the IA 1986, which applies to Northern Ireland as amended by the Order,[59] provides for co-operation between courts exercising jurisdiction in relation to insolvency law. In relation to bankruptcy this section replaces sections 121 and 122 of the Bankruptcy Act 1914.[60]

Enforcement of orders and warrants within the United Kingdom
28.43 An order of a court exercising jurisdiction in any part of the United Kingdom is enforceable in any other part of the United Kingdom as if it were made by a court exercising the corresponding jurisdiction in that other part, except that when the order relates to property situated in another part of the United Kingdom the court in that other part has a discretion as to whether, and if so how, it enforces it.[61]

28.44 Section 38 of the Criminal Law Act 1977 (execution throughout the United Kingdom of warrants of arrest of persons charged with an offence) is extended to warrants for the arrest of a person issued by a court exercising insolvency jurisdiction.[62] Such a warrant may therefore be executed throughout the United Kingdom. However, the former provisions of the 1857 Act for the execution in Great Britain of seizure and search warrants issued by the High Court in Northern Ireland [63] have not been continued. Where seizure or search in Great Britain is required, the procedure referred to below for seeking the assistance of a court in Great Britain should be invoked.

Mutual assistance between insolvency courts
28.45 The courts having insolvency jurisdiction in any part of the United Kingdom are required to assist the courts having the corresponding jurisdiction in any other part of the United Kingdom or "any relevant country or terri-

tory".[64] This last mentioned expression means any of the Channel Islands or the Isle of Man or any country or territory designated by the Secretary of State by statutory order.[65] The countries so designated to date [66] include the Republic of Ireland. As under section 122 of the Bankruptcy Act 1914 which provided for mutual aid between "British courts" [67] a court in the United Kingdom may request assistance from the relevant court in any other part of the United Kingdom or in any such designated country or territory.[68]

28.46 Thus, for example, where a person adjudged bankrupt in Northern Ireland or a person believed to have information relating to such bankrupt's affairs is residing in the Republic of Ireland or where property of the bankrupt is located there, the Official Receiver or the trustee may seek an examination of the bankrupt or other person or the recovery of the property by applying to the Northern Ireland Bankruptcy Court for an order requesting the aid of the court having bankruptcy jurisdiction in the Republic of Ireland.[69]

28.47 The IA 1986 imposes a duty on the court in any part of the United Kingdom from which assistance is sought to render assistance.[70]

28.48 Where the insolvency law of the other part of the United Kingdom or the country seeking assistance differs from that of the part of the United Kingdom or country in which assistance is sought, the assisting court has a discretion to apply the relevant insolvency law of either jurisdiction, such discretion to be exercised having regard to the rules of private international law.[71]

28.49 Whether or not the court outside the United Kingdom from which assistance is sought has a duty or a discretion to do so is determined by the law of that jurisdiction. Thus, under section 142 of the Republic of Ireland Bankruptcy Act 1988, the High Court in the Republic of Ireland may act in aid of any court in the United Kingdom, but is not obliged to do so.[72]

28.50 The insolvency law to be applied in relation to the United Kingdom is the statute law listed in IA 1986, section 426(10)(a)-(c). In relation to any designated country or territory it is so much of the law of that country or territory as corresponds to such United Kingdom statutory provisions.[73]

28.51 Where a trustee under the insolvency law of any part of the United Kingdom claims property situated in any other part of the United Kingdom, he may apply directly to the relevant insolvency court in that other part to give such assistance as it could have given on a request by the court in the trustee's own jurisdiction.[74] This is an important extension of the mutual aid provisions within the United Kingdom. Henceforth, if a Northern Ireland trustee in bankruptcy is claiming property of a bankrupt located, for example, in England and does not require any other assistance from an English court (e.g. does not wish to examine the bankrupt or other persons in England) he need no longer apply to the Northern Ireland Bankruptcy Court for an order seeking the assistance of the English court but may apply directly to the English court for such assistance.

28.52 IA 1986 section 426(3) enables the Secretary of State by statutory order to make provision to give a trustee under the insolvency law of any part of the United Kingdom the same rights (with such modifications as may be specified in the order) in relation to any property situated in another part of the United Kingdom as he would have in the corresponding circumstances if he were a trustee under the insolvency law of that other part. Such an order could, for example, give a Northern Ireland trustee in bankruptcy the same rights to deal with the bankrupt's property in England as if he were an English trustee in bankruptcy, without having to apply to an English court for an order. However, no order has yet been made by the Secretary of State under section 426(3).

28.53 Where a Northern Ireland trustee wishes to realise property belonging to the bankrupt located outside Northern Ireland he should, before considering resorting to any of these mutual assistance provisions (which inevitably involve additional expense to the estate) endeavour to obtain the co-operation of the bankrupt to execute such documents or take such other action as may be appropriate to enable the trustee to do so, and the attention of the bankrupt should be directed to the provisions of the Order requiring him to render such assistance.[75] The bankrupt may also be informed of the fact that failure to deliver up his property to the trustee is an offence[76] and that it may ground an application to suspend his automatic discharge (where applicable).[77] Failing voluntary co-operation, the trustee may, if the bankrupt is within the jurisdiction, also consider applying to the Court for an order requiring the bankrupt to do what is required, with the sanction of committal for contempt of court if he fails to comply with any such order.[78]

28.54 Orders may be made under IA 1986 section 426 in relation not only to a bankruptcy but to a voluntary arrangement or a deed of arrangement.

IV. VALUE ADDED TAX BAD DEBT RELIEF [79]

Value Added Tax Act 1983
28.55 Section 22 of the Value Added Tax Act 1983 provides for a refund of value added tax paid in respect of goods or services supplied to a person for a money consideration, all or part of which remains outstanding when that person becomes insolvent. In relation to proceedings under the Order this includes adjudication in bankruptcy, the making of a deed of arrangement for the benefit of creditors, the approval of a voluntary arrangement and the administration in bankruptcy of the estate of a deceased insolvent.[80]

28.56 A creditor wishing to claim a refund of value added tax under this provision must prove in the insolvency for the amount of his debt minus such tax and obtain from the trustee in bankruptcy, trustee under the deed of arrangement or supervisor of the voluntary arrangement an acknowledgement of claim specifying the total amount of the debt proved. The claim must be submitted to HM Customs and Excise in accordance with Regulations.[81] By the operation of section 11(9) of the Finance Act 1990 a refund may not be claimed under the Value Added Tax Act 1983 in relation to any supply made after 26th July 1990. Relief in respect of such supplies may only be claimed under the new system introduced by the Finance Act 1990. As noted below, a refund of tax under the 1990 Act may be claimed in respect of supplies made on or after 1st April 1989. In the case of supplies made between 1st April 1989 and 26th July 1990 the creditor may claim a refund either under the 1983 Act or the 1990 Act, but if a claim is made under the 1983 Act it may not be claimed under the 1990 Act.[82] If the supply was made before 1st April 1989 any claim must be made under the 1983 Act and not the 1990 Act.

Claim under Finance Act 1990
28.57   Section 11 of the Finance Act 1990 introduced new provisions for value added tax bad debt relief under which (as amended by the Finance Act 1991, section 15) a refund of tax may be claimed by the supplier in accordance with Regulations made by the Commissioners of Customs and Excise[83] where -
  (a)   goods or services have been supplied for a money consideration on or after 1st April 1989,
  (b)   the supplier has accounted for and paid tax on the supply,
  (c)   the whole or any part of the consideration for the supply in respect of which the claim is made has been written off in the supplier's accounts as a bad debt, and
  (d)   one year has elapsed since the date of the supply.

28.58   Such a claim may be made in these circumstances even if no formal insolvency proceedings have been commenced, but if the person supplied becomes subject to proceedings under the Order the supplier may claim in the bankruptcy or arrangement for the full amount of the debt written off, including the value added tax, but if he has received a refund under the 1990 Act and subsequently receives a dividend on his claim he must account for this to HM Customs and Excise.

V. SOME EFFECTS OF BANKRUPTCY PROCEEDINGS UNDER THE ORDER ON LAND OF THE DEBTOR

Introduction
28.59   No dealings in land are affected by the subsequent bankruptcy of the person whose estate is the subject of the dealing if the dealing takes place before the presentation of a bankruptcy petition by or against him, unless it becomes the subject of a disclaimer by the trustee in bankruptcy[84] or of an order of the Court under the provisions of the Order for the adjustment of prior transactions.[85] The title of the trustee no longer relates back to any date prior to the presentation of the petition, as it might have under the Bankruptcy Acts.

28.60   The power of a debtor by or against whom a bankruptcy petition has been presented to dispose of any of his property (other than property held by him in trust for another) is severely restricted from the date of the presentation of the petition. If he is subsequently adjudged bankrupt, any disposition made between the date of presentation of the petition and the vesting of his estate in a trustee (when he ceases to have any title to property so vesting) is void except to the extent that it is or was made with the consent of the Court, or is or was subsequently ratified by the Court. These restrictions are contained in Article 257.[86] In relation to dispositions of land, Article 257 must be read in conjunction with amendments made by the Order to the Registration of Deeds Act and the Land Registration Act.[87] The writer has attempted to analyse the combined effect of these provisions, which raise some problems of construction which may require judicial determination.

Contracts for sale of land
28.61   A contract for sale of land of which the vendor is the beneficial owner may be affected by Article 257 because it involves a disposition by him of the equitable interest in the land sold.

28.62   If the contract is entered into after the presentation of a bankruptcy petition by or against the vendor and before the vesting of the bankrupt's estate in a trustee following the making of a bankruptcy order against him, the trustee is not bound to complete the sale unless -
  (a)   the contract was entered into with the consent of the Court or was subsequently ratified by the Court,[88] or
  (b)   the contract was entered into in good faith -
      (i)   where it relates to unregistered land, before or within 21 days after registration of the petition in the Registry of Deeds and the purchaser did not at the time of the contract have actual knowledge of the petition,[89]
      (ii)   where it relates to registered land, before the entry of notice of the presentation of the petition in the relevant folio,[90] or
  (c)   the contract was entered into in good faith before the making of the bankruptcy order and the purchaser did not at the time of the contract have notice (actual or constructive) of the presentation of the petition.[91]

28.63   If the contract is binding on the trustee he takes the land subject to the obligation to complete the sale, unless the contract is unprofitable and he disclaims it under Article 288.

28.64   A contract for sale of land forming part of the bankrupt's estate made by the bankrupt after the vesting of his estate in the trustee is of no effect.

Title of purchaser/mortgagee
(a) Unregistered land
(i) Effect of bankruptcy petition

28.65   The title of a purchaser/mortgagee under a conveyance/mortgage by the vendor/mortgagor of land for valuable consideration is not affected by a bankruptcy petition by or against the vendor/mortgagor if the land is held on trust for another[92] or if -

(A)   the vendor/mortgagor is not adjudged bankrupt,[93] or

(B)   the purchase/mortgage is completed before the making of a bankruptcy order against the vendor/mortgagor and -

(AA)   the purchaser/mortgagee completes[94] the purchase/mortgage in good faith and without actual knowledge of the petition and registers his deed in the Registry of Deeds before or within 21 days after registration of the petition,[95] or

(BB)   the purchaser/mortgagee completes[96] the purchase/mortgage in good faith and without notice (actual or constructive) of the presentation of the petition,[97] or

(CC)   the conveyance/mortgage was made with the consent of the Court or was subsequently ratified by the Court.[98]

(ii) Effect of bankruptcy order

28.66   After a bankruptcy order has been made any purported conveyance or mortgage by the bankrupt of land forming part of his estate is void unless -

(A)   the purchase/mortgage is completed before the vesting of the bankrupt's estate in a trustee and the conveyance/mortgage is made with the consent of the Court or is subsequently ratified by the Court,[99] or

(B)   at whatever time the purchase/mortgage is completed the following conditions are satisfied -

(AA)   the purchaser/mortgagor completes the purchase/ mortgage in good faith and without actual knowledge of the bankruptcy petition or of the bankruptcy order, and

(BB)   at the time the purchase/mortgage deed is registered -

(AAA) the bankruptcy order has not been registered in the Registry of Deeds or such registration has been effected less than 21 days previously, or has ceased to have effect,[100] and

(BBB)   the bankruptcy petition has not been registered in the Registry of Deeds, or such registration has been effected less than 21 days previously, or is no longer in force.[101]

(iii) After-acquired property

28.67   Property acquired by a bankrupt after the making of the bankruptcy order does not vest in the trustee in bankruptcy unless and until he serves a notice claiming it.[102] Upon service of such notice the property vests in the trustee as part of the bankrupt's estate and the trustee's title relates back to the time at which the property was acquired by, or devolved upon the bankrupt.[103] However, if the bankrupt transfers the property (before or after service of the notice by the trustee) to a person who acquires it in good faith for value and without notice of the bankruptcy, the title of such a transferee or of any person deriving title from him is protected. [104]

(b) Registered land
28.68   The title of a purchaser under a transfer of registered land made in good faith for valuable consideration is not affected by a bankruptcy petition by or against the registered owner or by the making of a bankruptcy order against the registered owner unless, at the date of execution of the registered disposition, the purchaser had actual knowledge of the petition or of the bankruptcy adjudication or, at the date of registration of the transfer a notice of the presentation of the petition or, in respect of the bankruptcy order, a bankruptcy inhibition, has been registered. [105]

28.69   After the registration of a notice of the presentation of a bankruptcy petition by or against the registered owner and before the registration of a bankruptcy inhibition, any transfer of the land by the registered owner is subject to the rights of all creditors [106] and a note to this effect will be entered in the folio of the new registered owner.

28.70   After a bankruptcy inhibition has been registered and whilst it remains in operation no dealing affecting the land of the registered owner (other than the registration of the trustee in bankruptcy as owner) may be registered. [107]

28.71   These provisions are subject to the protection afforded to a purchaser by a priority search. [108]

28.72   A registered disposition of any registered land acquired by the bankrupt after adjudication is not affected by the bankruptcy unless a notice of the presentation of the bankruptcy petition or a bankruptcy inhibition is registered against the registered owner. [109]

28.73   The trustee in bankruptcy may be registered as owner of registered land forming part of the bankrupt's estate or, as the case may be, as a tenant in common of the land with another or others. [110] Where so registered as owner the trustee holds such land for the purposes upon and subject to which the land is applicable by law, and subject to all unregistered rights subject to which the bankrupt held the land. [111] Subject to this, the trustee as registered owner is in all respects, and in particular as respects registered dealing with the land, in the same position as if he had taken the land under a transfer for valuable consideration. [112]

Searches
28.74   A purchaser or mortgagee of unregistered land should search in the Registry of Deeds shortly before completion so that, if the result of the search is satisfactory and discloses no bankruptcy proceedings (and assuming that he completes in good faith and without actual knowledge of a bankruptcy petition

or a bankruptcy order affecting the vendor/mortgagor) he may be in a position to register his deed within 21 days thereafter and thus ensure priority over any bankruptcy petition or bankruptcy order registered in the meantime.[113] A purchaser or chargeant of registered land should protect himself against the consequences of registration of bankruptcy proceedings by procuring a priority search and having his transfer or charge lodged within the period of operation of the certificate of search.

28.75　　A purchaser or mortgagee of unregistered land should search in the Bankruptcy and Companies Office to ascertain whether or not the vendor or mortgagor or a predecessor in title had been adjudged bankrupt under the Bankruptcy Acts. However, in doing so he should avoid incurring the risk of acquiring actual knowledge of bankruptcy proceedings under the Order. New registers have been opened for such proceedings so the search should be confined to the old register. Once the search is made and no old proceedings are discovered there is no need to repeat the search.

Gifts of land
28.76　　The protection afforded by Article 315(2) to a purchaser of land from a person who acquired it by gift or at an undervalue against the risk that the transfer to the vendor may be set aside by the Court under Article 312 if the vendor becomes bankrupt within the relevant period[114] has been stated to be illusory in relation to gifts of land because it is not effective if the purchaser has notice of the gift, which in respect of unregistered land he will have from an examination of the vendor's title and in respect of registered land from an inspection of the folio (where the consideration or lack or consideration for the transfer to the vendor will in most cases be recorded).[115] This defect in the corresponding provision of the IA 1986 has been taken up by the Law Society in England. Any statutory amendment will, no doubt, be adopted in Northern Ireland in due course. In the meantime such a purchaser may consider it prudent to require adequate insurance cover against this risk to be provided by the vendor.

VI. SALE OF MORTGAGED LAND

Introduction
28.77　　A mortgagee of land forming part of a bankrupt's estate who wishes to realise his security and who does not have power to do so except under an order of a court (e.g. the holder of an equitable mortgage) or where the trustee in bankruptcy challenges the validity of the mortgage, may apply to the Court for an order for sale under the Rules as an alternative to such an application to the Chancery Division under the Supreme Court Rules or by equity civil bill in the County Court.[116]

Accounts and enquiries
28.78　　On the first hearing of the application, the Court must be satisfied that the applicant's title is valid.[117] If so, it will direct accounts to be taken and

enquiries made to ascertain the principal, interest and costs due under the mortgage and, where the mortgagee has been in possession of the land or any part of it, the rents and profits, dividends, interest, or other proceeds received by him or on his behalf.[118] Such directions may (and usually will) be given with respect to any mortgage (whether prior or subsequent) on the same property, other than that of the applicant.[119]

28.79 For the purpose of such accounts and enquiries and of making title to the purchaser, any of the parties may be examined by the Court, and must produce on oath before the Court all such documents in their custody or under their control relating to the bankrupt's estate as the Court may direct, and the service of interrogatories on any party may be ordered.[120]

28.80 The Court may order any further necessary accounts or enquiries to be taken or made under Order 43 of the Supreme Court Rules.[121]

Order for sale and possession
28.81 The Court may order that the land or any specified part of it be sold.[122] The order may also require any party bound by it and in possession of the land or part, or in receipt of the rents and profits from it, to deliver up possession or receipt to the purchaser or to such other person as the Court may direct.[123]

28.82 The form of order for sale may be either to permit the person having the conduct of the sale to sell the land in such manner as he thinks fit or that the land be sold as directed in the order.[124]

28.83 The order for sale will contain detailed directions, which may include-
  (a) appointing the persons to have the conduct of the sale;
  (b) fixing the manner of sale (whether by contract conditional on the Court's approval, private treaty, public auction, or otherwise);
  (c) settling the particulars and conditions of sale;
  (d) obtaining evidence of the value of the property, and fixing a reserve or minimum price;
  (e) requiring particular persons to join in the sale and conveyance;
  (f) requiring the payment of the purchase money into the Court, or to trustees or others;
  (g) if the sale is to be by public auction, fixing the security (if any) to be given by the auctioneer, and his remuneration.[125]

28.84 If the sale is to be by public auction, the Court may direct that the mortgagee may appear and bid on his own behalf.[126]

Proceeds of sale
28.85 The proceeds of sale must be applied -
  (a) first, in payment of the expenses of the trustee, of and occasioned by the application to the Court, of the sale and attendance thereat, and of

any costs arising from the taking of accounts, and making of enquiries, as directed by the Court; and

    (b)   secondly, in payment of the amount found due to any mortgagee, for principal, interest and cost;

and the balance (if any) must be retained by or paid to the trustee.[127] Where the proceeds of the sale are insufficient to pay in full the amount found due to any mortgagee, he is entitled to prove as a creditor for any deficiency, and to receive dividends rateably with other creditors, but not so as to disturb any dividend already declared.[128]

Footnotes

(1)   Companies (Northern Ireland) Order 1989, Art.14(1). See judgment of Murray J. in *Re McQuillan* (1988) 7 NIJB 1, (1989) 5 BCC 137,140/141.

(2)   Atkin Form 386.

(3)   R.6.200(1)-(3): Atkin Form 387.

(4)   R.6.200(4). The words "not less than" in the Rule appear to be erroneous.

(5)   MH 7-463.

(6)   R.6.200(5).

(7)   RR.6.201(1), 0.3(4).

(8)   R.6.201(2).

(9)   R.6.201(2),(3).

(10)   R.6.201(4).

(11)   R.7.02(1).

(12)   R.6.201(5).

(13)   Companies (Northern Ireland) Order 1989, Art.14(2).

(14)   R.6.202(2).

(15)   R.6.202(1): Atkin Form 388.

(16)   R.6.202(3).

(17)   RSC O.15, r.7(1): County Courts (Northern Ireland) Order 1980, Art.39(2)(d).

(18)   Hals 415, 423/426.

(19)   RSC O.15, rr.6(2),7(2): County Court Rules (Northern Ireland) 1981, O.3, r.23(1). Pending such a change of party the action is stayed - see case cited at fn.(25) below, at p.1027.

(20)   *Ramsey v. Hartley & ors.* [1977] 1 WLR 686.

(21)   *Afflick v. Hammond* [1912] 3 KB 162.

(22)   Art.318(4).

(23)   Art.258(1),(2).

(24)   R.7.51.

(25)   *Realisations Industrielles et Commerciales SA v. Loescher & Partners* [1957] 1 WLR 1026, 1028.

(26)   *Re Pitchford* [1924] 2 Ch 260.

(27)   RSC O.15, r.7(2): County Court Rules (Northern Ireland) 1981, O.3, r.23(2).

(28)   Art.318(4).

(29)   Paras.21.49/50: Atkin Form 455.

(30)   Art.258(3)(b).

(31)   Art.287(1), Sch.3, Pt.I.

(32)   Hals 429, 430.

(33)   Art.278(4). For precedents of writs of summons and statements of claim see Atkin Forms 451/454.

(34)   Art.258(3)(a),(4).

(35)   Art.258(5),(6),(7).

(36)   Art.258(1). Other forms of execution and "legal process" may also be stayed - see (1990) 3 Ins Int 73.

(37) R.7.51: para.28.17.
(38) JEO, Art.13(f).
(39) JEO, Art.67. See Atkin Forms 402/404 re charging order on surplus.
(40) Para.28.32.
(41) JEO, Art.88.
(42) JEO, Art.93.
(43) JEO, Art.90(1).
(44) *Ibid.*
(45) JEO, Art.90(1),(2).
(46) JEO, Art.90(3).
(47) JEO, Art.91.
(48) JEO, Art.92.
(49) Para.12.15.
(50) JEO, Art.90(3B).
(51) JEO, Arts 88(3A), 90(3A).
(52) RSC O.1, r.15(e).
(53) JEO, Art.94.
(54) Hals 120, fn.4: JH 29.028.
(55) Judgment Enforcement Rules (Northern Ireland) 1981, r.5(1)(b).
(56) Art.301(1): Atkin Form 385.
(57) Art.301(2).
(58) MH 3-480/3-481/3: Hals 713: (1988) 1 Ins Int 41: Smart "Cross-Border Insolvency" pp259/266.
(59) IA 1986 s.441: Sch.9, para.41.
(60) JH 34.06/15.
(61) IA 1986 s.426(1),(2).
(62) IA 1986 s.426(7).
(63) JH 34.08.
(64) IA 1986 s.426(4).
(65) IA 1986 s.426(11). The operation of the adaptation in Sch.9, para.41(b) (substitution of references to the Department for references to the Secretary of State in IA 1986 s.426) has been excluded from IA 1986 s.426(11)(b) - Insolvency (1989 Order) (Commencement No.4) Order (Northern Ireland) 1991.
(66) The Co-operation of Insolvency Courts (Designation of Relevant Countries and Territories) Order 1986 - MH 8-236.
(67) JH 34.09/15.
(68) *Re John Anderson Hunter, bankrupt* (1989) 4 NIJB 89.
(69) Atkin Forms 296/301.
(70) IA 1986 s.426(4). Re bankruptcies involving foreign revenue claims, see J.G. Miller, "Bankruptcy and Foreign Revenue Claims", (1991) JBL 144.
(71) IA 1986 s.426(5): MH 3-481/3.
(72) *Re John Anderson Hunter, bankrupt* (1989) 4 NIJB 89, 101.
(73) IA 1986 s.426(10)(d).
(74) IA 1986 s.426(6).
(75) Arts.285, 306.
(76) Art.325.

(77)   Art.253(3).
(78)   Art.334.
(79)   For notes on new regime (but written before amendment by Finance Act
        1991) see (1990) 3 Ins Int 79, (1991) 4 Ins Int 32, Tax Journal 17 Jan. 1991,
        16. See also VAT leaflet 700/18/91 "Relief from VAT on Bad Debts",
        available from HM Customs and Excise.
(80)   Value Added Tax Act 1983, s.22, as adapted by Sch.9 para.39.
(81)   Value Added Tax (Bad Debt Relief) Regulations 1986, Value Added Tax
        (Bad Debt Relief) (Amendment) Regulations 1989.
(82)   Finance Act 1990, s.11(8).
(83)   Value Added Tax (Refunds for Bad Debts) Regulations 1991.
(84)   Paras.14.056/085.
(85)   Paras.14.087/106.
(86)   Paras.7.022/023.
(87)   These amendments relate only to bankruptcies to which the Order
        applies and not to bankruptcies governed by the Bankruptcy Acts - Sch.8,
        para.8(2).
(88)   Art.257(1),(3).
(89)   R of D Act s.3A(5).
(90)   LR Act s.67A(1),(2).
(91)   Art.257(4). This proposition is based on the opinion that under R of D
        Act s.3A(5) when 21 days have elapsed since the registration of the
        petition it affects a purchaser in accordance with Art.257 of the Order, so
        that the protective provisions of Art.257(4) operate.
(92)   Art.257(6). See fn.(91) above.
(93)   Art.257(1). See fn. (91) above.
(94)   In this para. and at para.28.66 below it is assumed that as regards title
        under a conveyance/mortgage by the debtor the time at which good faith
        and absence of actual knowledge of the petition or bankruptcy order for
        the purposes of R of D Act ss.3A(5),3B(5),(6) is relevant is at the date of
        completion of the purchase or mortgage when the purchase/mortgage
        deed is delivered.
(95)   R of D Act ss.3A(5),(6),4(1).
(96)   See fn.(94) above.
(97)   Art.257(4): See fn.(91) above.
(98)   Art.257(1),(3).
(99)   Ibid.
(100)   R of D Act ss.3A(6), 3B(3),(5).
(101)   R of D Act ss.3A(6), 3B(5),(6).
(102)   Art.280(1),(2): para.12.15.
(103)   Art.280(3).
(104)   Art.280(4).
(105)   LR Act s.67A(6). This provision has not been applied to a mortgagee.
        Under the corresponding Land Registration Act 1925 applying to Eng-
        land and Wales the word "purchaser" includes a mortgagee (s.3(xxi)), but
        "purchaser" is not defined in the LR Act (cf. R of D Act s.3A(6)).
(106)   LR Act s.67A(2).

(107) LR Act s.67A(5).
(108) LR Act s.81(3),(4): LR Rule 171(2).
(109) LR Act s.67A(8).
(110) LR Act s.59(1).
(111) LR Act s.59A(2).
(112) LR Act s.59A(1).
(113) Paras.28.65/66.
(114) Para.14.093.
(115) Law Society's Gazette, 21 Sept 1988 (Vol 85/34 ,p.3), 22 Jan 1992 (Vol 89/3, p.2), and 5 Feb 1992 (Vol 89/5, p.13) but note that in England and Wales the consideration for a Land Registry transfer is not recorded in the register.
(116) R.6.194(1).
(117) R.6.194(2).
(118) *Ibid.*
(119) R.6.194(3).
(120) R.6.194(4),(5).
(121) R.6.194(6).
(122) R.6.195(1).
(123) *Ibid.*
(124) R.6.195(2).
(125) R.6.195(3).
(126) R.6.195(4).
(127) R.6.196(1).
(128) R.6.196(2).

See Ch.26.064

NOTICE OF MEETING OF CREDITORS IN INDIVIDUAL VOLUNTARY ARRANGEMENT
(Heading and title)

NOTICE IS HEREBY GIVEN that a meeting of creditors in the above matter is to be held at
on   day   19   at   am/pm to consider the proposal for a voluntary arrangement made by the above-named [debtor] [bankrupt].

A form of proxy is enclosed. This should be completed and returned to me by the date of the meeting if you cannot attend the meeting and wish to be represented.

In order to be entitled to vote at the meeting or to have your claim taken into account in the computation of the majority required to validate a resolution you must give to me or to the chairman of the meeting, either at the meeting or before it, details in writing of your claim. For this purpose a form of proof of debt is enclosed and I would ask you to complete and return it to me as soon as possible.

The following documents are also enclosed -
  (a)   a copy of the proposal;
  (b)   a copy of [the debtor's/bankrupt's statement of affairs][a summary of the debtor's/bankrupt's statement of affairs]; and
  (c)   a copy of my comments on the proposal.

My comments on the [debtor's] [bankrupt's] proposal has been filed in the Bankruptcy and Companies Office, Royal Courts of Justice, Chichester Street, Belfast, where it may be inspected by any creditor.

The voting rights of creditors and the majorities required to pass resolutions at the meeting are prescribed by Rules 5.20 and 5.21 of the Insolvency Rules (Northern Ireland) 1991. A statement of the effect of these Rules is attached, but any question which may arise in connection with these matters will be determined by the Rules and not by this statement, which is for general guidance only.
Dated   19 .

(Signed)

(Qualification)

A licensed insolvency practitioner, named as the nominee in the debtor's proposal.

Voting rights and requisite majorities at creditors' meeting

1. To entitle a creditor to vote in respect of a claim, written notice of the claim must be given, either at the meeting or before it, to the nominee or to the chairman of the meeting. The form of proof of debt enclosed with the notice of the meeting should be used for this purpose.

2. Subject to paragraph 3, votes are calculated according to the amount of the creditor's debt as at [the date of the meeting] [the date of the bankruptcy order].

3. A creditor's vote in respect of any claim or part of a claim is to be left out of account in the following cases -

(a)   where the claim or part is secured by property of the [debtor] [bankrupt];

(b)   where the claim is in respect of a debt wholly or partly on, or secured by, a current bill of exchange or promissory note, unless the creditor is willing -

(i)   to treat the liability to him on the bill or note of every person who is liable on it antecedently to the [debtor] [bankrupt], and against whom a bankruptcy order has not been made (or, in the case of a company, which has not gone into liquidation), as a security in his hands, and

(ii)   to estimate the value of the security and (for the purpose of entitlement to vote, but not of any distribution under the arrangement) to deduct it from his claim.

4. Subject to paragraph 5, the majorities required to pass a resolution are as follows -

(a)   in the case of a resolution to approve a proposal for a voluntary arrangement or any modification thereof, a majority of more than three-quarters, in value, of the creditors present at the meeting in person or by proxy who vote on the resolution and whose votes are not left out of account under paragraph 3;

(b)   in the case of any other resolution proposed at the meeting, a majority of more than one half of such creditors.

5. Notwithstanding that a resolution is supported by the majority required by paragraph 4, it is invalid if the creditors voting against it exceed one-half, in value, of those creditors -

(a)   to whom notice of the meeting was sent,

(b)   who have given written notice of their claims in accordance with paragraph 1,

(c)   who are not, to the best of the chairman's belief, associates of the [debtor] [bankrupt] (see note below), and

(d)   whose notes are not to be left out of account under paragraph 3.

6. Broadly stated, these provisions mean that a voluntary arrangement is not approved unless the resolution to approve it -

(a)   is supported by the votes of more than three-quarters, in value, of the unsecured creditors present or represented at the meeting, and

(b)   is not opposed by the votes of more than one half, in value, of all the unsecured creditors who are not associates of the [debtor] [bankrupt] to whom notice of the meeting was sent and who have duly notified their claims.

Note

The term "associate" is defined in Article 4 of the Insolvency (Northern Ireland) Order 1989. It includes the [debtor's] [bankrupt's] husband or wife, a relative (as widely defined) or the husband or wife of a relative of the [debtor] [bankrupt] or of the [debtor's] [bankrupt's] husband or wife, a partner of the [debtor] [bankrupt] and the husband or wife or relative of such partner.

James McCann

Index